Is for
SOUTHERN

Is for

SOUTHERN

A GUIDE TO **THE SOUTH, FROM ABSINTHE** TO ZYDECO

DAVID DI**BENEDETTO**

AND THE EDITORS OF GARDEN&GUN

HARPER WAVE

An Imprint of HarperCollins Publishers

HarperCollins books may be purchased for educational,
business, or sales promotional use. For information,
please email the Special Markets Department at
SPsales@harpercollins.com.

FIRST EDITION

Book design by Shubhani Sarkar,
sarkardesignstudio.com

Illustrations by Harry Bates

Library of Congress Cataloging-in-Publication Data has
been applied for.

ISBN 978-0-06-244514-8

17 18 19 20 21   LSC   10 9 8 7 6 5 4 3 2 1

CONTENTS

INTRODUCTION
by David DiBenedetto XIX

A

B

C

D

G

H

I-J

K

L

M

CONTENTS

N

O

P

Q-R

S

T

U-V

W

X-Z

A SOUTHERN TOUR

I DON'T KNOW IF YOUNG BOYS STILL FOLLOW coonhounds into the Ozark Mountains without a trace of adult supervision and without a touch of modern communication devices, but I hope they do. I didn't grow up anywhere near the Ozarks, but as a boy in the coastal environs of Savannah, Georgia, I happily got lost in the pages of *Where the Red Fern Grows* by Wilson Rawls. In my family, it was a reading rite of passage. The book, a tattered paperback copy, had been handed down from my three older brothers. When my turn came, I opened it up and couldn't stop reading, staying up well after I should have been asleep to find out if young Billy Colman got his coonhounds, if they treed that first raccoon, if the fabled ghost coon eluded Little Ann and Old Dan, if they won the coveted gold cup in the coonhound competition, and, in the end, if the mountain lion spelled the end to perhaps the most famous pair of hunting dogs in history. What I discovered then was that a book could rip your heart right out, causing you to shed tears, real sobbing tears, on those thin, yellowed pages.

So when the entire *Garden & Gun* editorial team held our first daylong brainstorming session to discuss what we'd include in this book, I suggested *Where the Red Fern Grows* when we hit the *W* chapter. The book's Southern setting made it a viable choice, and besides my own personal connection, its impact on readers across the South and beyond made it a worthy inclusion. The staff's passions informed many choices. Deputy Editor David Mezz, the new owner of a jon boat, felt the iconic watercraft deserved a spot in the book. Design Director Marshall McKinney made a strong pitch for the bar Earnestine & Hazel's (and its Soul Burger) in his hometown of Memphis. And Associate Editor Elizabeth Hutchison wanted to cover the Georgia/South Carolina peach wars. (A touch biased, Hutchison has three generations of peach farmers from Filbert, South Carolina, in her family.)

Of course, no one book could include every aspect of Southern life and culture. Rather than trying to make the book an all-encompassing academic and historical tome, we wanted it to take readers on a walkabout across the contemporary Southern landscape—its institutions, people, culture, and influences. You'll find entries on modern touchstones such as

Pappy Van Winkle and Waffle House as well as influential figures such as Edna Lewis and Ralph Stanley and insightful pieces on topics and events that shaped where we are today, from the Civil War to the lunch counter protests of the civil rights movement.

We also tapped some of the South's finest writers and prominent personalities for their expertise—Rick Bragg on Harper Lee; Southern Foodways Alliance founding director John T. Edge on his mentor John Egerton; singer-songwriter and Hank Williams's granddaughter Holly Williams on the Grand Ole Opry; food historian Jessica B. Harris on okra; and humorist Roy Blount, Jr., on humidity, among many others.

These days I'm a long way from my bedroom where I stayed up late reading *Where the Red Fern Grows*. Though I do keep a first edition of the book—a gift from my wife, Jenny—on my bookshelf. And one day I hope to find my children up past their bedtime reading it by the gleam of a flashlight, captivated by words on a page.

As for this book, I hope you'll find it both entertaining and informative, and that it sheds light on where the South has been and where it's going.

DAVID DiBENEDETTO
Editor in Chief, *Garden & Gun*
CHARLESTON, SOUTH CAROLINA

FOR THE RECORD, ABSINTHE WILL NOT MAKE you hallucinate forest elves or slice off your ear. More than a century after the European spirit's bohemian mystique begot a national panic in the United States, it isn't even illegal anymore. A New Orleans environmental chemist named Ted Breaux brought an end to its stateside ban with a series of studies in the early 2000s. His conclusion: the Green Fairy doesn't contain nearly enough toxic thujone—a by-product of one of its key ingredients, wormwood—to trigger hallucinations, and is therefore no more hazardous or morally degenerative than any other high-proof spirit. Sort of disappointing, no? But now, you can drink the herbal spirit as your ancestors did, free of gothic overtones. In the Crescent City, folks have long been fond of the slushy absinthe frappé—so fond that in 1934 they invented anise-flavored Herbsaint to replace the then-banned base spirit. The flip side of the standard baroque spoon-and-sugar-cube method of absinthe drinking, the frappé, a blend of absinthe, soda water, and mint over crushed ice, is wonderfully refreshing on a clear summer day.

ACADIANS CAME TO BE KNOWN AS CAJUNS after they moved to Louisiana and lost a syllable or two. *See Cajuns.*

ACCENT

by Daniel Wallace

THE SOUTHERN ACCENT IS ONE OF OUR nation's greatest treasures. Its beauty rivals that of a songbird or the most resonant cello. Had the Southern accent not been invented, our ears would have fallen off long ago, or become vestigial, fleshy cauliflowers hanging off the sides of our heads, for without the Southern accent there would have been nothing much worth listening to. Someone, somewhere, can make a case that I'm exaggerating its importance to us as a people and to America, but I can assure you I am not.

Maybe I am. But it's lovely, isn't it, the Southern accent? It's not because I have one myself that I say this, because my accent is not what it could be: years of watching *I Dream of Jeannie* growing up have me talking more like an out-of-work B actor than like my grandmother Eva Pedigo, who came from Savannah, settled in Birmingham, and sounded as if she marinated her vowels in butter overnight.

An accent is your vocal personality. It's like a hairstyle or a favorite pair of shoes, the only difference being that it's in your throat. There's a Northern accent as well, and it's easily distinguishable from a Southern accent the same way a paper bag full of broken glass is distinguishable from a cashmere scarf. But when you leave the South and head in other directions, accents tend to disappear, the song of language is lost, and what you're left with is bland communication, meaning without music.

It's amusing, at least to me, to hear scholarly argot used to understand and investigate our day-to-day lives, especially the most resolutely nonscholarly subjects, like Southern English. My wife, a Vermonter, had no idea what *fixin' to* meant when she first heard it. Had she researched the phrase, she would have learned that it indicated "immediate future action." I could have told her that. A *Southern drawl* is vowel breaking; that's what you call it if you're in the language business. Vowels are broken into *gliding vowels*, making a one-syllable word like *cat* sound as if it might have two syllables (something like *ca-yat*). People not from the South say that sounds stupid, but I say I'm rubber and you're glue, and anything you say bounces off me and sticks to you.

A Southern accent is not a single accent. There are many different Southern accents, some so distinct that an Alabama native like me will have no idea what that Carolinian might mean with the sounds coming out of his mouth. The Southern accent baseline is the merging of certain words—*pen* and *pin*, *cot* and *caught*. Why we talk the way we do is due to an ironic mélange of the speech of British immigrants in the seventeenth and eighteenth centuries and the Creole speech of African slaves. Today, believe it or not, Southern is the single most spoken accent in America. The rapidly growing number of Southern-accent speakers is due either to the fact that we're having a lot more children down here than they are anywhere else, or the fact that we're getting converts from Boston and New Jersey, seeking a better life. Probably both.

ACE BASIN

A WATERY WILDERNESS, THIS THREE-HUNDRED-thousand-acre natural preserve lies just south of Charleston, South Carolina—a mix of public, private, and corporate holdings where the Ashepoo, Combahee, and Edisto (ACE) Rivers meet the sea.

The ACE was passed over by developers the first time around—too hard to get to. But after the build-out of the nearby Hilton Head, Seabrook, and Kiawah Islands, they took a long second look. Come 1988, there was a quiet but determined revolt to keep the ACE wild. Ted Turner, the Coors brewing family, and heirs of the publishing magnate R. R. Donnelley led the charge, assisted by the South Carolina Department of Natural Resources, the U.S. Fish and Wildlife Service, Ducks Unlimited, and the Nature Conservancy. The upshot: private landowners would enjoy a considerable tax discount by not subdividing their properties and instead dedicating them to traditional uses, farming, logging, and hunting.

Though several state and county roads traverse the ACE Basin, you can reach most of it only by water. There are two dozen boat launches, several for kayaks only, and it lives up to its moniker: "One of the last great places." But the ACE is also alligator central—keep your toes in the boat.

AFRICAN METHODIST EPISCOPAL (AME) CHURCH

Considering that African Americans were often barred from meeting together in the South before the Civil War, it's no surprise that before emancipation, this religious sect—established in Philadelphia in 1816—spread largely in the North. Richard Allen, a former slave, formed the group after suffering racial discrimination at his local white Methodist Episcopal congregation. In the process, he founded the nation's first independent black denomination.

After the war, Union army officials allowed clergy to come down and promote their beliefs to former slaves. The AME Church then experienced its largest period of growth, opening not only churches across the region but also thousands of schools, including Allen University in Columbia, South Carolina, and Morris Brown College in Atlanta.

The oldest congregation in the South, however, had begun worshipping years earlier in Charleston, South Carolina. The followers who would come to form "Mother" Emanuel AME, including the Reverend Morris Brown and Denmark Vesey, had quickly joined the tradition the same year as its founding up north. No stranger to tragedy—including the church's being destroyed twice, once each by fire and earthquake, as well as Vesey's execution for his part in planning a slave rebellion—Mother Emanuel once again captured the country's attention in June 2015, when a twenty-one-year-old white supremacist shot and killed nine parishioners during a Bible study. In the immediate aftermath, the victims' families expressed forgiveness toward the shooter, prompting a nationwide conversation about race and the removal of the Confederate flag from the grounds of the South Carolina State House in Columbia.

Today AME congregations are still predominantly African American, although all are welcome.

THE ALLMAN BROTHERS BAND

IF THE GOOD LORD HAD A HAND IN CREATING the quintessential Southern rock band, he (or she) couldn't do any better than the Allman Brothers Band. Duane Allman and little brother Gregg were born in Nashville and later moved to Macon, Georgia, with fellow members Dickey Betts, Berry Oakley, Butch Trucks, and Jaimoe Johanson, eventually settling in at 2321 Vineville Avenue, aka the Big House, in 1970. Their self-titled debut and its follow-up, *Idlewild South*, were stiffs commercially, but the band had become dogged road warriors, playing some three hundred gigs a year with an improvisational energy fueled by family blood, booze, and copious amounts of drugs. In March 1971, they decided to record two nights in New York, and the resulting *At Fillmore East* became their breakthrough and remains one of the greatest live albums ever made, with searing versions of signature Allman tunes including "Hot 'Lanta," "In Memory of Elizabeth Reed," and an epic twenty-minute take on "Whipping Post." Tragically, Duane and Berry Oakley were killed in motorcycle accidents in 1971 and 1972, respectively. The band soldiered on with various lineups—highlighted by guitarist Warren Haynes and Butch's nephew Derek Trucks—packing venues for decades before finally calling it quits in 2014 with a final sold-out show at the Beacon Theatre in New York City. The Allmans detested the label "Southern rock" because they didn't feel it took into account their love of jazz, soul, and country music, but every band in the genre that has come after, from Lynyrd Skynyrd to ZZ Top, owes them a debt.

AMEN CORNER

THE MASTERS TOURNAMENT WAS ESTABlished in 1934 at Georgia's Augusta National Golf Club by the Grand Slam winner—and bow-tied walking archetype of the Southern sportsman—Bobby Jones. But Augusta's 11th, 12th, and 13th holes weren't granted their lofty title, Amen Corner, until twenty-four years later, the year Arnold Palmer won his first green jacket. (Strictly speaking, the phrase describes the approach shot on 11, all of 12, and the tee shot on 13, but it has gradually come to refer to all three holes in their entirety.) The term is credited to the sportswriter Herbert Warren Wind, who, looking for a phrase akin to baseball's "hot corner," wrote in the April 21, 1958, issue of *Sports Illustrated*: "On the afternoon before the start of the recent Masters golf tournament, a wonderfully evocative ceremony took place at the farthest reach of the Augusta National Course—down in the Amen Corner where Rae's Creek intersects the 13th fairway near the tee, then parallels the front edge of the green on the short 12th and finally swirls alongside the 11th green." But the nickname didn't entirely originate with Wind. He borrowed it from a jazz recording called "Shoutin' in That Amen Corner," which itself took the term from a New York City intersection frequented by lively Bible salesmen and preachers. At any rate, Wind's appending the name to Augusta stuck. And the green jacket bequeathed to those who pray successfully through Amen Corner endures as one of the most instantly recognizable symbols of victory in all of sports.

ANGEL OAK

THE WORD *MAJESTIC* GETS TROTTED OUT OF-ten in descriptions of the South's indigenous live oaks, but if ever a specimen deserved a breathless adjective, it's South Carolina's Angel Oak. Located off a dirt road on Johns Island, not far from Charleston proper, the tree looks like a character in a fairy tale (or a Tolkien fantasy) come to life—a wise and brooding presence. It's thought to be four hundred to five hundred years old; its massive trunk measures 28 feet around, and it stands an imposing 66 1/2 feet tall. But the tree's lateral reach is what boggles minds. Live oaks, built to withstand coastal winds, tend to have a branch span that greatly exceeds their height, and the Angel Oak's gnarled and massive limbs, rising and curving and dipping, snake out in every direction—the longest reaching *187 feet* from base to tip—and produce more than 17,000 square feet of shade. Perhaps there is a little magic in the oak's embrace as well. Even during the height of segregation, black and white families picnicked under its cooling shadow in close proximity. After centuries in which neither hurricanes nor floods nor earthquakes could fell this living monument, development threatened to—until a dedicated group of locals and conservationists, in 2014, raised funds needed for the City of Charleston to purchase more than eighteen acres surrounding it. *See Live Oak.*

APALACHICOLA, FLORIDA

THIS SMALL HARBOR TOWN PERCHED ALONG Florida's Panhandle coast is historic enough to have been the site of Native American settlements a few millennia ago, and more recently Spain, England, the Confederacy, and the Union took turns battling over it. It has been preserved enough to boast a main street and a waterfront that still look straight out of 1950s postcards, and the nearby pristine beaches are playgrounds of white-powder sand. But none of that is what starts Southerners' mouths watering whenever they hear the town's singsong name (locals refer to it simply as Apalach). It's the oysters—the briny, impossibly plump bivalves for which Apalachicola is so revered. Historically, Apalachicola Bay has produced as much as 90 percent of the state's harvest, and it's the last place in the country where men and women still harvest wild oysters using only small boats and handheld tongs. Let the New Yorkers have their adorable little bluepoints. We'll take a fat Apalachicola, on the half shell or a saltine with a dash of Tabasco.

APPALACHIA

by Allison Glock

GEOGRAPHY IS DESTINY. WHEN YOU ARE born, as I was, in the low beating heart of Appalachia, cosseted by the undulating green of the hollers, driving narrow strips of coiled roads that fall away on either side with the messy brutality of a severed limb, breathing damp, metallic air thick with the dust and fume of industry, you know your worth with firm certainty. Which is to say, not much.

Appalachia—which commonly counts swaths of North Carolina, Tennessee, Pennsylvania, and Kentucky, patches of Ohio, New York, Alabama, and Georgia, and every inch of West Virginia, my home state—can't help but make a person feel small, what with her glorious ancientness and indifference on display in every corner.

A single look at her mountains, formed 480 million years ago and rubbed smooth by centuries, renders any mortal ambition petty by comparison. So realized is her beauty it borders on cruelty. So defined is her landscape you are forced to become a part of it—via mining her ground, or milling her lumber, or spinning plates from her river clay—if you aim to stay within it. There are no other choices. You either leave, or become subsumed.

Not that one can ever *actually* leave Appalachia. Her essence embeds in your soul like tar on fur, sticky and impossible to ignore, even if you hightail it to New York City and pretend you never knew what it felt like to walk barefoot over root-strewn alleys.

It's enough to drive one mad, which is the other thing about Appalachia—we folks from there tend to have crazy in our blood. We aren't shy about violence. (There are statistics on this. This is a thing you can look up.) Call it hillbilly pride, a wry self-deprecation married to itchy trigger fingers. We know who we are, but don't you go trying to tell us.

Appalachia is a paradise of paradox: it makes you as it destroys you. And the people there follow suit, possessing deep wells of pride and humility, rage and tenderness. We love our stories, but we loathe pretending. We worship our mountains, even as we behead them. We praise the Lord, but more than half of us never attend church. We believe in haints, saints, and working-class heroes the rest of the world has forgotten. We play fiddles, not violins.

Appalachia is a breathtaking prison, and like all prisons, the confinement forges a gallows humor (seen clearly in our writers like James Agee, Jeannette Walls, and Breece D'J Pancake), and an unshakable mistrust of authority. Self-reliance breeds stubbornness, while self-awareness buoys the tendency to lead with our weaknesses and lampoon them into points of pride. Exhibit A: Dolly Parton. We taste our mortality on the regular—why not jump trains, or drink moonshine, or pick a fight, or howl at the moon, or get high, or love so hard our bones split?

Times are tough in Appalachia. Times have never not been tough in Appalachia. You feel alive there precisely because you never forget you are dying. Amid this fatalism survive hope, and fortitude, and fine, enduring music, and contortions of language so distinctive smarter people than we come and record the oldest of our voices, thinking them worthy of study. All the while the mountains sink deeper into history. And we along with them.

have left them unharmed. Along rural roads, it is common to find that someone has placed a beer can or bottle in the limbs of a dead armadillo. This is reprehensible but makes you think, however briefly, that it died happy.

ARMADILLO

WHILE THE HABITAT OF ARMADILLOS RANGES from South America to the American South, the nine-banded armadillo, *Dasypus novemcinctus*, is the one found in the United States. *Armadillo* means "little armored one" in Spanish, referring to the armor covering its back, formed of plates of dermal bone covered in relatively small, overlapping epidermal scales called "scutes." The Aztecs called armadillos *ayotochtli*, meaning "turtle-rabbit." At least one Arkansan calls them "possum on the half shell." The Texas legislature voted down repeated attempts to make the armadillo the state animal in the late 1970s, but in 1981 it achieved that status by executive decree. This is somewhat curious given that—while the animal has been a Texas souvenir since the 1890s—it is a known carrier of leprosy.

Burrowing, chiefly nocturnal, and solitary mammals, armadillos have few predators and are seldom eaten voluntarily by humans. One exception was during the Great Depression, when they were known as "Hoover hogs." When startled, armadillos leap three or four feet straight into the air, as if spring-loaded. This evolutionary reflex has not served armadillos well on roads, since they often leap up and are killed by vehicles that would otherwise

ARMSTRONG, LOUIS

(1901–1971)

by Daniel Wallace

AMERICA WAS BUILT WITH THE SWEAT and blood of millions of anonymous citizens, immigrants, and interlopers, but individuals whose names we will never forget authored the idea of America. Think of Washington, Jefferson, and Lincoln, if you will, but America is more—much more—than its presidents. There is a long list of writers, artists, and musicians, without whom we wouldn't be who we are. Near the top of that list—and not even necessarily alphabetically—is a man named Louis Armstrong.

Born in the first year of the twentieth century, in New Orleans, he had an early life that was as dark, desperate, and dismal as they come: He was abandoned by his father, his mother became a prostitute, and he had to leave school in fifth grade to collect junk and deliver coal. A little trouble with the law got him sent to the Colored Waif's Home for Boys, where he learned how to play cornet and play it well (he didn't play trumpet for years). By the time he was eighteen, he had married a prostitute himself and adopted a mentally disabled three-year-old boy named Clarence, whom he took care of for the rest of his life.

That paragraph alone could be turned into a novel—but there is so much more to come. His life deserves a quartet. It's natural to flash forward and consider a man's legacy, how Louis Armstrong became the most important influence on what we now think of as jazz, seeming to almost single-handedly create a new form of music. But, as with Elvis, who might be said to have done the same thing for rock and roll, there is a story behind the story that's as fascinating as the story itself, because it's our story, the story of America.

We know him as Satchmo, a nickname born of his very large mouth, which they said was as big as a satchel—the better to play trumpet with, my dear. He lived in New Orleans, Chicago, and New York City, and like heroes in the Grecian mode both triumphed and was beset by great misfortune. He invented scat singing; pop music became popular because of him. Then again, he had four wives and troubles with the mob, and in 1933 had to stop playing trumpet for a year because he played it so well he wore out his lips. He was the first African American to be featured in a Hollywood movie, the first to write an autobiography, and for decades the most famous African American in the world. Every time he was almost forgotten he came out with another song—"What a Wonderful World," "Hello, Dolly"—that made him relevant again. Beboppers abandoned and rejected him, but he persevered, and behind that grand smile we learned he had a deep moral center.

Though he eventually settled up North, the South never left him; he took it with him everywhere. But he was also, and most of all, American. From a junk collector to a musical demigod: What's more American than that?

ASHEVILLE, NORTH CAROLINA

by Hanna Raskin

THERE'S AN OLD JOKE IN ASHEVILLE THAT goes like this: "There are lots of jobs around here—a friend of mine has four of them."

That sounds about right, whether it's referring to a millworker who lives alongside a cold-water creek that bears his great-great-granddaddy's name and who picks up taxidermy jobs to pay the bills, or a surrealist poet who moonlights in acupuncture and jewelry design. This mountain town has been scrappy and scruffy since its founding in 1784.

Mired in debt from the Depression through the 1980s, Asheville was too impoverished to tear down the art deco buildings that had arisen before fortunes faded, but it kept chugging along in the manner of the road-making machines that grandly bore through Beaucatcher Mountain in 1928. When tourists came back to town, those architectural marvels were right there waiting for them.

Tourism has been central to Asheville from the start: travelers praised the healing qualities of its clean air and hot springs even before European settlers showed up. Thomas Wolfe, who had Asheville in mind when he decreed that you can't go home again, grew up in his mother's boardinghouse there. The minor-league baseball team is officially named the Tourists.

The wealthy and well known have always flocked here. F. Scott Fitzgerald stayed at the Grove Park Inn to rest his lungs, wracked by tuberculosis, while his wife, Zelda, checked into a nearby hospital to rest her mind. Decades earlier, George Vanderbilt had chosen 130,000 acres of woods just south of town for his country estate, Biltmore, which is now one of the region's biggest draws.

Visitors also gawk at the nightly drum circle, a quintessentially Asheville gathering that has steadily crescendoed from a few earnest sorts with bongos to a small colony of bohemians united in rhythm. It's a modern-day successor to Shindig on the Green, a set of informal ballad sessions, old-time banjo strumming, and impromptu flatfooting that has taken place in a downtown park on Saturday nights for more than half a century.

Asheville is alive with music, and it suddenly has countless new venues in which the pickers can play. In addition to the boutiques, restaurants, bookstores, and artisan food shops that populate downtown, a slew of microbreweries backs up the city's recent ascension as a craft-beer mecca. Oftentimes, you can find any given brewery's taproom spotlighting music from a bunch of bearded guys *this close* to quitting every last one of their day jobs.

ASPIC

ONCE UPON A TIME, ASPIC, A DISH IN WHICH ingredients are set into a gelatinous mold, required a serious time commitment. Cooks extracted the necessary gelatin from hooves or bones over hours of simmering. Then came powdered gelatin, which democratized the jiggly centerpiece. By the turn of the twentieth century, sweet and savory aspics were making statements in cafeterias and at cocktail parties all over the country. Southerners served them at white-glove luncheons alongside deviled eggs and finger sandwiches. In places, we still do. Classic tomato aspic remains the house specialty at Gilchrist Drug in Mountain Brook, Alabama, which opened in 1928, and at the Colonnade Restaurant in Atlanta, dishing it up since 1927.

ATCHAFALAYA BASIN

It might not encapsulate ALL of the Cajun world, but "the Basin," as locals call it, circumscribes the very heart and soul of Cajun Louisiana. It's a swamp nearly twice the size of Great Smoky Mountains National Park, alive with crawfish, alligators, wild hogs, swamp deer, and black bears, fed by a river that's not really a river. The Atchafalaya is a drain—a "distributary," in geologic parlance—of the Mississippi River. At Simmesport, Louisiana, the Mississippi takes an eastward turn, spilling much of its high-water flow into the Atchafalaya. Unraveling into braided channels, bayous, and swamp lake chains, the Atchafalaya River then wends for some 140 miles, eventually draining into the Gulf of Mexico. But it's hardly devoid of the hand of man. In 1876, South Louisiana's vast swamp woods were sold off to pay for levee construction. Having just leveled the big timber of Michigan, logging companies turned to the Basin, snapping up cypress forest for as little as twenty-five cents per acre. Tree by tree, nearly the entire Atchafalaya Basin fell to the saw. Still, the swamp's regrown forests are draped in Spanish moss and block out the Deep South sun. Hundreds of floating camps still draw Cajuns who hunt ducks, deer, and squirrels, and fish for crabs, catfish, bullfrogs, *gaspergou*, *choupique*, and buffalo fish. They cast their lines—and their hopes that the Basin's future is as rich as its past.

ATHENS, GEORGIA

by Matt Hendrickson

Southern football fans know Athens as the home of the University of Georgia Bulldogs and the hallowed hedges of Sanford Stadium. Foodies are probably familiar with the chef Hugh Acheson, who helped kick off the city's culinary cred with his restaurants 5&10 and The National. But there isn't anybody in the country who hasn't heard of a little band called R.E.M., which thrust this college town in the Georgia Piedmont to the forefront of the nation's musical consciousness.

The story of Athens's renown as a music incubator begins with a birthday party. On April 5, 1980, a UGA student named Kathleen O'Brien wanted her favorite local band—which had never played a real gig and was still nameless—to perform at the rundown St. Mary's Episcopal church. Led by a charismatic front man—Michael Stipe—the group would soon adopt the moniker R.E.M. and go on to become one of the biggest bands in the world. Along with R.E.M., the town has produced a slew of national acts, including Widespread Panic, the Indigo Girls, and the Drive-By Truckers. But, why, oh why, sleepy Athens?

The seeds were planted in the 1970s: in 1972, the UGA college radio station WUOG began broadcasting, exerting an outsize influence on the music heard in town. Wuxtry Records founders Dan Wall and Mark Methe opened the now-iconic shop in 1976, and it quickly became a gathering place for area musicians. R.E.M. guitarist Peter Buck was working the counter when he met Michael Stipe, and they bonded over a mutual love of the Velvet Underground. Art-poppers the B-52s played their first gig at a Valentine's Day party in 1977 before moving to New York and opening the door for other Athens bands like the seminal dance-rockers Pylon. Many of the town's music scenesters attended art school at UGA, and the nearby downtown offered practice spaces such as Stitchcraft, where bands would gather in cinder-block rooms. Maybe someone brought in a case of beer or a couch. From there, they'd get gigs at the I&I Club, Tyrone's O.C., and the 40 Watt, which after moving to several different locations found its permanent home at 285 W. Washington Street in 1991 and has become one of the country's premier music clubs. For Stipe, the whole scene seemed like a happy accident. "We just kind of created our own thing and that's part of the beauty of Athens," he told *Filter* magazine in 2003, "that it's so off the map and there's no way you could ever be the East Village or an L.A. scene or a San Francisco scene, that it just became its own thing."

For legions of Southern rock aficionados, though, perhaps the city's most beloved product is the jam band extraordinaire Widespread Panic. Two of Panic's founding members, John Bell and Michael Houser, met in a UGA dorm and picked up a couple of other musicians before starting out on the fraternity and bar circuit. And it was Panic that gave Athens its most crowded moment, when nearly a hundred thousand fans crammed onto city streets in 1998 to celebrate the release of the band's first live CD, *Light Fuse, Get Away.*

ATLANTA, GEORGIA

by Amanda Heckert

LIKE SHIFTING PATTERNS IN A KALEIDO-scope, Atlanta defies one definition. One quarter turn here, and it's the capital of the so-called New South, a transportation hub with sixteen Fortune 500 headquarters the likes of Home Depot and (of course) Coca-Cola, the planet's busiest airport, and the innovative new BeltLine greenway transforming the inner city. Another turn, and it's the seat of the civil rights movement, the "city too busy to hate" that produced Martin Luther King Jr., a thriving black middle and upper class, and the new Center for Civil and Human Rights. Keep turning, and you find a global melting pot with an international reputation burnished by the 1996 Olympic Games. The "A," a hip-hop mecca that fostered TLC, Outkast, India.Arie, and T.I. A welcoming LGBT destination. A genteel "city in the forest" crisscrossed by any number of streets dubbed Peachtree. The "Hollywood of the South" that has beckoned the film industry with tax breaks, turning leafy lanes into postapocalyptic streetscapes for *The Walking Dead*. A patchwork quilt of thriving neighborhoods, from Cabbagetown to Virginia-Highland. A sprawling web of suburbs crawling with soccer moms.

The Atlanta metro area is each of these things, and all of these things at once. The multidimensional ability perhaps stems in no small part from its relatively new arrival. Founded in 1837—a century, give or take, after other centers of commerce such as Charlotte and Savannah—the railroad stop situated in the Appalachian foothills zipped through a couple of names (Marthasville, Terminus) before landing on its present one. Burned to a crisp by General William T. Sherman during the 1864 Battle of Atlanta, the city perhaps then took its phoenix spirit animal a little too literally, bulldozing over one thing or another over the years in the name of progress.

Now six million people call this North Georgia megalopolis home, and when you're driving down 400 or around 285 past the new Atlanta Braves stadium or through the heart of the Connector on a Friday afternoon, it can feel like every single one of them is in his car and headed the same direction as you. Few are true natives of this transient city, but if you're visiting, they'll all probably tell you the same things, no matter how long ago they got here: the traffic *is* as bad as advertised. And don't call it Hotlanta.

ATLANTA BRAVES

by Jason Isbell

WHEN I WAS A KID IN NORTHERN ALABAMA, I spent a great deal of time with my grandparents Carthel and Louise Isbell. They lived next door to the school I attended from kindergarten through senior year, and since my parents couldn't really afford day care, I spent my time learning to play guitar from my granddad or helping him tend to the farm animals he kept out back. They had VHS tapes of old Westerns, and we watched them

at night, even though they'd seen them all at least a half dozen times. When I was seven, I started playing baseball for my local league (Dixie Youth, it was called). My grandparents made it to almost all my games. My grandfather would hand out two-dollar bills or ice cream sandwiches to my teammates and me afterward, while my grandmother would offer words of encouragement to the kids who hadn't played so well, or the ones who were afraid of the ball.

Until I started playing baseball, my grandparents had very little experience with the game. But once they watched me play for a season or so, they had learned the rules and were hooked. They were very religious folks, didn't curse or drink or watch R-rated movies, and other than old Westerns there was hardly anything on TV at night that we could all comfortably watch together. However, like pretty much everyone else in America in the eighties and nineties, we could watch Braves games on the Superstation.

I remember my grandmother's excitement every time Rafael Belliard came on the screen. She liked him best because he always had a smile. My grandfather made up nicknames for

almost all the Braves regulars. He called Bobby Cox "Wally Cox," after the old TV comedian, and John Smoltz "Smokes" for obvious reasons.

We spent a lot of summer days and evenings watching those games. They were exciting for me even up into my angry teens, and my grandparents never had to worry about graphic violence or nudity or profanity or anything evil coming through the television into their peaceful little home. I was sixteen when Atlanta won the Series in '95, and like a lot of sixteen-year-olds, I needed something to bring me closer to the elders in my family. Baseball, specifically Braves baseball, worked like a charm. For that, I will always be a fan.

AUSTIN, TEXAS

by Tom Foster

YOU MAY HAVE HEARD THAT AUSTIN (with apologies to Brooklyn) is the coolest city on the planet. Or that Austin is dead, a sellout to shameless real estate developers and California tech-bro transplants. Austin, that haven for pinko potheads in a deeply conservative state, is also the new Dallas, the new Silicon Valley, the new Hollywood. Austin is the breakfast taco capital of the world (apologies to San Antonio) and the live-music capital, too (though aspiring musicians struggle to scratch out a living here anymore).

Austin is all of the above, of course, the relative weights depending largely on how long you've been here. If you read the comments sections online, God help you, the flourishing garden of skyscrapers downtown, soon to include the tallest residential building west of the Mississippi, is both a sign of the apocalypse (or at least the end of slacker heaven) and a beacon of good times and long nights.

The surest statement about Austin is that it's a city in flux, though when the changes began is also a matter of debate. Was it in 1980, with the shuttering of the Armadillo World Headquarters, the legendary cavernous music venue in an old abandoned armory? Was it in the late nineties, when a software entrepreneur named Joe Liemandt, the founder of a company called Trilogy, lured a generation of tech kids to the city, a cohort that continues to drive much of its booming start-up scene? Was it in the late aughts, when South by Southwest's Interactive conference ballooned to what's now known, not always affectionately, as Geek Spring Break? Or maybe it's all Dell's fault, or Whole Foods's. Does it matter?

Cities evolve. Austin, the country's fastest growing, is a big-time boomtown, an international tourist destination, a lifestyle brand. The question is whether this new Austin still has its soul, whether it's just a scruffy-chinned University of Texas kid all grown up with a big job and a nice house but who still holds, deep down, to that stoner free spirit. One measure is the output of its creative class, and on that one Austin can still bring it. How else to account for Aaron Franklin's mastery of smoke and meat at Franklin Barbecue, which ignited a national fever for lowly brisket? Or Liz Lambert's inspired boutique hotels (Hotel San José, Hotel

Saint Cecilia), or Richard Linklater's movies (*Dazed and Confused, Slacker, Boyhood*)? Another measure is traditions carrying on. Stevie Ray Vaughan is long gone, but here's the new blues of Gary Clark Jr. A haze of weed smoke still fills the air above the swimming holes on Barton Creek on summer afternoons. Matthew McConaughey moved back. Willie, bless him, still throws his July Fourth picnic.

Where I live, along the old "hippie highway" that cuts through gentrifying South Austin, the forces of old and new coexist in what feels, for now at least, like balance. Every week another little bungalow or auto-body shop gets razed and replaced by something bigger and shinier. But one of our neighbors stills throws her rowdy full-moon parties in a crumbling barn that sits amid a row of angular modern homes, and the giant beer garden that sprouted next to the railroad tracks a couple of years ago is a draw for everyone.

In summer, we spend evenings around the pool at the High Road, a social club in a white midcentury building with peeling paint that used to be an Elks Lodge. Perched on a hill overlooking downtown, it sits on one of the best pieces of property in town. The club parted ways with the Elks when the organization tried to sell the building, and then the old-timers opened the membership to neighbors. The crowd is equal parts young families splashing in the water, tattooed hipsters smoking cigarettes, and ex-Elks lazing in the three-digit heat. As the sun sets and our new skyline shimmers violet, everyone orders another three-dollar beer and a neighbor plugs his guitar into an amp under the craggy canopy of live oaks. As one longtime local said to me recently, "How Old Austin is that?"

Very. And we will push forward and hang on to that through the next round of changes.

AVERY ISLAND

THIS IS THE MOST FAMOUS ISLAND YOU'VE probably never heard of, home to one of the signature flavors of the South. You can probably taste the inimitable Tabasco sauce in your sleep. It's the frankincense and myrrh of the region, with roots, literally, sunk into a marshy South Louisiana salt dome called Avery Island. It was here that the first *Capsicum frutescens* peppers for Tabasco sauce were grown, and it's here where every single Tabasco pepper plant is born today. While the demands of worldwide consumption now require peppers grown on small farms in countries from Honduras to Peru, and Zimbabwe to Zambia, the seeds for all those plants, each and every one, come from Avery Island. The McIlhenny family originally made the sauce in the late 1860s, marketing it in New Orleans groceries, and the company remains family owned and fills hundreds of thousands of bottles each day—the tail end of a long process. It takes five years to turn the seeds of *Capsicum frutescens* peppers and salt into Tabasco, fermented and aged in old wooden bourbon casks in a giant warehouse on Avery Island. Now sold in more than 180 countries, it's a true synthesis of Southern culture. *See Tabasco.*

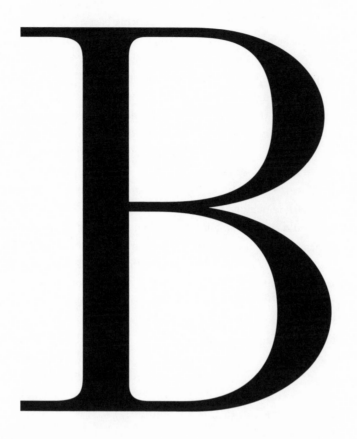

BACON

by Daniel Wallace

I REMEMBER WEEKEND MORNINGS ASLEEP IN my attic bedroom in Birmingham, Alabama, not exactly waking to the smell of bacon, but being awakened *by* it. Similar to that of freshly cut wet grass, the smell of bacon can travel for miles and never lose its potency. It was just like the cartoons I watched at the time—*Pepé Le Pew* I remember most vividly—in which you could *see* the smells; they wafted through the air like spirits. They could corral you like a lariat; they could capture you. That's what bacon did to me. Half-asleep, I would follow it downstairs and into the kitchen, and still half-asleep eat it until my mother slapped my hand. *Save some for the rest of us.* Only then would I open my eyes completely, a boy trapped in an unfeeling world where he had to share.

Bacon is a time machine for me to this day. I smell it and it's Saturday morning. My parents, dead now for many years, are seated around the morning room table. My beautiful sisters—one of whom is also gone—crowd around me, lunging for what is rightly mine, for what I very clearly had dibs on, being the first down. But they strike as fast as copperheads. Our dog Rudy, that little brown mixed breed, as long as a dachshund with the face of a beagle (we called him a dog, though no one was really sure), hid himself beneath the table, as still as a jungle animal, hoping for crumbs. Everyone is happy, everyone is young. Life is something that is just about to happen, and it's all good.

This is what bacon does to me.

Eating bacon is like dating Taylor Swift: it may not be good for you, but people just keep coming back for more, understanding that a life with a little bacon in it beats a life with no bacon at all. Bacon is full of saturated fat and salt, and yet unlike other foods makes no secret of it. Bacon is honest. Maybe this is one reason we've seen an *increase* in the popularity of bacon and recipes that call for it, such that we can now be said to be experiencing a "bacon mania." Those of us who were raised on a farm might count a piglet as a dear first pet and eat him later. That's because bacon is stronger than love itself. I wasn't raised on a farm but, rather, in front of a television, and yet I too counted a pig as my first virtual pet: Arnold Ziffel, on *Green Acres.* But that changes nothing. I would eat him if he were bacon. Bacon is not just bacon. It's bacon ice cream, bacon-infused vodka, chocolate-dipped bacon, and more. It's the meaty embodiment of Southern culture.

BANANAS FOSTER

THE ORIGIN STORY OF BANANAS FOSTER couldn't be easier to document, as it's one of those foundational recipes on which restaurant empires are built. This tale begins with three New Orleans siblings in the early 1950s. John Brennan, a produce supplier facing down a surfeit of bananas in his warehouse, gave the bananas to his brother, Owen, who was making the family name synonymous with fine Creole cuisine at Brennan's Vieux Carré Restaurant. Owen passed the bananas along to their sister, Ella, with instructions to create a dessert to honor a New Orleans civic grandee named Richard Foster. Working with the restaurant's chef, Ella devised the classic tableside preparation, which involves brown sugar, butter, a good splash of rum, a flick of the wrist, a tip of the pan, and a gleeful whoosh of fire. But the brilliance of bananas Foster is how it recasts cherries jubilee—a recipe invented fifty years prior by Auguste Escoffier in honor of Queen Victoria—with New World ingredients. And it left its imprint on a generation of American dinner-party hosts looking to dress up overripe bananas and a tub of vanilla ice cream.

wood charcoal, and that, to me, is it," chef John Currence of City Grocery in Oxford, Mississippi, once opined to *Eater*. "If you don't have both of those things, to my mind, you don't have what constitutes barbecue." Then there's Alabama's mayonnaise-rich white barbecue sauce and South Carolina's mustard sauce, both of which give purists fits. It's all in good fun, though. At its base, barbecue is a concept we can all get behind: big pieces of meat cooked low and slow in woodsmoke or over smoldering coals. Cheap, tough cuts, caressed by gentle heat and infused with sweet-tart sauces, improve like white lightning in an oak barrel. Nobody can argue with that.

BARBECUE

SOUTHERNERS LOVE TO ARGUE ABOUT BARBEcue. Take Eastern North Carolina whole hog, found at such shrines as Skylight Inn BBQ in Ayden and Jack Cobb and Son Barbecue Place in Farmville, versus Piedmont North Carolina shoulders, served in a ketchup-tinged sauce at joints like Red Bridges Barbecue Lodge in Shelby and Lexington Barbecue in Lexington. "People who would put ketchup in the sauce they feed to innocent children are capable of most anything," columnist Dennis Rogers once wrote in the Raleigh *News & Observer*. Or Southeastern pork versus Texas beef—smoked masterfully at Franklin Barbecue in Austin and Snow's BBQ in Lexington (the *Texas* Lexington). "I mean, pig and burned

BARRIER ISLANDS

THESE NARROW RIBBONS OF SAND THAT PARallel the mainland hold back hurricanes, spring tides, and nor'easters. The South boasts one of the longest single chains of barrier islands in the world, stretching from Cape Hatteras of North Carolina to Florida's Cape Canaveral, but they can be as different, one from the other, as a weeklong spring-break bender is from a quiet kayak paddle along an uninhabited shore. And barrier islands are alive; formed of sands and sediments moved by rivers and waves and currents and winds, they are in constant flux. They might be clad in dune and marsh and maritime forest, or be so overbuilt with condos and hotels that there's barely enough room for an oystercatcher to walk on two feet. Barrier islands host some of the South's wildest beaches and best-known coastal communities, and enclaves where the descendants of slaves still speak in the dialects of their forebears. They are where you find sea grass and sea-grass basket makers, nesting ibis, roosting pelicans, a Scotch bonnet, an empty beach. They're where you find some of our most garish human footprints and some of our wisest attempts to marry the built environment with the natural one.

BAYOU

THE WORD IS LOUISIANA CAJUN, BORROWED from the Choctaw *bajuk* for "small river," and refers to a body of water that flows slowly through low, swampy ground. But a bayou can be a substantial river, such as Buffalo Bayou, which flows from Houston to Galveston Bay; a braided channel to a larger stream; even a long skinny stretch of water that goes nowhere. A bayou can slowly flow in one direction, or carry currents that shift with the tides. Found most notably along the Gulf coast of Texas, Louisiana, and Alabama, and often linked to Cajun and Creole regions, bayous are as much a cultural feature as a physical one. They typically flow in places where a fisherman's lunch is likely to include boudin and cracklings, and where jokes about Boudreaux and Thibodeaux can send howls of laughter through shores armored with cypress trees and draped with Spanish moss.

BEER CHEESE

THE TRICK TO MAKING BEER CHEESE ISN'T Worcestershire sauce, Dijon mustard, or kosher salt, although every conceivable flavor enhancer has at least one ardent acolyte. To make true beer cheese, in the way the dip has been made along the banks of the Kentucky River since the 1940s, it's essential to mix together sharp cheddar, flat cheap beer, garlic, and hot sauce—and then not tell a soul exactly how you did it. Secret recipes have been part of beer cheese's allure ever since the snack was devised by the Kentucky restaurateur Johnnie Allman and his cousin, a head chef at an Arizona racetrack who had some bold ideas about spice. Originally known as Snappy Cheese, it's traditionally served cold with raw vegetables and crackers, but there's no shame in warming up a portion for a pretzel or stirring it into mac and cheese. High-end chefs who work in the Southeast (or admire its cuisine from afar) have lately taken notice of the simple dip, serving it with fancy sausages and tweaking its component ingredients. Or so we think; like all good beer cheese makers, they're not saying.

A BENNE SEED IS TO A RUN-OF-THE-MILL SES-ame seed as a juicy heirloom tomato is to the anemic supermarket variety. They may look the same, but there's a world of difference in taste. Benne came to the South from West Africa by way of the slave trade, the plant often grown in secret by the enslaved, who used the leaves, stems, and seeds as both a nutritional supplement and a flavor enhancer. Over the years, as benne became commoditized and was grown mostly for oil, those flavorful seeds became the more muted sesame seeds we know today. With a renewed interest among history-minded chefs and farmers, heirloom varieties of the seed have made something of a comeback in the South, though short of a trip to a Charleston-area farmers' market, your best bet is ordering a bag from culinary revivalist extraordinaire Anson Mills. So, no, the benne seed is not the sesame seed, exactly; the benne seed is living history.

(1947-)

ONE OF THE GREAT TORTOISE-AND-HARE STO-ries of the modern South began in Madison-ville, Tennessee, in 1973, when a high-school guidance counselor with a master's degree in psychology named Allan Benton bought a ham house from a local farmer. He never pursued his dream of eventually going to law school, instead running his roadside operation, Benton's Smoky Mountain Country Hams, through an era when most people took about as much interest in an aged haunch of hog as they did in possum potpie. Those were lean times for a self-described hillbilly selling old-timey cured hams and thick-cut smoked bacon. And he did consider caving to the pink, flabby standard that was then earning millions for the competition. As Benton tells the story, though, his dad offered one piece of advice that convinced him to keep the hickory fire stoked: "Son, if you play the other guy's game, you always lose." Benton stuck to what he knew, and when the fast-food fog cleared decades later, he was one of the few wood-burning cure masters left. The chefs found him: first, John Fleer of Blackberry Farm in nearby Walland, Tennessee, and then everyone from David Chang of Momofuku in New York City to Paul Kahan of the Publican in Chicago. By 2006, Benton was a national celebrity who could hardly keep up with his mail-order business. And it only took thirty-three years. *See Country ham; Cure masters.*

BERRY, WENDELL

(1934–)

by Erik Reece

I FIRST MET THE KENTUCKY WRITER AND farmer Wendell Berry in 2006, at a memorial service for another great Southern author, the reclusive polymath (and my mentor) Guy Davenport. I had just written a piece for *Harper's* magazine about mountaintop removal strip mining in central Appalachia. While about fifty of us gathered at the local arboretum to dedicate a sweet gum tree to Guy's memory, Wendell told me he approved of my reporting and would like to talk to me about moving forward on the problem—as writers. I felt on that day I had lost one mentor and gained another.

To oversimplify just a bit, I learned style and craft from Guy; from Wendell I learned responsibility. That is, I learned what it means to be a writer with an activist's commitment to one's home, one's native landscape. I could have written "native environment" there, but Wendell is deeply suspicious of that word—of its abstract nature and its inability to inspire dedication to a particular place, a dedication that might lead to an impulse to protect that place. Wendell has been writing in defense of Kentucky landscapes, and in support of their responsible use, since he returned from a teaching job at NYU in 1964. In New York, colleagues had tried to talk Wendell out of leaving. One even dug out the old you-can't-go-home-again saw, but Wendell knew better. Kentucky was "my fate," he wrote later in the essay "A Native Hill"—a difficult fate, but one that would not turn him loose. And far from meeting an intellectual wasteland upon his return, Wendell found living in Kentucky the Trappist monk Thomas Merton, the brilliant photographer Ralph Eugene Meatyard, the painter and printer Victor Hammer, the painter and shanty boat captain Harlan Hubbard, and the writers Guy Davenport, Ed McClanahan, and Gurney Norman. There is nothing, Wendell soon realized, quite so provincial as the New York literary world.

Wendell and his wife, Tanya, bought a marginal farm overlooking the Kentucky River, and they live there still. He reclaimed an old camp house on the banks of the river and converted it into his writing studio. There he has spent at least four hours a day, almost every day, composing what amounts to around fifty books of essays, poems, short stories, and novels. "I would not have been a poet," Wendell wrote in one of his many "Sabbath Poems,"

> Except that I have been in love
> Alive in this mortal world,
> Or an essayist except that I
> Have been bewildered and afraid,
> Or a storyteller had I not heard
> Stories passing to me through the air . . .

"In love" and "afraid"—that is the unfortunate dual nature of a man writing to preserve the land he was born to, the land he fears will be lost.

If Wendell Berry had spent the last fifty-some years writing in Vermont, his portrait would be on the state's money by now. Here in Kentucky, lawmakers hightail it for their offices and lock the doors whenever they see him coming. What it all means is that Wendell's work as a writer, a public intellectual, and a Kentuckian has been anything but easy. His early essay "The Landscaping of Hell: Strip-Mine Morality in East Kentucky" was written in 1966, but he could have written it yesterday, so stubbornly and ruthlessly has the coal industry held sway over our state. I have watched some environmental activists become eaten up with bitterness and frustration over such inertia. But Wendell has always balanced his righteous anger with affection for his fields, family, and friends. It has, I think, kept him sane.

Here's one more thing you need to know, and might not suspect, about Wendell Berry: he loves to laugh. It's a booming, shoulder-rolling laugh that escapes from his long, lanky frame like one of life's purest affirmations. His friend the late poet Jane Kenyon called it the greatest sound in the world.

BIRMINGHAM, ALABAMA

by Daniel Wallace

THE HEART OF THE HEART OF DIXIE. Other Southern cities may claim other organs—Atlanta, for instance, used to be known as the Kidney of the Confederacy—but Birmingham has always been at the center of everything good and everything bad that has happened in the South, ever since 1540, when Hernando de Soto made his

way through these parts, just for a bit, but long enough to have a cavern and a state park named after him. I'm not sure what all happened over the course of the next three hundred years or so, but I do know this: Birmingham didn't officially come into existence until 1871, six years after the Civil War ended, meaning it didn't really have anything at all to do with the Great Terribleness so stop looking at us like that.

Until the late 1960s, Birmingham *was* the industrial South. There were more steel mills and furnaces than barbecue joints and churches, so much so that for quite some time Birmingham was known as the "Pittsburgh of the South." I don't know who came up with this nickname and why they thought it was a good thing to want to be the diminutive Pittsburgh, when I have it on good authority that even Pittsburgh didn't want to be Pittsburgh at the time (they wanted to be called "Motown on the Monongahela").

At any rate, the steel that built the railroads that brought the South into the twentieth century was made in Birmingham. Kudos. And then . . .

Then, of course, came decades of segregation and racism and hate. I was born beneath that dark cloud. Many of the iconic images of that shameless era happened in Birmingham. Think of Bull Connor—the commissioner of public safety, of all things—who ordered the hoses and the dogs be used against black protesters, and who closed the city parks to prevent desegregation. That was Birmingham. Or "Bombingham," yet another nickname earned by my hometown, due to its habitual dynamiting of anyone working toward racial harmony, even children at the 16th Street Baptist Church.

Moral: When you're the heart of anything, you have to expect heartbreak. Birmingham has had its share, and caused its share, too.

But so much is different now. It's among the most beautiful cities in America. See for yourself. Many who go for a visit stay for a lifetime. The gentle slope of the Appalachian Mountains unrolls like a carpet to create green swelling hills. The steel mills are gone, the air and the water are clean, and it's where you'll find some of the best restaurants anywhere—Frank Stitt's Highlands Bar and Grill, Chris Hastings's Hot and Hot Fish Club, and more.

As if that weren't enough, rising above it all is Vulcan, at fifty-six feet tall the largest iron statue in the world. A refugee from the 1904 World's Fair, otherwise known as the Roman god of fire and metalworking, Vulcan is to Birmingham what the Empire State Building is to New York City, what the Eiffel Tower is to Paris—or, as the French call it, *le Birmingham de la France.*

BISCUITS

by Kathleen Purvis

LIKE A STAR WHO GETS REDUCED TO PLAY-ing the loyal sister as she ages, the biscuit lost its place for a while in the Southern food firmament. Biscuits became something we grabbed at fast-food windows or released from spiral tubes, while cornbread got the raves and appreciation. But there was a time when those roles were reversed.

Before the late nineteenth century, cornbread was everyday food, whipped together from ubiquitous cornmeal that anyone could buy or have ground from their own corn at the gristmills that were an essential part of any settlement. Corn-based breads and pones were easy to make and fast to cook early in the morning before a day of labor. Biscuits were special, the food of the owner's table. If you had biscuits at breakfast, it usually meant you had—or more likely, owned—a cook who rose early to make them. If you had biscuits, you had flour, ground from soft red winter wheat, less common and more costly than cornmeal. Parties featured beaten biscuits; making them was a truly sweat-inducing chore that involved repeatedly whacking the dough to break down gluten and create the right crisp texture.

Around the turn of the twentieth century, once railroads made it easier to get things like flour and when commercial baking powders became readily available, biscuits became food for everyone. Self-rising flour, with the baking powder already mixed in, made biscuits fast enough that anyone could whip up a batch for breakfast and tuck the leftovers in their pail for lunch.

The recent attention to the roots of Southern cooking, though, has restored biscuits to their starring role. Today, serious cooks are serious about biscuits. We pay attention to the flour, keeping low-protein winter-wheat flours on hand. We search out high-quality lard rendered from old-breed pigs. We look for good buttermilk, to give them tenderness and tang. And we take the handling seriously. Biscuits are less about recipe and more about touch, a deftness that comes only from repeated practice. There's a reason the finest biscuits were made by cooks and farm wives: the best way to learn to make good biscuits is to make biscuits. Over and over, every chance we get, until they come from muscle memory, not recipe.

Welcome back, biscuits. We missed you.

BISCUITVILLE

EVEN IN THE WORLD OF FAST FOOD, THERE are fancier joints. You'll often find Biscuitvilles situated in the same vicinity as junkyards and payday loan outlets. But the allure of all-day down-home Southern breakfast fare has helped the regional chain grow to fifty-four

locations in North Carolina and Virginia. At any one of them you're likely to encounter a mix of hungover frat boys, thrifty grandmas, and hungry construction workers waiting their turn to order. And at all of them you'll find an employee, in full view, hand making batch after batch of biscuits from just flour, buttermilk, and shortening—the way God intended. To dress those hot biscuits with country ham, a fried pork chop, or sawmill gravy is to visit the crossroads of comfort food and convenience. Recently, hard-core fans have noticed some new locations pop up with expanded lunch menus and suburb-ready stacked-stone exteriors. That's dandy, as long as none of this inevitable upscaling interrupts the never-ending flow of biscuits.

BLACKBEARD

(c. 1680–1718)

EDWARD TEACH HAD A BEARD. IT WAS BLACK. When he was in battle, he wove wicks laced with gunpowder into it and lit them on fire, surrounding his head with sparks and billowing smoke. It was part and parcel of what was perhaps the finest bit of pirate marketing ever, as Teach (or Blackbeard, as he became known) preferred fear and intimidation to outright violence, aiming to compel surrender before a fight even broke out. An Englishman by birth, Blackbeard began his career as a privateer during the War of the Spanish Succession and, after it ended in 1714, turned to piracy along the Carolinas and in the Caribbean.

When he captured a twenty-six-gun French boat named *La Concorde* in 1717, he refused an offer of amnesty from England and instead upped the ship's guns to forty, renamed her *Queen Anne's Revenge*, and carried on. *Queen Anne's Revenge* was sunk off Beaufort, North Carolina, seven months later, and within the year, in 1718, Blackbeard was killed in Ocracoke Inlet by forces sent by the lieutenant governor of Virginia. But only after he had taken five musket balls, endured twenty sword wounds, and fixed himself in the world's consciousness as the most famous pirate who ever lived.

BLACK BELT OF ALABAMA

IT MAY BE TRUE THAT "BLACK BELT" ORIGI-nally referred to the dark, rich topsoil blanketing nineteen counties that stretch across Alabama's lower half. But when tens of thousands of African slaves were forced to grow and harvest the cotton sprung from that fertile soil on plantations in the 1800s, the meaning inevitably shifted. After the Civil War, enough free blacks remained to work the land as sharecroppers that they still outnumbered the local population of white aristocracy. The harsh inequities of Jim Crow undoubtedly also helped make the region fertile ground for the civil rights movement in the 1960s, from the Montgomery bus boycott to the televised "Bloody Sunday" attack on peaceful marchers in Selma. Today, the Black Belt designation lives on, now used to define a "heritage area" that acknowledges its painful past while promoting its cultural and natural resources.

"BLESS YOUR HEART"

THE IDIOMS OF THE SOUTH VARY WIDELY based on location: phrases uttered in isolated mountain hollers differ from what's said in urban centers, farmlands, mill towns, water-locked bayous, and remote barrier islands. But there is one phrase that comes closer to being a universally recognized Southernism than most any other save "y'all": "Bless your heart." A colorful and handy parcel of verbiage, it can be a genuine expression of gratitude, but more often than not it's wielded to convey a veiled air of disdain with a tinge of pity. Still not getting it? Bless your heart.

BLUE CRAB

THE ATLANTIC BLUE CRAB, *CALLINECTES sapidus*, Latin for "savory beautiful swimmer." Mature, legal-size males and females are known as jimmies and sookies (respectively), and they're common in coastal waters from Maine to Mexico. They're hard to clean but easy to catch—chicken-wire box traps baited with bycatch: porgies, spots, yellowtail, grunts, and croakers, fish you wouldn't eat anyway. Deer liver works best when you have it, or trotlines baited with salt-cured bull nose—crabs love the stuff. Better yet, send the kids down to the dock with net twine, a bushel basket, a fistful of rusty bolts, a half pound of chicken necks, and a dip net. You stay home and boil the water, dusting a little Old Bay on top. (Unless you're anywhere near Chesapeake Bay, where about half of the country's commercial catch comes from and where crabs get steamed—never boiled.)

When it's time to eat the crabs, the claws are easy: pop them with pliers or a pecan cracker, slide the meat out, and dip it in butter—dark meat, the best. Bust off the legs, then peel the shell for white meat on either side. Little fingernails of shell there, but keep at it and suck the meat up if the picking gets too tedious.

Buying crabs? Make sure they're still alive. Ice on top will keep them stupefied till the water boils. You do not want a crab rodeo on the kitchen floor.

BLUEGRASS (MUSIC)

THINK OF BLUEGRASS AS THE COUNTRY cousin of jazz: a brother from another mother, so to speak. The name does not refer only to a particular sort of grass that grows in Kentucky, though one imagines that had to be involved at some point. The operative syllable here is *blue*, referring to the blue notes you find when you go looking in between the twelve main ones. In its origins, bluegrass is as messy and polyglot as jazz: some old-time music, some Irish fiddle tunes, a bit of gospel, a big injection of blues, some improvisation, and basically whatever else has caught the musician's fancy at that moment. You know it when you hear it—it's that mandolin, guitar, fiddle, and banjo, that twang, that whine, that drive. In 1946, Bill Monroe (a Kentucky native) recruited the banjo prodigy Earl Scruggs and the flat-picking guitarist Lester Flatt to form the Blue Grass Boys, and most point to this as the real moment when it all came together as a musical style. *See Monroe, Bill.*

BLUEGRASS (PLANT)

AN HERBACEOUS PERENNIAL THAT COVERS at least half the lawns in America, Kentucky bluegrass forms lush, soft fields of dark green turf. The common moniker (scientific name *Poa pratensis*, for the record) comes from the unmistakably blue seed heads that blossom atop the stems, appearing only on two- to three-foot unsheared grasses during spring and summer—so blame our obsession with painstakingly manicured lawns if you've never seen the tiny blue clusters. But the pioneers saw it all. European settlers named the Bluegrass region of northern Kentucky for its rolling meadows of this native grass. Although there are more than a hundred varieties of bluegrass nowadays, there's still a good chance the grass in your own front yard has roots in old Kentucky.

BLUE RIDGE PARKWAY

by Logan Ward

KNOWN AS "AMERICA'S FAVORITE DRIVE," this 469-mile back road ribbons through Virginia and North Carolina, high atop the spine of the Appalachian Mountains. But it's far more than a means from point A to point B. A jewel in the National Park Service's crown, the Blue Ridge Parkway is a finely planned unfurling of mountain meadows, scenic overlooks, old farmsteads, and split-rail fences designed by a landscape architect named Stanley W. Abbott. "The idea," Abbott explained, "is to fit the Parkway into the mountains as if nature has put it there."

The idea emerged during a Depression-era visit by President Franklin Delano Roosevelt to Virginia's newly built Skyline Drive, in Shenandoah National Park. Virginia senator Harry Byrd recommended extending the scenic road to Great Smoky Mountains National Park in North Carolina. Roosevelt's Interior secretary, Harold Ickes, approved the park-to-park roadway as a public works project on November 24, 1933.

Abbott, a twenty-five-year-old Cornell University graduate, started by making a long, rugged solo expedition to familiarize himself with the largely unmapped territory. As Civilian Conservation Corps crews surveyed deeper into the mountains, the challenges posed by steep terrain, rock outcroppings, winter snow and ice, and opposed landowners came into sharper focus. Undaunted, Abbott and his engineers made slow but steady progress. By the onset of World War II, 170 miles were drivable; a decade later, half the Parkway was done. By 1968, only seven miles of road remained unbuilt—a tricky stretch along the steep, ecologically fragile flanks of Grandfather Mountain, in North Carolina. The solution, a swooping 1,243-foot concrete segmental bridge known as the Linn Cove Viaduct, enabled crews to finish the Parkway in 1987. On September 11 of that year, fifty-two years after its groundbreaking, the Blue Ridge Parkway was officially dedicated.

The Parkway includes twenty-six tunnels, dozens of bridges, and more than two hundred parking areas, overlooks, and other areas of interest to passing motorists. The road reaches its lowest elevation, six hundred feet, at the James River in Virginia. At North Carolina's Richland Balsam overlook, the Parkway tops six thousand feet, its highest point.

In addition to providing a brilliant design, the tireless Abbott spent countless hours convincing skeptics "what a little ribbon of land a thousand feet wide and five hundred miles long could contribute to our major objective of conserving the fine landscape of America," he later recalled. One Michigan congressman called the Parkway "the most ridiculous undertaking that has ever been presented to the Congress of the United States." Time proved him wrong, of course. Today, the Parkway is one of the most beloved and widely visited destinations in the U.S. national park system. Drive it, and you'll witness the majesty of the world's oldest mountain range and better comprehend mountain life in the South.

BLUES

BLUES MUSIC IS BROADLY MARKED BY A SPE-cific chord progression over twelve bars, lyrical meter, a call-and-response vocal structure, and an individual series of flattened "blue notes," played at a slightly modified pitch. It's more viscerally marked by chilling loneliness, bad liquor, bad women, worse men, dirt-road vocals, and endless reserves of regret. The true origins of the blues are evocatively dusty. W. C. Handy is said to have discovered it in a Mississippi train station in the early 1900s via a traveler pressing his knife into guitar strings, and Handy later became one of the first to publish sheet music for it. But its roots extend deeper, to nineteenth-century Southern plantations, where slaves fought their days by

creating a powerful new mixture of African spirituals, folk songs, field hollers, work songs, and hymns, something that could conjure both deep pain and inextinguishable hope. However it happened, the blues came of age in the tents and juke joints of the Mississippi Delta before making its way up- and down-river and into cities that put their own stamp on the music: Kansas City blues is steeped in jazz, Louisiana blues is shot through with bayou feeling and harmonies, and Chicago blues became electric, both figuratively and literally, at the hands of John Lee Hooker and Muddy Waters. The true creators of the mid to late 1800s have largely been lost to history, but early recorded pioneers include Son House, Lead Belly, Mamie Smith, Blind Lemon Jefferson, Ma Rainey, and Bessie Smith, artists without whom there would be no R&B and no rock and roll.

BOILED PEANUTS

by Matt Lee and Ted Lee

BOILED PEANUTS SEEM TO OCCUPY A SPACE between a snack food and a habit, like chewing tobacco. As any fan can attest, the act of loosening the salty, wet little legumes from their shells inspires one's mind to take a leisurely walk. People eating boiled peanuts are usually engaged in other tasks—driving, chatting, fishing, watching a ball game. (Peanuts are most often boiled at home or purchased at roadside, and are almost never served in a restaurant.) The elusive, liminal nature of the boiled peanut—a strong touchstone of identity in parts of the South yet virtually unheard-of in others; a flavor worthy of highest exaltation in a package that's wet and messy; that anticommercial streak—is its only certain character trait.

There's an existential crisis, too. Peanuts (*Arachis hypogaea*) are not really nuts. They're legumes, from the family Leguminosae, which includes limas, favas, soybeans, and most any bean you've ever eaten. A peanut newly dug from the ground is as damp as a potato and has both the fresh aroma of mown hay and the pleasantly funky one of a dried leaf pile. Shell it and chew the medium-firm seed kernels and you'll discover a starchy, gently sweet flavor like that of a raw lima bean or sweet pea. It's a taste of high harvest, the end of August to mid-fall (in our native South Carolina; earlier to the south, later to the north). To us it seems logical—and not unusual—that you might want to boil them or steam them, the way most beans are boiled or steamed before they're eaten. (If instead you dry the peanuts and roast them in an oven, you will change their flavor, bringing out a nutty, buttery character that the legume doesn't possess in its raw state, and you'll have what most Americans recognize as peanuts—roasted peanuts.)

Peanuts came to North America from Africa and the Caribbean with the slave trade, sometime before the American Revolution. African Americans grew and popularized the peanut—both boiled and roasted/baked/parched—throughout the South. Eventually, by the early twentieth century, all Southerners took a widespread interest.

Boiled peanuts catch neophytes off guard, challenging them to think about a familiar food in a new way. And this miraculous transformation is accomplished not by adding any ingredient, but by simply taking the peanut *back* a step, toward its natural state. Not everyone falls for their distinctive bean-like flavor, but boiled peanuts are undeniably full of personality.

They couldn't be easier to prepare—if you can boil water, you can boil peanuts. It's a great activity for a Saturday or Sunday morning; all that's required is for you to get up from your primary occupation occasionally to maintain the water in the pot. The peanuts are incredibly tolerant, in the sense that they're difficult to overcook, which allows plenty of leeway for forgetfulness, distraction, and inebriation.

Eating the fragrant peanuts hot out of the pot is a wonderful way to approach them, but gobbling them at room temperature seems the quintessential experience, since they're most often purchased by the side of the road or in a gas station, in soggy brown kraft-paper bags. The briny peanuts seem to gain something from sitting in the fridge for a few days, too, so feel free to eat them cold, as we often do. Truly, boiled peanuts defy any attempt at gussying up, professionalization, or *expertise*, and that just might be their ultimate gift to those who love them.

ALBULA VULPES, OR "WHITE FOX," THE BONE-fish is also known as the phantom, silver ghost, ladyfish, grubber, and, inexplicably, as *banane de mer* (banana of the sea) by, naturally, the French. It is one of the most coveted of shallow-water sport fish and is usually found in areas with mangroves and sea grasses. For American anglers, that means southern Florida and the Bahamas, where you will be looked upon with a mixture of pity and contempt if you attempt to catch them on anything other than a fly rod. The fish has armor plates rather than scales, a sucker-like mouth, and a snout-like nose. With these it digs about for crabs, shrimp, and other small things, especially on rising tides and often in small groups. Bonefish startle like overcaffeinated guinea pigs at the slightest disturbance, so the angler must place his offering in the direction they're heading with precision. Too close, and they'll vanish. Too far, and they'll fail to register it. If you do get a strike, the fish typically bolts for up to a hundred yards. Then it may rest and bolt back, heading for the mangroves. Since motors frighten bonefish, the guide usually stands on an elevated platform and poles the skiff. When he spots one, he'll tell you where to cast, as in "Twenty-five yards at eleven o'clock," expecting you to instantly cast to that spot. When you fail to do this, he will often curse in the local dialect. You will not understand the literal meaning, but the message is unmistakable: the fellow you pay four hundred dollars a day has just called you one sorry-ass fisherman.

THE WOODEN SIGNS AND VINYL TARPS ALONG the back highways of South Louisiana that advertise the availability of hot boudin are typically worded so ecstatically (HOT BOUDIN + COLD BEER = GOOD COMPANY) that travelers might imagine they've stumbled across the only source of sausage in a pork-and-rice-deprived county. That's never the case, of course. Acadians are crazy about the delicacy, which is often the first thing they eat after arising: get yourself a cold Coke and a boudin link, and you've got yourself a Cajun breakfast, obligatory if you plan to spend the day fishing. Sold in butcher shops, grocery stores, and gas stations, boudin shares a name with French boudin blanc and not much more. Influenced by German immigrants' sausage-making mastery and the region's nineteenth-century rice economy, boudin is typically stuffed with ground-up pig parts, cooked rice, onions, green peppers, and spices, and then steamed for instant eating. Variations are endless: there's boudin stuffed with seafood, including alligator; grilled boudin; smoked boudin; and boudin balls. The most endangered of all the types is boudin rouge; health inspectors don't always take kindly to the amount of pig's blood required to produce its signature flavor and color.

BOURBON

by Kathleen Purvis

WHAT IS IT ABOUT THE SOUTH THAT drives us to drink? More specifically, what is it about the South that drives us to make the stuff everyone else wants to drink?

Ciders and fruit brandies were once common farm products, made anywhere peaches, apples, and grapes were grown. Rums and Madeiras were widely available wherever there was a port to bring them from the Caribbean or Portugal. But bourbon is so closely linked with Kentucky that many people still mistakenly believe it's the only place that creates the stuff. Truth be told, under federal standards set in 1964, bourbon can be produced anywhere in the United States as long as it meets a set of other criteria, including that the majority of the mash is made from corn and that it's aged in new charred oak barrels.

Still, corn grows well in many parts of the country. So why has bourbon always had such strong ties to the South?

A lot of factors played a part in the origins of Southern whiskeys, from clear corn liquor to barrel-aged bourbon. Early life in the South—when much of the region was far from population centers—required self-reliance, the ability to make whatever you would need. The Scotch-Irish settled much of the region, bringing whiskey-making know-how with them, so some form of high-octane alcohol was inevitable. Surviving here economically also meant the ability to turn anything you could grow into something that would bring the best returns in trade or usefulness. Corn

grows well even in slightly rocky soil, making it a reliable crop even in mountainous areas. Those mountains were also generally sources of excellent water, filtered through natural limestone so that it was free of iron and higher in calcium, making it perfect for use in distillation.

A bushel of dried corn is heavy. It's a lot easier to transport it and sell it for more money if you use that corn to make a mash and then distill that mash into alcohol. Pouring that alcohol into oak barrels that are charred on the inside will, over time, transform that raw, clear corn whiskey into something brown, smooth, and packed with flavor imparted from the wood.

From Kentucky, it could take months to transport those barrels by raft down the Ohio River to the Mississippi and on to New Orleans for sale, but even a few months in a barrel could nudge raw corn whiskey on its way to becoming something much more pleasant to drink—and that merchants were willing to buy and resell for a much higher price.

It is also worth remembering one other thing while contemplating Southern bourbons and whiskeys: the role of Southern isolation. Well into the twentieth century, the South remained rural, heavily wooded, and in many places mountainous. That made it possible to produce alcohol free from regulation and, more important, taxation.

The great irony is that the production of alcohol thrived in a place with such strong religious and social strictures against the consumption of it. Perhaps it's simply human nature: the more the fruit is forbidden, the more of a thrill it is to consume it.

BO WHOOP

No single firearm expresses the South's hunting heritage and history as completely as T. Nash Buckingham's monstrous 1926 12-gauge A. H. Fox Burt Becker side-by-side, dubbed "Bo Whoop" for its thunderous report. From the 1930s to the early 1960s, Buckingham published scores of hunting stories for major magazines, mostly tales of waterfowling and quail hunting. The tales filled seven book collections—the most famous was the first, *De Shootinest Gent'man & Other Tales*—and made Mr. Buck a near-household name across the region. The South's most famous shotgun won notoriety not only because of its featured role in many of the writer's famous stories, but because the gun vanished for half a century, fostering more fakes and false sightings than the Virgin Mary.

Buckingham lost Bo Whoop in 1948. As he and a buddy were being checked by a game warden, he leaned the shotgun against the car, then the pair drove off, the shotgun forgotten. The gun stayed lost for more than a half century, until 2005 when a gunsmith in Darlington, South Carolina, recognized the ancient blunderbuss when an anonymous owner brought it in to have the stock replaced. Once word got out that Bo Whoop had resurfaced, it didn't take long for the shotgun to hit the auction block. Buckingham's godson, Hal Howard Jr., bought it for $201,250, and loaned it for display at Ducks Unlimited's national headquarters in Memphis. *See Double guns.*

BOW TIE

Though it originated in Croatia, where seventeenth-century mercenaries wore scarves around their necks to hold their shirt collars together (the French word *cravat* literally means "Croat"), the bow tie has evolved into one of the South's ultimate sartorial expressions. The "string tie" first took root in the region—think Colonel Sanders—but Southerners today don't discriminate: from bolos to batwings to black-tie silks, in designs ranging from seersucker to turkey feathers, the humble bow tie has found a welcome home in the region.

BOXWOOD

The boxwood is a Southern garden icon, a small-leaved evergreen that thrives in a variety of soils, with minimal water, and in both sun and shade. While hundreds of box varieties exist, the two commonly associated with the American South are *Buxus sempervirens* (American boxwood) and a dwarf variety, *Buxus sempervirens "Suffruticosa"* (English boxwood). Many are surprised to learn that the so-called American box dominated the seventeenth- and eighteenth-century gardens of England. A fungal blight that originated in Europe in the 1990s now threatens both varieties of the historically hardy shrub.

Boxwoods are known for bringing order and symmetry to gardens, whether planted individually or in hedges. In gardens across the South, they form allées, perennial borders, and elaborate parterres. They're even orderly growers, requiring only one or two trimmings per year. The use of boxwoods reached peak popularity during the Colonial Revival movement of the late nineteenth and early twentieth centuries, especially in Virginia. Look for classic examples in and around Colonial Williamsburg. The restored box gardens at George Washington's home, Mount Vernon, are particularly impressive, with French influence plainly visible in the elaborately sculpted parterre fronting the conservatory.

BOYKIN SPANIEL

THE TRUE DEFINITION OF A POCKET RE-triever, the Boykin spaniel is a gundog that rarely tops forty pounds. It's also one of just a handful of truly Southern dog breeds. Established in the early 1900s near Camden, South Carolina, by a sportsman named L. Whitaker Boykin, the breed was developed to hunt the local swamps out of small boats. (This characteristic inspired an oft-used phrase describing the Boykin as "the dog that doesn't rock the boat.") These days hunters still take "the little brown dogs" into the swamps in pursuit of ducks and woodcocks but also into the field for quail and other upland birds. In 1985, South Carolina made the Boykin its state dog, even designating an official day to celebrate the breed, September 1. No surprise, that's also the opening day of dove season.

BROOK TROUT

THE ONLY SALMONID NATIVE TO THE SOUTH, found as far south as Georgia, the brook trout, technically, is no trout at all. It's a char more closely related to Dolly Varden and arctic char than rainbow and brown trout. Its Latin name, *Salvelinus fontinalis*, means "dweller of springs," and it is in high, pure, cold waters that it has remained since the last of the glaciers slid northward. It may not leap like the rainbow or run like the brown, but the brook trout gives no ground on beauty. In the hand, a wild brook trout is a riot of color, but in the water it utterly disappears. Blue-haloed red spots become tiny bits of stream-bottom stone. Yellow vermiculations across a moss-green back turn to spots of dappled sun. Every aspect of the fish's adornments is designed to keep it hidden, out of the clutches of otter, owl—and angler.

BROWN, JAMES

(1933–2006)

THINKING ABOUT SCULPTING A MOUNT Rushmore of American music? Start right here (and be sure to reserve enough granite up high for the hair). Born in 1933 in Barnwell, South Carolina, James Brown developed both an inhuman work ethic and the knowledge that in the 1960s you had to rattle stages not just with your music alone—though his would have sufficed—but with sweaty, glittery, flying, sequined, spinning, knee-dropping, screaming, unstoppable, and caped *style*. Brown's catalogue is an absurdly stuffed hit list of songs one can't imagine life without: "I Got You (I Feel Good)," "Cold Sweat," "Try Me," "Papa's Got a Brand New Bag," "Get Up (I Feel Like Being a) Sex Machine," "Say It Loud—I'm Black and I'm Proud." His self-assigned title, "the hardest-working man in show business," is an accolade no modern musician dare claim for himself—Brown will possess it eternally,

along with "Mr. Dynamite," "Soul Brother No. 1," and "the Godfather of Soul." That said, Brown also had more than his share of demons, which throughout his career led him to jail sentences, seemingly bottomless tax problems, a trail of broken relationships, and at least one mug shot gone viral. Yet through it all, driven less by financial requirements than a fierce need to perform, Brown achieved a standard that will be forever imitated. But never come close to being touched.

BROWN, LARRY

(1951–2004)

by Jonathan Miles

IN 1980, A TWENTY-NINE-YEAR-OLD Oxford, Mississippi, firefighter named Larry Brown decided to try writing stories. A father of two with another child soon to come, he'd been working odd jobs to make ends meet—building fences, hauling hay, painting houses—and figured writing might be an easier and more satisfying way to earn an extra buck. It wasn't. The more stories Brown wrote—more than a hundred, he later estimated—the faster they came boomeranging back into his mailbox affixed with rejection notes. Barry Hannah, then writer in residence at the University of Mississippi, took to hiding when he'd spot Brown coming his way with a manila folder under an arm, lest Hannah be served with yet another unsalvageable story. When Brown finally published a story, it was in *Easyriders*, a biker magazine known not for its writing but for the tattooed models and chromed-out choppers gracing its covers.

There seemed little to suggest, in this long and tortured start, that Larry Brown would go on to become a titan of Southern literature—a novelist, essayist, and short-story writer whose name is often and rightfully invoked in the same breath as Harry Crews, Cormac McCarthy, and Flannery O'Connor. But Brown was almost manically driven, and year after year of writing and reading and re-writing, along with the mighty artistic awakening it roused, eventually equipped him with the literary equivalent of perfect pitch: an astounding ear for the music of drawling speech, a keenly sensitive eye for the kudzu-riddled landscapes of his native countryside, and a breathtaking ability to render the foibles of human existence with warm but unblinking precision. Brown took a sledgehammer to Samuel Beckett's notion that the true artist comes from nowhere. Suffusing his work was what winemakers call terroir: the peculiar tang of a specific locale, the distinct and unfakeable flavors imparted by a collusion of factors such as soil (clay), climate (humid), and tradition (Faulkner et al., plus all the stories Brown heard traded at country stores and during quiet nights at the firehouse).

Brown's books—foremost among them *Dirty Work* (1989), *Big Bad Love* (1990), *Joe* (1991), *Father and Son* (1996), and *Fay* (2000)—were set mostly in the outer precincts of Lafayette County, and peopled with hard-living characters with a fondness or weakness (take your pick) for sex, cold beer, cigarettes, bare-knuckled violence, pedal-steel ballads, and riding the gravel back roads in a meditative funk. From the first page Brown liked to load his characters with trouble—"sandbagging," he once called it—and then chronicle their struggles to cast off this load, like the Old Testament's God lobbing ordeals at Job. Yet by gauging what they could endure, Brown showed what all of us can endure, calculating the carrying load of existence not unlike the way O'Connor, from another angle, charted the boosting powers of grace. His prose was lean but its effects were lush.

Those effects yielded Brown a devoted cult following—particularly among songwriters, ranging from the Texas legend Robert Earl Keen to the stadium-filling Tim McGraw, who saw reflected in Brown's work that bedrock definition of a great country song: three chords and the truth. At the time of Brown's sudden death in 2004—a heart attack claimed him in his sleep, at the age of fifty-three—he had exponentially exceeded those early firehouse ambitions. He had carved his name into the thick trunk of American literature, and had enriched that literature with a shatteringly singular voice that continues to be celebrated and imitated but—like the voice of Hank Williams, which often serenaded Brown as he'd roam the twilit back roads in his dun-colored truck—cannot ever be matched.

BRUNSWICK STEW

IF YOU'VE EVER EATEN A BRUNSWICK STEW made with squirrel, you won't forget the distinctive winey sweetness of the meat. That Brunswick stew—the one cooked in a cast-iron cauldron over an open fire—figures into many a multigenerational Southern family's mythology. But let's face it: people talk squirrel and cook chicken. Today's stews, unlike yesteryear's catchall of small furred game, usually combine long-simmered chicken along with its broth, corn, tomato, butter beans, and a few shakes of Worcestershire sauce. The farther south you head from Brunswick County, Virginia, to the coastal town of Brunswick, Georgia, the more likely you are to find threads and chunks of smoked pork in equal measure to chicken. The two Brunswicks, of course, have long fought over naming rights. Perhaps the Virginia stews are thicker and more simply seasoned, a one-dish meal. The more tomatoey Georgia stews tend toward soupiness and have a peppery bite and vinegary zing. Indeed, barbecue vendors throughout Georgia offer Brunswick stew as a thrifty side dish that uses up all the leftovers. Wherever Brunswick stew is claimed, there will be a full calendar of festivals and cook-offs.

BUFFETT, JIMMY

(1946–)

NO ONE HAS MONETIZED SUNSETS AND MARgaritas more than James William Buffett, whose island escapist sounds are played in every beach-bum bar from Hawaii to Aruba, not to mention his own restaurants. Born in Mississippi and reared in Mobile, Buffett began his career playing his folksy music on the streets of Nashville. After little success, he bought a one-way ticket to Miami, eventually ending up in Key West with his good friend Jerry Jeff Walker. There he found his muse. His 1977 breakthrough album, *Changes in Latitudes, Changes in Attitudes*, contained his now-ubiquitous single "Margaritaville," and subsequent hits like "Cheeseburger in Paradise" and the 2003 duet with Alan Jackson "It's Five O'Clock Somewhere" provided a rallying cry for happy hours in the sand. To his credit, Buffett was one of the first artists of the past forty years to recognize that the real money was in touring—he has hit the road every single year since 1976—and his die-hard fans, dubbed Parrot Heads, gather en masse wearing loud floral-pattern shirts and crazy hats, dreaming of ditching their day jobs for island life a few hours each night.

HERE'S WHAT A BUTTER BEAN MOST CER- tainly is *not*: a conventional lima bean that Southerners have given a more palatable moniker. Butter beans aren't green; they're creamy white. They should never be served from a can; look for them sold straight from a cooler in plastic bags along Southern roads for about a three-week period sometime between June and August. And they don't have any tartness; they're sweeter and smoother than their sometimes off-putting mass-market lima cousin. Also known as a Dixie bean or sieva, the butter bean has been a go-to hereabouts for succotash and stews since the 1700s. You can boil them until tender and dress simply with lemon zest, sea salt, and olive oil. Or cook them with a big ol' ham hock and spoon them over hot crusty cornbread for a classic helping of Southern goodness.

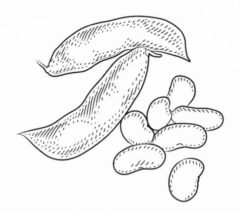

FOR ALL THE CONFUSION AROUND REAL buttermilk, its definition is simple: honest-to-goodness, farm-fresh, can't-buy-it-at-the-supermarket buttermilk is the sour liquid that runs off freshly churned butter. So why aren't we swimming in it? Because the way we make butter has changed. On a nineteenth-century farm, you would have made butter by leaving fresh milk out in the springhouse until the cream rose to the top and then churning it. As the milk sat out for twelve or fourteen hours, friendly bacteria would thicken and sour it. Once churned, it would have given you complex cultured butter and buttermilk that would have added zing to biscuits, pies, and fried chicken. Today, of course, most of our butter comes from factories. While cultured butter remains popular in Europe, stateside, we prefer it sweet. And if the cream doesn't sour, the buttermilk doesn't either. So modern dairies simulate old-fashioned buttermilk with cultured milk, which is a passable substitute but lacks the acid bite and butter flakes of the real deal. If you want to make biscuits that taste just like your great-great-grandma's, you'll need to either find an old-fashioned dairy or do as your ancestors did and churn your own butter.

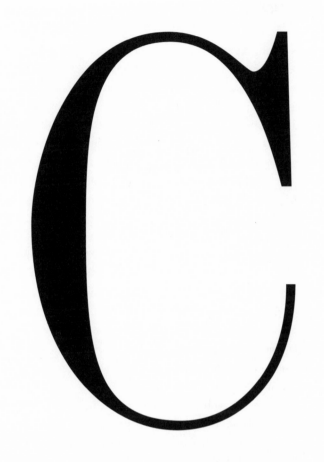

A FAMED NEW ORLEANS COFFEE SHOP, CAFÉ Du Monde opened in the French Market in 1862 not far from its current location just off Jackson Square. It's best known for café au lait made with chicory, and beignets, which are puffy fried dough related in concept and etymology to the Spanish *buñuelos*. While some other ordering options exist (hot chocolate, for instance), coffee and beignets are pretty much what's on offer.

Caffeine-deprived tourists often wait for an hour or longer for a seat at the French Quarter location (satellites exist in the suburbs and the New Orleans airport, but they lack the verve of the original). Therefore, a visit to Café Du Monde tends to be most successful when done opportunistically. That is, if you happen to pass by and see that it's line-free, it's advisable to walk in, sit down, and order coffee and beignets, even if you're not in the least hungry.

Unless you are wearing black. Then under no circumstances should you visit Café Du Monde. The beignets are piled high with powdered sugar and bring to mind Colombian drug cartels; a single poorly executed bite will result in a small avalanche, leading to a streaked, smudgy garment that will mark one for the rest of the day as a rank amateur.

A CAJUN IS THE ULTIMATE SURVIVOR, someone who not only eats anything that doesn't eat him first but also manages to make it taste good. In a fight, if you have a gun and he doesn't, you're still at a disadvantage. He will have at least three bateaux and an outdoor propane burner the size of an Atlas booster rocket in his yard for crawfish boils. *Cajun* derives from *Acadia*, the name of a French colony in northeastern Canada four hundred years ago. The Acadians refused to sign a loyalty oath, so the Brits kicked them out. Some rolled as far south as Louisiana, where they settled in the swamps and bayous that no one else wanted and did the work others wouldn't. Not even the resident French people wanted anything to do with them. Set apart by language, culture, and customs, the Cajuns did what they do best: survive. After World War II, Cajuns became more integrated into the larger world. But only to a point. Today, for the most part, they can pass in the larger culture. The reverse is not true. Remember that. Classic Cajun story: Each Friday night, Boudreaux would torture his Catholic neighbors by grilling a tantalizing venison steak. In time, he agreed to convert. The priest sprinkled him with holy water, saying, "You were born a nonbeliever and raised a nonbeliever, but now you are a Catholic." A week later, Boudreaux was once again grilling venison on Friday night. When the priest arrived, he found Boudreaux sprinkling water from a small bottle onto the meat and saying, "You was born a deer, you was raised a deer, but now you is a crawfish."

CAMELLIA

MUCH LIKE THE EARLY SOUTHERN COLONISTS who cultivated these pink-, red-, and white-flowering shrubs, camellias are "from off." Native to parts of China and Japan, the plants appeared in London in the early 1700s (and later the American colonies), courtesy of the East India Trading Company, when a bureaucratic goof resulted in a shipment of *Camellia japonica* rather than the expected *Camellia sinensis* (tea plants). A happy accident for Southerners from the eastern edge of Texas to the northern reaches of coastal Virginia, where the japonica thrived amid mild winters. The broad-leaved evergreens vary in size—they can grow as tall as thirty feet—as do their regal flowers, which range from feathery to almost perfectly symmetrical. Camellias prefer light shade, which protects them during hot summer months, and they bloom from October through April (even mid-May in places)—a reliable bright spot in winter gardens. Although the property takes its name from another Southern botanical darling, Magnolia Plantation and Gardens in Charleston, South Carolina, has the country's largest camellia collection, with more than twenty thousand plants and a special focus on ancient varieties, including the world's rarest—Middlemist's Red.

CANE SYRUP

AS THE STORY GOES, CHARLEY AND ELIZABETH Steen of Abbeville, Louisiana, founded their syrup company in 1910 as an effort to keep their cane crop from succumbing to frost. They purchased a mill to extract the juice, hitched it up to a mule, and were in business. More than a hundred years later, Steen's, in its iconic bright yellow can, remains a familiar brand and serves as one of the last reliable producers of all-natural cane syrup—once a staple of the Louisiana pantry but now in danger of being Karo'ed and Aunt Jemima'ed out of the kitchen. Like any reduction of natural plant juices (sorghum, maple), the syrup takes on a dark color and a bit of earthy, caramel bitterness as the sweet extraction turns to treacle. But it has a twang all its own, a flavor that likes baked beans and barbecue sauce as well as it does biscuits and pancakes.

CAROLINA DOG

WHEN SOMEONE SAYS HIS DOG IS A "CAROLINA Dog," the persistent assumption is that he means it's a good ol' mutt from the Carolinas. This drives owners crazy. Carolina Dogs are an honest-to-goodness breed. Recognized as such by the United Kennel Club only somewhat recently (in 1995), the Carolina Dog is known informally as the American dingo because, as with its Australian cousin, its natural habitat is the wild. Medium-sized and usually yellow (leading to another common nickname,

Ol' Yaller Dog), Carolina Dogs were "discovered" in the 1970s, when Dr. I. Lehr Brisbin Jr., an ecologist, spotted several of them roaming wild around the Savannah River. Noting their strong resemblance to the dingo, Brisbin began to investigate. Turns out Carolina Dogs, like dingoes, descended from the primitive dogs of Asia. Free-roaming mostly in the cypress swamps and longleaf pine forests of South Carolina and Georgia, Carolina Dogs are easily identified by their yellow coat, alert equilateral-triangle ears, and fishhook tail. They're sometimes shy and often gentle, and generations of Ol' Yaller Dog owners will assure you that they make great pets and have never been known to steal a baby.

CAROLINA GOLD RICE

IF YOU'VE EVER FOUND HOPPIN' JOHN TO BE lacking, you're not alone—and you're most likely missing a key ingredient: Carolina Gold rice, the grain that built Charleston, South Carolina. It was the foundation for a series of canonical dishes: rice and peas, rice pudding, rice bread. Enslaved Africans from rice-growing regions raised great fortunes for planters, sowing and tending it in marshy coastal fields. Then came a flurry of social and economic upheavals: war, emancipation, destructive storms, new planting and harvesting technologies that favored firm soil over pluff mud. In 1911, a hurricane wiped out the last operation growing Carolina Gold. So the rice essentially vanished, all but forgotten on the compost pile of history, until 1985, when an eye surgeon named Richard Schulze wheedled a couple of sacks from a USDA seed bank for his Hardeeville, South Carolina, duck-hunting plantation. Schulze resurrected the firm, nutty grain and opened the floodgates to a wave of vocal advocates of this and other heirloom foods. Among them: the miller Glenn Roberts of Anson Mills in Columbia, South Carolina, and the heirloom-obsessed chef Sean Brock of Husk and McCrady's restaurants in Charleston.

CASH, JOHNNY

(1932–2003)

JOHNNY CASH ALWAYS WORE BLACK ON-stage, from his early days as an upstart pop star to his late-in-life revival as a grizzled elder statesman. But there were many shades to country music's first outlaw. Although he famously performed for prisoners, he never actually served hard time himself. Dogged throughout his life by vice and addiction, he was also a man of deep religious conviction who ached to record simple gospel standards at the height of his stardom in the 1960s. A self-taught philosopher and poet, he once, in a drugged-up haze, carelessly started a fire that burned down five hundred acres of national forest and scared off forty-nine en-dangered condors. We all make mistakes, but his bleary-eyed deposition made sure that one went down in history: "I don't care about your damn yellow buzzards," he snarled. Cash's openness about his flaws and his ongo-ing quest for redemption, though, made him one of the most human and beloved figures in modern music. Just after his wife, June Carter, passed away in 2003, the seventy-one-year-old got a call from Rick Rubin, the producer re-sponsible for his popular late-in-life *American* albums. "Do you feel like somewhere you can find faith?" Rubin asked. Heartsick and ail-ing, Cash repeated a mantra that had seen him through a lifetime of joys and trials: "My faith is *unshakable*." Although his eyesight was dwindling and his baritone was wearing thin, the son of Arkansas cotton farmers kept re-cording until just three weeks before his death later that year.

CAST IRON

WHEN SORTING THROUGH FAMILY HEIR-looms, a savvy Southerner knows to *always* call dibs on that unassuming old cast-iron skillet, regardless of whether it has a perfectly smooth patina or looks like a rusty hunk of scrap. It may not flash the glitz of Grandmother's sil-ver, but it will sit on your stove top for decades ready to fry fish, bake cobbler, sear steak, sauté veggies, nail a frittata, caramelize on-ions, simmer a sauce—pretty much any cook-ing challenge you throw at it. An indestructible mash-up of iron and carbon, the skillet holds heat well and distributes it evenly (not to men-tion seriously works your biceps and forearms). Treated properly, it will outlive any of your other kitchen tools (and, truth be told, you). Cast-iron cookware originally came to the States with the colonists, and mass production in this country began more than a century ago in South Pittsburg, Tennessee, still the home of the iron cookware giant Lodge. You can easily clean a new, unrusted pan after each use: wash with warm water, dry completely, then rub it down with vegetable oil. Heat until it's smoking, then leave it on your stove top until you need it—most likely at your next meal. If it needs more of a scrub, use a little salt and a paper towel to dislodge gunk before rinsing. Inherited a rust bucket? You'll need to season it. Scour off the rust with steel wool, rub the pan down with vegetable oil, and place it upside-down in a 350°F oven for an hour.

CAST NET

THERE ARE A FEW SKILLS THAT MARK A CERtain elevated level of Southern sportsman, and the ability to hurl a cast net from the bow deck of a skiff is high on that list. It's a circular net, its outer margins weighted with lead, and when thrown correctly, the centrifugal forces of those edge weights pull the net into a disk shape that hovers aloft before hitting the water, edges sinking while the net floats, thereby capturing shrimp, finger mullet, and pilchards that you'd otherwise have to lay down some cash for at the bait shop. Problem is, it ain't easy to do, and when thrown incorrectly, a cast net wads up in midair, travels but half the distance you need, and crashes to the water as if you've hurled a sack of collards into the marsh, and you catch nothing but smirks of derision from all the real fishermen on the dock. Which explains why there are plenty of bait shops around.

CATFISH NOODLING

by Bill Heavey

CATFISH ARE NATIVE TO MOST OF THE eastern United States but, like magnolia trees—which they resemble in no other way—thrive best in the South. The three main species are channel cats, blue catfish, and flatheads. They can be caught on hook and line, in nets, or with "redstick" (dynamite, which can get you in legal trouble even if you don't blow up the boat and your friends). The most sporting way is *mano a pescado*, also known as noodling, grabbing, or grabbling. I once went grabbling with some Mississippians on the Big Black River, in which they had sunk cypress boxes that the local flatheads liked to nest in. One man would block the entrance with his legs while another poked a six-foot steel trident inside. If there was a flathead home, you could hear it slamming against the box five feet down. Holding a fish stringer in one hand, you held on to the blocker's legs to avoid being swept downstream and reached inside the box. For unknown reasons, a submerged catfish will often put up with a human fist in its mouth. Sometimes it won't, "logrolling" with sufficient vigor to remove the skin from your forearm. What you're trying to do is slip the stringer in its mouth and out a gill. You then wrap the cord around your wrist, hoping that the beast—mine was a fifty-pounder—won't dislocate your shoulder. Then you pull him out and up, attempting to lift the fish clear of the water, thereby robbing it of its power. Meanwhile, everyone helpfully yells, "Get 'im up! Get 'im up, boy!" just in case you've forgotten what to do next. It's tremendously exciting, and the kind of thing you later decide you really only need to do once.

CHARLESTON, SOUTH CAROLINA

by John Huey

CHARLESTONIANS HAVE LONG BEEN QUICK to tell you where their city lies on the map: at the point where the Cooper River meets the Ashley to form the Atlantic Ocean. That egocentric view has prevailed since 1663, when England's King Charles II granted the region to a group of eight Lords Proprietors—headed by Lord Anthony Ashley Cooper—who built a fabulously lucrative empire of rice, cotton, and indigo. All of it was made possible by the labor of thousands of African slaves shipped in for just that purpose.

The fruits of this wealth ripened into a glorious little port city in which to live and stroll. Majestic homes of Colonial, Georgian, and Federal styles, wrapped with classic English gardens and nestled under giant canopies of magnolia and live oak, still define the residential neighborhood south of Broad Street. Above Broad, grand Greek Revival temples of government emphasized the society's commitment to certain principles it believed hearkened back to Athens, namely a republic ruled by the oligarchy, and an intellectual and moral acceptance of slavery. Life was so good for rich Charlestonians that they barely joined the American Revolution. Not so the Civil War, the bloodiest in American history, which they famously started on April 12, 1861, when Confederate artillery fired on the Union garrison at Fort Sumter.

The next hundred years didn't go so well for Charleston, which after the war eschewed the whole "New South" scheme adopted by coarser towns like Atlanta and Charlotte. The town withdrew into itself. Great antebellum homes fell into paint-chipped decline. The city boasted no hotels or restaurants worth the trip. Most visitors arrived on shore leave from U.S. Navy ships calling at the now-defunct naval base.

Then, simultaneously, came a couple of unrelated events that would change everything. In 1974, the Kuwaiti Investment Company purchased a barrier island full of timber just south of Charleston. It aimed to develop Kiawah Island into a gated oceanside golf community, as the developer Charles Fraser had done at Hilton Head Island just down the coast. One year later, Charlestonians elected as mayor a thirty-two-year-old real estate lawyer named Joe Riley, who had a vision for reviving the city's struggling economy by restoring downtown to its former glory. As it turned out, Kiawah attracted well-heeled outsiders from all over the world who would fall in love with Riley's theme park of the new, old American city. Between days at the beach and rounds of golf, they would stroll through town, marvel at its charm, muse about rehabbing a home where George Washington slept, and long for better restaurants.

Forty-some years later, it's all come together, and Charleston is now recognized, by and large, as America's Prom Queen.

Condé Nast Traveler called it "America's Most Friendly City." *Travel + Leisure* raised that hand, declaring it "World's Best City." It's where you travel to get married in the glorious spring. Or bring your buds for the bachelor or bachelorette party. Or honeymoon. Or take your family to the beach. Or bring your grandma for a historic walking tour. Or shoot ducks and catch redfish by day, then barhop Upper King Street by night. It's where Bill Murray may drop by your table to nab a french fry. Where it's still fashionable to take your family to church. New hotels and restaurants are popping up like dandelions. James Beard Awards fall from the sky on its chefs. Citadels like Husk and FIG and a few others have received worshipful national attention. Not long ago a neighborhood soul-food fixture, Bertha's Kitchen, won a Beard America's Classic award for its fried chicken, okra soup, and neck-bone fare. High time.

Warning: the dream could fade. People don't just visit Charleston anymore. They move there, at the rate of thirty-five a day. With them come Atlanta-style apartments, traffic, a steady increase in horn blowing, and hedge-fund shoppers who buy $4 million teardowns (four-thousand-square-foot houses they bull-doze the day after closing) at the beach.

Hell, Scarlett, Rhett Butler would barely recognize the place.

CHARLESTON RECEIPTS

THE REIGNING QUEEN OF JUNIOR LEAGUE cookbooks, first published in 1950. *See Junior League.*

CHARLOTTESVILLE, VIRGINIA

by Steve Russell

THOMAS JEFFERSON WAS HERE. AND *HERE.* And *over there.* Indeed, sometimes it seems that ol' T.J. never departed this town, that he's still ambling between his imposing rotunda at the University of Virginia and Monticello, his tourist-magnet home atop a nearby mountain. But if he were still hanging around, he'd be wowed by so much more. He was a gourmand, after all, so would be astonished that a town of forty thousand can sustain such an impressive culinary scene, from the cherished neighborhood chicken joint Wayside Takeout to the special-occasion-worthy C&O Restaurant and its brethren—more chef-driven, farm-to-table eateries than you can shake a pastured pork belly at. Also quite the tippler, he no doubt would toast the area's award-winning wineries (especially since he could never get his own vineyard to thrive), not to mention the newer wave of craft breweries and hard cideries. His intellectual curiosity and fondness for entertaining would be sated by Charlottesville's shindig-a-week culture, including the Virginia Film Festival, the Foxfield steeplechase, and the always raucous bashes where the Charlottesville Lady Arm Wrestlers square off for charity. And like everyone else in town, he'd probably swear that he first saw the Dave Matthews Band back when it was playing parties on frat row, but now prefers any number of alt-folk acts that define today's local music scene. Given Jefferson's wondrous way with language, maybe he could even help coin a term to describe the undercurrent of energy that really makes Charlottesville hum—that certain friction between old money and disruptive technology, between townies and world citizens, between seersucker and blue collar, between academic idealism and rural pragmatism. Then again, maybe such intangibles are better left undefined, the better to let them continue morphing and shaping a random spot on the map into a unique place with a future that looks as striking as its history. So, Mr. Jefferson, how about we just grab a window seat at a downtown café for a while, local pint of Devils Backbone or Wild Wolf in hand, and revel in the people-watching paradise? Next round is on you.

CHASE, LEAH

(1923–)

by John Currence

Leah Chase walks between raindrops. Magic inhabits her domain. Though she's not immune to the tragedies, disappointments, and failures that touch the rest of us, Leah manages to find . . . no, *manufacture*, a silver lining for whatever dark cloud comes her way.

An attempt at full disclosure: I consider Leah my adopted grandmother. I spent fourteen months "after the storm" in the confines of a Katrina trailer arguing with her about how best to reopen her restaurant. (Dooky Chase's Restaurant first opened in New Orleans' Tremé neighborhood in 1941, and those who have been served Leah's Creole cooking range from Duke Ellington to Barack Obama to

Thurgood Marshall to Ray Charles.) At times during our discussions, I stormed out; at other times, she said the conversation was through. We laughed. We cried. In those moments, I realized we were family. No words can do justice to my admiration and love for her and the legacy she has etched in the oyster-shell concrete of the streets of New Orleans. To describe what she means to the city's socio-political, arts, and culture scenes in a few paragraphs is like trying to quickly sum up Martin Luther King Jr. or Gandhi or Lincoln: impossible. Leah Chase *is* New Orleans.

There is confidence in each measured syllable that emerges from her lips; she has a profound effect on people. She has scolded the city's mayor for not having formal enough place settings for his office entertaining, and presidents for their table manners or for mis-using Tabasco in her gumbo. She is a spirit unlike any other who has crossed my path.

An anecdote or two will have to suffice. In 2003, I got to spend a week cooking with her in Barbados. Each morning we had breakfast together, and for an hour I would quiz her over coffee—on characters from the civil rights era, sometimes, or black celebrities with whom she'd rubbed elbows. It soon dawned on me that I could not come up with a single person of influence whom she did not know and have an interesting story about. "Don't get me started on that rascal Cab Calloway." "Those marshals who ate breakfast with James Meredith at the restaurant every morning, while they were in New Orleans trying to get him in Ole Miss, could not have been any more kind." "It's a good thing Sugar Ray ate my chicken before that fight instead of a big ol'

steak down the street." It was an eternal loop of fascination.

About eight years later, the Charleston, South Carolina, chef Sean Brock and I were traveling, separately, to New Orleans to meet up during his first visit to the city. As I sat in Atlanta-Hartsfield that afternoon, my phone rang. It was Sean, excited: he was on the ground in New Orleans, and where should he go for his first lunch? Get a cab, I told him without hesitation, and go get a table at Dooky Chase's. Then go immediately to the kitchen to meet Ms. Leah. Tell her I sent you.

That was all I said. Sean is a rock; I have watched him sit steely-eyed across from Charlie Rose, trade intellectual punches with Anthony Bourdain and Heston Blumenthal. I wanted to see how the moment would strike him.

An hour and a half later, after my plane landed, Sean called again. He was laughing, but obviously through tears. "She hugged me, dude. . . . It was like meeting the pope. I literally don't know what to do right now. I'm stunned."

We caught up shortly afterward at a French Quarter bar. For an hour, Sean could say little more than, "You didn't tell me I was going to cry." And, "I just hope she remembers my name."

Trust me on this: Get to Dooky Chase's. Make your way to the kitchen. Spend a moment touching the hand of Leah Chase.

CHATTANOOGA, TENNESSEE

by Josh MacIvor-Andersen

WHEN HE WAS IN SIXTH GRADE, A teacher asked Ishmael Reed to name the world's highest mountain. "I didn't even hesitate," he wrote in his 1973 poetry collection, *Chattanooga*, "Lookout Mountain."

Reed, later the recipient of a MacArthur "genius grant," was a little off, of course. At 2,389 feet, Lookout is barely a blip on the topographical map. (There's a building in Dubai more than 300 feet taller.) But that tree-spiked Tennessee prow has a certain prominence, a grip on the local psyche, and a long historical shadow. Lookout's bluff once provided a perch for Confederate soldiers sniping at Union supply chains in order to starve away their enemies. For almost a century it has been home to perhaps our country's most classic (and kitschy) triumvirate of natural wonders turned tourist draws (the Incline Railway, Rock City, and Ruby Falls). Lookout was one of Martin Luther King Jr.'s mountaintops from which, in his "I Have a Dream" speech, he hoped, throughout the nation, freedom would ring.

And Reed was right about this: "Chattanooga is something you / Can have anyway you want it." The small Southern metropolis variegates and blossoms in any number of ways, although for Reed, a black man in a once deeply segregated city, there were thorns mixed in with the sweet. Chattanooga also once had the worst air quality in the country. It was all heavy industry and smokestacks, and the mountains trapped the pollution into a toxic pudding that filled up the valley, which for two decades emptied of those citizens who had the agency to leave.

But is this not *the* dominant story of the New South? How many nearby cities echo this exodus, and some similar, select resurrection?

Throughout the 1990s, a small army of ecominded entrepreneurs and visionary residents worked doggedly to transform their town from an industrial armpit into a global model for environmentally sound rejuvenation. Electric buses began carting people from downtown up the mountain. Razed factories sprouted into pedestrian parks and green space. Dilapidated mansions overlooking the river were reborn as the Bluff View Art District. Art is everywhere now, in fact, along with farm-to-table restaurants and fresh-brewed beer and the palpable buzz of possibility (accelerated by the country's fastest Internet connections). Chattanooga, by most current standards, is verifiably cool.

There's something more, though. A few years ago, on July 16, a date locals now know by its digits in the same way we're all stamped with 9/11, a disturbed young man opened fire on a military recruiting center, wounding one, and then blazed into a nearby Navy and Marine Corps storefront, where he shot down five service members. The shooter had attended a local mosque. Researchers had just named Chattanooga the most "Bible-minded city" in America. Some might describe the situation as volatile, a powder keg with a freshly lit fuse.

Then this happened: people leaned in, Muslims and Christians, believers and nonbelievers, and began to listen, to grieve, to reconcile. By and large, the aftermath of a violent, religiously charged tragedy smack in the middle of a religiously charged epoch unwound in a peaceful and conciliatory manner. There is a plaque now, outside the building where those victims lost their lives, that says that instead of erupting in violence, the city prayed. "We did not lash out at easy targets for revenge," it reads. "Instead, we invited each other into our lives, homes and places of worship."

Chattanooga is something you can have any way you want it. A stopover for Northerners migrating south to Disney World. A mecca for rock climbers hunting toothy, chalk-marked boulder fields. A city healing over its wounds past and present, breathing fresher air, always looking toward what's next.

CHEESE STRAWS

Open a drawer in any well-stocked Southern kitchen and you will find a cookie press, an industrial-looking steel extrusion tube with a lever and fitted dies. One could make fancy sugar cookies with these precision-engineered tools, but really the only action the gadgets generally see is for the production of cheese straws. These long, ridged wafers that look like bread sticks and taste infinitely richer are—axiomatically—the most beloved party snacks of all time. No one says no to a cheese straw. With scant variation to the recipe, the dough consists of copious amounts of

grated sharp cheddar cheese mixed with soft butter. The cook works in just enough flour to set the short dough and adds an all-important pinch of cayenne pepper, which races through the straw like Tinker Bell through the forest, leaving a sparkle of bright spice. The Southern cheese straw is the very glory of what is dismissed as bridge party food.

CHICKEN AND WAFFLES

If chicken and waffles were the cue in a word association test, a healthy number of respondents would probably come back with Roscoe's, the black-owned Los Angeles restaurant that's been supplying syrupy plates of drumsticks, thighs, and buttered waffle rounds to celebrities since the 1970s. But the concept of combining fried chicken with waffles, instead of the biscuits that fast-food chains have designated poultry's constant companions, originated half a world away in Germany. Creamed chicken and waffles was a popular dish there in the 1700s, when residents started boarding boats bound for America. They brought with them their chicken-and-waffle recipes, which survive in Pennsylvania Dutch cookbooks. Soon the dish was being served in wealthy Philadelphia homes, and the fad wended its way south, where plantation owners made it a centerpiece of their Sunday menus. After emancipation, African American cooks recreated the meal for their families, imprinting the memories that would inspire restaurateurs and jazz club owners in 1930s Harlem to offer it on their menus. One of their customers, Herb Hudson, went west to open Roscoe's House of Chicken and Waffles.

CHICKEN MULL

MULL IS A BUTTERY STEW of chopped or ground chicken thickened with milk, cream, and crackers, or a combination of two of those. Kin to burgoo, hash, and fish stew, it's an iron-pot dish that often stars at church fund-raisers and other community get-togethers. Bear Grass, North Carolina, hosts an annual Chicken Mull Festival, and mull is also on the menu at barbecue joints around Athens, Georgia—and, passing as "chicken stew," at Midway BBQ in Buffalo, South Carolina. Wherever you encounter it, be sure to shake a little hot sauce over the top before you spoon it up.

CHICK-FIL-A

LIKE WAFFLE HOUSE, CHICK-FIL-A HAS A special resonance for Southerners, blending the modern American idea of industrialization with the timeless identity of the South. The family-owned business traces its roots not just to Baptists, but Southern Baptists. Its founder, S. Truett Cathy, was the sort of man who didn't work Sundays, Christmas, or Thanksgiving, a tradition that continues in its more than 2,100 restaurants today. Cathy is considered the inventor of the fast-food chicken sandwich. He'd started running the Dwarf Grill in an Atlanta suburb in 1946. In 1961, after buying a shipment of chicken breasts deemed too large to be served as airline food—there was never much room on those little trays—he found that a pressure fryer could cook a boneless chicken sandwich as quickly as a fast-food hamburger. This changed the industry and led to the trademarked slogan, "We Didn't Invent the Chicken, Just the Chicken Sandwich." (The capitalized *A* in the name was meant to symbolize "Grade A" or "superior quality.") The business juggernaut appeared to stumble when CEO Dan Cathy set off a public controversy in 2012, when he told a radio announcer that ". . . we are inviting God's judgment on our nation when we shake our fist at Him and say, 'We know better than you as to what constitutes a marriage.'" It was also revealed that the company had donated millions to Christian groups opposed to same-sex marriage. Many people boycotted Chick-fil-A. Counter-boycotts ensued. Within a month, however, the company issued a statement saying that it would henceforth leave the debate to "the government and political arena." Then it got back to doing what it does best, turning out those sandwiches, nuggets, sweet tea, and waffle fries. By the way, every time a new restaurant opens, the first one hundred customers receive "a year's worth" (fifty-two, to be precise) of free meals. A St. Petersburg, Florida, man, Richard Coley, has stood in line for the privilege at least 110 times.

CHITLINS

As the old chestnut goes, the best way to cook chitlins is outside—at someone else's house. Pigs' intestines aren't a side dish for the faint of heart, and even if you can handle the concept, you might not be so amenable to the offal stink. They weren't always so divisive, though. Both planters and the enslaved once valued chitlins before the modern era consigned them to the gallery of offal curiosities along with brains and lungs. Nowadays, they still surface at soul-food joints where cooks employ generations-old tricks to neutralize the odor. Soaking them in vinegar helps, and so does cooking them with potatoes and onions. At the table, you can smother them with hot sauce and slaw. Ultimately, though, chitlins are an acquired taste—centuries in the making.

CHRISTENBERRY, WILLIAM

(1936–2016)

Coming off the tongue of some of its inhabitants, the pronunciation of Hale County, Alabama, can easily be mistaken for "Hell County." And surely many have thought of it that way. It became a symbol to the world of deep Southern poverty after being documented in the 1941 book *Let Us Now Praise Famous Men*. But while Walker Evans took the photographs for that volume as an outsider looking in, his future protégé—William Christenberry—came from Hale County itself. He began with

pictures he took with a Brownie camera given to him as a child and developed the film at drugstores. His unpretentious straight-ahead photos of rural buildings and landscapes soon became some of the most celebrated works of photography in the twentieth century, helping to elevate color photography to the level of fine art. Returning to Hale County every year, Christenberry marked the passage of time by documenting the same buildings again and again—the door of his grandparents' house, his uncle's country store, a green warehouse. "I guess somebody would say I am literally obsessed with that landscape where I am from," he once said. "I don't really object to that. It is so ingrained in me. It is who I am. The place makes who you are."

THE CIVIL WAR

by Jon Meacham

In 1955, nearly a century after Appomattox, the writer Shelby Foote was just beginning work on what would become a massive three-volume history of the Civil War. In a letter to his friend Walker Percy, Foote spoke of being consumed by the story of the conflict. "I'm living a hermit's life," Foote told Percy. "Whiskey bores me. Movies are no damned good. The War is all."

As it was for Foote, so it has long been for the American South. Note the capitalization: it wasn't the "war" but the "War," as if there had never been any other—a common enough view shared by many Southerners from Fort Sumter down to the present day. As Foote remarked, the "War" was the "crossroads of our being" not only as a region but as a nation. "It is an irrepressible conflict between opposing and enduring forces," said the New York politician William H. Seward, "and it means that the United States must and will, sooner or later, become either entirely a slave-holding nation or entirely a free-labor nation."

Seward's observation came in 1858, but the origins of the conflict he believed inevitable stretched back to the beginnings of the American experiment in republican government. Slavery and its implications played essential roles in the American Revolution; it was only after the Virginia royal governor, Lord Dunmore, issued a proclamation offering freedom to those enslaved persons who joined the British in resisting colonial pressure in November 1775 that the whites of Virginia, a critical colony, united in their push for independence. A dozen years later, after military victory but a failed attempt at living under the Articles of Confederation, the framers of what became the Constitution wove concessions to the slave interest into the nature of the government, including a compromise providing that the enslaved be counted as three-fifths of a person for purposes of apportioning federal power, including the presidency of the United States. (Thomas Jefferson was derided as "the Negro President" since he owed his electoral majority to the slave states.) And forty years on from Philadelphia, Andrew Jackson faced down nullifiers in South Carolina over a tariff controversy that he knew was but prelude to a coming storm. "The tariff was only the

pretext, and disunion and southern confederacy the real object," Jackson said. "The next pretext will be the negro, or slavery question."

Jackson was right. The expansion of American territory westward gave the ancient debate over slavery new force and urgency, and Abraham Lincoln's refusal to allow what was euphemistically known as the "peculiar institution" to take root beyond the existing Southern states led to secession and war in the spring of 1861. The ensuing cataclysm was bloody and prolonged, claiming the lives of roughly 620,000 men. With the struggle came what Lincoln called a "new birth of freedom," but only slowly. Despite emancipation and the passage of subsequent constitutional amendments, the South reverted to prewar form as soon as it practicably could, imposing Jim Crow laws to segregate a society that slavery had once defined.

Generations of white apologists would argue over the relative roles of slavery and "states' rights" in the Civil War, but a fair-minded reading of history leads to the inescapable conclusion that the conflict was chiefly about race and white power. And while it is true that not every Southerner who fought consciously did so for slavery, the fight was nevertheless over the future of an old and discredited order.

The North fought a total war against the South, often treating civilian assets as combatant forces—a precursor of the nature of the world wars of the twentieth century. The vestiges of inequality, most vividly addressed during the civil rights movement of the 1950s and '60s, can be traced to the events of 1861 through 1865 and beyond. And the politics of white nostalgia even into the twenty-first century are inextricably bound up with the "Lost Cause" mythology of the postwar period. "In that furnace (the War)," Foote told Percy in 1955, "they were shown up, every one, for what they were." And so we are still, all these years distant.

CLAPPER RAIL

THE CLAPPER RAIL, OFTEN CALLED THE MARSH hen, is the most democratic of Southern game birds. Hunting wild quail generally requires owning a large plantation (or scoring an invite to one); shooting doves, a summer spent toiling over fields to grow rows of sunflowers and millet that attract the birds come fall. But the rail lives in the coastal environs of the Southeast, where its call—often described as the sound of a children's wooden clapping toy—can be heard chattering across Lowcountry marshes. Hunters pursue rails from small boats that they can row or pole through the endless flooded acres of spartina grass during full- or new-moon tides. They

are not known for blazing flight speed or for gustatory excellence on the table, but they inhabit some of the most beautiful environs in the country. And hunting them is a throwback to a simpler time. As one early devotee of the game bird once wrote to John James Audubon, "It gives variety to life; it is good exercise, and in all cases affords a capital dinner, besides the pleasure I feel when sending a mess of Marshhens to a friend such as you."

CLARK, SEPTIMA

(1898–1987)

THE LIST OF VOCABULARY WORDS THAT LEADS off a 1962 Citizenship School workbook hints at what Septima Clark aimed to accomplish by teaching African American adults across the South to read: arranged from *A* to *Z*, the entries include *constitution*, *election*, *justice*, *knowledge*, and *rebellion*. Within three years of Clark's launching her first Citizenship School, designed to help black Southerners pass the literacy tests intended to disenfranchise them, the grassroots program had produced fortytwo thousand new African American voters. As Myles Horton, founder of Tennessee's Highlander Folk School, said, Clark "had as much to do with getting the civil rights movement started as anybody else." Born in 1898 in Charleston, South Carolina, Clark attended Avery Normal School, the city's first African American school. She took her first teaching job on nearby Johns Island, holding classes for adults at night. Clark joined Avery's faculty in 1919 and taught at a handful of South Carolina schools for decades before being fired in 1956 for belonging to the NAACP, leading her to join the staff at Highlander; while there, she developed the Citizenship School, modeling it after her Johns Island sessions. Eventually, those schools were absorbed by the Southern Christian Leadership Council, which invested in the training of tens of thousands of volunteer teachers.

CLERMONT LOUNGE

by Allison Glock

Located in Atlanta, on Ponce de Leon, in the seedy basement of a now-shuttered motor lodge, the Clermont has been "alive since '65." Not much has changed.

Tattered velveteen paper clings to the walls amid band flyers and warnings from management not to bring cameras. No need, really. What you see will be seared into your eyes. Both a dance club and a club with dancers, the Clermont is an intimate smoke-filled shrine to raunch. The square footage is tight. The dance floor tighter still. If you plan to exhale, you will have to brush up against your fellow man. Or stripper. It's like Delhi. With nudity.

Less a dive than a complete submersion, the Clermont is not clean. (If you drop something on the floor, best just to leave it, eyeglasses, wallets, and pants included.) Nor is it

pretentious. The dancers feed their own quarters into the jukebox to perform. The cups are plastic. Cash only.

The performers, many middle-aged and up, look like real people. With real parts. If you want to be seen or meet the real estate agent of your dreams, best to head to any other bar in Atlanta. Unlike those so-called hot spots, the Clermont is inspiringly democratic. On any given night you will see college kids, hipsters, retirees, Navy SEALs, artists, stockbrokers. You will also see veteran dancer/poet Blondie crush a PBR can with her breasts. (Cash only.)

As with the best Southern haunts, continuity counts. Most of the dancers have been around for decades. Saturday's disco night has been happening virtually since disco was a thing. Same DJ. Same bartenders. Same toilet shared with the talent, who more often than not chat you up and tell you how pretty you are, the way grandmothers are supposed to, except not naked.

Thing is, no one cares at the Clermont. About how you look. Or what you earn. Or the mistakes you've made. There is nothing you can do at the Clermont that 1) hasn't been done and 2) will offend anyone in the joint. How many places can you say that about? Cover charge: free to ten dollars. Absolute abandon? Priceless.

CLINE, PATSY

(1932–1963)

In 1957, not long after Virginia Hensley had parlayed performances on radio stations around her hometown of Winchester, Virginia, into a recording contract, the twenty-four-year-old appeared on Arthur Godfrey's televised variety show. Producers insisted she trade her cowgirl getup for a cocktail gown and requested a song that didn't twang as fiercely as the piece she had planned on playing. "Walkin' after Midnight" became an instant hit, charting with both country and pop listeners at a time when genres rarely mixed. Renamed Patsy Cline by a manager, Hensley went on to defang more taboos with her perfect pitch and husky voice, which she swore came from a childhood bout with rheumatic fever. Cline was the first woman to wear pants onstage at the Grand Ole Opry, and the only person ever to petition her way into the elite organization. She was the first female country singer to be billed above the men on her tour, and the first to perform at Carnegie Hall, an ideal setting for her polished Nashville sound. The definitive interpreter of "Crazy," "Sweet Dreams," and "She's Got You" died at the age of thirty when the private plane flying her home from a benefit concert crashed in the West Tennessee woods.

COCA-COLA

It might be forcing the metaphor to call John Pemberton and Asa Candler the Romulus and Remus of Atlanta. The city had been incorporated nearly forty years prior to Pemberton's 1886 introduction of his soda-fountain beverage as a patent medicine, and Candler's subsequent marketing and branding innovation that made icons of both the drink and its curvaceous bottle. But Atlanta's personality—its distinctive admixture of small-town pride and global aspiration—started with Coca-Cola, still its best-known ambassador. You can't go far without witnessing the imprint of the Candler family's philanthropy and civic engagement. And you can't leave without visiting the World of Coca-Cola, the ne plus ultra of corporate museums. This effervescent exhibit teaches you all you can ever know about Coke's global presence, its advertising, and its misguided foray into New Coke. A massive tasting of global Coke brands sends you out on a sugar high.

COLLARDS

The *Oxford Dictionary of English* notes that collards are "a cabbage of a variety that does not develop a heart," which is somewhat harsh although not wholly inaccurate. *See Greens.*

COMEBACK SAUCE

Kin to Louisiana rémoulade and Thousand Island dressing, comeback sauce originated at the Greek-owned Rotisserie restaurant in Jackson, Mississippi, in the 1930s. It spread quickly from there. Although the Rotisserie closed years ago, comeback remains a staple at nearby haunts like the Mayflower Café, Crechale's, and Walker's. It is an all-purpose special sauce, good for anything from salads to fresh shrimp to burgers to fried fish. Ingredients vary, but the basic components are mayonnaise, garlic, paprika, and chili sauce, and it's now traveling far beyond Mississippi. Today you'll find it on menus from Portland, Oregon, to New York City.

CONCH

When the micronation of Key West, Florida, proclaimed on April 23, 1982, that it had "seceded" from the United States, it chose the name the Conch Republic. (The government of the mother country, in turn, reacted with decades of silent indifference.) The rogue breakaway nation took its name from the big spiral-shelled sea snails commonly known as conchs (pronounced *konks*) or conches (*konchez*), which many a Floridian and Caribbean islander enthusiastically consumes. Because the dense meat of the snail is so tough, it typically gets beaten with a tenderizing hammer, cooked in a pressure cooker, and then minced or ground before anchoring such popular dishes as conch chowder, conch fritters, and conch ceviche. After cleaning, the shells can be turned into deep-resonating horns (years ago on Grenada, the man delivering ice used to blast a loud note from one to announce his arrival to island villagers). To this day, on the official Key West website, you can purchase a Conch Republic passport—a splendid conversation piece, although you probably shouldn't rely on it to get you through airport security.

CONFEDERATE JASMINE

So it's native to Asia and not a true relative of real-deal jasmine. Pah. The fragrant plant has snaked its way into the Southern consciousness in much the same way as those other Asian-born knockouts camellias and gardenias have. Stroll the streets of Charleston, South Carolina, come April and you'll see foot-traffic jams of both residents and tourists snapping photos of archways, porch rails, mailboxes, and even entire potting sheds draped in the flowering vine. Tiny five-petal pinwheels bloom out from every inch of the dark green foliage in spring and early summer, and the aroma suggests a cross between

nutmeg and the sultry summer evenings of your dreams. When the writer Eudora Welty became homesick for her Jackson, Mississippi, garden (as anyone transplanted up to the University of Wisconsin would have), she included a character in her thesis novella, *Kin*, who visits Mississippi and notes Southerners' habit of enjoying one another's gardens: "Bloom was everywhere in the streets, wistaria just ending, Confederate jasmine beginning. And down in the gardens! . . . Everybody grew some of the best of everybody else's flowers." Few Southerners would disagree: Confederate jasmine smells like *home*.

COOKE, SAM

(1931–1964)

OTIS REDDING HAD THE BRAWN, AL GREEN had the slinkiness, but no one combined them better than Sam Cooke. His string of hits was a murderers' row of chart toppers including "You Send Me," "Chain Gang," and "Twistin' the Night Away." In 1963, the Mississippi native's infant son, Vincent, drowned in the swimming pool at the Cooke family home in Los Angeles. Cooke was devastated, and in the tragedy's aftermath he shifted his focus from romantic love songs to something more impactful and profound. He had also become obsessed with Bob Dylan's "Blowin' in the Wind," confiding to friends and relatives that he felt a black man should have written the song. Cooke eventually tried to do Dylan one better. In late 1963, he entered

an L.A. recording studio and recorded the soaring, socially charged "A Change Is Gonna Come," released after his death and arguably the greatest soul song ever recorded, one that laid the groundwork for other politically minded singers including Marvin Gaye and Curtis Mayfield.

COON DOG CEMETERY

by Daniel Wallace

THE COON DOG CEMETERY IS ON A GENtly sloping rise in the Freedom Hills of North Alabama, prolific with hardwoods—elm, oak, ash—and pine trees too, but with enough open space left over to walk between them, even with a dog. The rise falls like a slide into a holler, thickly wooded and dark. Way back when, at certain times of the day when the sun cut through the treetops, there was a winking glint off a moonshiner's still. Beyond that nothing but green, an ocean of forest, and all the critters you'd expect to find there: the barred owl, kestrels, fox squirrels, deer. Raccoon.

In 1937, Key Underwood buried his dog, a coonhound, here, because this is a place they loved to hunt. The dog's name was Troop, and he carved that name into a chunk of sandstone from the chimney of an old cabin with a screwdriver and a hammer, and below that the essential information, the only indisputable facts of existence: the day he was born and the day he died.

4-1-22

9-4-37

This is what was happening in September 1937 on a mountaintop in Cherokee, Alabama. Since then, more than three hundred dogs have been buried here. And not just any dogs: they are, each and every one of them, coonhounds. Redbone, black-and-tan, English bluetick, English redtick, Plott, Treeing Walker, and various combinations of the above. It's a place that's known as—well, what else could it be known as?—the Coon Dog Cemetery (officially the Key Underwood Coon Dog Memorial Graveyard), and there is no place like it anywhere in the world. One of the best places on the planet, I think, so peaceful, the spirits of dogs who lived their fullest lives lingering there, wind blowing through the oaks, you can almost hear them howl.

In some respects, the Coon Dog Cemetery looks a lot like other cemeteries in which there are not coon dogs. Traditional rectangular sandstone gravestones are inscribed with names, dates, and sometimes a pithy remembrance: "He wasn't the best, but he was the best I ever had," or simply "In Loving Memory." But there is more than one way to mark a grave, and in the Coon Dog Cemetery you might could see them all. Some are just pieces of wood or rocks, or combinations of both; one looks like the other side of a car tag, one a small piece of a wrought-iron fence, and one—"Bear"—a rusting piece of soldered metal on a pole.

The Coon Dog Cemetery has its own road—Coon Dog Cemetery Road—a ten-mile-long stretch of winding rolling beauty, a barely paved one-and-a-half-lane road with steep hills and sharp curves sketched through a thousand acres of nothing much. You're never going to get there without *going* there, because it's not on the way to anywhere else. That said, the space here feels more sequestered than it does isolated. I won't call it holy, because that's a big word that brings a lot of baggage with it. But hallowed? Sure. It's a hallowed spot. A place like this *shouldn't* be too close to anything else. It's one of those places you wish you couldn't find with a GPS.

CORNBREAD

THE SIMPLEST DISH IN THE WHOLE SOUTH IS pinto beans, simmered with lard and paired with cornbread, just as it's served at the Bean Barn in Greeneville, Tennessee. Then again, maybe the humblest of them all is crumblin', the Texan term for a tall glass of buttermilk with cornbread broken into it, the way the onetime Speaker of the House Sam Rayburn liked it. Or perhaps it's a mess of vinegary South Carolina greens, with a thin sliver of cornbread alongside. Starting to detect a pattern? Cornbread, affordable and pleasing, defines Southern cuisine from one end of the region to the other. Eaters of European and African ancestry were latecomers to the dish, of course: Native Americans had been cooking with corn for thousands of years when they arrived. Europeans were initially unimpressed, comparing corn pone unfavorably with fluffy wheat breads. They ultimately decided that dense cakes cooked in ash were preferable to starvation, and corn crept into their diets. Benjamin Franklin was an early cornbread champion, calling johnnycakes a sight better than Yorkshire muffins. But Southerners grew especially fond of ground cornmeal, which they ate until after the Civil War without the embellishments of eggs, butter, and milk. Many cornbread fans prefer it that way still.

COTTON

At the 1963 Newport Folk Festival in Rhode Island, a seventy-some-year-old man known as Mississippi John Hurt spellbound the crowds with his fingerpicking guitar style and his Delta blues and field ballads—and then returned home to Avalon, Mississippi, where he had long worked as a sharecropper, to pick cotton for four dollars a day. His fellow blues-man Lead Belly famously sang that when he was "a little baby, my mother rocked me in the cradle, In them ole cotton fields back home" (in his folk classic "Cotton Fields," which has been covered by everyone from Elvis Presley to Johnny Cash to Creedence Clearwater Revival to—go figure—the Beach Boys). Cotton is indelibly woven into the South's past and its present. There's no excusing the commodity's dark past—its planters were among those who perpetuated slavery, and the crop begot the "King Cotton" rationale for secession and later tethered sharecroppers to bottomless debt. There's also no dismissing its enduring status as an economic engine; even now, cotton clothes the world, and the United States exports more of

it than any other country. Drive through most any state below the Mason-Dixon—especially Texas, Georgia, Mississippi, or Alabama—and it's not hard to find seas of white bolls. Nowadays, much like Southern foodways, Southern cotton has begun to tilt toward the local and artisanal; witness the locally milled denim revival in North Carolina, for instance, and the artist collective Alabama Chanin's insistence on growing and harvesting its own organic varieties. For better and for worse, it's hard to find a Southern narrative that doesn't have cotton threads running through it.

COUNTRY CAPTAIN

British seafarers brought not only Indian spices but also a recipe for this simple chicken curry dish to the port of Savannah. While versions of it appear in both the United Kingdom and India, it has taken on a special Lowcountry flavor, and today there's nary a community cookbook in Savannah or nearby Charleston without a recipe. Pieces of bone-in chicken simmer until tender with tomatoes, onions, dried currants, and the gentlest possible hit of curry powder. The chicken and its thin sauce get ladled over the kind of fluffy white rice that has long gone out of style, and diners pass garnishes that must include crumbled bacon, chopped parsley, and toasted almonds or peanuts. Though few cooks turn up the heat on the curry, many like rococo flourishes for garnish, including toasted coconut, sieved hard-boiled egg, fried onions, and mango chutney. But as with any oft-reproduced canonical recipe, the variations are tiny but endless.

COUNTRY HAM

Country ham is the common name for the dry-cured hind leg of a pig. Born out of hardscrabble necessity, perfected over centuries, this salty delicacy has long been the pride of the Southern table. Whether skillet fried in redeye gravy for breakfast, boiled and slipped into buttermilk biscuits on Christmas Eve, or shaved dry and served alongside figs and cheese in a Michelin-star restaurant, country ham can go high or low. Its appeal is universal, cutting across racial and class divisions. Patrick Martins, founder of Heritage Foods USA, calls country ham "one of the South's most important contributions to the American table."

Country ham is as old as the South itself. British colonists brought hogs to Jamestown along with the old-world know-how to salt-cure their flesh. Pioneers pushing west survived on boiled bear and deer meat until they could establish a herd of swine. Frontier hogs were mostly feral and fleet of foot. Settlers rounded them up each fall during the first extended cold spell, killing some and capturing others to fatten on corn.

As the South became more established, the region's hogs grew tamer and rounder, but the seasonal rhythms of the smokehouse remained the same. After the autumn slaughter, hams (and shoulders, jowls, and bacon) were packed

in salt for four to six weeks, hung in a smokehouse for weeks to keep away spring flies, and left hanging through the hot months to sweat out the last drops of moisture. Conditions are best in a swath of the South—Virginia, Maryland, North Carolina, Tennessee, and Kentucky—that falls within the world's ham belt, a distinct climatic zone where temperatures get neither too cold nor too hot.

A country ham is more precious today than ever before because dry-curing is no longer a necessity. But the slow-cured ham tastes better thanks to the salt, the earthy hickory smoke, and the twang of proteins left to break down over time by natural enzymes. Hams by legendary cure masters—Broadbent, Benton, Edwards—stand hock to hock with the great dry-cured hams of Spain and Italy. *See Cure masters; Benton, Allan.*

CRACKER COWBOYS

Cracker is one of those powder-keg words that can sound harmless when bandied by a friend, or blow up big-time if mumbled by a stranger to imply that someone is uneducated, backwoods, or otherwise overly fond of his cousins. In Florida, however, the term offers distinctive shades of meaning and is often deployed with a sense of ironic pride. Back in the 1800s, the term *cracker cowboy* was coined to describe frontiersmen who, unlike their Western counterparts, used dogs and whips to round up cattle scattered over the state's vast, untamed scrublands. The famed artist Frederic

Remington even sketched some classic images of these hardworking, hard-drinking souls in 1895, though he lamented their lack of lassos. Nowadays, some Floridians use *cracker cowboy* or *Florida cracker* to claim descent from these long-ago settlers, as opposed to the waves of newcomers who migrated to the Sunshine State after World War II (and, more to the point, after the invention of air-conditioning). The term has even been normalized enough to be lent to the Cracker Trail Annual Cross-State Ride, a heritage-honoring event held near Bradenton every February. You know—just in time for all the snowbirds from New York to saddle up, too.

CRACKLINGS

ANYWHERE THAT PEOPLE RENDER LARD, they make cracklings. As the white fat liquefies, bits of fatty tissue brown and rise to the surface, ready to scoop out. Skinless cracklings can emerge from the hot grease as puffy and crumbly as Cheez Doodles, while those with the rinds still on pack a powerful head-ringing crunch. Most people eat them out of hand, or crumble them into cornbread, where they form pockets of savory, porky goodness. There is one important regional variation. If you buy a bag of cracklings in Louisiana, you will end up snacking on chunks of fried pork belly, with streaks of meat to wash down all that tasty fat and crunchy rind. Sometimes called grattons in Cajun country, these cracklings are often sold alongside and consumed with boudin.

CRAWFISH

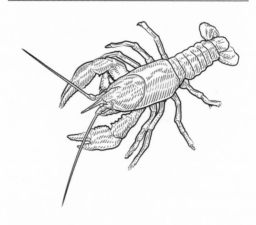

AFFECTIONATELY KNOWN AS MUDBUGS OR crawdaddies in the South, and formally as crayfish in the British Isles and the *New York Times*, these freshwater crustaceans are treasured for their lobster-like flavor and appearance. *Procambarus clarkii*, or red swamp crawfish, is the species harvested wild by the Cajun natives of western Louisiana's Atchafalaya Swamp; they are especially abundant during the flood stages that occur between late winter and early summer.

Cajun-style crawfish are typically boiled in a spicy stock with small potatoes and corn on the cob, then dumped on a picnic table spread with newspapers. At community events called crawfish boils, diners assemble their own plates by reaching into the help-yourself heap. Restaurants called boiling points sell cooked crawfish by the pound. Along the Gulf coast, waterfront crab shacks now offer freshwater crawfish on the "seafood" menu. Seafood experts suggest that increasingly scarce Gulf crabs are being replaced by abundant crawfish, which are now available farm raised as well as wild.

Beginning around 2001, Vietnamese-owned restaurants in Houston and elsewhere with names like Cajun Kitchen and Cajun Corner opened, largely drawing clients of Southeast Asian descent and ushering in a new style of Asian-Cajun crawfish. Cooks spike the boiling pot with Asian lemongrass and ginger, and the crawfish appear at the table in a plastic bag, swimming in garlic butter or spicy sauce. More mouthwatering globalism: a few years ago, a Vietnamese American woman opened a place called the Cajun Cua in Saigon. She calls it a Vayjun restaurant. *See Cajuns.*

CREEPING FIG

THE CREEPING FIG—*FICUS PUMILA,* ALSO known as the climbing fig—grows across the South. Its tiny, oblong, heart-shaped leaves and vines wrap around wrought-iron gates, stencil the facades of brick houses, and bring lacy patterns to concrete garden walls. Like many Southerners, this evergreen member of the mulberry family doesn't fare well in cold temperatures, but it can withstand saltwater spray from Virginia to Florida and the scorching sun of the Gulf states. Once you've planted it, let creeping fig climb wildly, but keep your pruning shears handy—left to its own devices, the feisty ficus will embrace everything it can wrap its tendrils around, and has been known to inflict damage on stucco and wooden structures as it's removed. Creeping fig requires no trellis to climb; it always finds a way to make a home its own.

CREOLE

CREOLE IS A SHAPE-SHIFTY TERM THAT HAS meant different things to different generations since the early 1700s, most notably in New Orleans. "The slippery nature of this term continues to produce confusions, controversies, and conflicts in New Orleans," the historian Rien Fertel has written. ". . . Its 'meaning differs according to location, as it does with historical period and from one [scholarly] discipline to another.'"

Creole initially described someone who had been born in the colonies, differentiating him or her from a neighbor who may have been born in France or Spain and subsequently immigrated. This definition wavered as more Creoles populated the city, and the word instead came to mean chiefly those who identified as being of French or Spanish descent, and usually practicing Catholicism. This was a point of status for those who did not want to be confused with barbaric Americans. After the Civil War, the term came to be more loosely applied to African Americans, often of mixed race, whose ancestors had arrived with the French or Spanish settlers (sometimes as slaves, sometimes as freemen) and who identified with old-world culture rather than the culture of newly freed American slaves.

Today people often use the term culinarily to describe a cuisine linked to French culture (cream sauces, lots of butter). This is not to be confused with Cajun cooking, which is distinct and plagued by its own confusions, controversies, and conflicts.

CROSSROADS

THE MISSISSIPPI DELTA INTERSECTION WHERE bluesman Robert Johnson made his deal with the devil (or so the story goes). *See Johnson, Robert.*

CUBAN SANDWICH

by Rick Bragg

THIS, TILL THE DAY I DIE, IS WHAT FLORIDA tastes like.

Old Cuba, it is said, gave birth to it, in the cigar factories and sugar mills, and sent it across the waters by sail and steam, to Ybor City and Key West, then, after Castro, to Miami, but you will play hell getting Miamians to say it did not belong to them all along.

People will fight you over a Cuban sandwich. They will shout you down over who invented it, who perfected it, who has the best one now, and what the traditional ingredients should be. To tinker with it too much is like painting a mustache on the *Mona Lisa*. It is best, being an interloper, to be neutral, or try to be.

I could not be more neutral. I fell in love with the Cuban sandwich in territorial waters, watching the shallows for sharks and rays, sacrificing baitfish to the trout, and ladyfish, and now and then a mangrove snapper. But if I was going to be honest, I'd have to say that I was mostly waiting for lunch. I knew that, when the sun looked right to him, the boat's

captain, Joe Romeo, would nod to me, the dead weight, and ask me if I was hungry. He would hand me an ice-cold Coca-Cola from the chest; I am far too poor a fisherman, and seaman, to even consider fishing drunk, and since I would have made two of Joe, I am certain he would have been unable to hoist me back into the vessel if I had fallen out, and it was too far to swim or wade back to Anna Maria Island.

Then he would toss me lunch. This time, it was a foot-long foil-wrapped parcel that had been ruminating on the deck since dawn, a beautifully simple sandwich of roast pork, sweet ham, Swiss cheese, and pickles on buttered Cuban bread dressed in only a little mustard, then heated through in a sandwich press till the cheese melted and the crusty bread was flat and crispy. It was the perfect thing to keep warm on the deck.

The fine Florida writer Marjorie Kinnan Rawlings wrote once that a cold biscuit in the woods is better than cake indoors, and it may be that it is the same on the water. I remember, once, seeing a hammerhead glide across the sand in water no deeper than my thigh. What restaurant, in any land, has that view?

I took a bite of that sandwich and, in that place and moment, was convinced it was the best thing I ever ate.

A year or so later I moved to Miami, which was a little like finding heaven on the other end of the Tamiami Trail. In every Cuban restaurant, market, and quite a few gas stations, you could find a good Cuban sandwich, but when I made the mistake of telling people I had come from across the state, they had to set me straight.

"That's not a real Cuban," people sniffed.

"Why?" I asked.

It had to do with salami. When the cigar factories migrated from Key West to Ybor City in the late 1800s, thousands of Cubans moved to Tampa, and Ybor City in particular. A strong Italian influence, it is believed, also influenced the sandwich.

"They put salami on them," an old Miamian told me, and made a face.

That, it was explained to me, made the west coast's claim to the sandwich null and void.

Miami did not claim the sandwich so much as conquer it. On Calle Ocho, on Coral Way, on every paved road, I found delicious Cubanos, and my favorite meal quickly became a sandwich and a café con leche, preferably eaten in a cool place on a hot day, reading a *Miami Herald* or a *St. Petersburg Times*, people-watching, wondering if a slice of *tres leches* might make life just too good to bear.

This Cuban, the Miami Cuban, was the true Cuban, I was lectured, but I remained neutral, having no dog in this fight.

Instead, I wandered off to try to write stuff, about something, and wait till another lunch, which had a pretty good chance of being a Cuban sandwich, unless I had my mouth set for a grouper sandwich, or some black bean soup with ham *croquetas* and sweet plantains. Because, deep in my heart, I knew I would leave this place someday, and that outside Florida it would not be the same.

I read that at least one Cuban sandwich emporium will make you a traditional Cubano with a ham *croqueta* on it. I would be willing to risk a fistfight to get one of them.

CURE MASTERS

IN PRINCETON, KENTUCKY, NANCY NEWSOM Mahaffey of Col. Bill Newsom's Aged Kentucky Country Ham cures haunches the same way her family has since the 1600s. Each winter, she packs them in salt, then smokes them over nineteenth-century iron kettles. At the end of each summer, she releases another year's batch. Mahaffey is a purist, but she isn't alone in her painstaking old-fashioned approach. Allan Benton of Benton's Smoky Mountain Country Hams, in Madisonville, Tennessee, learned to cure hams in a log smokehouse on his grandparents' property in Scott County, Virginia. Along the Virginia coast, Sam Edwards III carries on a tradition that dates back to the earliest days of the republic at Edwards Virginia Smokehouse in Surry. Lately, our homegrown cousin to prosciutto has undergone a renaissance. Cure masters who've held on to this labor-intensive tradition over the years have become national celebrities. Having persevered through thankless decades, though, none of them are in it for the glory. Southern country ham producers do what it takes to keep a tradition on the table. Here's how to honor them: vow never to overcook their product; all it needs is a quick sear on each side. Shaved thin, it requires no cooking at all. *See Benton, Allan; Country ham.*

CURSING

by Guy Martin

COTTON FARMER, TOWNSMAN, OR TRANS-planted Atlanta-based victim of sprawl trapped in a split-level overlooking I-85, any given Southerner's relationship with the land is the gift that keeps on giving to the language. Southerners have an easy command of what a covey of quail does on the rise, how to hot-walk a horse, or what a copperhead lounging out back under the blackberry bushes can do if you poke it with a stick. The bounty of flora and fauna and their behavior only expand the field of wordplay. When Southerners speak editorially of their fellow citizens, even the most basic agrarian similes—*she's common as pig tracks*, or *he's crooked as a dog's hind leg*—can be used to great effect.

When more forceful comparison is required, a Southerner undisturbed in his natural habitat will resort to the known, and technically profane, classics. These beloved old tools have been handed down in a treasure chest of expression from all ancestral streams that fed the mother tongue, namely, Latin, Saxon German, Norman French, and Middle English, as we can easily read from snapshots of our young language in Chaucer's or Shakespeare's deftly bawdy sections. (See Iago's malicious spreading of the gossip in Act IV that Othello and Desdemona are "making the beast with two backs.") During the Hundred Years' War, the French dubbed their fourteenth- and fifteenth-century English enemies *les goddamns*, which sprang from the English troops' robust custom of taking the Lord's name in vain. The British etymologist Geoffrey Hughes notes that the French continue to vamp on that six-hundred-year-old bit of cussing today, calling the British by the phrase they hear them screaming at one another on long, drunken weekends in France, *les f**koffs*.

The durable Anglo-Saxon verb at the root of that term, which inspires so much off-color creativity, seems to have come to us from the Norse and Swedish verbs *fukka* and *focka*, respectively, presumably describing some of what took place during Viking incursions into what later became Scotland and England. As refracted through a few hundred years of English satire and derogation since then, the word is a staple of the Southerner's linguistic patrimony in crafting profanity, arguably because there is so much blunt poetry that is right with it. Although the old words themselves may be thought of as "careless" language, they have very much been cared *for*. Accordingly, Southerners treat the act of cursing as eminently social, and thus worth attending with an old, mannerly code.

No rules can be followed to the letter in heated moments, but boiled down, the cursing code follows that for every other Southern circumstance, from stirrup cups on a fox-hunt morning to barbecues and garden parties: when cursing, mind your manners. This seeming oxymoron is not just about the use of coarse language in mixed company, although it does apply to that. Rather, it's about heeding the fact that, much as we love their many rainbows of connotation, the old four-letter

Anglo-Saxon words have stopping power. They strongly punctuate whatever sentence they live in. Like our better chefs, the speaker wants to use the peppers sparingly, lest they overpower the gumbo.

A second important aspect to the code is that a curse should not be an invitation to a pig wallow so much as an invitation to elevate the discourse. You're not in it to invite your listeners to "go low." Not so long ago, the curse was actually a *curse*—a sentence to doom, as with Macbeth's three witches. One should strive to use metaphor, rhythm, and simile to lend context and drive to any bit of coarse speech. It's a Southerner's social duty to curse with whatever fleeting literary beauty can be mustered—welcoming and entertaining folks, not putting them off. This is an ur-Southern contradiction, something to be embraced, not solved. My formidable mother parses the distinction well: "Curse all you want; just don't be vulgar about it, goddammit."

D

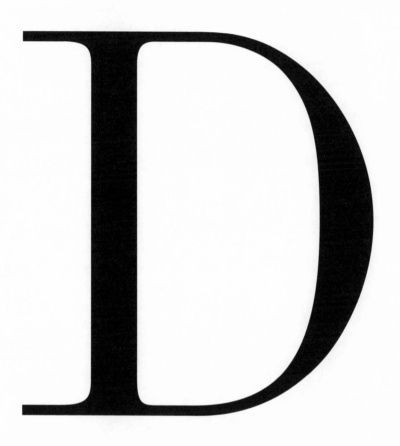

DANCE, BILL

(1940–)

Bill Dance is America's Favorite Fishin' Buddy. His TV fishing show, *Bill Dance Outdoors*, has been on the air since 1968 and made him a cult figure in the bass-fishing world. From his home in Collierville, Tennessee, Dance oversees a fishing empire that includes not only television but also tackle endorsements, how-to seminars, his own magazine, and a series of popular "blooper" videos, compiling his legendary pratfalls from the show (*Fishing Bloopers, Volumes 1, 2, 3,* and *4*). There's even a Bill Dance app.

This level of popularity results from a happy convergence of several factors. It doesn't hurt to be a superb angler. Before retiring from competition in 1980, Dance won twenty-three National Bass Titles, qualified for the Bassmaster Classic (the Olympics of bassdom)

eight out of nine years, and was three times named B.A.S.S. Angler of the Year. It's even better if you're a down-to-earth guy whom people enjoy having in their living rooms. And if you have a wet sense of humor (there is no dry humor among anglers) in which you are frequently the butt of your own jokes, better still. Dance's *Fishing Bloopers* are consistently best sellers—a four-minute clip from *Volume 1* on YouTube has exceeded two million views (and counting) over three years. Even all these ingredients, though, can't fully explain Dance's enduring appeal. There's that certain intangible, something you can't describe but recognize when you see it: authenticity. Whether you see him in person or on-screen, you immediately sense that the unpretentious, outgoing fellow signing autographs or talking to the camera is exactly who he appears to be. He's Bill Dance.

DARK 'N STORMY

The Dark 'n Stormy is to the gin and tonic what whole wheat is to white bread: both drinks may be highballs garnished with a lime, but the former is possessed of more grit and gumption than its milquetoast cousin.

The Dark 'n Stormy is often served in bars in coastal areas, likely the effect of sailing culture and the rum's long ties to the island of Bermuda. It's made—by law—with Gosling's Black Seal Rum, a dark, funky liquor made in Guyana and bottled by the Gosling family in Bermuda, as it has been for two centuries.

The Dark 'n Stormy cocktail was apparently invented on the island after World War I and is one of the few cocktails that's trademarked by a distillery.

The construction of a Dark 'n Stormy—er, make that a Dark 'n Stormy®—is simple. Start with a tall glass and mix spicy ginger beer with a jigger of dark rum—use Gosling's unless you enjoy corresponding with attorneys. Add a few ice cubes and a healthy squeeze from a wedge of lime. Then sip, preferably with a view of sun-dappled water that's at the very least brackish. Bonus points are awarded if the water is full-on briny and framed by teak planks with brass fittings.

DAUBE GLACÉ

PRIOR TO REFRIGERATION, MEAT DIDN'T LAST too long in the swelter and humidity of New Orleans. So nineteenth-century cooks got creative to keep meat from spoiling: they jellied it. Originally, this meant simmering down the continental beef-and-vegetable stew known as daube to make it last for multiple nights. A chef would reconstitute it before serving. In time, some savvy cook realized that concentrated daube glacé was a worthy dish by itself. Traditionalists still serve slices of the old-school terrine as a holiday hors d'oeuvre, with garlic croutons or crackers.

DAUFUSKIE ISLAND

HERE'S DAUFUSKIE ISLAND BY THE NUMBERS: 32°6'47" N, 80°51'59" W. All of fifteen square miles, it's the southernmost inhabited spot in South Carolina. Population three hundred, made up of descendants of slaves, sundry Georgians who blew ashore here for reasons about which you do not casually inquire, and shell-shocked Northern transplants who imagined they were moving to the next Martha's Vineyard. Six thousand acres of high ground—on a raucous holiday weekend, *very* high ground. (Listen to Jimmy Buffett's song "Prince of Tides" for reference.)

You could call Daufuskie a world apart: no bridge, no problem. It's fourteen miles from the nearest traffic light, with yoga infrequent and frozen yogurt nonexistent. The fast food has fur, fins, or feathers. Two beer joints: come July, you can't see the bars for the bikinis, the gumbo makes you sweat, and they sweep up the eyeballs come closing time. Naked on the beach? No problem with that, either.

A great time warp—instant 1956—Daufuskie boasts America's largest collection of freedman architecture, the homes, churches, and schools of the first generation up from slavery. The entire island was declared a National Historic Landmark District in 1982; tours daily. Notoriously independent locals call Daufuskie "the right side of the river." By implication, the entire North American continent is the wrong side.

DELIVERANCE

NEARLY HALF A CENTURY AFTER THE PUBLI-cation of James Dickey's 1970 novel (and the 1972 movie classic whose screenplay he co-wrote), banjos, Southern white water, and backwoods savagery remain, in American pop culture, inseparable. "My story is simple," Dickey once told an interviewer, "there are bad people, there are monsters among us. . . . I wrote *Deliverance* as a story where under the conditions of extreme violence people find out things about themselves that they would have no other means of knowing." *See Dickey, James.*

THE DELTA

by Julia Reed

A FEW YEARS AGO, I WAS ON A BOOK TOUR that took me everywhere from Knoxville, Tennessee, to Manchester, Vermont, and I found myself having to explain—a lot—what I meant when I referred to the Mississippi Delta, where I was born and raised. Usually I made like a first-grade teacher and held up my forefingers and thumbs in front of my face in the shape of a diamond. "This is Memphis," I'd say, tapping my fingers together at the top. "Down here, where my thumbs meet, is Vicksburg, and over here on the right is the Yazoo River. The Mississippi is on the left, to the west." I repeated what the Greenville-born novelist David Cohn said, about the Delta be-ginning in the lobby of Memphis's Peabody

hotel, where ducks—descendants of live de-coys left there by long-ago Delta hunters—still swim in the marble fountain.

I explained that the Delta is not an actual delta but one of the richest alluvial flood-plains in the world—one pretty much unin-habitable until well into the 1820s, when a handful of folks rich enough and crazy enough (Cohn called them "pioneers with means") turned up to literally hack it out. They'd al-ready built their grand houses in other parts of the South, where the land was beginning to tap out. Now they were willing to risk yel-low fever and countless slaves and members of their families to clear the oft-flooded tangle of primeval swamp and hardwood forest that had been all but untouched for thousands of years by anyone except the mound-dwelling "Indians." Necessarily adventurers and gam-blers at heart, they were anxious to get at the sandy loam that became known as Delta Gold.

By that time, my audience was transfixed, so it became more personal. My hometown of Greenville, I said, is the most sophisticated place I've ever lived. It's where I got my first byline, for a review of a book written by my next-door neighbor, the *National Geographic* contributor Bern Keating, in our newspa-per, the *Delta Democrat-Times.* I told them how Hodding Carter II, the paper's found-ing editor, had won a Pulitzer Prize for writ-ing a series of editorials in support of racial and religious tolerance as early as the 1940s. Carter, a crusading young newspaper editor from Louisiana, had been lured to Greenville by William Alexander Percy, the poet and planter whose literary influence on the region is enormous. He inspired countless writers, including Walker Percy, his much younger cousin whom he adopted, and Shelby Foote, Walker Percy's best friend.

I reminded them that we'd never had much truck with the "moonlight and magnolias" Old South, and repeated what Shelby Foote once told an interviewer: "The Delta is a great melting pot." Foote's grandfather was one of a thriving group of prominent Jews who came to the Delta from Austria, Poland, and Russia. When Greenville was incorporated after the Civil War, the first elected mayor was Jewish, as were the first businesses to open. There was also a sizable Syrian population, who, like most of the Jews, had arrived as traveling salesmen, as well as a large influx of Chinese, whose influence, Foote said, was "considerable." Arriving in the area as itinerant railroad workers, they drew the line at picking cotton and chose instead to open small businesses (primarily grocery stores) catering to the Delta's majority African American population.

Finally, I told them that we have always, from the get-go and by necessity, been seriously adept at making our own fun. And that everywhere there are reminders of that ancient forest from whence we sprang. Before my parents bought our house, there had been a yellow-fever cemetery just beyond our backyard; even now my mother yells at me to shut the door lest a snake get in. In high water, the odd black bear, the population of which once numbered in the tens of thousands, has been known to wander into civilization.

The latter is the kind of stuff that always left them wide-eyed. But there was lots more that I couldn't explain, the stuff better written about in songs or fiction. The way my heart skips a beat every time I drive over that last hill outside of Memphis and into what feels like an enormous dome turned on its side. That earthy chemical smell more powerful than any of Proust's madeleines. The signs naming towns that read like reassuring mantras as I blow by: Rena Lara, Midnight, Nitta Yuma, Louise.

There's the breathtaking starkness of the landscape in winter, the sunsets that drench the sky, my favorite stretch of blacktop connecting 61 to Old Highway 1 at Duncan, not far from where Robert Johnson is said to have sold his soul. There's the memory of just-caught brim and crappie frying in a black-iron skillet at the Highland Club on the banks of Lake Washington, one of the many oxbow lakes formed by the Mississippi, or the first time I ate a hot tamale at the legendary Doe's Eat Place. No matter what, there's the soundtrack: Johnson, Albert King, B. B. King, Bobby "Blue" Bland, Son House, John Lee Hooker, Charley Patton, Muddy Waters, Son Thomas. The list goes on and on. More recently, there's been Eden Brent channeling Boogaloo Ames on the piano or Duff Dorrough bringing me to my knees with "Rock My Soul." I listen to it all and realize that what I should have said to everyone who asked is that the Delta is a great gift, from thousands of years of flooding and all those who carved it out and worked it afterward in conditions so insufferable that it gave us the blues. It's also inseparable from who I am.

(1928–2016)

(1923–1997)

THORNTON DIAL HAD ENORMOUS HANDS. For many decades, he put them to singular use, crafting found objects—including doll parts, metal scrap, paint, old shoes, and springs—into works of art now coveted by such institutions as the Metropolitan Museum of Art. For most of Dial's life, though, such acclaim must have seemed about as likely as aliens touching down in his Alabama front yard. Born to an unwed teenager in Emelle, Alabama, in 1928, Dial dropped out of school in the third grade and never learned to read. He moved to Bessemer, Alabama, in 1941, and after working a variety of odd jobs, Dial found work building boxcars for the Pullman Standard Company, where he remained until retirement. Throughout it all Dial made art but remained in essence unknown until his fifties, when a collector named William Arnett visited him on a tip. In time Dial became one of the rare African American self-taught (or "outsider") artists to find success within the traditional spheres of "insider" tastemakers.

JAMES DICKEY WOULD HAVE BEEN A LEGEND even if he hadn't written *Deliverance*, the 1970 novel and subsequent film for which he is best known. He was a National Book Award winner and a poet laureate of the United States. Yet strike even *that* from his record and the epic stories of the man would most likely still be floating around simply because of his larger-than-life personality. The author Pat Conroy, a former student of Dickey's, once said Dickey made Ernest Hemingway look like a florist from the Midwest. Large, loud, and preternaturally talented, Dickey was born in Atlanta, served in the Air Force, and later quit his job as an advertising executive in order to write. His widely celebrated poetry—a high-test vernacular concoction Dickey dubbed "country surrealism"—became even more powerful when read aloud in his booming voice. Yet it was his first novel, *Deliverance*—a spare, testosterone-driven tale of Atlanta suburbanites caught in a backwoods Appalachian hell—that made the biggest impression. Ironically, the line Dickey is perhaps most identified with—"squeal like a pig"—wasn't even his. It was an inspired bit of perverse improv delivered on the film set. But that seems fitting too, for in the end, James Dickey was nothing if not an inspiration.

DIDDLEY, BO

(1928–2008)

by Matt Hendrickson

Bo Diddley passed away from heart failure on June 2, 2008, at age seventy-nine, and it's easy—in the aftermath of his death—to bestow lofty titles on him. But the reality is that Diddley *was* the originator of rock and roll, the most influential figure in the history of popular music. Muddy Waters and Chuck Berry came from straight-up blues, but Diddley was different: something more primal, evil, and dangerous. The Bo Diddley beat—bonk, ba donk, donk donk donk—is the most frequently borrowed riff of all time, showing up in songs such as Buddy Holly's "Not Fade Away" and U2's "Desire." Elvis Presley, it has long been supposed, copped his stage moves from Diddley. Sure, Berry was a monumental figure in rock and roll, but his keyboardist Johnnie Johnson cowrote many of his hits. The Stones wouldn't exist without Bo Diddley, and even John Lennon, when asked what he wanted to do when he arrived in America for the first time, said: "I want to meet Bo Diddley." The Clash asked him to tour with them. U2 adored him. Only Little Richard comes close to Diddley's significance, and until the good reverend passes on, let's just anoint Bo as the king.

But Diddley never reaped the full benefits of his influence. He signed away the publishing rights to his music for a $10,000 down payment on his first house, a bitter pill that he swallowed until his death. He once famously said: "Don't trust nobody but your mama, and even then, look at her real good." Until his stroke in 2007 shortly after a show in Council Bluffs, Iowa, Diddley played about a hundred dates a year, each a lesson in the theatrics of rock and roll with its ruckus of high kicks and searing work on his custom-made cigar-box-shaped guitar.

By all accounts, Diddley loved being just an average joe to the residents of Archer, Florida, where he lived on a seventy-six-acre farm. "He always loved doing regular guy stuff," says his band member Frank Daley. "We were in Santa Barbara and he called me up and said, 'Let's go to the hardware store.' He was looking for a big tarp to cover God-knows-what at his farm. He found this big blue thing, rolled it up, and put it in his suitcase." Diddley loved to cook chickens and turkeys in a smoking pit on his property, and drive around in his tractor moving earth around.

"I'd do his taxes, and every year there was an expenditure for sand," says Diddley's co-manager Faith Fusillo. "He would get piles of sand and just move them from spot to spot. I was like, 'How am I going to write this off?'"

Through his music, Diddley did move heaven and earth, and though his influence as Bo Diddley was never far from the minds of the people attending his funeral, it was the life of Ellas McDaniel—father, grandfather, and great-grandfather—that was celebrated during a four-hour "homegoing ceremony" at the Showers of Blessings Harvest Center in Gainesville. As the choir and band cooked up a chills-inducing spiritual, Diddley's casket was wheeled in, followed by more than forty family members chanting "Hey, Bo Diddley" and led by his oldest daughter, Evelyn, or

"Tan," who danced maniacally behind the slow-moving casket.

Once most of the overflow crowd was seated, the testifying and singing began. City officials read proclamations from Gainesville and Archer—Gainesville's mayor announced to raucous applause that the city's downtown square would soon be renamed Bo Diddley Plaza. Diddley's grandson Garry Mitchell—wearing Diddley's black leather cowboy hat with a silver eagle medallion in the front and two small badges on the side—spoke for the family. "Many times Grandpa and I would talk, almost in secret," Mitchell said. "Our conversations on his life and mine were almost intertwined. I thank God for that cycle, because his legacy shall live on. Grandpa was awesome; he was way before Elvis Presley. He always got up way early, so early that he tapped the roosters on the shoulder and said: 'You forgot to crow, because I'm already here.'"

Though Diddley didn't succumb to the pitfalls of rock and roll—he never did drugs, and drank only occasionally—religion was never a huge part of his life until near the end. "The night he died, all of us were gathered around him," says his comanager Margo Lewis. "He grabbed my hand, told me he loved me. His friend Sam Green began singing the old spiritual 'Walk Around Heaven.' He was in and out, but when Sam finished, he sat up, shook Sam's hand, and said, 'Whoa.' He knew he was on his way."

And Diddley was truly sent out in style. As his longtime backing band—led by Debby Hastings, his bandmate of twenty-five years—softly played his signature song, "Bo Diddley," his casket was wheeled out into the steamy Florida sun. Brushing past flower arrangements sent by such admirers as Tom Petty and the Heartbreakers, George Thorogood, and Jerry Lee Lewis, Diddley's casket was loaded into the hearse as tears streamed down many faces. He was gone, but the originator of rock and roll was finally going home.

DISMALITES

TEN MILES BEYOND THE SIPSEY WILDERNESS and sunk more than a hundred feet from the surrounding forest, Dismals Canyon looks more like something out of Jurassic Park than Northwest Alabama. Dump-truck-sized sandstone boulders furred with moss form dozens of shaded, fern-filled grottoes on the canyon's eighty-five-acre floor. The gorge is so remote, the notorious traitor (and original Southern separatist) Aaron Burr hid out there while plotting his takeover of Texas before the law caught up with him in 1807. Jesse James reportedly did the same after an 1881 robbery in Muscle Shoals. But all of that pales in comparison to the main event: the show put on by the larval form of *Orfelia fultoni*, a relative of fungus gnats, known as Dismalites. Just after sunset on spring and summer nights, the tiny bioluminescent creatures begin to glow, covering the canyon's cliff faces in galaxies of pale blue lights. Outside of New Zealand, Australia, and a few isolated pockets of the Southern Appalachians, Dismals Canyon is one of the only places in the world where the insects are found. Luckily, taking in the

Dismalites' glow is easy: following the installation of a staircase, visitors no longer must squeeze through Fat Man's Misery—a sixteen-inch-wide crack between two boulders—to take a guided nighttime tour.

DOE'S EAT PLACE

by Julia Reed

THE FIRST MEAL I EVER ATE AT DOE'S EAT Place, the legendary steak and hot tamale restaurant in my hometown of Greenville, Mississippi, was, as it happens, in utero—there's a photo of my mother sitting on the slightly sagging front steps when she was seven months pregnant with me. My first actual memory dates from at least two years later, when a plate of unshucked "hots" was placed before me, commencing a love affair that continues apace.

The hot tamale is a product of the extraordinary commingling of cultures that has marked the Mississippi Delta from its earliest days and of which Doe's itself is a prime example. The father of Dominick "Doe" Signa arrived in Greenville in 1903, part of a wave of Southern Italian immigrants to the area, and opened a grocery store in the same building that now houses the restaurant. Located on Nelson Street, the city's unofficial African American Main Street, it was part of a bustling scene that included late-night barbershops, blues clubs, sidewalk craps games, fish markets, and more than a dozen grocery stores

operated by Chinese Americans who arrived around the same time as the Italians.

When the devastating 1927 flood all but shut down the grocery store, the young Doe turned to bootlegging. In 1941, after selling his still for three hundred dollars and a Model-T Ford, he turned the store into a honky-tonk and takeout joint featuring fried buffalo fish, chili, and the now-famous hot tamales (made from a recipe Doe acquired from a friend and that his wife, Mamie, improved). In an arrangement that turned segregation on its head, African American customers came through the front door, while the occasional white customer entered through a side door into a back room, where Doe served steaks grilled on the mammoth broiler up front. Within a few years the back room, or "eat place," became so popular that Doe shut the tonk and developed a "menu." While there has never been a paper or even a blackboard version, regulars know that it consists of chili and tamales, spaghetti and meatballs, fried shrimp, hand-cut french-fried potatoes, salad, garlic bread, gargantuan sirloin and porterhouse steaks, and, until the shucker (Doe's older brother Jughead) died, oysters on the half shell.

Doe's gained national renown in the 1960s and '70s, when Greenville became a magnet for national reporters covering the region's civil rights and political upheavals—in no small part because my father, then the chair of the fledgling Mississippi Republican party, and Hodding Carter III, the editor of our Pulitzer Prize–winning newspaper, the *Delta Democrat-Times*, invariably took them to Doe's for dinner. Bowled over by the food and free-flowing whiskey and wine (customers bring their own bottles, a holdover from the fact that until 1966, the whole state was officially, though not remotely in reality, dry), they returned to their various editors with tales of the exotic "eat place." The *Washington Post* and *New York Times* followed up with profiles, and since then, Doe's has appeared in countless publications.

From the get-go it was a family operation. Doe's sisters ran the "dining rooms," while Jughead's wife, Florence, manned the fry "station" (three heavily encrusted black iron skillets on a four-burner gas stove) until she was put in charge of the iceberg lettuce salad. Such is the magic of its dressing—an ineffable combination of olive oil, garlic, lemon juice, and salt—that customers have been known to drive long distances to leave their own wooden bowls for Florence to "season" over time. When Doe retired in 1974, his two sons, Doe Jr. ("Little Doe") and Charles, took over. These days the steaks are cooked mostly by their sons, Charles Jr. and Doe III, who stand on the same worn floorboards in front of the same broiler their grandfather did. Florence still turns up a couple of nights a week to make salad. Even the waitresses are part of the dynasty. Judy Saulter, who's been waiting tables since 1970, recruited her daughter Debra to join her in 1988.

A side room (where the family once slept) was opened up in the 1960s, and another back room around 1980. Otherwise very little has changed, though the broiled shrimp Big Doe once offered to regular customers on Friday nights was formally added to the menu sometime in the 1980s, and the steak selection now includes filets and rib eyes. Though credit cards are now taken, regulars can still simply sign the ticket before they depart; reservations are still taken on the black rotary phone and written down in a spiral notebook. Until the recent addition of Sysco cheesecakes, dessert consisted of the lollipops in a glass jar by the cash register. I've celebrated many a birthday with a Doe's "cake," a loaf of French bread stuck with lollipops and candles, and I'm relieved to know I can count on many more.

DOGWOODS

SOME HERALD DOGWOOD TREES AS THE MOST breathtaking plants in the South—they put on a year-round show, with fragrant spring blooms, gorgeous branch sprays in summer, turning leaves and bright berries in fall, and lovely buds come winter. Although today we may regard them mainly as eye candy, to Native Americans they were a whole lot more. When the dogwoods' lovely white flowers burst into bloom, they knew it was time to plant corn. They also used the hardwood to make daggers and arrows (which is why the English initially called the tree a "dagwood"), toothbrushes, a tobacco mixture for pipes and sacred religious ceremonies, and even poison to use against rival tribes (the sap can be toxic). It wasn't until the 1600s that the tree became known as the dogwood, most likely because the wood was boiled to create a medicinal wash to treat skin conditions like mange in dogs. (A less likely but more cocktail-party-suitable tale of the name's origins: on windy days branches knock into each other and sound like barking.) Today the tree—native to the eastern United States, and the state tree of

North Carolina—remains a beacon of spring and its bounty. Those first blossoms' arrival signals to knowing fishermen that the spring bite is on. Tip for a worthwhile detour: in eastern North Carolina's Sampson County, north of Wilmington, the nation's largest dogwood—certified by none other than the National Register of Big Trees—boasts a branch spread of forty-eight feet. Pretty as a (panoramic) picture.

DOUBLE GUNS

DOUBLE-BARRELED SHOTGUNS, WHETHER SIDE-by-sides or over-unders, are de rigueur in the quail fields of the South. They have long been known as gentlemen's guns, handmade for dukes and barons who would tolerate only the finest, a tradition continuing in bespoke British Best shotguns today. American doubles experienced a golden age from the early 1900s until World War II, from makers such as L. C. Smith, A. H. Fox, Ithaca Gun Company, and Parker Bros., and have come down through the generations. The most famous double in Southern lore is known as Bo Whoop, a 1926 A. H. Fox Burt Becker side-by-side belonging to the writer T. Nash Buckingham, which was lost for more than half a century before being rediscovered. *See Bo Whoop.*

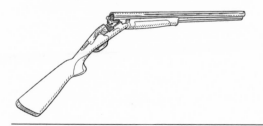

DOUBLE NAMES

by Daniel Wallace

To BEGIN WITH, DOUBLE NAMES ARE NOT middle names. Double names function as single names do—one is not to be spoken without the other. Middle names, on the other hand, are only used when you're signing contracts or in big trouble. For example:

Kayla Jane, get your butt downstairs right this minute! That's a middle name.

Hey everybody, Kayla Jane's here! That's a double name.

Double names are exactly what they say they are. They are one name, but two words. Like one cone with two scoops of ice cream on it.

Why do double names exist, and why especially in the South? Some explanations are even less meaningful than others.

1. Everything in the South is about heritage and family and family inclusiveness bordering on the insane. In some cases, a double name is derived from the single names of two people. Let's say you want to name your daughter after your aunt Mary but don't want to offend Aunt Lucille, so you'd name the daughter Mary Lucille. Not Lucille Mary, because that doesn't sound right, and in most double names in which Mary takes part, Mary comes first. No one knows the why about that.

2. Double names point to the dichotomy of self, the bringing together of our inner lives and our outer *presentation*

of self, the face we put on for others to see. I made that up.

3. It's just something that happens. It is what it is.

Like chess moves, the variety of double names is infinite. Here are just a few: Alva Grace, Ida Bell, Jancy Jane, Olivia Faye, Oscar Ray, Joe Ben, Joe Don, Joe Jim, Joe Bill, Phoebe Lynn, Queen Anne, Sadie Bell, Sammie Lou, Twila Fay, and Zippornia Lee. I could go on, but after Zippornia Lee they let you down.

Here's a true story. In high school I was in love with two girls at the same time and they were both named Mary. They were friends. I needed ways to differentiate between the two, even in my own head. This is where the double name came in handy. The double name made it easy, because one was named Mary Clayton and the other was Mary Catherine, which is much more elegant than Mary No. 1 and Mary No. 2. I ended up dating both of them, by the way, one after the other, but in the end neither worked out. Happy ending: two or three decades later, I met the woman who would become my wife.

Laura Anne.

DOUGLAS, MARJORY STONEMAN

(1890–1998)

"THERE ARE NO OTHER EVERGLADES IN THE world," reads the famous opening line of *The Everglades: River of Grass*, a galvanizing book authored by a woman who had an intimate understanding of singularity. Marjory Stoneman Douglas fought unceasingly for the protection of South Florida's natural resources, insisting just years before her death at age 108 that the urban ills that had infringed upon her beloved wetland network's purity and span had not dissuaded her. "I say it's got to be done," she said of the Everglades' defense. Born in Minneapolis in 1890, Douglas joined her father in Miami in 1915 after her husband proved to be a pauper and a cheat. Frank Stoneman, the editor of the town's leading newspaper, assigned a gossip column to his daughter; within a few years, she was writing about the need for women's suffrage and abolition of the convict lease system. Despite believing the Everglades was a buggy and unwelcoming swamp, she accepted an invitation to chronicle its natural and political history. *The Everglades*, published in 1947, is considered a masterpiece of environmental literature. Although she stood just five feet two, generations of activists have hailed Douglas as a giant, declaring that, if not for her pioneering work, there would be no Everglades left to save.

DOVE SHOOT

Despite the somewhat unsavory term, the Southern dove shoot is a fairly refined affair, part tent meeting and part camo-clad cotillion, an annual debutante ball of sorts for the hunting set. And while a dove shoot can take place on any day during the legal hunting season for mourning doves, it is the opening-day festivities that lend the term its real significance. It works like this: across most of the South, hunting season for mourning doves opens on the Saturday before Labor Day, which is preceded by a few weeks of brownnosing, chit calling in, and desperate glad-handing as hunters suck up to friends, colleagues, and distant family members for an invitation to a coveted shoot. It's often a daylong affair. A pig pickin' isn't required but is nearly customary. Hunters spread out in cornfields and sunflower patches, hunkered down on five-gallon buckets with Labrador retrievers panting at their sides. Doves are notoriously challenging targets to hit, with an average ratio of far below 50 percent, and yet words of encouragement and support are rarely heard in the field. But the ribbing is all good-natured, and at the end there is often cold beer and homemade banana pudding to soothe any sunburn and bruised egos.

DRESSING

Is it dressing in the South and stuffing in the North? Or is it dressing when baked in a pan and stuffing when baked in the cavity of a turkey? It depends on whom you ask, as both explanations have elements of truth. Stuffing, when prepared outside of the South, counts as a seasonal holiday treat. A buried treasure to be excavated from the Thanksgiving or Christmas turkey, it is limited by capacity, a bowlful gone until the following year. Dressing dresses a full table that holds a bounty of vegetables and side dishes. It may accompany turkeys, as well as chickens, ducks, and the occasional smothered pork chop, and consists primarily of cornbread (not bread), a tradition derived from making the most of stale leftover cornbread. Dressing is further prone to assuming the local accent of wherever it lands. It likes oysters near the shore and fruit in the mountains, and it never says no to a pecan.

DRY COUNTY

The Twenty-first Amendment to the Constitution, passed in late 1933, repealed Prohibition after fourteen long years. While the federal government got out of the temperance game, the amendment left open a back door for local bluenose authorities. In the ensuing years, hundreds of counties declared themselves "dry" and prohibited the sale, consumption, and transportation of alcohol. Others became so-called moist counties, which may make exceptions for private consumption, sales in licensed clubs, or even the presence of a local winery. Some counties may be dry, but cities within them have voted to allow retail sales. It gets confusing. While dry counties are scattered throughout the South and, to some degree, the Midwest, many are concentrated in the states of Kentucky, Mississippi, and Arkansas. Interestingly, Lynchburg, Tennessee, home to the Jack Daniel's distillery, is located within a dry county. So while you can tour the distillery, you can't legally buy Jack Daniel's in the Jack Daniel's gift shop. Though you can purchase a special commemorative bottle that coincidentally comes filled with, you guessed it, Jack Daniel's. Get it?

DUBOIS, BLANCHE

IT MEANS, SHE INSISTS (INCORRECTLY, AS IT happens), "white woods." Blanche DuBois is Tennessee Williams's most famous heroine: a fallen aristocrat come to live with her sister in the New Orleans slums of *A Streetcar Named Desire*, undone by her new status in life and brought to brutal conflict with her brother-in-law, Stanley. She's caught between fantasy and reality, and the audience is never quite sure which one she should choose. *See Williams, Tennessee.*

DUELING

WHILE DUELING WAS NEVER EXCLUSIVELY Southern in eighteenth- and nineteenth-century America, its most passionate and effective advocates were. Our nation's Code Duello was published in 1838 by a former South Carolina governor, John Lyde Wilson. In other words, just a few scant years before dueling was outlawed in the mid-nineteenth century, Southern politicians were busy codifying the practice. Everybody who was anybody erred, and incurred a challenge. Never shy to whip out his sidearm, Andrew Jackson killed a rival planter in Tennessee after the neighbor made the mistake of accusing Jackson's wife, Rachel, of being a bigamist and Jackson himself of cheating on a horse-racing bet. (The latter was most likely correct.) Jackson missed once but shot twice, killing his opponent, considered a huge, virtually criminal violation of etiquette by the men attending on the field. The future president escaped being prosecuted for murder.

Of New Orleans, the site of Jackson's career-sealing military victory five years after that duel, it was said that you could face a morning challenge from a Creole aristocrat if you so much as moved the wrong chair at a dinner party without apology, or even with one. The court at Versailles was the model. Dueling was done under the live oaks out by the Bayou St. John. *Salles d'armes*, or fencing schools, were ragingly popular. The ruling late-eighteenth-century fencing master was Don José "Pepe" Llulla, a Minorcan said to be so adroit that he would indicate to his seconds on the field the exact button on his challenger's waistcoat through which he would run his saber. Llulla engaged in some twenty-plus duels over a long life, preferring actually to use his superior talent to spare his opponents—he killed only two men. In the eighteenth- and early-nineteenth-century South, that rated as excellent manners.

DUKE'S MAYONNAISE

THE FRENCH INVENTED MAYO, BUT IT TOOK Eugenia Duke to perfect it, whipping up her own recipe to dress sandwiches she sold to World War I doughboys in Greenville, South Carolina. Duke's is still eggier and zestier than other mayos, is still sold to fierce loyalists primarily below the Mason-Dixon Line, and still elevates a simple tomato sandwich into a memorable occasion. *See Mayonnaise.*

DUPREE, NATHALIE

(1939–)

WIDELY RECOGNIZED AS ONE OF THE GRANDES dames of Southern cooking, Nathalie Dupree never refuses to pose for a picture with one of her fans. And she says the same thing every time she smiles for the camera: "Sex!" Born in New Jersey in 1939 (and a longtime resident of Charleston, South Carolina), Dupree has never shied away from subjects that make some people uncomfortable, including kitchen mistakes (she's a vocal advocate) and the challenges of being a woman in the food-and-beverage industry. She started cooking in her college dormitory dining room, and—over her mother's objections—trained as a chef at London's Cordon Bleu school. In the 1970s, she opened a restaurant in rural Georgia, then founded the cooking school at Rich's Department Store in Atlanta. She filmed her first cooking show in 1986 at the request of White Lily flour, and went on to become the first woman since Julia Child to host more than a hundred cooking programs on public television. She's written fourteen cookbooks, including *Mastering the Art of Southern Cooking*, which won a prestigious James Beard Foundation Award. Although she lost her write-in bid for the U.S. Senate in 2010, she's won countless lifetime achievement awards from organizations that include Les Dames d'Escoffier International, the James Beard Foundation, and the Southern Foodways Alliance.

EARNESTINE & HAZEL'S

THERE ARE THREE THINGS YOU NEED TO know about this gloriously shabby Memphis watering hole. First, it is frequently touted as the best dive bar in America. Second, the Soul Burger, as it's dubbed, is greasy nirvana at 2:00 a.m. after a night of getting soused on Beale Street. Fried in a squirt of pickle juice, the patty holds only onions, cheese, and "Soul Sauce." Third—and this is where it gets weird—they say Earnestine & Hazel's is haunted. Employees swear that the jukebox will fire up on its own, say like the time a group of women came in celebrating a divorce and Tammy Wynette's "D-I-V-O-R-C-E" popped on. Upstairs lie a set of rooms with paint peeling off the walls that at one point were inhabited by ladies of the evening. Rumor is that some met an unfortunate demise between those walls. But not to worry. When it's hopping downstairs, as it usually is come late night, the bar is just the thing to raise the spirits.

EARTHQUAKES

IN 1886, TWO DECADES BEFORE THE GREAT QUAKE of 1906 leveled San Francisco, Charleston, South Carolina, experienced the largest earthquake ever to hit the eastern United States (then or now). It would have registered 7.3 on the Richter Scale had that measurement been around at the time—a seismic disaster that wrought untold damage and prompted the widespread installation of earthquake bolts, metal reinforcements designed to brace buildings against future quakes. Earthquakes have plagued the South throughout its history, and since 1970, destinations as widespread as Alcoa, Tennessee, and Fort Payne, Alabama, have felt the ground shake at a magnitude of 4.6 or higher. Earthquakes still pose a real and persistent threat across the region: coastal South Carolina, for instance, averages ten to fifteen quakes a year, and though there has yet to be one that measures up to the 1886 disaster, experts say it could happen again.

EASTERN SHORE

REMOVED, REMOTE, A WORLD ALL ITS OWN, the eastern side of the Chesapeake Bay is a 175-mile-long landscape of marsh and protected coves, bay islands, and barrier islands. Composed of seven Maryland and two Virginia counties, the Eastern Shore has a mash-up of colonial history and commercial fishing, sprawling fields of corn and soybeans, wild beaches, and maritime forests all within an oyster shell's throw of each other. To get there most often involves one of two epic drives. From the south, you take the soaring—and at times, underwater—twenty-three miles of the Chesapeake Bay Bridge Tunnel. Or drive from the north via an island-hopping highway from the Washington, D.C.–Baltimore megalopolis to Annapolis to Kent Island and then the Eastern Shore proper. There, cultural icons are scattered like driftwood in a marsh: the wild ponies of Chincoteague and Assateague Islands, soft-shell-crab shedding shacks, the Chesapeake Bay Maritime Museum in St. Michaels, and decoy shops from one end to the other.

EDMUND PETTUS BRIDGE

IN THE WEEKS LEADING UP TO MARCH 7, 1965, tensions were running high in Alabama. Two civil rights groups—the Student Non-Violent Coordinating Committee and the Southern Christian Leadership Conference—had joined the Dallas County Voters League to help with a voter campaign in Selma, where only 2 percent of African Americans were registered due to discriminatory barriers such as literacy tests. Thousands of people had been arrested already, and at the end of February, a state trooper shot and killed a church deacon peacefully demonstrating in nearby Marion, causing the SCLC's James Bevel to call for a march from Selma to Montgomery to bring attention to voter rights and police brutality. And so on what would come to be known as Bloody Sunday, John Lewis, then the chairman of SNCC (the acronym is pronounced "snick") and now a U.S. congressman, and Hosea Williams of the SCLC took their places at the front of roughly six hundred people to march the fifty-odd miles to the state capital, many of them wearing overcoats and backpacks full of reading material and snacks in case they were arrested. As they approached Selma's Edmund Pettus Bridge—named for

a Confederate brigadier general, U.S. senator, and Ku Klux Klan Grand Dragon—they couldn't see the other side, because of the way the bridge arched upward at its longest span. They couldn't see the line of 150 Alabama state troopers—some of whom had been deputized that day, just for the occasion—waiting with their gas masks and billy clubs on the orders of Governor George Wallace. When they did spot the policemen, Williams asked Lewis if he knew how to swim, indicating the Alabama River, one hundred feet below. Watching footage of what happened next is enough to make you weep, even more than fifty years later. The troopers advanced, beating and gassing the protesters, fracturing Lewis's skull and causing him and sixteen other people to be hospitalized. As images of the violence raced across America, the nation largely was aghast. Two more marches and a little more than a week later, President Lyndon B. Johnson sent a voting rights bill to Congress, and the Voting Rights Act was signed into law in August of that year.

In the decades since, Lewis has reenacted that march annually. The entire route is now designated as a U.S. National Historic Trail, which passes by the National Voting Rights Museum, and in 2013, the bridge was honored as a National Historic Landmark. In 2015, Lewis walked hand in hand with President Barack Obama and First Lady Michelle Obama as they led a crowd of forty thousand back over the span to honor and remember the fiftieth anniversary of that day. "That's why a march is such a good metaphor, because the march is one that always has a new leg to it, a new twist to it, a new bridge to cross," the president said in a speech that day at the foot of the Pettus. "Each generation, each successive generation, has to walk that mile." *See Lewis, John.*

EGERTON, JOHN

(1935–2013)

by John T. Edge

JOHN WALDEN EGERTON, BORN ON JUNE 14, 1935, in Atlanta, grew up in Cadiz, Kentucky, where his father was a traveling salesman and his mother was a shopkeeper. Egerton showed early talent for writing, covering high-school sports for the *Cadiz Record* while still in grade school. After serving in the army and earning two degrees from the University of Kentucky, he worked for the University of Kentucky and the University of South Florida before moving to Nashville in 1965 to write about school desegregation efforts for the Southern Education Reporting Service.

By 1971, Egerton had established himself as an independent journalist and author. Over forty-plus years, he wrote hundreds of magazine and newspaper articles and ten books of history and literary nonfiction, focused on the American South. In *The Americanization of Dixie*, published in 1974, he foretold a future when the South would adopt the North's brusque and industrial ways. The North, he wrote, would soon buy into the South's worst instincts, born of slavery and nurtured by Jim

Crow. He described the process as a mutual exchange of sins and predicted "deep divisions along race and class lines, an obsession with growth and acquisition and consumption, a headlong rush to the cities and the suburbs, diminution and waste of natural resources, institutional malfunctioning, abuse of political and economic power, increasing depersonalization, and a steady erosion of the sense of place, of community, of belonging."

Egerton served the South as a moral bellwether, writing about cultural identity, race relations, and what we now know as foodways. At a time when most food books celebrated mint juleps and skillet-fried chicken, *Southern Food: At Home, on the Road, in History*, published in 1987, read like a social history. Egerton paid homage to the working-class folk on whose backs Southern food culture was built. And he claimed food as a talisman for the region, arguing that "no other form of cultural expression, not even music, is as distinctively characteristic of the region." As interest in Southern foodways accelerated in the twenty-first century, *Southern Food* served as a road map for the next generation of writers.

Speak Now Against the Day: The Generation Before the Civil Rights Movement in the South, published in 1994, was his second big book. As with *Southern Food*, Egerton focused on Southerners who had not previously gotten their due. *Speak Now* explored how progressive blacks and whites had conspired in the 1930s and 1940s to break the back of Jim Crow. A mix of personal narrative and deeply researched history, it won the Robert F. Kennedy Book Award and was a finalist for the Pulitzer Prize.

Later in his career, Egerton emerged as a public figure, called to give talks about the state of the region. Dressed often in gray slacks and a blue button-down, looking like a rumpled college professor, Egerton extolled the virtues of Southern food and spoke truths about race, class, gender, and ethnicity. In that role as public intellectual, Egerton, along with forty-nine other cooks and writers whom he recruited to the cause, drove the 1999 founding of the Southern Foodways Alliance at the University of Mississippi.

His belief in the possibilities of welcome table conversations inspired the nonprofit. "Even if this is the best regional food in America," Egerton would say, "it's still endangered by genetic modification, mass production, focus group marketing, modern technology, accelerated living, family disintegration, cultural homogenization, celebrity chefs, yuppie gazers, scientifically raised hogs, shellfish depletion, politically correct tofu, and instant grits."

At times, Egerton seemed to pine for a time past, when smokehouse-cured country ham and skillet-fried chicken were birthrights, not artisanal goods. "When the chemistry is right, a meal in the South can still be an esthetic wonder," he wrote, "a sensory delight, a mystical experience." But he was no fabulist. Egerton was critical of this place he loved. "I'm not advocating a return to 'the good old days' of some mythic past," he said. "For most people, they were never all that good to begin with." In his writing and thinking, John Egerton, who died on November 21, 2013, challenged the region and its people to realize its long-deferred promise.

EGGLESTON, WILLIAM

(1939–)

THERE WAS A TIME WHEN COLOR PHOTOGRAphy was considered trash, good for nothing more than snapshots. Then came William Eggleston. By shooting the very things that made up snapshots—parking lots, teenage girls on a sofa, an exposed lightbulb against a red ceiling, a tricycle in an empty suburb—Eggleston turned color photography into high art. When the Museum of Modern Art first featured his work, in a 1976 solo exhibition, his distinctive dye-transfer colors and Delta vernacular subject matter flipped the art world upside down. Reportedly proud to have never owned a pair of blue jeans, Eggleston was born to a wealthy family in Memphis and raised in Sumner, Mississippi, and by the time he was a teenager was cruising around town in matching baby-blue Cadillacs with his girlfriend, Rosa, who later became his wife. He attended Vanderbilt, Delta State College, and Ole Miss but refused to take tests and never graduated from anywhere. Now the ultimate art-world insider-outsider, Eggleston is known for an aloof Deep South elegance attuned to the region's grit—but not so much grit that he'd ever need to wear denim.

ÉTOUFFÉE

Étouffée is a dish so good it straddles Cajun and Creole cuisines—surfacing everywhere from the small-town Café des Amis in Breaux Bridge, Louisiana, to the New Orleans fine-dining mecca Galatoire's. The original French *étouffer* means "to smother," in this case in a gravy that often begins with a tan roux and ends in a buttery stew of well-seasoned crawfish, shrimp, or crab; the holy trinity of bell peppers, onions, and celery; and chopped parsley and green onion, all served over rice. Other ingredients, such as tomato or cream, vary from family to family and arouse passionate debate.

THE EVERGLADES

by Monte Burke

DEEP IN THE LARGEST SUBTROPICAL WIL-derness in the United States, the great fishing guide Steve Huff tells me it's time to reel up and stow the rod. He eases the boat down Lost Man's River, headed for the wide-open Gulf of Mexico. But when we reach the *boca*, we are blasted by the wind. The once-drowsy Gulf—our fastest route home—is now frothed by rolling whitecaps. Huff's flats skiff is the perfect vessel for stalking laid-up tarpon—stealthy and shallow-drafting. It's not much good, however, in an angry sea.

"We'll take the back way," he says. By that,

he means traveling through the mangrove-lined backcountry of the Everglades, that seemingly inscrutable labyrinth of creeks, rivers, lagoons, and black-water lakes. Huff navigates it all without a map or GPS. Going this way adds an extra two hours to the trip, but the time passes unnoticed, as if in a dream.

We stop once. Deep in a tangle of mangroves, Huff points out a nearly extinct type of vanilla orchid. Its hanging vines are adorned with buttons of startlingly white petals. It is the Everglades in microcosm: beautiful, rare, and threatened.

The Everglades are true, unbridled nature, where Melville's "great floodgates of the wonder-world" swing wide open. Swallow-tailed kites, man-o'-war birds, great horned owls, ospreys, and roseate spoonbills, in their psychedelic pink, own the skies. Insects thrum in the mangroves. Nine-foot-long crocodiles sun on the beach, unnerving in their serene nonchalance. A copse of tall skeletal trees, bleached by the sun, stands decades after Hurricane Andrew swiftly slayed them.

Then there are the fish, the reason that many of us visit the Everglades and swing open those floodgates. The ever-willing sea trout. The flats-cruising redfish. The surly snook hanging tight to the mangroves. And, of course, the tarpon—glowing like a precious metal in the sheet of ever-moving brackish water, a jungle fish entirely in its element.

The Everglades are the last true frontier in the American South, and one of the last in the country. They are a sanctuary in more ways than one: your cell phone will not get service in the backcountry. Even the towns—Everglades

City and Chokoloskee—have an outpost feel, their legions of mosquitoes having successfully defended them from high-rises and resorts. It's no accident that self-reliant people like Huff call this place home. He's never had an email address.

Despite the mosquitoes, the Everglades remain under siege, in ways both substantial and petty. Pollution from the sugar industry poisons the headwaters. Politicians have been known to shirk their duty as stewards of this public land, one of the last best places on earth. Orchid thieves selfishly poach beauty. But nature persists, for now, anyway.

The Everglades matter. They are worth fighting for. "Man only cares for things he knows," said Aldo Leopold. Go there, and lose yourself within the wilderness.

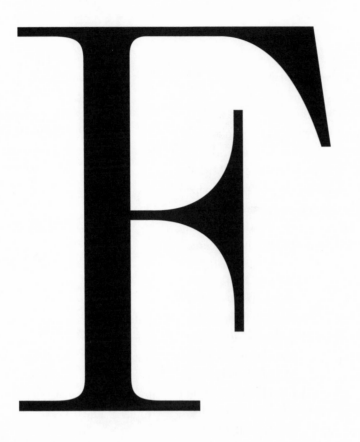

THE DENSE BLOCK OF FAT CARVED FROM A pig's back presents many tempting options to the frugal cook. It can be cut into cubes and rendered into lard. Cured, it becomes salt pork, which seasons pots of greens, field peas, summer squash, and corn. Some cooks simmer it with vegetables and water until the fat softens and gives its porky essence to the pot-likker. Others will fry it until crisp, leaving the liquid fat for the vegetables and snatching the golden-brown strips for snacking. Indeed, for many poorer Southerners, slices of cured fatback have long provided a less expensive alternative to bacon. Streak o' lean, in fact, is a cut of fatback that looks like the mirror image of pork belly bacon: a white strip shot through with a wispy ribbon of pink meat. Cooks sometimes fry up these rashers after a soak in milk to leach out the excess salt, often coating them in flour before slipping them into a pan of hot peanut oil. After all, if you're going to eat fried pig fat, might as well go whole hog.

(1897–1962)

ARGUABLY THE GREATEST TWENTIETH-CENTURY American writer, and hands down the least finished, William Faulkner wrote novels, short stories, poetry, essays, and—when he needed the money—Hollywood screenplays. Influenced by James Joyce, he frequently wrote in a stream-of-consciousness style, previously unknown in this country, that confounded and repelled many readers. He didn't care. Asked what he would advise readers who had slogged through one of his books two or three times and still didn't understand it, Faulkner replied, "Read it four times." In just fourteen years (1929–42), he produced ten novels and collections of short stories, including three novels frequently regarded as among the best ever written: *The Sound and the Fury*, *As I Lay Dying*, and *Absalom, Absalom!* By 1945, however, his novels were out of print. Much of his work is set in Yoknapatawpha County, a fictionalized version of Lafayette County, Mississippi, where he lived. Faulkner wrestled with questions of race, class, and the vagaries of Southern families. He wrote about the decay and tragedy of the South after the Civil War. But his dense prose was also compassionately alive to the humor, energy, and endurance of the human spirit. If you've never read him or have made frustrating attempts, try his 1942 collection of seven short stories, *Go Down, Moses*. It's more linear. Faulkner is worth the whistle.

FIELD PEAS

by Jessica B. Harris

IN 2015, A FIELD-PEA TASTING TOOK PLACE in South Carolina. The table and sideboard in the dining room of a grand Charleston double house in the heart of the Holy City displayed Old Paris tureens and Limoges serving dishes filled with more than twenty varieties of the Southern staple, prepared in myriad ways. The tasting celebrated the diversity and the taste range of the legumes, named for the way farmers traditionally planted them at the edges of rice and corn fields to replenish nitrogen in the soil. Some varieties are also known as cowpeas, because harvesters left the stems, vines, and remnants of the crops for livestock to forage.

The black-eyed pea is undoubtedly the best known of the lot, but in fact there are hundreds of varieties: crowder peas, named for the way that they "crowd" the pod; pinkeyes, so called for their distinctively colored "eye"; and the genteelly named lady pea, to mention a few. Field peas, it would seem, have moved Southerners to waves of poetic fantasy, inspiring fanciful names like Wash Day, Mississippi Silver, Polecat, Turkey Craw, and Big Red Ripper. In color they range from light buff to deep burgundy, with spots, speckles, and eyes of different hues.

Field peas are thought to have originated in Africa, and few foods are more connected to African Americans. In their New World context, the peas are linked to enslaved African Americans but have been eaten in various ways throughout the South for more than three hundred years by Southerners of all stripes. No one knows exactly when or how they arrived, but prior to the early 1700s, they were growing at the edges of rice fields in the Carolina colonies before becoming one of the area's first cash crops. Early American farmers, including George Washington, recognized their ability to improve the soil, and in 1797 he mentioned using them both as a crop and "for plowing in as manure." They were in widespread cultivation in Virginia by 1800 and were called Indian peas there. They were grown in the slave gardens in Monticello, where Thomas Jefferson also used them as a field crop and experimented with new varieties. In 1798 he extolled their virtues, describing them as "very productive, excellent food for man and beast, [that] awaits without loss our leisure for gathering and shades the ground for the hottest months of the year." They also appear in early cookbooks such as *The Virginia Housewife*, in which Mary Randolph suggests making a fried bean cake that is garnished with "thin bits of fried bacon."

More than one hundred years later, George Washington Carver, through his work at Tuskegee Institute, encouraged farmers to use black-eyed peas to fix nitrogen in the soil. In 1903's "Bulletin No. 5 Cow Peas," he reminded them that "as a food for man, the cow pea should be to the South what the White Soup, Navy, or Boston bean is to the North, East, and West; and it may be prepared in a sufficient number of ways to suit the most fastidious palate." He also published a second bulletin listing more than forty recipes including croquettes, griddle cakes, baked peas, and a cow-pea custard pie that seems to be a cousin to the Muslim bean pie. Carver didn't have to tell anyone that field peas, especially black-eyed peas, come into their own on New Year's Day. Whether solo, with greens (turnip, mustard, collard, kale, or even cabbage), or with rice as in South Carolina's hoppin' John, eating black-eyed peas or some form of field pea at the start of the year brings luck and prosperity. It is a tradition that few would dare to contravene.

FIREFLIES

A backyard flickering with fireflies—better known in certain circles as lightning bugs—is as quintessentially Southern as lemonade on the porch. The winged beetles bring romance to the dusk, and not just figuratively: using the bioluminescence of their glimmering lower abdomens, they wink messages to potential mates.

Fireflies have long thrived in our temperate climate, at least until the kids get ahold of them; well before the advent of Day-Glo, preteens smeared them onto their T-shirts and ran around in the gloam glowing in the dark. The classic (kinder) method is to capture them in mason jars to create a makeshift lantern, or to just gaze out at them from the porch. The seriously committed hit the road, traveling to Great Smoky Mountains National Park near Elkmont, Tennessee (after booking parking spaces online months in advance), where thousands of *Photinus carolinus*—the only species in the Western Hemisphere that can synchronize its flashing patterns—put on a blockbuster mating-season light show for about two magical weeks, typically kicking off in late May.

Nowadays, firefly numbers are dwindling, perhaps because of development and light pollution. So if you want to attract them to your own little piece of paradise, cut the motion sensors and let nature's fairy lights take over.

FITZGERALD, ZELDA

(1900–1948)

IT'S HARD TO FAULT PEOPLE FOR TURNING Zelda Sayre Fitzgerald into a symbol: her life was madcap and messy, making her the ideal warm-blooded representation of intangibles such as Jazz Age decadence and the destructive power of art. But before she was a cultural icon, she was a little girl in Montgomery, Alabama, admired for her pluck and good looks. Although her father, a state Supreme Court justice, was dour and straitlaced, Sayres and her pal Tallulah Bankhead liked to smoke, dance, and prance about in flesh-colored bathing suits. In 1918, she met F. Scott Fitzgerald, who was stationed at a nearby army camp. Two years later, he published his first book; the success of *This Side of Paradise* persuaded nineteen-year-old Zelda to accept his marriage proposal. The couple chased glamour from New York City to Paris but spent much of their time together drunk and unhappy. F. Scott Fitzgerald was baffled by his wife's growing obsession with ballet, which wore out her body and mind; she was first institutionalized in 1930. Despite being diagnosed with schizophrenia, she arranged in 1932 for the publication of her fictionalized memoir, *Save Me the Waltz*. It flopped. Discouraged and mentally deteriorating, Zelda retreated further into her fantasies. She died in a fire in 1948 at Asheville's Highland Hospital, where she was locked in a room, awaiting electroshock therapy.

FLASK

A FLASK IS AN ESSENTIAL ACCESSORY IN A VAriety of Southern social circumstances. While flasks come in many styles and materials— hammered pewter, polished silver, leather encased—all share similarly occult properties in that they can make a long and tedious occasion seem briefer, and a blissful occasion more prolonged and enjoyable. Examples of events that call for a flask include college football games (especially those in stadiums that prohibit alcohol or sell only overpriced beer); weddings of somewhat distant relatives where the quality of liquor is suspect; hunting trips with former college friends; and social gatherings involving your children's current college friends.

A flask should fit a rear pants pocket or inside jacket pocket comfortably and invisibly. In appearance, it should reflect one's personality— rugged, discreet, rakish, or what have you. For men, who now must grope their way through an era in which cuff links, tie clasps, decorative hatbands, and cigarette cases have become vanishingly rare, few accessories allow one to convey a sense of both style and status, and do so understatedly. A flask serves admirably; it should be chosen with care.

The contents of a flask are entirely a matter of personal preference, as long as one prefers a quality sipping bourbon.

YOU KNOW IT WHEN YOU SEE IT—USUALLY AT an old-time bluegrass festival. The fiddle and banjo really get cooking, and a few folks down front are compelled to abandon their seats for some open space. With their backbones straight and their arms hanging loose at their sides, their feet start slapping the floor in jerky sweeps. Knees jut up and out, but never too long before heels fly back down with force enough to add syncopation to the music. The enthralling effect suggests a marionette with strings attached only below the waist. Whether it's called flatfooting, clogging, or buck dancing, it has been a dance form passed down by Appalachian settlers since . . . well, since there have been settlers in the Appalachians. It has roots in English, Irish, and Scottish folk dances but, this being America, also freely absorbed moves from minstrel shows and Native American ceremonial dances. Today trained groups flatfoot with fine-tuned choreography on big stages like the Mountain Dance and Folk Festival in Asheville, North Carolina. But for many the real joy is in watching freestyle flatfooters channel traditional music to their toes and heels. Go ahead, join them. Just know that, as with most things having to do with mountain life, it's harder than it looks.

THE FLEUR-DE-LIS DATES TO 1967, THE YEAR the New Orleans Saints football franchise was established. It has long been emblazoned on helmets, jerseys, banners, and bumper stickers, which are frequently flaunted to show one's allegiance to "Saints Nation." More recently, the fleur-de-lis has also become available as an emoji (Unicode U+269C).

Oh, all right, just kidding: the fleur-de-lis actually goes back a bit further than that. Lore has it that the symbol may date to an earlier epoch in Europe—perhaps as early as AD 400 and involving someone with the improbable name of Clovis. Or maybe AD 800, when Charlemagne was crowned emperor and took the symbol as his own. It is said to represent a stylized lily with three petals, and to symbolize purity. In the medieval era, the fleur-de-lis was reportedly adopted by the Bourbon dynasty and then came to be seen as the symbol of France, and by extension its colonial holdings, including eventually the city of New Orleans. Frankly, this all seems suspect, given that American football would not be invented for another half millennium.

FLORA-BAMA

WHEN THE FLORA-BAMA WENT UP IN 1964, the lounge's position on the Florida-Alabama state line was a pragmatic solution to laws that prohibited liquor sales in the latter state's Baldwin County. Now, though, the proudly tattered collection of drinking decks and live-music stages needs at least two states to contain the full slate of high-spirited fun on its calendar, which begins with a Gulf of Mexico dip on New Year's Day and winds down with Santa Claus parachuting onto the Flora-Bama's stretch of beach. (The bar's renowned Interstate Mullet Toss comes around in the spring.) As Kenny Chesney describes the Hurricane Ivan survivor in his song "Flora-Bama," "There's ball caps, photographs, dollar bills and bras; license plates from every state nailed up to the wall." Yet to fully appreciate the boozy charms of this good-time institution, which hosts honky-tonk church services on Sunday mornings, a few more accessories are required: namely, a pound of peel-and-eat Royal Red shrimp; a chocolate milk shake-esque Bushwacker, stiffened with five different kinds of liquor; flip-flops; and a Sharpie. You'll want to scribble your name on a blank bit of wall, table, or rafter, since if you Flora-Bama correctly, you otherwise may not remember you were ever there.

FLORIDA HIGHWAYMEN

IMAGINE YOU'RE ON VACATION. IT'S FLORIDA in the 1960s and you're driving along Route 1. Suddenly you spot a young man parked on the side of the highway, his car trunk overflowing with lush oil paintings of idealized Florida landscapes. You pull over. The paintings—no more than twenty or thirty dollars apiece—pop from the canvases with life, depicting palm and poinciana trees in dream inlets under bird-filled skies of tropical pinks, oranges, and blues. They have an undeniable power. You buy one. And thus did it occur that thousands of paintings by the Florida Highwaymen—a group of twenty-six talented and entrepreneurial young African American artists who made their living this way in the Jim Crow South—ended up in homes across the country. Now their works hang in the White House, in museums, and on the walls of such luminaries as Steven Spielberg. Working in oil on industrial surfaces like Upson board, the Highwaymen produced paintings at such a rapid pace that Alfred Hair, the originator of the movement, was said to have started lifting weights just so he could keep painting long enough to keep up with the feverish demand.

FLOUR

SOUTHERNERS SPECIALIZE IN PIES AND BIS-cuits for a reason. Our hot, sticky climate isn't amenable to the high-protein wheats that grow out on the prairie and make hardy loaves. What thrives here is the more genteel soft winter wheat, which makes a low-protein flour that delivers light, flaky results—cake flour, in other words, rather than bread flour. Southern bakers are thus rightfully loyal to such home-grown brands as White Lily, Martha White, and Southern Biscuit, and more regional flours like Kentucky's Weisenberger and South Carolina's Adluh. *See White Lily flour.*

(1916–2005)

Decades ago, folklorists traveled up into the Blue Ridge Mountains and down into the Mississippi lowlands in search of sounds they feared would be forever lost. More recently, scholars have started fretting about flavors—which are in many ways more challenging to document and disseminate than shape note hymns and work songs. The concern that contemporary palates might never get acquainted with the tang of sassafras tea, the sweetness of a rhubarb cobbler, or the rich grease of a freshly fried quail motivated students at Rabun Gap-Nacoochee School in Georgia to ask people living in North Georgia to recount their traditional practices, from dressing hogs to pickling cabbage. Those interviews formed the basis of *Foxfire* magazine, first published in 1966 and eagerly absorbed by back-to-the-landers. Eventually, a reverence for old recipes sparked an interest in heirloom ingredients, which were vanishing in the age of industrial agriculture. Prodded by chefs such as Charleston, South Carolina's Sean Brock; food preserver April McGreger of Farmer's Daughter in Carrboro, North Carolina; and grain evangelist Glenn Roberts of Anson Mills in Columbia, South Carolina, along with University of South Carolina professor David Shields, farmers in the 2000s started again cultivating formerly abandoned varieties such as Carolina Gold rice, Sapelo Island red peas, Bradford watermelons, purple ribbon sugarcane, and Seashore rye. *See Foxfire.*

There are history books, and then there's *The Civil War: A Narrative*, a sprawling record of the war by Shelby Foote, who drew on his own roots in the Mississippi Delta to pen his three-thousand-page masterwork. A novelist and fiction writer, Foote had been tapped by Random House to produce a short history of the Civil War, an assignment that expanded into a three-volume opus that commanded twenty years of his work life. Famously, Foote wrote everything in longhand with a dip pen, only going back later to type it all up. But while the trilogy won him acclaim, his fame came more from Ken Burns's documentary *The Civil War*, a PBS smash that brought Foote's Southern drawl, pipe, and personality into the living rooms of countless history buffs. Foote's volumes have come to be considered definitive, and though critics claimed the series was light on the political and economic causes of the war, and cringed at his lack of footnotes, few could argue with the force of his narrative and the vividness with which he brought history to life on the page. *See The Civil War.*

Long before the do-it-yourself movement got self-styled urban homesteaders fermenting their own mead and pouring organic soy wax candles, residents of a tiny mountain community on the Georgia–North Carolina border distilled moonshine, warmed their hands over bubbling pots of hominy, and hand strung box banjos to entertain themselves on bitter cold nights. Trendsetting was the furthest thing from their minds, but the collected wisdom of the Foxfire folks remains influential decades later. Beginning in 1966, high-school students in Rabun County, Georgia, ventured out of the classroom to interview the elders of their mountain communities. The oral history project wound up becoming a social documentary on an epic scale, catalogued in more than a dozen best-selling *Foxfire* books now considered an invaluable archive of Southern Appalachian life and culture. More than fifty years later, Foxfire is a nonprofit with a museum and heritage center in Mountain City, Georgia, devoted to preserving Appalachian foodways and customs. "There are still people, both old-timers and new-timers," the editor Kaye Carver Collins writes in the series' most recent volume, "who believe in close-knit families, in kindness to their neighbors, and who take tremendous satisfaction in how they construct meaning from their corner of the world." With help from Foxfire, that flame still burns brightly, and the torch keeps getting passed. *See Food revivalists.*

(1942–)

The Queen of Soul, with hits including "Respect," "Chain of Fools," and "Think" woven into the fabric of American culture, Aretha Franklin has a fearlessness and sheer power that make even the strongest of her fellow singers seem tepid. Born in Memphis, she moved to Detroit at the age of four, honing her vocal and piano skills by traveling the country as part of her preacher father's touring gospel revival show, befriending legends like Mahalia Jackson and Sam Cooke. Her list of hits continued in the 1960s and '70s (the latter decade includes "Don't Play That Song" and "Spanish Harlem"), before she hit a career lull in the late 1970s. But you can't keep the Queen down for long: a part in the classic comedy *The Blues Brothers* gave her a career reboot, and she followed it up with two of her biggest hits, "Freeway of Love" and the international smash "I Knew You Were Waiting for Me" with the late George Michael. In early 2017, she announced her retirement after the release of a new album featuring Stevie Wonder.

Freedman's cottage is the somewhat mis-leading term for a type of small, vernacular dwelling found in the Lowcountry, and especially associated with Charleston, South Carolina. More than a thousand were built throughout the Charleston peninsula from the 1860s to the 1930s, though many have been lost in the decades since. Like the Charleston single house, the cottage is only one room wide with a side piazza. It's topped with a gable roof, but unlike the single house has no upper floors. The cottage's narrow side typically faces the street, with a false front door opening onto the piazza.

Contrary to long-held belief, the cottages were not the exclusive domain of emancipated African Americans. More accurately called Charleston cottages, the small domiciles were popular among people of many ethnic backgrounds, including Irish and German immigrants. Built in rows and blocks of rows, they were often rented out to mill or phosphate-industry workers. They were cozy, typically 300 to 500 square feet and rarely more than 1,200 square feet. Though long underappreciated—and unprotected, because of their location outside official historic districts—Charleston cottages have become prized among historic preservationists and tiny-house lovers.

The French 75 is a spirit-and-champagne cocktail named after the 75-millimeter M1897, a fearsome field gun the French deployed during World War I. The name of the drink, it's said, reflects its potent kick. Most recipes call for London Dry gin, lemon juice, and sugar, making the drink essentially a Tom Collins topped with champagne rather than seltzer. Lore suggests it was first served in Paris, at Harry's New York Bar.

This is not, however, the universally preferred recipe. Chris Hannah, the head barman at the authoritatively named Arnaud's French 75 bar in New Orleans, insists, with some logic, that anyone who makes a French 75 with gin is being willfully ignorant or unnecessarily adversarial. The French would not use the iconic British spirit, Hannah sensibly points out; they would choose to use their own spirit, which is to say cognac (or some other fine French brandy).

In truth, a French 75 may be made with either liquor, and both have merit. It's best to try both and determine your own preference. Unless you're ordering one at Arnaud's French 75, in which case you order the gin variant at your own peril.

FRENCH QUARTER

by *Guy Martin*

THE FEDERAL GOVERNMENT STILL RECOG-nizes New Orleans as a municipality subject to the laws of the United States, and the city still posts representation to Washington. But its driving loyalties lie in fortifying its global renown for laissez-faire French-colonial excess—in the astronomical calorie count of its cuisine; in its innate fondness for any sort of business on the down low; in the hubba-hubba encouragement of casual sex and mistress-keeping in all social strata; in the routine elevation to public office of minor despots who are then just as routinely jailed; and, not least, in alcohol consumption. Three hundred years after its founding by Jean-Baptiste Le Moyne, the Sieur de Bienville, New Orleans' ties to the social and legal fabric of the United States are gossamer at best. The French idea is bedrock.

The wellspring of that otherness is the postage-stamp-sized, ninety-two-square-block Vieux Carré. Literally the "Old Square" to the colony's founding eighteenth-century Creole families, the Vieux Carré *was* the city. The square, as such, is the grid laid out at Bienville's behest by Adrien de Pauger in 1721 on that slightly higher landing (elevation: one foot) tangential to the river. Aboriginally, it had been a portage point for the Houma tribe on their commute down Bayou St. John between the river and what became Lake Pontchartrain.

The French had staggering good luck in their choice of this portage. The Vieux Carré quickly became its own vastly rich, independent city-state, sitting astride a continent-spanning aquatic superhighway through the most fecund agricultural river delta known. Fortunes lay for the taking—on the backs of the thousands of slaves brought in by the French corsairs, of course. The town was second only to New York as an eighteenth-century market power on the continent. Indigo, rice, King Cotton, a robust slave market, warehouses along the levee, government houses around the Place d'Armes (now Jackson Square), and the glittering parties at the Philippe de Marigny mansion—these were the lodestones. The gilded age lasted just four generations, about eighty years, but long enough to cement an unassailable boomtown confidence in the city's crazy-quilt DNA.

It stupefied the American envoys who arrived in France to buy it in 1803 that Napoleon would actually include New Orleans, and the rest of the huge territory, in his fire sale, but he had expensive wars still to lose. There was, instantly, a business war between the old Creoles and the Anglo-Saxon usurpers. The more-than-slightly derogatory sobriquet "French Quarter" came into play after the American influx, just as the old Creole families derided "the American city" springing up below Canal Street.

The section has had many masters. Not one of them ever quite managed to bend the Quarter to whatever he had in mind—neither the French, nor the Spanish, nor the super-crusty wheeler-dealer Andrew Jackson, nor the infamous 1930s governor-demagogue Huey Long, nor the dapper and deadly Mafia don Carlos "the Little Man" Marcello, who remains on the short list as a mastermind of the

JFK assassination. Eros and Thanatos danced their own jig in this original corner of New Orleans, under the thumb of no man.

The Quarter lost its long, slow battle against the American takeover, but became along the way a neighborhood of pirates—literally and metaphorically. Any attempt to mess with or, worse, legislate any business or social curlicue in the Quarter usually backfired. A backward American "foreign" trade embargo in 1807 led the privateer brothers Pierre and Jean Laffitte (later Americanized to Lafitte) to establish their "free city" of Barataria downriver, fencing contraband goods and luxuries back in the Quarter. Trying to banish prostitution from the Quarter in 1897, a Sisyphean project from the get-go, city fathers gerrymandered it two blocks west, along Basin Street to Storyville (later Tremé)—the birthplace of Louis Armstrong to a prostitute mother in 1901. But the concentration of brothels—Mahogany Hall was the most opulent—brought enormous custom, which brought bars, which brought musicians. And so the aldermen accidentally manufactured precisely the rich cultural loam in which the fathers of American popular music—Kid Ory, King Oliver, Lawrence Duhé, Sidney Bechet, and the young Armstrong—could grow their great gift of jazz. When Storyville was shuttered in 1915, the prostitutes moved back to the Quarter with no fanfare.

People washed up like flotsam, for many reasons, but mainly because the place was both insular and forgiving. During Prohibition—which in New Orleans was regarded more as a bizarre joke staged by clinically insane people in a faraway country than as legislation pertaining to real life—one young part-time worker on a Lake Pontchartrain bootlegger's boat was William Faulkner. By 1925 he was penning *Soldier's Pay*, his first novel, in the little house at 624 Pirate's Alley, just off Jackson Square. Later in the century, Tennessee Williams took up the mantle of *the* New Orleans writer, spending years in the Quarter—cane, great panama hat, and all.

Since the invention of jazz a century ago, the Quarter has served America as an ad hoc sensory-rehabilitation clinic for hordes of pilgrims—about ten million per annum—from the sadder monochromatic corners of the country, who visit inchoately yearning for something different to see, hear, eat, and drink.

There, they get it.

FRIED CHICKEN

Fried chicken was once a luxury. Crisped in a bath of bubbling fat by those sought-after cooks who could deliver a golden crust and tender meat from a heavy cast-iron skillet, it came to the table only on the occasion that a family managed to finagle a tender spring chicken. The tough old chicken-and-dumplings birds laying eggs in the coop out back wouldn't do. In 1952, everything changed. That was the year the first KFC franchise opened in Salt Lake City. More important, though, it was the year when a growing population of mass-produced young birds finally overtook those older laying hens as the country's most popular poultry.

Chicken prices plummeted. Deep fryers proliferated. Southerners didn't lose their respect for proper skillet-fried bird, though. Today fried chicken is a dish for all occasions. Under a gas-station heat lamp, it's late-night salvation. On a fast-food biscuit, it's a hangover-busting breakfast. From the grocery-store deli counter, it's a make-do lunch. And in white-tablecloth restaurants, it comes artfully fried in heritage fats and garnished with sprinklings of delicate herbs. Like a devilish debutante with a trunk full of camo and cheap beer, fried chicken today straddles the high and the low with grace—and grease.

FRIED GREEN TOMATOES

The pickup trucks in *Fried Green Tomatoes*, the 1992 movie based on a Fannie Flagg novel, were definitely Southern. And to Northern audiences, the shotguns and Klan references seemed pretty Southern, too. So it stood to reason that fried green tomatoes must be an iconic Southern dish. Prior to 1992, though, when anyone ate green tomatoes at all, it was early-frost-afflicted Midwesterners, who may have been influenced by Jewish immigrants who came from old-world places where people commonly pickled them. Southerners generally preferred to let their 'maters ripen so they could slice up the bright red fruit for sandwiches. But once the movie achieved blockbuster status, savvy Southern chefs decided to profit from the myth. Within the year, the dish was so widespread that Flagg heard its

popularity had disrupted the region's tomato market, much like what *Sideways* would later do to pinot noir. Condemned to careers of frying green tomatoes, chefs in cities hailed for their Southernness, such as Charleston, South Carolina, and Atlanta, now do their best to reinvigorate the dish with sophisticated sauces and fresh seafood. Usually, though, the tomatoes end up plated with pimento cheese.

FRITO PIE

No, it's not really a pie—more like a junk-food lunch in a bag. The recipe is uncomplicated: tear open a one-ounce package of Fritos, ladle some chili right into the bag, top it with grated cheddar and chopped onions, and go to town with a plastic spork. That's Frito Pie, the high-school football concession-stand classic that Southerners love and Northerners misunderstand. On his TV series, Anthony Bourdain once compared a freshly made Frito Pie to a warm colostomy bag. Maybe he would have taken to one of the many upscale restaurant versions—such as a fine-china soup bowl full of corn chips covered with venison chili and topped with goat cheese and chopped Vidalia onions. Also known by Tex-Mex aficionados as a "walking taco," the Frito Pie has given rise to less highfalutin spin-offs as well, including the Cheeto Pie, made by layering chili into a bag of . . . you guessed it.

FROGGING—OR FROGGIN', IF YOU HAVE A Cajun outdoors TV show or want to sound as if you might—is the hunting of wild bullfrogs. The practice is particularly popular in the Deep South where French influence is more prominent. Froggers go out at night in jon boats or other shallow-draft craft. Serious froggers wear hard hats to which they attach powerful sealed-beam headlamps that connect directly to a motorboat's 12-volt battery. (They prefer aircraft landing bulbs—such as the GE 4405 or H 4405—over automobile lights, which cast a more diffuse beam.) Frogs freeze when illuminated. It is not known whether the light blinds or otherwise paralyzes them or whether they are simply overconfident about their natural camouflage. Froggers gig their prey with pronged forks on poles or grab them by hand—the latter having the advantages of keeping the frog alive and saving money on ice. Frog eyes reflect whitish yellow in the light's beam, while the eyes of alligators—which are also out hunting frogs at night—show up red. You don't want to grab anything with red eyes. A good-sized frog can match the size of a rotisserie chicken and weigh two pounds, though most are in the one-pound range. They don't taste like chicken. They taste like frog and are delicious.

YOU WON'T FIND ANY FROGS IN FROGMORE stew, a Lowcountry classic with origins in the Gullah Geechee community of Frogmore on South Carolina's St. Helena Island. Nor is it a stew by most definitions. You don't slurp the one-pot boil out of a bowl. Traditionally, you scoop it by hand off a newspaper-covered table onto which a cook has heaped the imposing piles of shrimp, corn on the cob, sausage, and often potatoes and onions. It's a coastal celebration of summertime that feeds a crowd without much trouble. Be sure to add plenty of seasoning to the boiling water, and don't dare sully this bare-bones feast with seafood that's anything less than superfresh.

(1933–)

AS A CHILD IN RURAL POINTE COUPEE Parish, Louisiana, Ernest Gaines picked cotton and fished the bayous on the same plantation where five generations of his family had been born and raised before. There was no high school for black children in that parish, though, and so at fifteen Gaines moved to California. There he spent hours absorbing books in the Vallejo public library, and because he lived across the bay from the infamous San Quentin State Prison, he developed a fascination with the idea of death row. Gaines found success writing and publishing fiction over the years, but it was that lingering interest in capital punishment that eventually helped form the novel for which he is best known: *A Lesson Before Dying* (1993). The story of a young black man railroaded into a murder conviction in rural Louisiana and sentenced to death for it won the National Book Critics Circle Award for fiction and brought Gaines wide acclaim. Now living on the same plantation where he was born, Gaines has said the most important moves in his life were "the day I went to California and the day I came back."

WHILE YOUNGSTERS ELSEWHERE MARVEL AT pictures of dinosaurs in books, children in the Deep South dodge them on the way to school. *Alligator mississippiensis* has made itself comfortable in the wetlands of what became the Southeast United States since the Jurassic period, surviving three mass extinctions and at least eight seasons of *Swamp People*. That other top threat, *Homo sapiens*, converted nearly the entire species into luggage in the 1950s, but protections have allowed populations to rebound—gators now flourish in Florida, South Carolina, North Carolina, Georgia, Alabama, Mississippi, Louisiana, Texas, Arkansas, and even Oklahoma. Stealthy predators of everything from minnows to deer, they can grow to a whopping thirteen feet long and eight hundred pounds, and they don't always confine themselves to remote swamps. As human habitat continues to encroach on their domain, close encounters of the reptile kind become more and more common. Granted, it may be inconvenient (and hair-raising) to stumble across a gator on a putting green or in a backyard swimming pool, but just remember—they were here *waaaay* before us.

GEE'S BEND QUILTS

ORIGINALLY PIECED TOGETHER FROM THE scraps of old work clothes, overalls, dresses, feed sacks, and other fabric remnants marked by stains reflecting hardscrabble life in the rural South, these one-of-a-kind textiles are abstract works of modern art. Gee's Bend quilts stand apart for their simple yet vibrant patterns, reminiscent of Amish quilts but with an improvisational flair. That the rural African American community tucked into a bend in the Alabama River has produced five (and in some families six) generations of enviably talented quilt artists is due in large part to their isolation, which helped foster a unique artistic voice—each maker's design reflecting both her singular experience and that of her community as a whole. Even the notoriously snooty New York City art crowd was wowed by the designs when the Whitney Museum of American Art introduced a collection of the hand-stitched throws in November 2002. Today a Gee's Bend quilt can fetch between $1,000 and $20,000.

GINGHAM

WHY HAS GINGHAM BEEN A STAPLE OF Southern life since early colonists brought this English and French cloth to the region? For one, the cotton fabric is thin and breathable (ideal for humid summers and hot kitchens). It is also eminently versatile: the signature cross-check pattern goes with everything, has

no right or wrong side, appearing the same whether worn outside-in or inside-out, and transcends occasion, making it appropriate for tablecloths and aprons, dress shirts and summer dresses, Texas bandannas and Patsy Cline's stage costume.

GIZZARDS

by Roy Blount, Jr.

THAT THING GRABBED MY CHICKEN BY THE tenders and held him underwater till he like to drowned." I'll bet you have never heard anybody say anything like that. Partly because nobody would ever volunteer that his fighting rooster was nearly killed by a duck. But mainly because "chicken tenders" are not parts of a chicken. And yet pretty nearly everywhere fried chicken is sold, one way it comes is in these boneless, gristle-less, anatomy-unrelated "tenders." Like so many other things today, tenders are about 10 percent chicken and 90 percent marketing.

I was reflecting on this fact in a Popeyes in Greenville, Mississippi, recently, when my eyes strayed over to the buffet. Not every fried-chicken outlet has a buffet, but this did, perhaps because it was Southern, and on that buffet was a big pan of things that are very much actual working parts of the actual birds known as chickens: chicken gizzards.

And I bought me some. And I chewed. And chewed.

The gizzard is what a chicken has instead

of teeth. When you are chewing a gizzard, you are having the rare experience of chewing what chews. Where else in the food chain are you going to get an experience like that? If eating pigs' feet puts a spring in your step, you might in effect be trotting on the trotters; but that's a big if.

Here's how chicken digestion operates. When a chicken pecks up a bug, say, it swallows it down to the crop, also known as the craw, as in "This whole concept of chicken tenders just sticks—figuratively speaking—in my craw." The crop holds the bug and marinates it in digestive juices until the gizzard croaks (or maybe not croaks, but some kind of gravelly tone), "Okay, gimme what you got." And the gizzard's wrenchy slaunchwise muscles and its "horny callosities" (to quote one technical description), and the bits of grit and gravel that the chicken swallows in order to assist the gizzard, go to work on that bug until it turns into . . .

What would you say it turns into? I would say it turns into proto-chicken. Let's set aside that old conundrum of which came first, chicken or egg. The chicken gizzard is where chicken begins.

Here, from *The Birder's Handbook: A Field Guide to the Natural History of North American Birds*, is a tribute to the gizzard: ". . . objects that required more than four hundred pounds of pressure per square inch to crush have been flattened within twenty-four hours when experimentally fed to a turkey."

Aside from Molly Bloom saying Yes and Yes and Yes so expansively at the end, what does any reader of *Ulysses*, by James Joyce, remember? "Mr. Leopold Bloom ate with relish the inner organs of beasts and fowls. He liked thick giblet soup, nutty gizzards . . ." and so on. Joyce himself obviously relished that passage, because further along in the book he's still tasting it: "As said before he ate with relish the inner organs, nutty gizzards . . ." and so on. What a comedown it would be if *Ulysses* were written today, and Mr. Bloom ate without effort odd notional figments of fowl.

There's an Uncle Remus story, "Brother Rabbit and the Gizzard-Eater," which ends (spoiler alert) in Brer Rabbit cackling:

"You po' ol' Gator, ef you know'd A fum Izzard,

You'd know mighty well dat I'd keep my Gizzard."

But gizzards are not always cherished things, in literature. For a serious person to concern himself with conventional politics, wrote Henry David Thoreau in his essay "Life Without Principle," would be "as if a thinker submitted himself to be rasped by the great gizzard of creation. Politics is, as it were, the gizzard of society, full of grit and gravel, and the two political parties are its two opposite halves . . . which grind on each other."

I hear that, all right. And maybe a chicken would rather have some slicker method of digestion. Peel the outer layer off an uncleaned gizzard and you are likely to find all manner of inorganic detritus. Human heartburn must be a piece of cake compared with chicken gizzardburn.

But that's the chicken's problem. The toughness that the bird requires in this vital organ translates into this indubitable virtue for whoever undertakes to eat one: the longer you have to chew on something, the longer you get to taste it.

GONE WITH THE WIND

THIRTY MILLION OR SO COPIES LATER, Margaret Mitchell's sweeping 1936 historical novel, and its Oscar-winning film adaptation, leave a complicated legacy. Opening at the outbreak of the Civil War, the thick tome follows the Georgia belle Scarlett O'Hara from her Clayton County plantation through Reconstruction in a torched-by-Sherman Atlanta. The tale often gets dumbed down to that of an epic love quadrangle between Scarlett; her scoundrel husband, Rhett Butler; her first love, Ashley Wilkes; and Ashley's wife, Melanie. Or boiled down to its indelible lines, from "Fiddle-dee-dee" to "Tomorrow is another day" to "My dear, I don't give a damn" (a screenwriter added the "frankly" later). But the onetime Atlanta reporter saw the novel's theme as survival—not just of the "Lost Cause" Confederate mythology that permeated her upbringing and spurred the book. Mitchell actually seems to reject romanticizing of the Old South through her heroine, who largely forsakes antebellum social expectations and post–Civil War pouting in favor of making money and moving forward. That mindset becomes an apt metaphor for the "New South" itself, the ideals of which were perhaps best embodied by the city where Mitchell lived, worked, and wrote. But critics have noted Mitchell also treats slavery and the plight of African Americans as a one-dimensional backdrop to the action, using racist epithets and perpetuating stereotypes, like that of the loyal, master-loving slave.

Ironically, Hattie McDaniel became the first black actor to win an Academy Award for her portrayal of one of those devoted slaves, Mammy, in the director David O. Selznick's 1939 film—the Atlanta debut of which the city's segregation laws barred her from attending. Still, Vivien Leigh's Scarlett and Clark Gable's Rhett immortalized Mitchell's memorable duo for decades to come, inspiring official and unofficial sequels, spin-offs, parodies, painted porcelain, dolls, conventions, doodads, gewgaws, a famous Carol Burnett sketch, and legions of superfans called Windies. A 2014 Harris Poll reinforced the story's unfading popularity, ranking *GWTW* as the second-most-popular book in America—just behind the Bible.

GOOBERS

LIKE THE NAMES OF SEVERAL OTHER TASTY Southern staples—okra, gumbo, yam—this term for peanuts got its name from West Africa. Scholars generally trace the word back to *nguba*, which originally meant "kidney" (and then referred to the kidney-shaped legume) in the Bantu languages Kikongo and Kimbundu, and which slaves brought with them around the 1830s. (On a much more recent trip to Africa, the travel writer Paul Theroux learned a Kikongo proverb—*Ku kuni nguba va meso ma nkewa ko*—that recommends discretion: "Don't plant peanuts while the monkeys are watching.") During the Civil War, some people referred to North Carolinians as "goobers"; at times, natives of Georgia have been called "goober grabbers." *See Peanuts.*

GOOD OLD BOYS

by John T. Edge

Last night I saw Lester Maddox on a
  TV show
With some smartass New York Jew
And the Jew laughed at Lester Maddox
And the audience laughed at Lester
  Maddox too
Well he may be a fool but he's our fool
If they think they're better than him
  they're wrong.

THOSE WORDS OPEN THE SONG "REDNECKS"
on Randy Newman's 1974 album *Good Old
Boys*, one of the most insightful musical med-
itations on Southern identity the twentieth
century ever produced.

Born in Los Angeles, Newman, who went
on to win fame as a movie composer, knew
the South. He had spent his youth bouncing
around Alabama, Mississippi, and Louisiana,
visiting his mother Dixie's family in New
Orleans, while his father served as a doctor
in World War II. Newman, whose parents
were raised Jewish, conceived "Rednecks" after watching the talk-show host Dick Cavett
berate Maddox, the segregationist governor
of Georgia, during a televised conversation
in 1970. "The audience hooted and howled,
and Maddox was never given a chance to
speak," Newman said later, explaining his
motivation.

On *Good Old Boys*, Newman channeled
various Southern personas. Foremost among

them: a white Birmingham steelworker who
witnessed Maddox's televised embarrassment,
and Huey P. Long, the demagogue Louisiana
politician who favored silk pajamas and luxurious hotel suites but proclaimed himself a
man of the people. Through those characters,
he told a complicated story of a conflicted
South.

Warner Bros. Records described the album
as a "collection of Newmanesque glimpses into
the collective mind and past of a maligned,
neglected and vital portion of America: the
South." Released in September 1974, it reached
No. 36 on the *Billboard* charts. That October,
Newman, accompanied by guitarist Ry Cooder
and the Atlanta Symphony Orchestra, pre-
miered the work at Symphony Hall in the
South's capital city. Maddox, elected governor
in 1966 after infamously refusing to integrate
his restaurant, passed on an invitation.

At a time when dramatic changes buffeted
the region, Newman connected the fates of
poor whites and poor blacks, historically pit-
ted one against another by power brokers who
divided to conquer. In "Rednecks," Newman
also targeted the hypocrisy of Northerners
who convinced themselves that the South was
a hive of racism outside the virtuous North.
He mocked the idea of a Northern promised
land, likening the ghettos of the Hough in
Cleveland and Boston's Roxbury to cages.

Good Old Boys also critiqued the American
experiment. Newman recorded "Mr. President
(Have Pity on the Working Man)" on the
night in 1974 when Richard Nixon resigned
the presidency. A plea to embattled president Herbert Hoover, who failed Louisiana

voters after the Great Flood of 1927, the song sounded to listeners like a takedown of Nixon. Circa 1974, Newman was hip, the literate auteur of the rock-and-roll set. Glenn Frey, Don Henley, and Bernie Leadon of the Eagles, the American supergroup of the moment, accompanied Newman on "Rednecks."

While many albums sound dated a year after their release, *Good Old Boys* has remained relevant. In the wake of Hurricane Katrina and the man-made disasters that followed, the song "Louisiana, 1927" became a favored dirge for a deluged people. Simple in structure, the song drives its message with a repeated couplet, "Louisiana, Louisiana / They're trying to wash us away."

Newman argued, through songs buoyed by wry humor, that if you love a place, you have a responsibility to criticize it. *Johnny Cutler's Birthday*, the original title for the material that would become *Good Old Boys*, sounded like a modern opera for the years after the civil rights movement. When Newman released a remastered version of *Good Old Boys* in 2002, he included the demo tapes for that earlier version of the album. They showcase the breadth of his vision. They make clear, too, his aim to create a kind of Southern pageant.

"Sail Away," the title track on the album of the same name, broadcast a similar ethic. Released two years before *Good Old Boys*, the song offered a prelude of what was to come. Written from the perspective of a slave master recruiting laborers from the Rice Coast of West Africa to board a ship bound for Charleston Harbor, it's one of the harshest indictments of the South ever written:

Ain't no lions or tigers, ain't no mamba
    snake
Just the sweet watermelon and the
    buckwheat cake
Everybody is happy as a man can be
Climb aboard, little wog, sail away
    with me.

Like much of the Newman oeuvre, it's a pleasant little ditty, layered with lacerating observations.

GOO GOO CLUSTER

WHEN DOLLY PARTON SENDS HER HOLLYWOOD friends a gift, it's often a box of Goo Goo Clusters, Nashville's famous candy bar—created by the Standard Candy Company with layers of marshmallow nougat, caramel, and roasted peanuts draped in milk chocolate. In the era B.G.G.C. (before Goo Goo Clusters), candy bars had only one main ingredient, so the arrival of the hand-dipped disk-shaped treats in 1912 blew the minds of sweet-toothed Southerners, who picked them up at local pharmacies. They were such a hit that the company became the main sponsor of the Grand Ole Opry radio broadcast for forty years ("Get a Goo Goo . . . it's gooooood!"). During the Great Depression, the slogan became the quaint (though in hindsight preposterous) "A nourishing lunch for a nickel." Originally the Goo Goo was sold without a name, but as legend has it the candy's coinventor Howard

Campbell was riding on a streetcar and telling fellow passengers of his infant son's first words—"goo goo"—and had an epiphany of sorts. The recipe has remained nearly the same for more than a century, though the company now uses fancier peanuts and offers versions with pecans and peanut butter. There's even a Goo Goo Finder app to locate your nearest fix.

GRACELAND

GRACELAND IS THE 17,000-PLUS-SQUARE-foot home in Memphis where Elvis Presley lived for twenty years, until his death in 1977. It is now a museum, a historical landmark, and the second-most-visited private home in America (after the White House), with 650,000 visitors annually. Visitors have included George W. Bush, Jimmy Carter, and Japanese prime minister Junichiro Koizumi. Graceland has been deservedly ridiculed for looking more like a movie set than a home. Elvis's bedroom (pink bedspreads, red telephone, stuffed hound dog) is often compared to a teenage girl's boudoir. The TV room featured three television sets side by side, an idea inspired by Lyndon Johnson, who wanted to monitor all three major networks at once. Living in the era before remote control, Elvis once shot a TV rather than leave his chair. "Let's face it," said one longtime associate of Presley's, "if something wasn't overdone, it was abnormal to Elvis." True enough. But to visit Graceland is also to encounter a fundamental innocence suddenly given free rein, as if a twelve-year-old had suddenly come into great wealth. The breathtakingly garish Jungle Room—arguably the proto–man cave—is an example. In one account of its creation, Presley's father said he'd just seen a window in Donald's Furniture Store of Hawaiian-themed furnishings, the ugliest thing he'd seen in his life. Upon hearing the details, Presley said, "Good, sounds like me." The next day, his father returned to find that the entire display had been installed in Graceland, where the boy king sat laughing.

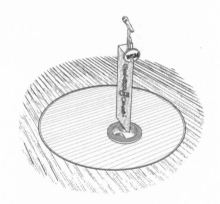

GRAND OLE OPRY

by Holly Williams

IN LESS THAN A DECADE, THE GRAND OLE Opry—the longest-running radio broadcast in U.S. history—will celebrate its one hundredth anniversary. This may seem like a long time to some. I've played the Opry many times, and when I think about what a cultural legend the show has become, a century sounds surprisingly young.

The program began on November 28, 1925, as an hour-long radio "barn dance" produced by an outspoken radio personality named George D. Hay; by the 1930s, it expanded to four hours, and the signal reached more than thirty states. Many people are still around to reminisce about gathering near the radio on Saturday nights, tuning in to WSM-AM. It seems like such a sweet and simple time: families connecting by sitting together and listening to country, bluegrass, folk, gospel, comedy—sounds that made them laugh, cry, dream, and feel certain they knew exactly how the singer felt in that moment. Sometimes when I'm on tour, I'm lucky enough to meet one of these old-timers. They tell me stories of Mama sewing and Daddy tapping his feet to the big sounds coming from their little radio. Today it seems mind-boggling to think that people had nothing else to do on Saturday night but sit and listen with the ones they loved the most. But to me, nothing sounds sweeter.

Of course, over the years millions have also attended the Opry in person, and if you never have, you should—you just might witness history in the making. After the show moved to a more permanent home in downtown Nashville, the famed Ryman Auditorium, aka the Mother Church, in 1943, that venue hosted some pretty incredible moments. Here's a sampling:

June 11, 1949: My grandfather Hank Williams made his Opry debut. (He had first auditioned nearly three years earlier, but was rejected.) The crowd went wild, and he ended up playing six encores, the first and to this day the only Opry performer to do so. Sadly, he was fired in July 1952 over his ongoing struggles with alcohol, and never reestablished his connection to the Opry. He died just six months later. Today he's regarded as one of the show's first worldwide stars: the "Hillbilly Shakespeare."

October 2, 1954: A nineteen-year-old boy from Mississippi appears for the first time on the Opry stage. Although the audience reacted politely to his rockabilly tunes, after the show Opry manager Jim Denny told the young man's producer, Sam Phillips, that the singer's style did not suit the program. Elvis Presley never performed at the Opry again.

January 20, 1973: Jerry Lee Lewis used his forty-minute Opry slot to wreak revenge on certain Nashville music-industry people who he felt had shunned him some eighteen years earlier. The producers laid down stern ground rules before Lewis's performance: no rock and roll, and no profanity. Onstage, Lewis proceeded to play plenty of rock and roll and to refer to himself as a "motherf**ker." He was not invited back.

I have released three albums and had the good fortune to tour around the globe, but there's nothing like coming home to that Grand Ole Opry stage. In 1976, the Opry House opened nine miles from downtown Nashville to accommodate larger crowds. A circular wooden piece of the original stage at the Ryman was transplanted to the front and center right of the Opry House stage, where the musicians stand and sing. Brad Paisley once said that the dust from my grandfather's boots could still be on that hardwood floor. Every time I stand there, I look a little harder.

GRAVY

Whether dressing a holiday feast or partnering with ham at breakfast, gravy usually starts with pan drippings. Sawmill gravy calls for a fat-and-flour roux, milk, and crumbled sausage. Cornmeal gravy substitutes a more affordable starch for flour, while tomato gravy has long drawn on the bounty of the garden or a well-stocked pantry. Appalachian cooks make redeye gravy from country ham drippings, coffee, and brown sugar. Then there's rich, syrupy chocolate gravy. You can hardly go wrong pouring any of them over a hot biscuit. *See Redeye gravy; Sawmill gravy.*

most of the rest of his career to gospel music. If you're in Memphis on a Sunday, a stop at his Full Gospel Tabernacle church in South Memphis is a must no matter what you believe.

GREEN, AL

(1946–)

With his silky, seductive vocals and production by Memphis's Hi Records boss Willie Mitchell, Al Green had a run of hits in the early 1970s that has fueled jukeboxes and wedding bands all over the world. "Let's Stay Together," "Here I Am (Come and Take Me)," and "I'm So Tired of Being Alone" propelled Green to superstardom, with his devastating falsetto and intimacy replacing the heft of predecessors Otis Redding and James Brown. In 1974, a jealous girlfriend, Mary Woodson, poured boiling grits on him while he was in the bath—she would shoot herself in the head shortly after—and Green took that as a sign from God that he needed to change his life, going on to devote

GREENS

Collard, mustard, turnip, cabbage. We all know those greens, but the Southern roster doesn't end there. Cabbage collards are the sweet, tender pride of Ayden, North Carolina. Appalachian cooks celebrate winter's end with foraged wild varieties such as creasy greens, poke sallet, and sochan. Sweet potato greens are finally catching on with a wider audience. Not all leafy vegetables get the same treatment. Some simmer for hours, yielding a dark, nutritious potlikker, while others only need a quick toss in the skillet. But if you're getting greens, you can usually count on a warm, soul-satisfying side. Because around here, the word *greens* rarely refers to salad.

GRITS

GROUND CORN OF THE DENT (OR FIELD) VARI-
ety, simmered in liquid until porridge-like, grits
have been a part of mealtime in the Americas
since before the first European explorers set
foot in Florida. More than rice, they are the
foundational starch of the Southern diet,
mixed with anything from butter to cheese to
shrimp and sausage, and they can ignite the
sort of controversy that also dogs the likes of
buttermilk biscuits and pimento cheese. Some
cooks simmer grits with milk or cream, others
settle for tap water, still others insist on spring
water. The only required seasoning is salt. And
although menus rarely distinguish between
white and yellow grits, many cooks do. Grits
milled from white corn traditionally serve as
a discreet backdrop for the likes of tomato-
sauced shrimp and the pounded and braised
hunks of meat known in New Orleans as *grillades*. Yellow grits are generally sweeter and
taste more like corn. One higher-end purveyor
has recently introduced blue corn grits, which
have a nutty flavor. So say the connoisseurs,
anyway; plenty of others insist they can't taste
the difference. But whether a professional chef
or a casual eater, no self-respecting Southern
cook will defile a cooking pot with instant
grits, which are to the genuine article what
Tang is to fresh-squeezed juice. To paraphrase
the great Leah Chase, a ninety-something chef
who still presides over the kitchen at Dooky
Chase's Restaurant in New Orleans: if you
can't take the time to make grits the right way,
fix a ham sandwich or fry an egg and get out of
the kitchen.

GROUPER

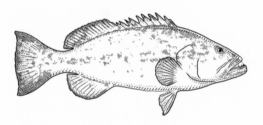

GOLIATH GROUPERS ARE THE GIGANTIC FISH
seen hanging next to fishermen half their size
in old snapshots and postcards from the Gulf
Coast. The world record, a 680-pounder, was
caught on May 20, 1961, off Fernandina Beach,
Florida. Nearly wiped out by overfishing, goliath groupers are now a protected species; but
recreational fishermen still catch many other
varieties, including red, black, yellowmouth,
and Warsaw groupers, especially in Florida.

Stricter limits on commercial grouper fishing have made the once cheap and plentiful
fish more expensive. Chefs prize grouper for
its mild and sweet flavor and heavy-flaked
dense meat. The grouper sandwich was once
an icon of Old Florida cuisine, but nowadays
the genuine article is harder to find. In August
2006, the *Tampa Times* reported that out of
eleven "grouper" sandwiches purchased at local Tampa Bay restaurants and turned over to
scientists, only five actually contained grouper. The six impostors contained tilapia, Asian
catfish, hake, and an unidentified species. The
researchers found that expensive restaurants
advertising "bronzed grouper" were also serving tilapia. Caveat emptor. And it's almost
certain that none of them contained "square

grouper," a nickname the U.S. Coast Guard coined to describe bales of marijuana floating in the Gulf of Mexico after being thrown from airplanes for retrieval by boat, or abandoned by smugglers trying to avoid arrest.

GRUENE HALL

H. D. Gruene built Gruene (pronounced: *green*) Hall in 1878 as a small spot for local farmers, cowboys, and families to gather and dance the weekend away to German-style polka music. Today, Texas's oldest operating dance hall is a country-music holy site, annually drawing thousands of the honky-tonkin' faithful to a tiny town (not even a stoplight) wedged between San Antonio and Austin. Gruene has hosted the likes of Willie Nelson, Kris Kristofferson, Jerry Lee Lewis, Merle Haggard, and many more—and hasn't much changed since its construction. The high-pitched tin roof still rattles when it rains (seldom), a cold-beer-stocked bar sits up front (with plenty of Lone Star), and holes in the original oak floors are patched up with old license plates. And no, there's no AC. But within the 6,000-square-foot, 800-person-capacity hall lives an energy that continues to attract, and attract again, country music's most fabled artists, and newcomers to boot.

GULF COAST

For a good chunk of those below the Mason-Dixon Line, going to the beach means going to the Gulf Coast, accessible to many Southerners by a drive of three hours or less. Five states—Florida, Alabama, Mississippi, Louisiana, and Texas—share its 1,680 miles of U.S. coastline. To many, however, the Gulf Coast refers to the Redneck Riviera (or Emerald Coast, depending on your net worth). As Tom T. Hall put it in his song of the same name, "Gulf Shores up through Apalachicola they got beaches of the whitest sand / Nobody cares if gramma's got a tattoo or Bubba's got a hot wing in his hand." This 100-mile stretch of the Florida Panhandle is a democratic place. You can hole up in a multimillion-dollar gated community or plunk a folding chair right down in the water at a public beach where they're not sticklers about alcohol or, in some cases, clothing. Either way, you're wiggling your toes in the finest, purest, most powdery white sand in the country, according to "Dr. Beach" (aka Dr. Stephen Leatherman, director of the Laboratory for Coastal Research at Florida International University). It's because wave action has ground to dust the softer minerals, leaving only the hardest—quartz crystals. And those it has pounded to "terminal size," meaning as small and uniform as possible. Which is why it's so damn hard to wash them out of certain parts of your body, be you male or female.

THE TERMS REFER TO THE DESCENDANTS OF enslaved West Africans along the Lowcountry coast—Gullah in South Carolina, Geechee in Georgia—and may have been derived from Gola and Kissi, West African tribes. They still retain their own language, culinary traditions, music, art, and beliefs—a unique treasury of culture that has survived centuries.

Justice Clarence Thomas is Geechee. Tim Scott, the only black man in the U.S. Senate, is Gullah. So is Michelle Obama, with grandparents hailing from the South Carolina rice fields. Ditto Darius Rucker and Smokin' Joe Frazier, who grew up in Beaufort County.

Assimilation worked its dubious ways, and by 1970, Gullah/Geechee culture seemed destined for the scrap heap of American history. But growing awareness has helped protect it. There are university classes now, and even a Gullah New Testament. Most notably, there's Beaufort, South Carolina's Gullah Festival each Memorial Day, "Decoration Day" to the Gullah. A brass band leads a parade to the riverbank, where people toss extravagant garlands upon the waters, honoring the Union Navy that set their forebears free in 1861.

PEOPLE WHO ORDER GUMBO IN RESTAURANTS distinguish different versions by the kind of protein used. They may prefer the gentle spice of, say, chicken and andouille gumbo to the oceanic funk of crab and oyster gumbo. People who actually prepare gumbo, however, classify it by the thickener used. Different gumbos get their spoon-coating texture from filé (ground sassafras leaves), roux, okra, or some combination of the three. Rules exist—use okra with oysters, roux with wild turkey—but these rules aren't broken so much as beset by endless fractal variation. The Creole gumbo of New Orleans tastes stylistically different from the Cajun gumbo of the country. Coastal gumbos almost always pool around a mound of rice, but the Cajun cooks of inland Avoyelles Parish will more likely serve their gumbo with a roasted sweet potato. Just remember: if you are in New Orleans and someone is having a gumbo, by all means go. Having a gumbo in the Crescent City is like having a barbecue elsewhere; it's a feast with roux-dark soup as the centerpiece.

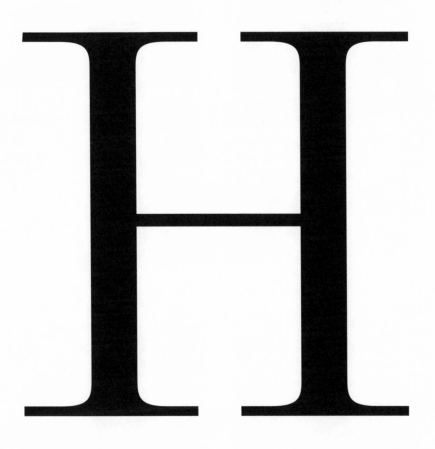

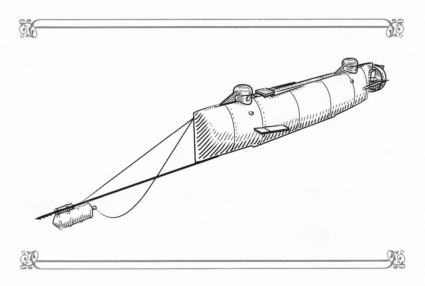

HAINT BLUE

IF YOU THINK YOU'RE PREVENTING WASPS from nesting on your porch by painting the ceiling blue to mimic the sky—a common Southern practice, especially in Georgia and the Carolinas—you might want to stock up on calamine lotion. Perhaps prior to the Civil War when milk paints, often containing lye (a known insect repellent), were used, that theory might have held a small kernel of truth. But even that's a stretch. The tradition actually originated with the Gullah Geechee people of the South Carolina and Georgia Sea Islands, who called the color "haint blue." They believed the blue-green hue protected a home from troubled spirits (or "haints")—and often used it to paint doors and window trim as well as porch ceilings. The preferred Gullah shade is typically a bright Caribbean blue (almost turquoise), but you can spot dozens of variations ranging from robin's egg to ice blue.

HALF-AND-HALF

A TERM THAT CAN REFER EITHER TO A BALanced blend of sweet and unsweet tea *or* to the popular mixture of sweet tea and lemonade. *See Palmer, Arnold.*

HANDY, W. C.

(1873–1958)

WAY BEFORE THE MUSCLE SHOALS SOUND was a thing, a fellow named W. C. Handy had an even greater impact on popular music. Born in Florence, Alabama, in 1873, Handy is often dubbed the "father of the blues" for his role in bringing a regional style (Delta blues) into the national consciousness. Handy traveled all over the South, playing with local groups, before settling in Memphis and then New York City. He composed a number of songs that became hits, including "Memphis Blues" and "St. Louis Blues," with Bessie Smith's version of the latter becoming one of the seminal recordings of the 1920s. Handy was also a musicologist, publishing blues anthologies and sheet music and diligently documenting the rise of the blues as an art form.

HANNAH, BARRY

(1942–2010)

PATRON SAINT OF POSTMODERN SOUTHERN literature, Mississippi's Barry Hannah was a comic prose stylist, a wild man, a motorcycle rider, a trumpet player, a drunk hilarious jerk, and, in the end, a sober literary legend. Perhaps best known for his short story collection *Airships*, Hannah was the writer in residence at the University of Mississippi for decades, and, while he may not have achieved the sales numbers of some of his contemporaries, he is revered by generations of his peers as the finest and most lovable of them all. Of his seemingly effortless and unmatchable talent, the late author Jim Harrison once said that Hannah was "brilliantly drunk with words and could at gunpoint write the life story of a telephone pole." *See Brown, Larry; Oxford, Mississippi.*

HASH

EATERS WHO ARE JUST STARTING TO APPRECIate the diversity of Southern barbecue sometimes flinch at the notion of mustard sauce, one of four sauces traditionally associated with South Carolina. But if you really want to blow the minds of barbecue beginners who think the gamut of smoked meat sides runs only from hush puppies to mac and cheese, tell them about hash. Like burgoo in Kentucky or Georgia's Brunswick stew, South Carolina hash is a one-kettle wonder dreamed up to use parts of the pig that no one could easily or attractively serve any other way. As the hash historian Robert Moss has put it, "You shouldn't inquire too closely as to what goes in the hash pot." But it's safe to assume that onions, potatoes, and spices are simmering down with the offal; just as with barbecue sauce, ketchup or mustard sometimes finds its way into the mix too, meaning the hash served at a church in the Pee Dee region may taste slightly different from the hash spooned out at a volunteer fire department fund-raiser in the Midlands. The end product—too thick to be called gravy, too thin to qualify as a stew—is always paired with rice, a vestige of its plantation origins.

HATCH SHOW PRINT

WHEN THE REVEREND HENRY WARD BEECHER, Harriet Beecher Stowe's brother, came to Nashville to speak in 1879, Charles and Herbert Hatch printed the handbills. The brothers laid out carved woodblocks, inked them by hand, and ran them through a letterpress. It was their very first job. Almost 140 years later, Hatch Show Print still makes posters exactly the same way. In the meantime, it has become a cornerstone of Southern culture by creating thousands of pieces of graphic perfection, promoting more than a century of Nashville performances. Originally naming their company CR and HH Hatch, the brothers changed the name to Hatch Show Print to prevent people from mistakenly thinking they ran a hatchery. By the time Charles's son Will T. Hatch took over in the 1920s, Nashville had become a show town, and business was flourishing. Hatch Show Print has cranked out thousands of hand-printed posters for circuses, vaudeville acts, sporting events, and, of course, the golden age of country music. Now part of the Country Music Hall of Fame, Hatch Show Print designs some six hundred new posters a year, its work coveted by performers, collectors, and graphic designers the world over.

HELLBENDER SALAMANDER

by Daniel Wallace

THE FIRST THING YOU NEED TO KNOW about the hellbender is that it exists. It's not some sitting-by-the-campfire creation your troubled scoutmaster invented, he whose second-greatest pleasure came from supplying bad dreams to young minds. The hellbender is out there. You probably won't ever see one, but if you do, it will be a terrifying confrontation and you will have every reason to believe you have stumbled through a rift in time and find yourself feeling a bit Jurassic.

The hellbender is a giant salamander. It's been around for about sixty-five million years, and there's a reason for that: It's the only thing that's both giant *and* a salamander, traits that don't often go together. It's the largest amphibian in North America, growing up to three feet long and sometimes weighing six pounds. With beady eyes, a wide-gaping biting mouth, and wrinkly skin, covered in slime, it has been called the ugliest animal on earth. It looks like a Komodo dragon run over by a car. On the other hand, it has a great sense of smell and photosensitive skin, so it knows when the entire length of it is concealed beneath a rock, because there's nothing more embarrassing than to think you're concealed beneath a rock and to not be. Hellbenders can live for fifty years and love nothing better than crawfish for breakfast, lunch, and dinner.

The hellbender lives a long, solitary life, and in fact does spend most of its time under rocks. The only time a male and a female get together is to breed, and even that takes place externally: the boy hellbender gets the girl hellbender under his rock, and she lays her eggs and leaves, whereupon the boy hellbender disperses his sperm above them, hopes for the best, and guards the eggs until they hatch. You never want to mess with a hellbender when he's guarding his eggs. There's no telling what he might do.

Then there's the name. Hellbender. To be called a hellbender, no matter what kind of animal you are, is a lot to live up to; for a salamander, no matter how large, it would appear impossible, which may explain why the hellbender salamander lives under a rock. The name suggests a power greater than Satan's, as if the salamander were saying, "I ain't scared of hell. Hell, I can *bend* hell. That's why they call me—"

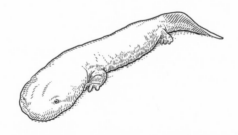

Or maybe it's not that but something else. Maybe it's called that because it's so ugly that it could only have come from hell and is *bent* on returning there. But it's been called all kinds of other things, too, none of them much more affectionate: snot otter, mud-devil, devil dog, grampus.

As a boy I spent a good part of my summers in creeks. This was in Alabama. I was a salamander and crawfish hunter, and I was pretty good at it, adept even, capable of lifting rocks from soft sediment without disturbing the clarity of the water. Hellbenders live under big flat rocks, the kind I would carefully pry my little fingers beneath and lift with the studied care of a safecracker. I never saw one. Alabama is about as far south as they get, though, and they are very sensitive to changes in water quality, to mining, and to sedimentation, so they're becoming endangered. Some people keep them as pets. I don't suggest keeping a slippery flat-headed creature from hell in your bedroom aquarium. That's not a good thing, not for the hellbender and certainly not for you. I'd worry about after nightfall, the two of you alone, and you learning, finally and for certain, where the slimy little rascal gets its name.

HIAASEN, CARL

(1953-)

INEXPLICABLY, IT TOOK FOREIGNERS (*The London Observer*) to point out that Florida-born Carl Hiaasen is "America's finest satirical novelist." Born in 1953 and raised in Plantation, Florida, by twenty-three, Hiaasen was a reporter for the *Miami Herald*. He still writes a regular column for the paper, which, according to his website, "at one time or another has pissed off just about everybody in South Florida, including his own bosses." He has also produced fifteen novels (virtually all best sellers), including *Skinny Dip*, *Bad Monkey*, *Lucky You*, and *Native Tongue*, five children's books, and five nonfiction books. Like that of

all satirists, his work is fueled by righteous anger. Unlike most, his home state provides him with endless material. "This is an economy based on growth for the sake of growth . . . we don't produce anything except oranges and handguns." He acknowledges that it's difficult even in fiction to do justice to the world around him. "There has been more than one occasion," he told *60 Minutes* in 2005, "where I wrote what I thought was the sickest possible scenario . . . only to have real life come along and trump me shortly afterward." His novels do offer the satisfaction—as so seldom happens in real life—of bad people getting what they deserve. One villain was speared on the bill of a stuffed marlin. A few have been eaten by alligators. One was "romanced" to death by an amorous sea mammal, Dicky the Friendly Dolphin (based on an actual event, although that one only injured the man involved, but one doubts he has swum with dolphins since). Until Judgment Day, Hiaasen may be as close to justice as one can hope for.

THE *H. L. HUNLEY*

ON FEBRURY 17, 1864, A STEAMBOAT ENGI-neer turned Confederate lieutenant named George E. Dixon steered the Civil War submarine *H. L. Hunley* toward its final mission. His target: the *USS Housatonic*, a 205-foot Union sloop that held the northernmost point in the blockade of Charleston, South Carolina. When the *Hunley* first launched in 1863, she was considered by many to be a strange contraption (as submarines mostly were in those days); her slender forty-foot hull and protruding latches made for an unusual sight. By the end of her first year, she would earn the nickname "Little Devil" after sinking and killing thirteen crewmen during two test runs. Dixon, however, wasn't thinking of the past on that fateful night; his mission was clear. With a single torpedo in its arsenal, the *Hunley* attacked, becoming the first sub in history to defeat an enemy ship (a feat that went unmatched until World War I) before sinking with her eight-man crew into the Atlantic and immortality. A protracted recovery effort—in which both the showman P. T. Barnum and, later, the author Clive Cussler were invested—lasted 131 years before the vessel was finally discovered and raised in 1995. Today it is permanently docked and open for tours in North Charleston—proving that even a ghost ship can remain undercover for only so long.

HOECAKE

CONTRARY TO RUMOR AND SPECULATION, it's doubtful the hoecake's name owes anything to farming implements. *Hoe* is an antiquated term for *griddle*. Adapted from indigenous recipes, the proto-cornbread flapjack serves as a vehicle for any number of toppings. George Washington ate his with butter and honey; in twenty-first-century Nashville, Pat Martin of Martin's Bar-B-Que Joint heaps them with pulled pork and slaw to make his Redneck Tacos. In Lumberton, North Carolina, members of the Lumbee Tribe eat hoecake-and-collard sandwiches at the annual Robeson County Fair. A versatile role player in Southern foodways, the hoecake has long been the anchor for a workingman's lunch.

HOLLER

Holler IS THE VERNACULAR FORM OF *hollow*, a narrow, steep-sided valley. Hollers are often reachable only by single-lane roads that cling to slopes or trace winding streambeds. These isolated coves are significant for the way they shaped the culture and language of a broad swath of the South, the region known as Appalachia. Formed eons ago by continental upheaval that folded the land into accordion-like ridges and valleys, hollers have, for better or worse, served as redoubts against the onslaught of urbanization and cultural homogeneity.

Providing plenty of water, timber, and arable land, hollers have long bred self-sufficiency. When other parts of the antebellum South were given over to vast plantations producing commodity crops such as cotton, Appalachian hollers remained home to fiercely independent economic generalists, who hunted, trapped, gathered, farmed, and kept hogs and milk cows. The rise of industrialization and urbanization that followed the Civil War reached the hollers only slowly. Outside encroachment finally came during the twentieth century. Extractive industries such as timber and mining hit Appalachia hard, driving many inhabitants to pick up and move west. But the hollers' culture of kinship, feuds, folktales, and hardscrabble self-reliance—not to mention one of the country's most distinctive dialects—lives on.

HONKY-TONK

BORN IN THE BAWDY BARS OF THE SOUTH, honky-tonk music pairs the raw, ragged sounds of guitar, fiddle, steel guitar, and string bass with lyrics about broken hearts and drinking. Ernest Tubb jump-started the genre in the 1940s, and Lefty Frizzell and Hank Williams brought it to ubiquity in the 1950s, setting the standard for "real" country music. The term can also refer to a bar in which such music is played, as in "I'm going to drink my way through all the honky-tonks on Lower Broadway." And it's sometimes turned into a verb, as in "My head hurts real bad from honky-tonkin' all night."

HOOVER SAUCE

AFTER EMANCIPATION, COTTON GROWERS IN the Mississippi Delta were desperate for cheap labor, so they recruited men from Sze Yap, an area in South China. The Chinese workers weren't pleased with the state's treatment of nonwhites or satisfied with the pay. But they realized there was money to be made in grocery stores; the first Chinese-owned grocery

in Mississippi likely opened in the 1870s. In the early 1900s, Hong Lee followed his countrymen to Mississippi from Canton, opening a general store in the Delta town of Louise. His son, Hoover, inherited the store, and in the 1980s started selling his signature blend of soy sauce, garlic, and sugar. (Before the sauce became available online, Lee advised curious eaters elsewhere to imitate the flavor by combining hoisin sauce with onion powder, minced garlic, and chopped cilantro.) Delta residents, who got to know Hoover Sauce in the 1970s when Lee first served it at community events, say the salty-sweet condiment perfectly complements steaks, wings, venison sausage, and just about anything else that might end up on your plate.

HOPPIN' JOHN

ON NEW YEAR'S DAY IN THE SOUTH, resolutions traditionally come with a generous helping of hoppin' John, a pork-flavored stew of rice and black-eyed peas, which are thought to bring good luck. The recipe itself varies from cook to cook. The James Beard Award–winning chef Sean Brock, who routinely obsesses over the history of Southern ingredients and flavors, believes Lowcountry cooks originally prepared hoppin' John with Sea Island red peas and Carolina Gold rice. Robert Stehling, the chef and owner of Hominy Grill in Charleston, South Carolina, adds a secret ingredient, Benton's hickory-smoked bacon. No matter how you tweak it, serve the dish with a heap of slow-cooked greens (which represent money in New Year's tradition) for a belly that feels—on January 1 or any other day—very fortunate, indeed.

HOT BROWN

No offense to Fred Schmidt, the chef at Louisville's Brown Hotel who back in 1926 came up with the Hot Brown as a late-night snack, but the first people to sample his open-face sandwich most likely didn't realize they were beholding a local legend in the making. After all, Hot Brown is close kin to Welsh rarebit, a chafing-dish classic that became a party fixture after John Jacob Astor's wife in 1914 treated guests to melted cheese on toast, iced eggs, and hot coffee in between dances. Smart hostesses across the South followed her lead, but Schmidt adjusted the basic recipe so it would counterbalance high-octane hooch even more forcefully, piling sliced

turkey, bacon, Mornay sauce, and broiled tomatoes atop thick-cut bread. Imaginative Kentuckians have since tinkered with the basics, incorporating avocados, mushrooms, and American cheese, but the Brown Hotel hasn't wavered in its allegiance to tradition. The hotel serves about eight hundred Hot Browns a week (always with a knife and fork, since the sandwich is meant to be a molten mess)—and during Derby Week, closer to four hundred a day.

HOT SAUCE

by Roy Blount, Jr.

Most people can't imagine why anyone would ingest anything that makes them go NYAUGGHHH NYAUGGHHH and spit spit spit and WHOOO WHOOO as the tears roll down and their faces go numb. And yet the hot-sauce industry keeps turning out products with names like (and these are imaginably *actual* names) Aunt Mamie's Burn Your Guts Out You Crazy Doomed Bastard You or Sold for Treatment of Parasites Only.

There are *metrics* involved. Something known as the Scoville scale ranks hot sauces according to how many units of sugar water you would have to add to a drop of a given hot sauce in order to dilute it enough to take the hot out of it. The hottest possible sauce is *sixteen million* Scoville units, which is achievable only artificially, by reducing the sauce to pure capsaicin, the chemical compound that causes the burn. There exists, available, on the open market, a hot sauce called Get Bitten Black Mamba Six, which packs a hit of six million Scovilles. To one drop of that, most people would want to add a couple hundred thousand drops of water. With a quart of milk, because capsaicin is fat soluble, so a dairy product better cuts the painful effect.

Even a sanely snappy hot sauce like Tabasco (2,500 to 5,000 Scovilles), or a more moderate popular sauce like Crystal (I don't know how many Scovilles; I like it), can be run into the ground. Before you put any hot sauce into your oyster stew at Casamento's, in New Orleans, you'll want to ask your server for guidance, because a more vinegary sauce will curdle the stew. You might not want to add *any* hot sauce to gumbo, if it's good gumbo. Leah Chase of Dooky Chase's Restaurant, in New Orleans, stopped then president Barack Obama from adding hot sauce to the gumbo served him there, because if it had needed hot sauce, Mrs. Chase would have put it in there already.

However, and this is a big however, hot sauce does sharpen up a lot of good old originally-poor-folks' food like rice and beans, it surely does.

In Louisiana, not in Minnesota. In Bolivia, not in Sweden. It may seem counterintuitive that hot sauce is big in places that are already hot. You'd think Minnesota would need hot sauce. But no, hot sauce is a hot-location thing.

Why is that? Not, as people will try to tell you, because it makes people sweat. Not, as people will try to tell you, because it masks the taste of spoiled food. No, it's a pre-refrigeration thing. People in sultry climes, where microbes abound and breed fast, came evolutionarily to like the taste of hot-pepper sauce because it protected them from disease-causing bacteria. And the peppers were there already; they weren't one invasive species brought in to stop another. People just had to take a little, *whoof,* a little hit.

Biologists have worked this out. Chiles kill microbes. But, by the way, they have established that hot sauce, however strong, is not the most powerful antibacterial spice. Garlic is, and then onion. Chile pepper is down at twelfth, just barely ahead of rosemary. Can you imagine old boys doing tequila shots and then bracing themselves against the challenge of rosemary hits?

It must be said that the biologists referred to above have inferably not consumed a lot of hot sauce in their lives, because they are at Cornell University, where it's seldom very hot and often very cold. The Scoville scale itself was devised by Wilbur Lincoln Scoville, a product of, oddly enough, Bridgeport, Connecticut, which is a far piece from tropical. Maybe in the study of hot sauce, geographical detachment is an advantage.

HOUSTON, TEXAS

by Robb Walsh

Houston is the city that turned "feeder roads," those access lanes that run alongside major highways, into real estate gold mines. Fast-food franchises, big-box stores, and all manner of businesses that thrive in high-visibility locations flocked to the city's elaborate grid of crisscrossing highways, complete with three interstates, an inner loop, an outer loop, and a few extra ten-lane limited-access thoroughfares thrown in for good measure. In a 1975 *New Yorker* article, Calvin Trillin coined the term "Houstonization," which became a synonym for unsightly sprawl resulting from an utter disdain for urban planning.

Houston's style, or lack thereof, made it the butt of jokes. It was (and still is) the only major American city without any zoning laws. Then the development frenzy came to an abrupt halt when the 1980s oil bust left real estate developers holding 187,000 unsold new homes and 116 million square feet of brand-new un-rented commercial space. All that cheap real estate, along with the hot and sticky climate, the bustling port, and the piquant cuisine, made Houston attractive to immigrants from Mexico, Central America, Asia, and Africa, transforming what was once a typically bira-cial Southern city into a multicultural mecca. Today Houston has no "minorities" per se, but a population of Hispanics, Anglos, and res-idents of African or Asian descent, none of them constituting an ethnic majority. The fu-sion of ethnic foods emerging from this great

bubbling gumbo of cultures inspired John T. Edge of the Southern Foodways Alliance to call Houston "the South's new Creole city."

Also, it turns out that a dense urban core connected to outlying suburbs by a hub-and-spoke rapid-transit system is fine for New York, Boston, and other cities that arose in the horse-and-buggy era. But forcing this model on Houston, Los Angeles, and cities of the American West that were built to accommo-date automobiles is a matter of round pegs and square holes. In fact, after years of Houston's drawing ridicule as the nation's sorriest example of endless sprawl, Stephen Klineberg, a profes-sor of sociology at Rice University, says that ur-ban planners now hold up Houston as a model of a "Multicentered Metropolitan Region"—an urban area with lots of smaller, pedestrian-friendly town centers scattered throughout its own unique transportation grid.

So there: these days, they come to Houston to see how it's done.

HUMIDITY

by Roy Blount, Jr.

If fish had a literature, you wouldn't find the word *water* there, and in classic Southern fiction you won't find *humidity*. It's just assumed. What you will find is *sweat*. Not just atmospheric sweat, but sweat as the outward and visible sign of lust, fear, oppres-sion, shame—all the eternal verities that peo-ple try to hide. Eudora Welty: "Sweat in the airless room, in the bed, rose and seemed to weaken and unstick the newspapered walls like steam from a kettle." Tennessee Williams: "Your husband sweats more than any man I know and now I understand why." In William Faulkner we find sweat like blood and sweat like tears; "sweet, sharp" horse sweat and "the ammonia-reek" of mule sweat; proprietary sweat, "to bind for life them who made the cotton to the land their sweat fell on." And in "Dry September," a story about a lynching, unnatural sweat: "Where their bodies touched one another they seemed to sweat dryly, for no more moisture came."

Near warm water like the Gulf Stream and the Gulf of Mexico, hot air holds more water, or anyway more of the gases that are close to combining into water. Something like that. Let's just say this: when you sweat into Southern air, it is already close to sopping. The 100-plus temperatures of, say, Arizona, may sound hot, Southerners will say, dismissively or wistfully, "but it's that *dry* heat." Some will maintain that humidity makes heat more bearable, because it brings out the sweat. But no. In Welty's story "No Place for You, My Love," a would-be-adulterous couple are "bathed in sweat and feeling the false coolness that brings." What truly cools is rapid evaporation of sweat, not sweat that flows and lingers. Humidity makes sweat stick.

Which works not only in literature but in music. Louis Armstrong's brow-mopping handkerchief was as much a trademark as his smile. James Brown was not only the hardest-working but the hardest-sweating man in show business. Muddy Waters paid this tribute to Howlin' Wolf: "Some singers they's

cool . . . They too *nice* to sweat! But Howling Wolf now he *works*. He puts everything he's got into his blues. And when he's finished, man, he's sweatin'. Feel my shirt, it's soaked ain't it? When Wolf finishes, his *jacket*'s like my shirt."

Some of the grit of early blues recordings may derive directly from humidity. When RCA Victor was in New Orleans recording Rabbit Brown, a street guitarist and singer (he would also charge to row you out into Lake Pontchartrain, serenading as he rowed), for a 1928 album, the heat and humidity shorted some microphones out and made others sizzle and hum so much, they had to be packed in ice before use.

The old saying, of course, is that Southern ladies don't sweat or even perspire, they glow. But in *A Streetcar Named Desire*, Blanche DuBois reassures her feckless suitor (a type that in Tennessee Williams always sweats heavily), that "perspiration is healthy. If people didn't perspire they would die in five minutes." Think of all the Southern things connected with humidity: porches, juleps, seersucker, halter tops, the blessed sweetness of a breeze, levees, powder, oppressive closeness, rot, the expression "freshen up," crawfish, mosquitoes, fever, high ceilings, and heat that thickens, that casts a sheen, that comes in waves, that picks colors out of the air like a prism. Humidity humanizes the air, drawing out pheromones, bacteria, semidigested gravy, bacteria, gossip—the funk of what people breathe of each other. Today air-conditioning drastically limits the impact of humidity. So we're all more comfortable. And what we get in the way of cutting-edge culture is

Sweating Bullets, a book about the invention of PowerPoint.

HURRICANE KATRINA

What began in August 2005 as a tropical depression in the Bahamas went on to ravage parts of Louisiana, Mississippi, and Alabama, the deadliest U.S. hurricane in nearly eighty years, the costliest one ever to hit the United States, and what a former official with the National Oceanic and Atmospheric Administration called "a defining moment in U.S. history." *See Katrina.*

HURRICANES

Admittedly, Southerners are sometimes known to prepare for natural disasters by stocking up on more liquor than plywood. But when the big storms hit, they're hardly anything to celebrate. In 1900, the Great Galveston Hurricane's 145-m.p.h. winds and massive storm surge killed an estimated eight thousand Texans (still the deadliest single day in U.S. history). Later hurricanes were given personalized names but were no better behaved: category-five Camille smashed the Gulf Coast and drowned hundreds from Mississippi to Virginia in 1969. Hugo turned coastal South Carolina upside down in 1989,

and Andrew ravaged twenty-five thousand homes in Dade County, Florida, alone in 1992. As for 2005's Katrina, well, we all watched live as she broke a beloved city—and our hearts. Hurricanes spin up from the tropics aimed at Southern shores (Florida is basically a big middle finger daring them to muss up its white-sand beaches), so, yes, living in the coastal South greatly increases the odds of meeting one of these monsters face-to-face. But it also means that your neighbor is likely to help dig you out of the debris, a coworker is likely to loan you a chainsaw, and a local church group is likely to hammer the last nail that gets you back on your feet. *See Katrina.*

HURSTON, ZORA NEALE

(1891–1960)

While living in Harlem at the height of the Manhattan neighborhood's storied artistic renaissance, Zora Neale Hurston was known for her parties. Langston Hughes, the poet Countee Cullen, and the actress and singer Ethel Waters would congregate in the living room, and Hurston would sit in her bedroom, typing. Although the folklorist's legacy is complicated by her conservative politics and contrarian positions on race-related issues, the scene of Hurston writing in the vapor of celebrity comes closest to an image upon which biographers and critics can agree. Born in Alabama in 1891, Hurston at a very young age moved to Eatonville, Florida, a town founded by African American men. When she was thirteen, her mother died, forcing Hurston to ramble the South in search of work. At twenty-six, she declared herself sixteen again and enrolled in a Baltimore high school; she continued her studies at Howard University, where she joined up with literary figures and hatched a plan to move to Harlem. During the 1920s and 1930s, Hurston wrote short stories and conducted fieldwork. But her professional peak occurred about a decade later, when she published the novel *Their Eyes Were Watching God* to critical acclaim. Hurston never profited from her books, though; her neighbors in Fort Pierce, Florida, took up a collection for her burial in an unmarked grave after she died of a stroke in 1960.

HUSH PUPPIES

SOME PEOPLE WILL TELL YOU THAT COOKS came up with hush puppies to keep hungry dogs from howling their way through fish fries. This backstory has its charms but probably isn't true. For generations, humans have been too fond of these deep-fried balls of cornmeal batter to throw them to the dogs. Hush puppies unquestionably do quiet stomach rumblings, though, whether as bare-bones cornmeal croquettes or more elaborate appetizers spiked with onion, garlic, or whole kernels of corn. Commonly served alongside fried seafood and barbecue, they come in the shapes of golf balls and cheese curls and hark back to centuries of deep-fried cornbread tradition.

I - J

ICEBOX DESSERT

SOUTHERN HOSPITALITY OWES A LOT TO ICE-box desserts. Frozen concoctions of gelatin, condensed milk, and whipped cream some-times shot through with fruits and nuts, they don't need a hot oven. That's a blessing on steam-bath summer nights. And there's no struggling with burned crusts or underbaked fillings, as cooks raised on pies and puddings discovered after the midcentury advent of the refrigerator. Like ice cream, icebox lemon pies and strawberry-and-cream delights exit the freezer ready to be divvied up and enjoyed. What's more, they tend to be multicolored, multilayered showstoppers worthy of a dinner party finale.

ICED TEA

A FOREIGN-SOUNDING TERM THAT OFTEN RE-fers to a peculiarly sugarless beverage that is unfamiliar, unpalatable, and possibly incom-prehensible to many native-born Southerners. *See Sweet tea.*

INDIGO

THE DARK BLUE DYE EXTRACTED FROM IN-digo grown in the Carolina colony was once one of the most sought after commodities in the world, second only to rice as South Carolina's foremost plantation cash crop in the years before the Revolutionary War. Historians have compared its profitability to the silver mines of Mexico or Peru during the same span. But selling indigo was the easy part; cultivating it was another matter alto-gether, relying heavily on slaves' labor and skillful knowledge to produce the prized dye. A few notable eighteenth-century planters, including a teenage Eliza Lucas Pinckney, achieved success and fortune, contributing to an annual export that reached more than a million pounds by 1775. The industry declined rapidly following the Revolution, giving way to cotton by the 1800s. In recent years, how-ever, a few devoted small-scale producers have begun experimenting with the dye, which for all its dark history produces an undeniably beautiful color.

INDIGO SNAKE

FIRST OF ALL, THIS DARKLY GRACEFUL REP-tile is actually a glossy black or metallic purple, making the indigo snake one of nine million American things that are named in a way that is abjectly misleading (see: pineap-ple). But aside from that, it has earned a repu-tation as being mythically, almost spiritually alluring. Indigo snakes are nonvenomous and generally friendly, though you'd be forgiven for not immediately wanting to cozy up to an iridescent eight-foot-long metallic purple predator. In addition to their docility, they're defined by unhingeable jaws (which dislodge to make it easier to gulp down frogs, rodents, and other snakes), intelligence (which is noted by fans and collectors), and status as the country's longest native snake species. But mostly, it's the look: dark and radiant, a glowing black with crimson-orange touches on its face. That look is also partly why they're vanishing. Indigos are on the brink of extinction, displaced by development, reduced by hunters who damage their habitats in search of rattlesnakes, and depleted by the pet trade. The species was granted federal protection in 1978, and remains listed as federally threatened in its usual home states of Georgia and Florida.

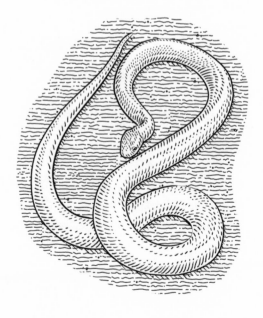

INSECTS

by Guy Martin

INSECTS THAT EXIST FOR REASONS OTHER than to suck the blood of people have a multitude of uses. The main daily quandaries of any Southern rural childhood are twofold: Where are the snakes one has to kill today, and where are some june bugs, so that they can be captured, have strings tied around their legs, and then "flown" on the leash? Those insects that can be bent to one's will are the mainstay of constructive biological experimentation for the Southern child in the wild—for instance, catching a cricket, which can then be used to motivate a fish to take a hook in a creek. Tying strings around a june bug's legs—without ripping them out—was the more difficult trick.

The nuanced, experienced june-bug torturer—such as my brothers and me—quickly noted that success was often built on the thinness and flexibility of the string. This would be the early-school theory of fishing lines of different weights for different fish, because the play is not to inhibit their flight by weighing the tiny beings down with a heavy line. Thus if one sacrifices a few to the learning curve, one gains a kind of fly-tying expertise, and june bugs, in particular, will survive for hours to become one's very own Beelzebub, the little green devil's helper buzzing around on its leash from the hole in your T-shirt. It was an early badass move, walking through the day having a june bug fly around your head, the eight-year-old's equivalent of having a live-action miniature green motorcycle on your shoulder.

JACK-MULATER—ALSO KNOWN AS WILL-O'-the-wisp, fox fire, and jack-o'-lantern, of which the term is most likely a Gullah variation—is one name for the ghost light of Southern swamps and hills. Theories and haunting legends abound. A Confederate soldier looking for his lost head on Land's End Road (in Beaufort County, South Carolina)? Cherokee maidens seeking out dead warriors by torchlight up and down the east side of Brown Mountain (along the Blue Ridge Parkway in North Carolina)? Many have seen it, but few can explain.

Scientists tried, but the closest they got was to give ghost lights a name: *ignis fatuus*, Medieval Latin for "foolish fire." The Italian physicist Alessandro Volta, the Englishman Joseph Priestley, and the Frenchman Pierre Bertholon de Saint-Lazare, great minds of the late 1700s, pegged it as methane gas from decaying vegetation ignited by static electricity. Modern science suggests most ignis fatuus results from the oxidation of phosphine (PH_3), diphosphane (P_2H_3), and methane (PH_4), which can cause photonic emissions. Got that?

Something else to consider: Chemistry fails to account for the ghost light's apparent intelligent behavior. It rarely appears to large groups, mostly to lone travelers. When approached, it retreats, often leading the unwary to peril. If the traveler retreats, the light is sure to follow.

Maybe sometimes it's just easier to believe in ghosts.

(1911–1972)

DESPITE BEING BORN INTO A NEW ORLEANS household so poor that her longshoreman father had to moonlight as a barber, Mahalia Jackson held on to hope. "Blues are the songs of despair," she explained when asked why she didn't chase money in the secular sphere. "Gospel songs are the songs of hope. When you sing gospel, you have the feeling there is a cure for what's wrong." In 1927, at age sixteen, Jackson moved to Chicago, where she cleaned hotel rooms, washed clothes, and sang with the choir at the Greater Salem Baptist Church. By the mid-1930s, she was touring with Thomas A. Dorsey, who introduced jazz rhythms and the autobiographical language of the blues to gospel music. His "Take My Hand, Precious Lord" became Jackson's signature song, although she sold more copies of "Move On Up a Little Higher." Jackson's faith in better days ahead remained so sturdy that she took notice when a Southern preacher sermonized about his utopian vision. A few weeks later, seated behind him on the dais at the March on Washington, Jackson urged, "Tell them about the dream, Martin!" Martin Luther King Jr., departing from his prepared remarks, did just that. More than six thousand people attended Jackson's funeral in 1972 in her adopted home of Chicago. Her friend Harry Belafonte called her "the single most powerful black woman in the United States."

JAMBALAYA

JAMBALAYA IS THE PAELLA OR PILAU OF bayou country. Cajun and Creole recipes follow the same steps: First, sauté the holy trinity of bell peppers, onions, and celery with the meat—chicken, smoked sausage, and shrimp are popular choices. Then add rice and stock and simmer until done. Creole cooks might add a few urban flourishes along the way, such as chopped vegetables and tomato. Cajun cooks might add wild game. Whatever recipe you follow, this is a rice-and-seafood dish fit for beginners—made in one pot, and easier to master than a roux-based étouffée or gumbo.

JAZZ

THE BEST DEFINITION OF JAZZ IS SAID TO HAVE come from none other than Louis Armstrong, the New Orleans trumpeter who arguably served as a definition of the thing in himself. "If you gotta ask," he supposedly said, "you'll never know." Most say it grew out of the singing, dancing, and drumming at Sunday slave gatherings in New Orleans' Congo Square, where African rhythms began to form the backbone of a new style that drew on traditions from all over the world. But one reason jazz is hard to define is its utter disregard for convention: Jazz likes to bend notes out of shape; it uses offbeat, syncopated rhythms to keep you on your toes; it prefers a loose structure full of improvisation over anything

too regimented. Jazz absorbs influence, from Africa, from the Caribbean, from the Mississippi Delta; from chamber, classical, and marching music; from everything else. It uses a lot of brass and woodwinds but also might not. Jazz might be the big bands of the 1920s, the hypercool virtuosos of the sixties, or those soft tones leaking out of elevator speakers. It has been called the only true American art form, the baseball of music. It's a distinction to which jazz, by nature, would most likely pay little heed.

JAZZ FEST

by Wayne Curtis

TO BE OFFICIAL: IT'S THE NEW ORLEANS Jazz & Heritage Festival Presented by Shell, which nobody ever calls it except the local papers, and one suspects they only do so under some pecuniary duress involving threat of withheld advertising. Everyone else just calls it Jazz Fest, as they have since it was first staged in 1970.

The festival was initially conceived by the New Orleans Hotel Motel Association to boost tourism. The association sagely hired George Wein, the producer of the Newport Jazz Festival, which started in 1954, to organize it. Wein, in turn, recruited help from the Hogan Jazz Archive at Tulane University, which lent him a staffer, Allison Miner, and a student intern, Quint Davis. Both assisted in producing the event the first year; both joined the staff to oversee the festival's tremendous growth thereafter. Miner worked for the festival until her death in 1995; Davis is the current producer and director.

The first festival took place at Louis Armstrong Park at the edge of the French Quarter and featured a gospel tent and four stages. Performers the first year included Mahalia Jackson, Fats Domino, the Preservation Hall Band, Duke Ellington, Clifton Chenier, and Al Hirt. Admission was three dollars. Approximately 350 people attended.

Word spread about the quality of music, and the festival quickly outgrew the park, moving after two years to Fair Grounds Race Course, about three miles from downtown, where it remains today. The event now takes place over seven days at the end of April and the beginning of May. It unfolds across a dozen stages of varying size, plus several more intimate stages where musicians are interviewed and cooks demonstrate recipes. Nearly a half million people now attend over the course of the week, with ticket prices running about seventy-five dollars for a full day.

Jazz Fest features headliners whose connection to jazz is not immediately evident: Paul Simon, Drake, Elton John, Willie Nelson, Bruce Springsteen, Kenny Chesney. Longtime fest veterans shrug this off, noting that the one Springsteen attracts thousands of attendees who effectively subsidize the dozens of local trad-jazz performances staged with less fanfare at the smaller venues. Anyway, the festival was started to celebrate jazz's birthplace, but it has always encompassed all forms of music—rock, pop, blues, gospel, and country.

The "heritage" part of the festival takes several guises. Artisans from Louisiana and beyond vend their creations at booths, and craftsmen display forgotten skills such as ironmongery and violin making. The grounds often erupt in music and dancing as Mardi Gras Indians and "second-line" bands parade through. Food is also a significant draw—dozens of vendors hawk local specialties, including many perennial favorites available chiefly at Jazz Fest, among them the Cochon de Lait po'boy, Crawfish Monica, and Mango Freeze (a tasty sorbet).

Critics sometimes gripe that Jazz Fest has settled into a slightly slouchy middle-age rhythm, which is not surprising for an event well into its fifth decade. While it still attracts attendees of all ages, gray-haired folks dressed in floppy straw hats and bright aloha Jazz Fest shirts visually dominate (new official patterns are released annually). Fest veterans often wear their old shirts as badges of honor, like tattered rock tour T-shirts, although Jazz Fest shirts look more laundered and one guesses that plastic storage tubs may be involved. As such, Jazz Fest has evolved into something of a secret society of baby boomers who still appreciate a good tune.

JAZZ FUNERAL

OVER THE LAST THREE HUNDRED YEARS, THE art of celebrating the end of a life by staging a catharsis of music and dance has been honed to perfection in New Orleans. Sundays were days off under the eighteenth-century Code Noir, the French-colonial body of law governing slavery, so that Congo Square, the plaza within today's Louis Armstrong Park in Tremé, could host fabulous West African orchestras and dance-offs. The brass band entered the African American musical lexicon with military marches in the 1800s. By 1900, what outsiders called a "jazz funeral" had taken on the soaring narrative architecture we know today. The slow march out to the grave site musically states the passing, after which the body is, in New Orleans parlance, "cut loose," or severed from the embrace of the community at burial. Exuberantly, with flourish and flair, the band and procession then work back to a boisterous wake, followed as ever by the "second line," who promenade with their own drummer. Taken as a dramatic progression from a state of grief to the state of joy—a wholesale reversal of tragedy—the jazz funeral mimics the soul's imagined arc from the body to the heavens. In doing that, it has become one of this world's most eloquent, defiant essays on Death's own march, addressed to the celestial powers and to those left behind.

JEFFERSON, BLIND LEMON

(1893–1929)

A PILLAR OF COUNTRY BLUES, WITH A LEGACY OF both influence and a string of hits in the 1920s,

Blind Lemon Jefferson was born on a cotton farm outside of Couchman, Texas. Known as the "father of Texas blues," Jefferson was blind from birth and one of seven children, and though exact dates are hazy, around 1912 he began playing guitar at area picnics and gatherings, taking cues from local players but also absorbing the flamenco-influenced sounds of Mexican workers. His eerie, lonesome-sounding voice, ribald (for the time) lyrics, and intricate guitar work on songs like "That Black Snake Moan" and "Matchbox Blues" brought him success from Dallas to Chicago and directly impacted the works of fellow bluesmen including Lead Belly and Lightnin' Hopkins. He cut more than a hundred original songs during his run, one that was tragically cut short when he was found dead on a Chicago street in 1929.

JEFFERSON, THOMAS

(1743–1826)

by Logan Ward

FOR MANY, THOMAS JEFFERSON EMBODIED the ideals of the Southern gentleman. A Renaissance man brimming with curiosity and passion, he was an agrarian innovator, garden tinkerer, naturalist, philosopher, inventor, public servant, architect, writer, and able musician, equally as fond of wine and warm company as intellectual pursuits. Jefferson, more than any other founding father, shaped the future trajectory of the United

States. He authored the U.S. Declaration of Independence and served his young democracy in many roles, including Virginia governor, U.S. vice president, foreign ambassador, and president for two terms. In 1803, he led the purchase of the Louisiana Territory from France, a masterstroke that gave the United States control of the Mississippi River.

A Southerner, Jefferson was a fierce advocate for his region following independence, when distinctions between North and South came into sharper focus. He opposed Federalism, fearing the agrarian South would lose influence. Still, he could be self-deprecating and hard on his kind. In a 1785 letter to the Marquis de Chastellux, Jefferson wrote that "in the north" people were cool, sober, laborious, and chicaning, while "in the south" they were fiery, voluptuary, indolent, unsteady, generous, and candid.

Jefferson was far from perfect. Though he was a visionary leader and artful politician who fiercely defended individual rights and intellectual freedom, he kept upwards of two hundred enslaved blacks as property. They boosted his bottom line while working without compensation, tending his fields, laboring in his nailery, and keeping house. He kept one, Sally Hemings, as a concubine and fathered six of her children. In his writings, Jefferson condemned slavery as "this great political and moral evil," yet throughout his life he freed only seven males, all members of the Hemings family.

For all his brilliance and worldly refinement, Jefferson was not a fancy man. He felt that the president should dress and act in a way that reflected the simplicity and informality of the country. Leave the pomp and circumstance to European royalty. Dinner guests arriving at the White House were often shocked by his disheveled appearance and threadbare slippers. He seated dinner guests, regardless of social status, on a first come, first served basis. On one notorious occasion, the wives of British and Spanish diplomats had to scramble for the best seats.

Two centuries later, Jefferson's practicality and humility come off as refreshingly authentic. He was down-to-earth. Offered a third chance at the presidency, he declined, writing to a friend: "Never did a prisoner, released from his chains, feel such relief as I shall on shaking off the shackles of power. Nature intended me for the tranquil pursuits of science, by rendering them my supreme delight."

At sixty-five, Jefferson returned to Monticello, his beloved Virginia mountaintop estate, but his ambition never diminished. Among other things, in his later years he founded and designed the University of Virginia, which accepted capable students, both wealthy and poor.

The university opened in 1825. Jefferson died in 1826. He left directives for his burial at Monticello, stipulating a simple monument made of coarse stone. It was to read:

Here was buried Thomas Jefferson
Author of the Declaration of
American Independence
Of the Statute of Virginia
for Religious Freedom
And Father of
the University of Virginia

And "not a word more . . . ," Jefferson instructed, "because by these, as testimonials that I have lived, I wish most to be remembered."

JIM CROW

by Amanda Heckert

A SONG, A CHARACTER, AN EPITHET, A SYS-tem of oppression—that's the evolution of Jim Crow. Named after a racist tune and archetype created by a white minstrel performer named Thomas Dartmouth "Daddy" Rice in 1830s New York, the term became synonymous with a series of laws and customs that disenfranchised, terrorized, oppressed, and segregated African Americans from white populations, largely in the South, for almost a century.

After the Civil War, Reconstruction—the federal military occupation of the Southern states that had seceded from the Union—forced Southerners to grant voting rights to black men per the Thirteenth and Fourteenth Amendments, and entities such as the Freedmen's Bureau, which sought to help former slaves make the transition to freedom, fueled white resentment. After the troops withdrew in 1877, Jim Crow rules reared their heads. An 1890 Louisiana law separating blacks and whites on railroad cars provided the first test. When the U.S. Supreme Court upheld that discrimination in the landmark 1896 case *Plessy v. Ferguson*,

its decision cemented the acceptance of "separate but equal."

From there, Jim Crow seeped into every aspect of daily life. In various cities and states across the South, the list of things blacks and whites could not do together ranged from rules imposed and enforced by law—marrying; attending school; serving in the military; riding a bus; being buried in the same area of a cemetery; living in the same neighborhoods; and even playing checkers—to unwritten codes of "etiquette" meant to underscore white supremacy (a black man, for instance, couldn't offer his hand first to shake with a white man). Breaches of those customs were often met with intimidation and violence such as lynching, or the threat thereof, by groups such as the Ku Klux Klan. In the meantime, black voting rights took a substantial hit, thanks to expensive poll taxes and laws that excluded, for example, those who couldn't read. In 1954, the Supreme Court finally overturned *Plessy* with its decision on *Brown v. Board of Education of Topeka*, ruling that the "equal" part of "separate but equal" was rare and that segregated schools were *inherently* detrimental to minority students.

Over the years, influential civil rights activists emerged from efforts to fight Jim Crow, including Ida B. Wells, a Mississippi native who condemned lynching through her newspaper column; Rosa Parks, whose refusal to give up her bus seat to a white person sparked the 1955 Montgomery bus boycott; and Martin Luther King Jr., whose nonviolent protests sparked the beginning of the end of Jim Crow, culminating in the Civil Rights Act of 1964 and the Voting Rights

Act of 1965, both of which greased the wheels of desegregation first set in motion ten years earlier.

JOGGLING BOARD

A HISTORICALLY INSPIRED PIECE OF OUTDOOR furniture—part garden bench, part rocker, part swing—the joggling board has long been a fixture on porches and piazzas in Charleston, South Carolina. Simply made, it's a long, pliable pine plank, traditionally thirteen inches wide, supported by rocking legs on either end. The effect: a bench that bounces and sways—but doesn't break—when you sit.

Popular local lore contends that the first joggling board appeared in 1804 at Acton Plantation, the home of Cleland Kinloch, in Sumter County near Columbia. When Kinloch's wife passed away, his sister Mary Benjamin Kinloch Huger arrived to help care for the household. At the time, she suffered from debilitating rheumatism that prevented her from exercising, and so after relatives in Scotland, as the story goes, sent plans for a bench on which she could gently bounce, the plantation carpenter got to work. Before long, the narrow bouncing boards were gracing porches across the Lowcountry. One hundred fifty years later, they were nowhere to be found. If not for Tommy Thornhill, a Charlestonian who began building them in his basement in 1959 after a fruitless search of antique and furniture stores, they might have vanished altogether. Thornhill, who founded the Old Charleston Joggling Board Co. in 1970, not only helped revive them, he also gave them their now-signature color: the not-quite-black historic hue known as Charleston green.

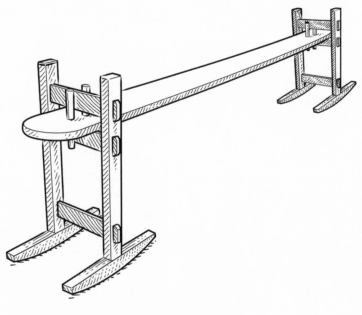

JOHNSON, ROBERT

(1911–1938)

AT THE INTERSECTION OF ROUTES 49 AND 61 IN Clarksdale, Mississippi—probably the world's most famous crossroads—the legendary bluesman Robert Johnson is reputed to have sold his soul to the devil in exchange for mastery of the guitar. Myths and stories about Johnson abound, mostly because he left little behind but two (definitive) photographic portraits and twenty-nine recorded songs. In the 1997 film *Can't You Hear the Wind Howl?*, Johnson's friend and fellow musician Johnny Shines took issue with the most famous legend. "He never told me that lie," Shines said. "If he would've, I would've called him a liar right to his face. You have no control over your soul." Another Mississippi-born bluesman, Son House, claimed that Johnson actually annoyed audiences with his poor guitar playing in his early days. Johnson fled "to Arkansas or someplace," returning six months later a changed player. What remains today is the singularity of both his guitar playing and his almost terrifyingly haunting voice. Both of them have influenced generations of musicians. Eric Clapton calls his singing "the most powerful cry that I think you can find in the human voice." When Brian Jones played Keith Richards a Robert Johnson record, Richards's first question was "Who is the other guy playing with him?" There was no other guy playing.

JON BOAT

WHAT THE HUMBLE JON BOAT LACKS IN LUXury, it makes up for in utility, a floating testament to the adage that less can indeed be more. Typically made of aluminum, with a flat-bottomed hull, square nose, one or more bench seats, and a slight updrift at the bow, a jon boat is lightweight, maneuverable, and ideally suited to shallow waters, where it can get to places bigger, fancier boats often can't. And while you'll find these nearly indestructible workhorses from coast to coast, they're a mainstay of hunters and fishermen across the South.

The origin of the name is a matter of some debate, though a popular theory traces it to a variation of "jack boat," a flat-bottomed craft popular in the Ozarks in the early twentieth century. However, it may also relate to its longtime reputation as an everyman boat—a boat for every John. Regardless, the jon boat has survived the test of time, favored by those who don't require a boat to look sexy as long as it gets the job done. Which accounts for an oft-repeated bit of Southern wisdom: if you really want to figure out where the fish are biting, follow the guy in the jon boat.

JONES, GEORGE

(1931–2013)

FRANK SINATRA ONCE SAID THAT GEORGE Jones was the second-best vocalist he'd ever heard, and there is perhaps no more adored male country singer. With an unbelievable delivery that soared and rumbled with equal aplomb, Jones's voice was spectacular, milking every syllable for sonic gold on hits like "White Lightning" and his 1980 smash "He Stopped Loving Her Today," which topped the country charts for eighteen weeks. He was just as adept at singing harmony, sharing the microphone with stars such as Waylon Jennings, Buck Owens, and Merle Haggard, along with recording nine albums' worth of collaborations with his onetime wife Tammy Wynette. Jones—given the nickname "Possum" by two radio programmers because of the shape of his nose and facial features—was also infamous for his struggles with alcohol, including the oft-told legend of him driving his riding lawn mower to the liquor store after his second wife, Shirley Corley, took away the keys to all of their cars.

JOWL

SOUTHERNERS COOK WITH A CORNUCOPIA OF salt pork products: bacon, hocks, fatback, and jowl. Cut from the cheek, jowl is a cured and smoked product that's kin to continental guanciale. Fried like bacon or diced as seasoning for pintos and field peas and other vegetables, it's a versatile ingredient in the traditional pantry. Meatier than bacon, it contributes more flavor and has a richer texture, making it a popular partner for first-of-the-year greens and peas.

JUBILEE

IF YOU'VE EVER BEEN FORTUNATE ENOUGH TO experience one of Alabama's Mobile Bay jubilees, you'll understand exactly why Spanish explorers christened the body of water Bahía del Espíritu Santo. The rare natural phenomenon, when marine life swarms ashore for the taking, has a mystical, almost religious quality. On warm summer nights when conditions align, the shallow bay—its average depth is only ten feet—can experience a dramatic drop in oxygen levels. Coinciding with a predawn rising tide and gentle easterly wind, hypoxic water wells up and moves west, herding all sorts of marine life before it. Rendered nearly catatonic, shrimp, anchovies, rays, and flounder crowd along the shoreline; blue crabs cluster up the sides of dock pilings; and gasping eels poke their heads out of the water. They're all searching for oxygen, and once word of their arrival spreads, locals descend with gigs, nets, and buckets in hand. Filling a freezer with an entire summer's worth of seafood in mere minutes is certainly cause for celebration, thus the name, which dates to a 1912 report in Mobile's *Daily Register*, though records of jubilees go back to the 1600s, when settlers first colonized the area. Sometimes a jubilee may be highly localized in a 100-yard-long stretch of the eastern shore; in rare years, one might extend fifteen miles from Daphne down to Mullet Point. It may occur a dozen times from June to September, or only once. But as quickly as it happens, the jubilee ends, departing with the tide—and leaving a few lucky folks who heeded the call with laundry baskets full of the bay's bounty.

JUKE JOINT

JUKE JOINTS AROSE AS THE AFRICAN American nightclubs of the rural South, and they're where the blues was born. Lightnin' Hopkins, Robert Johnson, and B. B. King all cut their teeth in juke joints with names like back-roads poetry: Marion's Place, House of Joy, Simmons Fish Camp, Po' Monkey's.

In 1928, Justus P. Seeburg, a builder of player pianos, combined a loudspeaker with a coin-operated phonograph that played eight selections. Within a dozen years, three-quarters of all records produced in the United States wound up in such "automated music vending devices," and every juke joint had to have one. That's how we got jukeboxes.

JULEP

JULEPS ARE A CLASS OF LAVISHLY ICED ADULT beverages associated with the Old South of verandas and the New South of the Kentucky Derby.

The julep's heritage is long and widely traveled. The word comes from the Persian word for rosewater, *gulab*, which the French called *julep* and which migrated as such into English. It evolved in America to describe a morning medicinal drink, made of spirit (often brandy) infused with botanicals (often mint) to keep away diseases borne on fogs and miasmas.

In the first half of the nineteenth century, ice inundated the South, shipped to icehouses aboard a growing fleet of insulated ships filled with pond ice cut during Northern winters. Soon ice made a lasting and fortuitous acquaintance with the julep. The first such drinks were often called "hailstorms" after the crushed, hailstone-like ice that adorned the inside and (often) outside of julep cups.

In the years leading up to the Civil War, the julep was the most popular drink in America. Then it fell from fashion, most likely owing to the labor involved. While juleps are experiencing a revival in some of the South's better bars, today they are chiefly associated with the annual running of the horses at Churchill Downs. Some claim that more juleps are served in that place on that day than in the rest of the year in the rest of the South combined.

JUNETEENTH

SCHOOLCHILDREN LEARN THAT ABRAHAM Lincoln "freed the slaves" in 1862 by signing the Emancipation Proclamation, which stipulated that all enslaved people in rebelling Confederate states would gain their freedom on January 1, 1863. But war combatants don't take kindly to their enemies' decrees, so the measure worked only where Union troops were on hand to enforce it. Fearing that situation, huge numbers of slaveholders marched their slaves deep into Texas, where slavery persisted even after Robert E. Lee surrendered. Then, on June 19, 1865, Union general Gordon Granger arrived in Galveston with an occupying army and announced, "All slaves are free." The following year, African Americans marked the occasion with the first Juneteenth, singing songs and playing games. Celebrations, often featuring barbecue, baseball, and red soda, grew in size and magnitude until Jim Crow laws systematically deprived black Texans of anything that resembled freedom. But those who moved north carried the anniversary with them. In the late 1960s, it emerged as a national holiday, superseding smaller observances in places that freedom reached sooner. As the Harvard scholar Henry Louis Gates has written, "By choosing to celebrate the last place in the South that freedom touched, we remember the shining promise of emancipation, along with the bloody path America took by delaying it."

JUNIOR LEAGUE

FOUR COUNTRIES AND 291 CHAPTERS. A who's who roster of illustrious alumni—including Ann Bedsole, the first woman to serve in the Alabama State Senate, former First Ladies Barbara Bush and Laura Bush, and Eudora Welty—and a tradition of civic leadership dating back to 1901. The all-female Junior League, officially called the Association of Junior Leagues International, originated in New York City, to address issues of poverty and affordable housing. Soon its scope broadened, both geographically and philosophically, and Junior League members began creating community cookbooks (first popularized in the 1800s) to fund their various projects. The Dallas chapter claims the oldest version, published around 1920, followed by a collection from Augusta, Georgia, around 1940. From there, it's impossible to count the number of spiral-bound cookbooks produced by Junior League members. Popular Southern titles include *Stop and Smell the Rosemary: Recipes and Traditions to Remember* (Houston), *Southern Sideboards* (Jackson, Mississippi), and *With Our Compliments* (Charlottesville, Virginia). But the undisputed sales leader is *Charleston Receipts*. First printed in 1950, it is the League's longest-running and most-purchased title, having netted $1 million and counting for local charities.

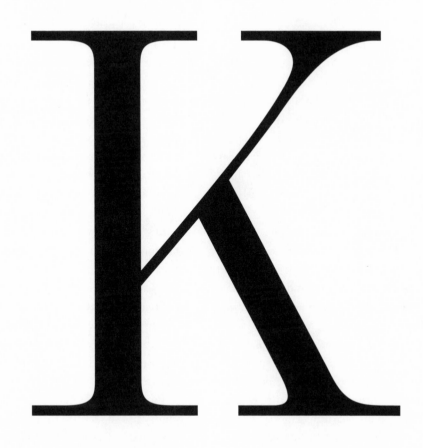

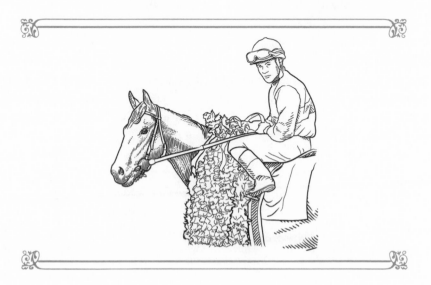

KATRINA

by John M. Barry

THE STORM BEGAN SMALL, CHEWING ITS way across Florida like a teething baby, then, suddenly broad-shouldered and bullying, as big as the Gulf, it came howling at a stretch of the Mississippi and Louisiana coast with a storm surge twenty-eight feet high, sweeping away homes that ocean had never before touched.

More than a decade after Katrina—no one on the Gulf Coast says "Hurricane Katrina," it's just "Katrina"—people here use it as a reference point. There is *before the storm* and *after the storm*. In Mississippi rebuilding was simpler—not easier, just simpler. Everything was gone. Few had to decide whether to restore or tear down because there was nothing left to tear down. And there were resources. Mississippi's governor, Haley Barbour, the plugged-in former Republican National Committee chairman, got Mississippi far more than its share of federal dollars, enough so that places like Starkville, two hundred miles from the coast, got $8 million to build a parking garage, and nearly a decade after the storm $872 million remained unspent.

New Orleans was where the complexity— and much of the horror—was. Katrina killed 1,833 people, 1,577 of them in New Orleans. And betrayal began before the storm. Most of the city flooded from the rear, from Lake Pontchartrain, where storm surge was much lower than on the coast—not high enough to overtop flood walls the Army Corps of Engineers had built. Yet those same flood walls—some completed only five years before Katrina—collapsed because of poor design. Later, the Corps itself conceded it had provided flood protection "in name only."

The horror came with the chaos, the political gamesmanship, the extraordinary incompetence of the Federal Emergency Management Agency—for example, holding search-and-rescue teams in Atlanta to hear lectures on sexual harassment instead of letting them save lives—and the ensuing breakdown of order. City government was worse. Mayor Ray Nagin gave incompetence a bad name: while cutting illegal deals unrelated to Katrina that sent him to jail in 2014, he took almost a year and a half to name a rebuilding "czar," who two years later, after accomplishing exactly nothing, was laughed out of town.

Yet New Orleans did recover. Ten years after the storm, it had far exceeded the most optimistic predictions for its recovery. There are two reasons for this.

First, *it's New Orleans*. No other city in the country has so identifiable a culture, a culture that emanated from the city's intricate histories and made it a prime world tourist destination, a culture that, combined with a lack of economic opportunity over many decades, also made it the country's major city with the highest percentage of people living there who had been born there. Though the city may have been insular, its citizens loved it, and fought for their home. They had to. As Harry Shearer said, "The illusion of leadership is much more dangerous than no leadership. We had no illusion of leadership." So people did things themselves, rebuilt homes and neighborhoods themselves. And grassroots leadership defined what happened, and to hell with planners.

Second, plenty of outside help arrived. Tens of thousands of volunteers and tens of billions of dollars came; young people in their twenties came. Before the storm, those few who moved to New Orleans had sought to fit into what was. These new immigrants, invigorated by possibility and entrepreneurial spirit, were determined to make space for themselves. Suddenly trendy, in 2013 New Orleans became the nation's most popular destination for working-age Americans; in 2014, it led the nation in growth in college graduates. They changed the city, made it greener, more dynamic, more sophisticated; typically, one neighborhood restaurant removed shrimp, crab, and crawfish from its menu, replacing them with such items as oxtail soup. And neighborhoods changed.

Indeed, two parallel universes developed. Gentrification had moved slowly in New Orleans, creating mixed neighborhoods; now, suddenly, it accelerated, pushing the black community out of its neighborhoods. If for whites New Orleans is doing better than it has in decades, African Americans have yet to find enough places for themselves.

And for both communities, there's one great overhang: the threat of the next storm and the dissolution of coastal Louisiana. The state has lost roughly two thousand square miles of land—equivalent to the state of Delaware—since 1932. Chief causes are levees, which prevent a flooding river from depositing sediment, and the oil and gas industry, which dredged thousands of miles of canals. That land once provided a protective buffer to absorb hurricane storm surge. Land loss continues, and sea level rise is coming.

The state has a plan, but no money to fund it. The city has a new levee system—one that will perform as designed this time. But will these things protect the city into the future, or is New Orleans the next Atlantis?

KEEN, ROBERT EARL

(1956–)

A SONGWRITER'S SONGWRITER, ROBERT EARL Keen Jr. is Texas through and through. Raised in Houston and steeped in the work of fellow Texans Townes Van Zandt and Guy Clark, Keen—along with his best pal and fellow A&M Aggie, Lyle Lovett—has made his name by writing literary, sweeping songs full of rich Lone Star characters. Over the course of nearly thirty years and twelve studio albums, he's become one of the preeminent alt-country artists, staying firmly outside of the Nashville machine while garnering plaudits from everyone from George Strait to Dave Matthews. His live chops are unquestionable, honed by playing the Texas dance-hall circuit, with his amiable storytelling and sizzling backing band captured not once, but twice at the legendary Gruene Hall for 1996's *No. 2 Live Dinner* and the 2016 sequel, *Live Dinner Reunion*.

KEENELAND

A RACETRACK AS WELL AS A THOROUGHBRED auction house, Lexington, Kentucky's Keeneland lies in the red-hot center of what's called the Inner Bluegrass, a stretch of God's country where the flinty, limestone-tinged water yields smooth-strong racehorses and smooth-strong whiskey. The greatest Thoroughbred-breeding farms in the world—Calumet, Lane's End, Claiborne, Gainesway, among others—are within a stone's throw of town, and during Keeneland's famed September Yearling Sale, the private jets stack like sardines out at Lexington International. Over the years, the September sale and Keeneland's two other annual auctions have produced twenty-one Kentucky Derby winners, twenty-three Preakness winners, and nineteen Belmont Stakes winners, not to mention the ninety-five horses that have won, more than a hundred Breeders' Cup series races. The track's spring and fall meets certainly hold their own, too, providing the stages for eleven Grade I stakes races.

Keeneland came to be in 1936, after a group of Bluegrass horsemen purchased the property from Jack Keene—whose breeding farm upon which the track and sales barns were built had been in family hands for more than a century—to construct the world's first racetrack with a strong sales component. Globally renowned for a half century, a national landmark since 1986, and relatively unchanged since its founding, Keeneland remains extraordinarily beautiful and thus served as a set for the film *Seabiscuit*. It is that rare, organic thing among sporting institutions: it had to occur where the horses were born, in this precise limestone-fed chunk of their Kentucky home, and nowhere else.

KENTUCKY DERBY

by Guy Martin

EACH MAY, AS MILLINERS ACROSS AMERICA and around the globe sweat bullets over the last little insouciant flicks and upturns of their fascinators, it behooves us to remember that the roots of all Kentucky Derby madness lie in the towering equine passions of a prescient Southern madman, Meriwether Lewis Clark Jr. A Kentuckian and horseman of distinction, Clark was the grandson of the explorer William Clark (yes, of *that* Lewis and Clark). In 1872, he succumbed to his familial DNA for travel and struck out for Europe. His notion was to take in the great European horse races—first at Epsom Downs for the Derby, which had been run since 1780, and then at Longchamps, where the French Jockey Club had organized the Grand Prix de Paris just ten years earlier.

Lit up by these great races and the culture surrounding them, Clark returned to Louisville in 1873 to devote himself to bringing events of similar magnitude to Kentucky. His social reach spanned the young continent, which is another way of saying, as a descendant of one of the first families of Kentucky—his mother was a Churchill—and since he belonged to American royalty as a Clark, he had what the Bluegrass horse breeders would today call the right pedigree to arrange a fine horse race.

It didn't take him long upon his return from Europe to do that. He quickly formed the Louisville Jockey Club and leased the hundred acres for what became Churchill Downs from his uncle John Churchill (hence the name of the track). A scant two years after his return, in 1875, Clark produced the very first Kentucky Derby, with a fifteen-horse field. In a moment of pure athletic and political poetry, America's first Derby, run at a brutal mile and a half, was won by Aristides, who was exquisitely trained by the subsequent Hall of Fame trainer Ansel Williamson, one of the rare African American trainers in the fledgling industry. Aristides was ridden to his win by the star jockey Oliver Lewis, also African American. In other words, a short ten years after the cessation of hostilities of the Civil War, two superbly talented African Americans won America's premier race at America's premier track.

For his part, Clark, a man of ferociously short temper and enormous competitive drive, did not let the Derby's spectacular beginning be the end of the story. Year after year, he roped in the owners who brought the horses. As with so much in Clark's turbulent life, what follows may be legend, or it may be fact, but according to the legend, at a post-Derby party in 1883 hosted by the so-called King of the Dudes, Evander Berry Wall, an extravagant New York socialite and a founding father of the Belle Époque's café society, Clark noted well that Wall handed out roses to every woman he had invited to the party. What is indisputably in the historical record is this: by 1896, the famous garland of several hundred roses was being tossed over the winner of the race.

Since then, the race has grown to occupy its pride of place in what by 1930 had become the Triple Crown. As the big inaugural race for three-year-olds, the Derby has become the debut for a global crop of superb young athletes at the beginnings of their careers. The names of the winners alone are a record of the sport's last 142 years, from 1930's Triple Crown winner, Gallant Fox, to Secretariat, who still holds the track record from his Derby win in 1973, to 1978 Triple Crown winner Seattle Slew, and on up to 2015's American Pharoah.

The Derby is the big, bold, ripping renewal of an athletic season and brings us the flower of youth, who contest in it with furious grace. In this, at bottom, Meriwether Clark's race has become the Southern stage for a national rite of spring.

KEY LIME PIE

Small, tart key limes made their way across the Atlantic with the Spanish conquistadores, and groves were already well established in the Florida Keys by the end of the Civil War. Around the same time, condensed milk became a pantry staple and a welcome source of shelf-stable dairy. The eureka moment didn't take long. Before the turn of the century, locals were combining the puckery juice with the milk and some beaten egg in a crumb crust. A hurricane wiped out most of the groves in the 1920s, killing the trees if not the recipe. For decades, key lime pie was made with the larger, ubiquitous Persian limes or bottled, pasteurized juice, cases of which line the pantry of any coastal seafood shack. Fresh key limes are now available year-round, though they spoil quickly. So when you get ahold of some, have your pie (and perhaps daiquiri) ingredients ready.

KEY WEST, FLORIDA

by Amanda Heckert

PITY THOSE WHO ONLY SEE THE SOUTHERN-most point of the continental United States after spilling off the gangway of a cruise ship onto the main drag to do the Duval Crawl for piña coladas or catch the daily Sunset Celebration at Mallory Square. Small as Key West is—an easily biked or walked four miles across by one mile wide, with just 25,000 or so residents—this island deserves more than the few hours afforded the 800,000-plus passengers who disembark every year to sample the original Margaritaville.

Key West owes much of its import to its "end of the earth" location—the terminus of the Florida Keys, where the shipping lane known as the Straits of Florida and the Gulf of Mexico meet the Atlantic, ninety miles this side of Cuba. Once inhabited by indigenous Calusa people, the island was first "discovered" by Juan Ponce de León in 1521

and settled by Spaniards, who christened it Cayo Hueso ("bone cay"). It changed hands several more times before the United States planted its flag in 1822. Trade ships and pirates swarmed, often getting trapped in the coast's expansive coral reef, and shipwreck salvage became a leading industry (visit the Mel Fisher Maritime Museum to see some of the booty). When the Civil War began, the Union retained control of Key West thanks to the recent construction of Fort Zachary Taylor, one of several military outposts (and namesake of a state park that today offers beach access—the real southernmost point open to the public, no matter what that giant buoy monument at the corner of South and Whitehead Streets claims). Thanks to salvaging and the cigar industry, by the mid-1800s the city of Key West ranked, per capita, as one of the richest in the country.

Walking around, you'll most likely see flags heralding the island as the Conch Republic, so-called by locals in 1982 when the city announced its "secession" from the States after a tourism-hampering roadblock aimed at foiling drug smugglers in the Upper Keys. Other island hallmarks include tours of Hemingway's French Colonial home, where the author lived from 1931 to 1939, complete with his standing desk and descendants of his mysterious six-toed cats. A lookalike contest devoted to Papa every July at his favorite bar, Sloppy Joe's. Harry S. Truman's "Little White House," where the president spent 175 days of his terms in office. The zero mile marker of U.S. Highway 1. Rainbow flags. Chipped beef on toast at Pepe's Café. Sportfishing for sailfish, tarpon, and permit, among other species.

Sunbathers at Smathers Beach. Quaint B&Bs with rocking chairs on porches in genteel Old Town. Loose roosters in the streets. Key lime pie at Blue Heaven. Key lime pie everywhere.

KIL'T GREENS

TENDER SPRING GREENS CAN'T STAND UP TO hot bacon fat. They wilt—get "kil't"—under the dressing of bacon, onion, and vinegar that makes this traditional Appalachian dish. *See Greens.*

KING, B. B.

(1925–2015)

HE SOMETIMES SEEMED TO BE LISTENING TO Lucille, his guitar, as if translating her emotions rather than his. Born Riley B. King, B. B. King was perhaps the last of the great bluesmen, the self-created ones who rose from sharecropping in Mississippi to worldwide acclaim. Playing in town for tips on Saturday afternoons, he soon found that gospel songs elicited compliments, while the blues got money and beer. "Now you know why I'm a blues singer," he told an interviewer.

He blended the blues with gospel and country. By 1970, with his hit "The Thrill Is Gone," he'd become an idol to legions of long-haired rockers: Eric Clapton, Billy Gibbons, Jimi Hendrix, Duane Allman, and countless others. His licks, phrasing, and facility for bending notes were singular. But it was his inimitable vibrato—stinging, vibrant, alive—that made it possible to hear two notes and instantly know who was playing. He could tear your head off with his guitar or voice, as Bono learned at close range while recording U2's 1988 duet with King, "When Love Comes to Town." Bono recalled how he'd given the song's opening howl everything he had. "And then B. B. King opened up his mouth and I felt like a girl." Who didn't? No serious rocker even tried to compete with him.

What King is less credited for is just as important: his subtlety, restraint, what he didn't play. It made what he did play that much more meaningful. The guitarist Derek Trucks said King's playing "was just the cold hard truth—like hearing Martin Luther King speak. You just needed one word, one note with B. B. No one has that."

KING, CORETTA SCOTT

(1927–2006)

"OFTEN, I AM MADE TO SOUND LIKE AN AT-tachment to a vacuum cleaner: the wife of Martin, then the widow of Martin, all of which I was proud to be," Coretta Scott King told her friend Barbara Reynolds, a writer and minister. "But I was never just a wife, nor a widow." A civil rights fighter who boycotted, marched, and spoke out for social justice, King devoted much of her adult life to Atlanta's Martin Luther King Jr. Center for Nonviolent Social Change, which she founded to pro-mote her late husband's philosophy of peace and methods of resistance. Born in Marion, Alabama, in 1927, Coretta Scott won a schol-arship to the New England Conservatory of Music, where she trained to become a classical singer. A mutual friend set up her first date with Martin Luther King; the two married in 1953 and moved to Montgomery, where violent threats by racist whites loomed over their home. Coretta Scott King realized just how much she was willing to sacrifice for the movement when in 1956 a man threw a bomb through their front window. She called on that courage decades later when she was ar-rested for protesting apartheid, and when she denounced homophobia, a stance that many black pastors then rejected.

KING, MARTIN LUTHER, JR.

(1929–1968)

FROM 1955 UNTIL HIS ASSASSINATION IN 1968, the most prominent and widely known leader of the American civil rights era, the struggle to attain legal equality and economic justice for African Americans; an Atlanta-born Baptist pastor and president of the Southern Christian Leadership Conference; spokes-man for the 1955 Birmingham, Alabama, bus boycott that led to the U.S. Supreme Court's ruling racial segregation on transportation unconstitutional, and leader of the 1963 cam-paign in Birmingham, the televised images of which—showing police responding to demonstrations with fire hoses and attack dogs—helped prompt landmark federal civil rights laws; acclaimed orator of the "I Have a Dream" speech during the 1963 March on Washington; winner, at age thirty-five, of the Nobel Peace Prize; and, as his biography at Atlanta's Martin Luther King Jr. Center for Nonviolent Social Change (an archive and memorial to his legacy) concisely summa-rizes, "one of the greatest nonviolent leaders in world history." "King was trying to tell the nation something it didn't want to hear," the journalist Taylor Branch (who spent more than two decades researching and writing the three-volume history *America in the King Years*) told *Smithsonian Magazine* in 2015, "that we can't put race on the back burner. That race isn't just a Southern problem or a problem of segregation, it's an American problem at the heart of American history and the measure of American democracy." *See Lorraine Motel.*

KING BISCUIT TIME

Inside a small studio in downtown Helena, Arkansas, just across the Mississippi River from the crossroads where Robert Johnson may or may not have sold his soul to the devil, DJ Sunshine Sonny Payne just said, "Pass the biscuits, cause it's King Biscuit Time!" It's what he says at the start of every *King Biscuit Time* radio show, which just aired its 17,737th episode. Who knows how many more will have run by the time you read this, but you could tally it up: one show for every day of the workweek since the show's debut on November 21, 1941, making this blues program the longest running daily radio show in America. Named for King Biscuit flour, a local brand that provided the original financing, *King Biscuit Time* airs on KFFA, which in 1941 was the only station in the area to broadcast music by African Americans; the show took on its unusual 12:15 p.m. time slot to coincide with the lunch hour of black laborers in the Delta. (Nowadays listeners outside the station's range can stream or download episodes on kffa.com.) Members of the original live band included Sonny Boy Williamson and Pinetop Perkins, and the show's influence has been profound, shaping the early musical tastes of such icons as B. B. King, Levon Helm, and Ike Turner.

KING CAKE

New Orleanians can come to blows over which neighborhood bakery—Gambino's, Randazzo's, Dong Phuong's—makes the tastiest king cake, but the truth is that the cherished confection is little more than a gaudily iced coffee cake. Hardwired tradition and ritual—that's what really prods the Crescent City to devour 750,000 of them each year. Cakes containing a hidden prize actually may predate Christianity; by the late nineteenth century, Mardi Gras krewes used them to pick who would preside over the next pre-Lenten soiree. (Lore also holds that an early Mardi Gras king established the cake's purple, green, and gold color scheme to denote justice, faith, and power.) Along the way the coin hidden inside gave way to a tiny baby figurine, and the "reward" for finding the tot in your slice (hopefully without cracking a molar) became the obligation to purchase the next cake. Hence the perpetual supply of king cake in every employee break room in New Orleans during Mardi Gras season—and the reason that giving up dessert is the go-to choice of Lenten penance.

KOLACHES

Kolaches arrived in Texas about a century before Interstate 35, but it's the highway that helped make the yeasty pastry famous. Traveling Texans know to stop in West, about halfway between Austin and Dallas, for its bakeries' interpretations of the Czech sweet—although which bakery makes kolaches best remains a matter of fierce debate. Closely related to Danish, hamantaschen, and other filled pastries with old-world heritage, kolaches arrived in central Texas in the 1850s with immigrants drawn by the promise of cheap land. Soft and puffy, kolaches are typically filled with apricot, prune, poppy seeds, or sweetened farmer cheese, and if they're not hot when you buy them, most kolache bakers will point you toward the microwave. Beyond West, kolaches are sold at gas stations, doughnut shops, and groceries all over Texas, alongside tightly wrapped meat rolls that are classified as kolaches, too. Technically, the sausage version is a klobasnek, but as long as there's not a Czech speaker within earshot, it's fine to ask for a sausage kolache. Heck, ask for two.

KOOL-AID PICKLES

Kool-Aid pickles—a typical recipe mixes four packets of cherry-flavored Kool-Aid with two cups of sugar and a jar of whole dill pickles—originated in kitchens and corner stores of the Mississippi Delta as a quick and cheap method for a sweet-and-sour snack. But

they've since surfaced everywhere from Dallas to the Carolinas, including even fancy restaurants that are experimenting with the form. Eat carefully, lest you end up with electric-red fingers.

KRISPY KREME

As the story goes, a pack of Camels, made in Winston-Salem, North Carolina, inspired Vernon Rudolph to seek his destiny in the city where he would go on to launch an empire. Armed with a yeast doughnut recipe procured from a New Orleans chef, the Marshall County, Kentucky, native set up what was initially a wholesale operation in 1937. But it wasn't long before he cut a hole in the side of the building to sell doughnuts directly to people drawn to the bakery by their noses. Southerners have been lining up ever since, and so has the rest of the world: today Krispy Kreme has more than a thousand locations as far afield as Bangladesh, Saudi Arabia, and Singapore, the smell of those featherlight rounds a persistent come-on for millions who insist that the only doughnuts worth the calories are hot and fresh.

KUDZU

Pueraria lobata: THE VINE FROM HELL, the plant that ate the South. Kudzu was introduced at the Japanese pavilion of the 1876 Centennial Exposition in Philadelphia, for livestock feed and erosion control. It looked real good on paper: kudzu grows in all kinds of dirt, even gummy red clay. A legume like peanuts and clover, it has deep roots that add organic tilth to the soil, hosting bacteria that put nitrogen back in the ground. Starting in 1935, the U.S. government's Soil Conservation Service paid farmers as much as eight bucks an acre to plant it.

Fast growing, propagating by root, seed, and tendril, kudzu has since become the South's most noxious weed, taking over (by some estimates) eight million acres in the last century. Grazed, mowed, and sprayed to scant effect, it spreads across 200,000 new acres annually. It was declared a Federal Noxious Weed in 1998—too late. Entire stands of pine succumbed to kudzu's smothering embrace, as did power lines, phone lines, railroad lines, abandoned farmhouses, entire run-down small farm towns. Goats love kudzu, but, alas, there just weren't enough goats. Giraffes would have helped, but there were none.

During summer, kudzu can grow as much as a foot a day. Doze off on the front porch too long and a kudzu vine will lash you to your rocking chair. True? Almost.

LAKE FLATO

(1959–)

HE IS A BIG MAN, AND HE SAYS "BAM" A LOT. For most people, that's enough to instantly conjure an image of the outsize chef that sent a shock of the South through mainstream American cuisine in the nineties, a man no less Southern for being born in Fall River, Massachusetts, some thousand miles north of the Mason-Dixon. Emeril Lagasse is indelibly linked to his adoptive home of New Orleans, where he took over the legendary Commander's Palace at twenty-six, reshaping the revered but stodgy New Orleans culinary scene. His seems to be a simple, if maximalist, philosophy: that food could be made more exciting with the unrestrained application of spices, hot sauce, and catchphrases, as well as a liberal sampling of global cuisine. His particular brand of New Orleans cooking, dialed to eleven, rolled through the country by way of his TV show, and he happened to become the archetype of the modern celebrity chef in the process. "Kick it up a notch" became a culture-wide tagline for a reason: Emeril asked, and taught his audience to ask, how whatever dish they had in their kitchen could be elevated to some next level. And once it was there, hey, why not kick it up another notch?

LAKE FLATO IS A SAN ANTONIO ARCHITECTURAL firm lauded for its designs that blend groundbreaking sustainability and place-specific, down-to-earth modernism. Lake Flato buildings often incorporate skillfully welded structural steel—a material as indigenous as lumber in oil-field-rich Texas; some Lake Flato buildings incorporate salvaged drill-stem pipe—and always prioritize outdoor living. The firm's first commission, a weekend retreat in South Texas, was "more porch than house," according to Ted Flato, who cofounded the firm with David Lake in 1984. Fresh out of the University of Texas at Austin School of Architecture, the pair worked for the legendary Texas architect O'Neil Ford, a self-professed "pre-modernist." Like their mentor, Flato and Lake put great stock in the wisdom of their antecedents—reliance on local materials and craftsmen, and the ways older shelters overcame the Southwest's blistering summer sun, winter winds, and long dry spells. You could call Lake Flato "pre-green," since the firm's sustainable leanings predate the green-building revolution. Since then, the firm has evolved to incorporate the most advanced technology to model and measure buildings' impact on the environment. But the original instinct—responding to place with simple, beautiful, meaningful designs—still drives the work. Rather than beat back sun and wind with energy-intensive mechanical systems, Lake Flato designs often harness and leverage those natural forces using breezeways, covered outdoor kitchens, courtyards, and porches.

The firm is known for its Porch House concept, which involves site-designing a compound of modular rooms linked by breezeways and other connective tissue. Lake Flato even managed to apply its philosophy to San Antonio's ATT Center, home court of the NBA's Spurs. The architects designed tall porches, loggias, and deep overhangs to soften the coliseum's exterior. Corner stairs wrapped in perforated metal, like sunscreened silos, pull in air for better circulation. An exterior plaza invites visitors outside for beer and tacos. The metal *sombrilla* shading the plaza—a classic Lake Flato detail—was inspired by something Lake saw while driving past a hot, dusty cattle yard: a makeshift shade strung up with cables and cast-off sheets of roofing tin.

LANE CAKE

HARPER LEE PUT LANE CAKE ON THE CULI-nary map in 1960, when *To Kill a Mockingbird*'s heroine, Scout Finch, describes her neighbor's booze-soaked confection as "loaded with shinny." But actually this decadent cake, layered with bourbon, butter, and raisin filling and topped with fluffy egg-white icing, dates back to the late nineteenth century. Originally a West Georgia treat, having first appeared in Clayton native Emma Rylander Lane's self-published 1898 cookbook, *Some Good Things to Eat*, the Lane cake's popularity eventually spread into Alabama and its surrounds. More than a century later, it remains a staple of church socials and other community gatherings. No need to serve it with an after-dinner drink—this spirited dessert stands firmly on its own.

LARD

A PIG STORES FAT ALONG ITS LOINS, IN ITS shoulders, and in a thick casing along its back. There is ruffle fat by the intestines and caul fat near the stomach. But the finest porcine blubber is soft, pure white leaf fat from around the kidneys. Once rendered, it becomes the king of lard. With its high smoke point, leaf lard makes an excellent frying fat, yet its greatest value is to pastry makers. Generations of Southern bakers became masters of piecrust and biscuits thanks to its mild flavor and creamy room-temperature texture. For decades, lard served as the primary cooking fat in the South, cheaper and more readily available than butter or nut oil. But amid misguided health concerns, many bakers switched their allegiance to hydrogenated vegetable oil, aka shortening, in the mid-twentieth century. It wasn't until dietitians and health experts let out a collective "oops" in the 1990s amid studies showing the health risks of trans fats that home cooks began returning to animal fats like lard and butter. You can find jars of leaf lard in gourmet shops; alas, it has become an expensive alternative.

LEE, HARPER

(1926–2016)

by Rick Bragg

Writers, I hear, get to be famous in a quiet kind of way. I have yet to see one depicted on a T-shirt. Their posters appear mostly in libraries, bookstores, and orderly literary festivals, printed with good grammar and dignified fonts. People *will* applaud them, with polite enthusiasm, and might even line up to see them, for a signature or a handshake, but rarely do they push, hoot, or jostle, even for the most famous of them. Nelle Harper Lee was too private, much of her life, even for such as that, and this was part of her great mystery.

I knew a young writer who wanted to meet her. To him, as with so many of us who call ourselves writers, she stood at the zenith of what we wanted to be, for she had written a book that mattered, that had, even in some small way, changed the world. The young writer just wanted to step onto her porch in Monroeville, and, in a perfect world, see the lady herself open the door and say . . . well, anything, "Hello," or "May I help you?" or even "Get off my damn porch." I cannot recall exactly what happened, but I believe he did seek her out, and she was polite to him, as I recall.

Me, I was too proud. I waited till I was almost an old man myself, to go see her. And when I did, I spoke just a few moments about nothing at all and then left too soon, because I was too polite. I left with questions unasked

and the great mysteries unsolved. I doubt if she would have told me any of them anyway, if I had been of a pushy mind. But she was kind, and complimentary, and told an Auburn joke, and though it was already clear that macular degeneration and a profound deafness had begun to imprison her, her legendary wit was still there, and that was a fine gift on a spring afternoon, in a small, hot room in a quiet retirement home in Monroeville, Alabama.

It is widely known that people who knew her called her Nelle.

I think I never called her anything but ma'am, and mumbled that. And then, not long after, in February of 2016, she was gone.

But this, in remembering your idols, may not be the worst it could be.

Published in 1960, *To Kill a Mockingbird* was a kind of gospel, north and south, appealing, through the beauty of story, for us to be better than we were, to live up to our finer natures, and not our baser ones, to rise inside our own consciences and not wallow in the mob. I have written that it was not a cure. The meanness depicted in its story endures and, in the modern day, still often triumphs. Yet the hope in it lingers on, and on.

One of the few who did know her, who shared his thoughts with her in writing, was the respected professor, historian, and author Wayne Flynt, who, with his wife, Dartie, corresponded with her across decades, beginning in 1993. In that fine meantime, they wrote of the world as they saw it, of catfish, Mobile eye doctors, Hebrews 13:8, hateful infirmity, C. S. Lewis, Zora Neale Hurston, whether or not Baptists will tell a lie, and if someone told

Truman Capote that Kennedy had been shot, he would have claimed to have been driving the car. She asked, in writing, if he would preach her funeral.

He did know her.

"Two things I talked to her about," Dr. Flynt said, "I could never tell while she was alive."

One would seem easy, yet has been debated by scholars for decades: What was *Mockingbird*'s theme?

To her, it was simple. It was not just about race, though that will always be the part we most cut ourselves upon, but about all kinds of justice, and fairness, and a sorting out of what it means to get into someone's skin and walk around in it. You never gain any understanding, in a pluralistic society, until you do. She expected smart people, like Flynt, to know this.

In a time "when we needed it as an insight to race, she told it to us in a way that seared our conscience," said Flynt, who is also an ordained Baptist minister.

The other one, of why she did not more quickly follow with another book, is still not perfectly clear, even after years of friendship. He believes it is not one answer but many, including the fact that she was never sure she could write a book of such quality.

"Then she looked at me with those sparkling, inquisitive eyes," he said, and told him, more or less, she didn't have to. Then, only at the end of her life, came the sequel, written not after *Mockingbird*, but before.

Flynt put his and his wife's correspondence with Harper Lee into a lovely book called *Mockingbird Songs*, to, finally, "let her voice become part of the conversation," he said.

The best thing about that long friendship was its depth, and that was also its pain. It broke his heart as her deafness and blindness closed in, and confusion followed, to the point she could not always recognize the people she knew that she should know. It is the price you pay, for the joy of it.

Most of us have only what Harper Lee gave us, which was 376 pages, in paperback.

My niece, Meredith, read the book for the first time recently. When I asked what she would remember, she said "the knothole," where Boo Radley left the treasures for the children to find, before it was filled in with cement, to try to kill a friendship that could not be so easily killed.

Everyone has something that stays inside them, from this book. I hear that when Tennyson died, they rang the bells in London all day, longer. Every time I hear a bell, I think of Tennyson.

Every time I hear a mockingbird, I wish I had stayed longer in that hot little room.

LEWIS, EDNA

(1916–2006)

by Randall Kenan

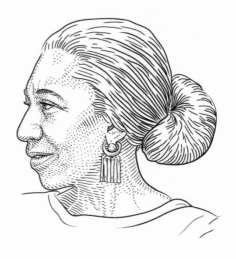

AMONG PEOPLE WHO MET THE CHEF AND author Edna Lewis or who knew her, there's a constant refrain: how regal she was. Very like a queen. Tall, erect, strikingly beautiful, with a beatific smile and a great mane of steel-gray hair, often swathed in a shawl of West African pattern, she did fit that description. And, like her British royal counterpart, soft-spoken, a very decorous, calm, and courteous queen. Imposing but never imperious. This natural nobility sprang from two sources: a pedigree of rich American roots, and an imaginative and skillful culinary mastery.

She was born in 1916, in a small part of Virginia founded and occupied by former slaves and their descendants, appropriately known as Freetown. Freetown gave her the gifts of a lifetime. As her classic 1976 book, *The Taste of Country Cooking*, makes abundantly clear, it gave her a heritage not just of food, but also of traditions and community. The people of Freetown ate sustainably, locally, and farm to table long before those became marketing buzzwords. In direct, supple, and elegant prose, Lewis took the reader to the groaning board of the African American picnic. *The Taste of Country Cooking* is recognizably Southern, but even more, recognizably American, which is the generous lesson Lewis gave us. That book was published well before the renaissance of Southern cooking in the 1980s, when it came to the forefront on

the world stage as a legitimate fine cuisine— before chefs such as Larry Forgione in New York, Stephan Pyles in Dallas, Jeremiah Tower in San Francisco, Mark Miller in Santa Fe, Paul Prudhomme in New Orleans, Jasper White in Boston, and Bill Neal in Chapel Hill, North Carolina, received international recognition and won major awards. Lewis's book also seemed to rhyme with what the Berkeley, California, chef Alice Waters had been doing and saying about using fresh, local, organic foods—ushering in a new American whole-foods diet.

Edna Lewis, it would seem, was destined from early on to become a legend, in culinary circles at least. Having left home at sixteen, she wound up in New York by way of Washington, D.C. In the late 1940s, at Café Nicholson on East Fifty-Eighth Street, she was cooking for Southern expatriates (the likes of Truman Capote, Tennessee Williams, and

William Faulkner) and for other bigwigs—Marlon Brando, Richard Avedon, Gloria Vanderbilt, Eleanor Roosevelt, Greta Garbo, Salvador Dalí. She was known for simple yet dynamically delicious fare: perfectly roasted chicken, seafood prepared with wine, cheese and chocolate soufflés; always mindful of what vegetables were in season, of freshness, and above all of flavor. It would take decades, though, for Lewis to receive the broader recognition befitting her accomplishments. After Café Nicholson closed, she would go on to cook at Gage & Tollner in Brooklyn, the Fearrington House Restaurant outside Chapel Hill, and Middleton Place in Charleston, South Carolina.

Her legacy goes beyond her books, which include (in addition to *The Taste of Country Cooking*) *The Edna Lewis Cookbook* (1972), *In Pursuit of Flavor* (1988), and *The Gift of Southern Cooking*, which she cowrote in 2003 with the lauded chef Scott Peacock before her death in 2006. Now we have the Edna Lewis Foundation, a nonprofit (in the words of its founder, the chef Joe Randall) "dedicated to honoring, preserving, and nurturing African Americans' culinary heritage and culture." And a generation of chefs, cooks, and food writers—some of whom are only now coming to recognize her regency, their debt to her, and her great good gifts.

LEWIS, JERRY LEE

(1935–)

TAKE A GANDER AT THE ICONIC 1956 PHOTOGRAPH taken at Memphis's Sun Studios of the "Million Dollar Quartet"—Elvis Presley, Johnny Cash, Carl Perkins, and Jerry Lee Lewis—and it's hard to square that Lewis is the last surviving member. Already known as a hell-raiser both on the piano and in his personal life, Lewis shot to early rock-and-roll superstardom with the indelible hits "Whole Lotta Shakin' Goin' On" and "Great Balls of Fire" before scandal erupted over his marriage to a thirteen-year-old cousin. Years playing in the beer-joint wilderness followed, punctuated by the deaths of two later wives under mysterious circumstances, his conspicuously dropping an f-bomb at the Grand Ole Opry, and an infamous arrest for ramming his Lincoln Continental into the gates at Graceland. Induction into the Rock and Roll Hall of Fame in 1986 helped return Lewis to the firmament, followed by a 1989 biopic in which he was portrayed to the hilt by Dennis Quaid. These days, the octogenarian formerly known as the Killer likes to watch old *Gunsmoke* episodes at his ranch near Memphis, but when he takes the stage at a Mississippi casino or a hip London club, it doesn't take long for that old fire to light up his eyes—and the ivories.

LEWIS, JOHN

(1940-)

HE WOULD LATER SAY IT WAS THE MOST frightened he'd been in his life. Which was saying something. As twenty-five-year-old John Lewis led six hundred people across the Edmund Pettus Bridge in March 1965 to walk from Selma, Alabama, to the capital, Montgomery, to protest barriers to black voter registration, he had already endured round after round of violence in his quest to defy injustice. Inspired by the Montgomery bus boycotts and their engineer, Dr. Martin Luther King Jr., he was hit while sitting in at segregated Nashville lunch counters as a college student, punched in the face in Rock Hill, South Carolina, and knocked unconscious with a Coca-Cola crate in Montgomery as one of the first thirteen Freedom Riders testing the Supreme Court ruling that barred segregation of interstate transportation hubs. As one of the organizers of the Student Non-Violent Coordinating Committee, he refused to strike back every time he was threatened, or beaten, which was often; still, he was arrested some forty times in the sixties alone. But on that Bloody Sunday in Selma, when his skull was fractured by the business end of a billy club as a line of 150 Alabama state troopers brutally advanced on the peaceful marchers, horrifying a nation, his courage helped lead to, days later, President Lyndon B. Johnson's taking landmark voting rights legislation to Congress—the Voting Rights Act was signed into law that August.

Heroes are often defined by one act. One bout of bravery, whether on the battlefield or at a burning car on the highway. But John Lewis never stopped to rest on his laurels. Instead, this son of Alabama sharecroppers dedicated his life to securing human rights and civil liberties, driven by his moral convictions and his desire for what he calls "the beloved community"—a society free from the burdens of race. In 1986, more than twenty years after he helped MLK organize the March on Washington, at which he gave a keynote speech at age twenty-three, he brought the movement back to the nation's capital when he was elected to the House of Representatives representing an Atlanta district. There, he has served for three decades, fighting for the likes of health care for the uninsured, LGBT rights, and a museum to honor the contributions of black Americans. That dream was finally realized in the fall of 2016, when the Smithsonian's National Museum of African American History and Culture opened on the Mall. President Barack Obama added the highest civilian honor, the Presidential Medal of Freedom, to Lewis's cavalcade of honors and awards over the years, a list that now includes a National Book Award, for the third in his coauthored best-selling trilogy of graphic novels called *March*, which depict the civil rights movement through Lewis's eyes. Not bad for a man who was once denied a library card as a boy in Troy, Alabama. *See Edmund Pettus Bridge.*

LIONFISH

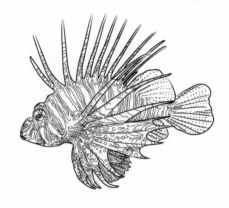

Ornery fish with venomous spines, lionfish don't play well with others. The invasive swimmers—natives of the South Pacific and Indian Oceans and popular aquarium specimens—are spreading like the plague: first spotted off the coast of Florida in 1985, they're now established as far up the Atlantic coast as North Carolina, and throughout the Caribbean. Scientists say they're feasting so ravenously on native fish including grouper and snapper that they're becoming obese. Now, humans are biting back. Fishermen gather for lionfish derbies in Florida and elsewhere, and coastal chefs have begun putting them on the menu in an effort to dent the population. Given that the fish must be speared one at a time, they don't come cheap or easy, and the outlook for eradicating them from the reefs they've colonized is pessimistic at best. On the upside, their light, buttery meat is positively luxurious.

LIVE OAK

Officially the Southern live oak, *Quercus virginiana*, the beloved and iconic coastal hardwood spreads its blessings from Virginia to East Texas. It's a shade provider, an air-conditioner, and a source of provender for wildlife—woodpeckers, fish crows, sundry ducks, turkeys, squirrels, bears, coons, deer—and in the olden time, people (their crushed acorns make tolerable mush and passable flatbread, once you get the bitter leeched out).

A live oak can take a lightning bolt, droop and wither a few days, then come back as good as new. Wildfire can burn the heart right out, roaring up into the trunk, throwing smoke and sparks like a steam engine at full throttle . . . and the tree will still live another century.

Colonial shipbuilders loved live oaks, hewing the gentle swoop of the limbs into ribs, and making the crotches into brackets and the trunk into hull planking. Live oaks from Georgia's St. Simons Island built the *USS Constitution*, laid down in 1797 and named by George Washington. Sailors called her Old Ironsides after British cannonballs bounced off her live oak in 1812. She's still afloat.

Cut a live oak at your peril. The trees are often protected, and the law might make you replace it "inch for inch." A sixty-inch live oak equals eight saplings at about two grand each. Plus freight. Plus labor.

LIVERMUSH

You've probably heard the old chestnut about American Indians using every part of the bison, from hide to horns. Below the Mason-Dixon, the hog is our *tatanka*. You name it, we've eaten it: ears, snout, feet, tail, and, yes, liver. In and around Shelby, North Carolina, the pork-liver-and-cornmeal loaf known as livermush in fact remains a staple. Fans keep the product on supermarket shelves in both Carolinas, even as a new generation far removed from the family farm and menus that make the most of the hog finds it hard to swallow. Most people eat livermush on a plate with grits and eggs, or on biscuits with mustard or jelly, but it isn't just for breakfast. At Mush, Music & Mutts, an annual livermush festival in Shelby, you'll find everything from livermush pizza to livermush fried rice. One thing all livermush lovers can agree on, though: it should be sliced thin and fried hard, in plenty of butter. Because despite the name, "mush" isn't the goal.

LOMAX, ALAN

(1915–2002)

The South's indigenous sounds—blues, gospel, jazz, bluegrass, zydeco—are such an integral soundtrack of the region that we've sometimes taken them for granted. God bless Alan Lomax for knowing better. Starting out at the age of seventeen with his father, John, the native Texan spent much of the 1930s and 1940s documenting the various strains of American folk music for the Library of Congress. He was exhaustive to the point of obsession, happily hauling a bulky three-hundred-pound recording machine deep into Appalachian hollers and Delta cotton fields if tipped off that there was an authentic voice to be found there. His so-called field recordings captured prison work songs and sacred choirs, banjo pickers and slide-guitar innovators, and, incredibly, he was the first to record the seminal figures Lead Belly, Muddy Waters, and Woody Guthrie. The interviews Lomax also conducted showed the artistry of his subjects *and* his deep respect for them. To help folk music find an audience (as Lomax put it, give "a voice to the voiceless"), he became a radio host and record producer, but continued his forays afield into the 1990s. Today, the Association for Cultural Equity has digitized more than seventeen thousand audio files from his collection. Ethnomusicologists (as they are now called) will study those recordings forever—though Lomax would most likely tell his acolytes to get out and spend some time on the back roads, too.

As state nicknames go, the Lone Star State beats the hell out of Land of Enchantment and America's Dairyland. (Sorry, New Mexico and Wisconsin, you had your chance to do better.) It helps that the nickname's origin predates the state of Texas itself, even if the meaning is a bit fuzzy. What historians do know is that when early Texans fought to gain independence from Mexico (you remember the Alamo, right?), they devised flags bearing a single large star. To some that star may have represented Texas's brief status as an independent republic; to others it may have expressed a desire to join the United States. Texas did just that in 1845, and in 1889 adopted an official flag that prominently featured a lone star. Today it represents the still stubbornly independent spirit of Texans, but it is ubiquitous, emblazoned on everything from license plates to steakhouses. You can even ask about the state nickname in just about any bar in Texas and be handed a cold beer. Which probably doesn't work in Oregon—the Beaver State.

Once the dominant tree of Southern coastal plains, longleaf covered ninety-three million acres from Virginia to Texas, forests that were dependent on brush fire for their regeneration (longleaf seeds will not germinate unless cracked by fire). It takes a century to grow a longleaf sawlog, but it's worth the wait. The wood of *Pinus palustris* is fine grained and beautiful, unbelievably strong, rot resistant, and termite proof. In 1538, the de Soto expedition walked for days through cathedral groves.

Today the trees are mostly gone. The forests were stripped after the Civil War and longleaf timber went around the world, shoring up European mines and framing Buckingham Palace. An entire ecosystem went with it— panthers, bears, ivory-billed woodpeckers. A scant million acres of longleaf remain, the rest replaced by yellow pine planted and harvested like corn. It takes only twenty-five years to make a crop of yellow pine, fated to become toothpick timber, chipboard, and paper. But groups such as the Longleaf Alliance are pushing to bring the original trees back—five acres, ten, a hundred at a time. Meanwhile, there is a booming business in recycling longleaf timbers from factories, warehouses, and mills into flooring, wainscoting, and countertops. Run your hands across a thirty-inch board and count the rings: right back to de Soto.

LORRAINE MOTEL

by Hampton Sides

THEY LEFT THE ROOM UNTOUCHED, JUST the way it looked on that terrible day. The rumpled bedspread. The old rotary phone. The scattered coffee cups in their saucers. The mod sixties furniture, set against a wall of knotty prefab paneling. The black-and-white TV, rabbit ears tuned to the staticky world. You stand behind the Plexiglas divider, and see the room more or less the way Martin Luther King Jr. left it when he cinched his tie and headed out the door—and into martyrdom.

The tableau is simple, even mundane, and yet it grabs you: personal effects transform into relics; period pieces become stand-ins for the souls who last occupied the space. A freeze-frame of the precise moment an era ended.

At a little before six o'clock in the evening, on April 4, 1968, the civil rights leader emerged onto the balcony and stood in front of the now-iconic turquoise door, Room 306. Did he realize how vulnerable he was up there? Did he have a premonition of his own death? "I may not get there with you," he'd said the night before. But "we, as a people, will get to the Promised Land."

From a motel corridor, you gaze at the brick rooming house where James Earl Ray brandished a .30-06 rifle from the window of a grungy bathroom. You look down at the balcony floor, where King fell with a ragged wound to his neck and jaw. You try to imagine what really happened at that moment, and what larger plots may have been churning in the margins of history.

The Lorraine Motel—home of the National Civil Rights Museum, which has recently undergone a $27.5 million renovation—is something every Southerner, every American, every human, needs to see. Any place erected on the site of an assassination is liable to skew toward the macabre, but somehow the Lorraine doesn't. Set among warehouses and railroad depots in downtown Memphis's South Main Historic Arts District, the Lorraine is a pilgrimage shrine—holy ground with an ineffable power.

For a long time, through the seventies and eighties, many of the town fathers lobbied to tear down what was then a ratty, vice-ridden haven for addicts and prostitutes—an embarrassment, they said, and an eyesore. But for a handful of forward-thinking people, the Lorraine would have succumbed to the wrecking ball. Dedicated in 1991, the museum has become one of the city's greatest attractions, with more than 265,000 yearly visitors. "This is everybody's museum," the NCRM's president, Terri Lee Freeman, has said. "What it should do, frankly, is light a fire under us."

And it does. People come here from around the world to contemplate the power of nonviolent protest. Others come to enact rituals, exorcise demons, and expiate sins. There's a reason the Lorraine has been visited by the likes of the Dalai Lama and Nelson Mandela and Bono. The museum—and especially Room 306, the heart and soul of the enterprise—has a haunting potency that must be experienced to be understood.

Just below the balcony, beside a finny vintage Cadillac permanently parked in the lot, a stone marker proclaims: "Behold, here cometh the dreamer . . . let us slay him . . . we shall see what will become of his dreams." And yet it's here, at the very spot where he fell, that his dreams feel most emphatically alive.

LOWCOUNTRY

SACRED GROUND IN SOUTH CAROLINA AND Georgia, the Lowcountry hugs the coast, stretching from the Sea Islands to the Sandhills (the eastern edge of South Carolina's Midlands). Roaring surf, pungent dead-end creeks, bright brimming inlets, and lazy rivers. Blue crabs, mullet, redfish, sea trout, and shrimp. Oaks, plantations, palmettos, pine, porpoises, and 7,500 square miles of some of the loveliest country on earth. Charleston, the Holy City, is its undisputed capital.

Beauty was nearly the Lowcountry's undoing, as several hundred thousand folks have relocated here, making it the fastest-growing region in the country many years running. But thanks to public/private initiatives, half this coast will remain forever wild.

LUNCH COUNTER

by John T. Edge

THE LUNCH COUNTER, ONCE COMMON IN DEpartment stores across the region, was not a Southern innovation. Like the space itself, the foods typically served there, from club sandwiches to hamburgers and fries and apple pies, were more broadly American than specifically Southern. Lunch counters became sacred Southern spaces on February 1, 1960, when four black college students at North Carolina A&T—Ezell Blair Jr., Franklin McCain, Joseph McNeil, and David Richmond—took seats at a Woolworth's lunch counter in Greensboro and ordered coffee and pie that never came.

Blacks had previously protested segregated service in Southern restaurants. Perseverance distinguished this effort. When they were rejected, the students didn't leave their counterstool perches. They literally sat in, determined to wait out the white waitresses who refused them coffee and subvert the Jim Crow laws that dictated second-class treatment of black citizens.

Woolworth's closed early on that winter day. Twenty more students joined the next day. By the end of the week, the crowd of activists neared three hundred. Word of the sit-ins spread, and demonstrations began in Winston-Salem, Wilmington, and south of the border in Rock Hill, South Carolina. Within two months, students in more than fifty cities had staged sit-ins.

There was power in their protest. Reflecting on the moment, McCain, who died in 2014, said, "Fifteen seconds after I sat on that stool, I had the most wonderful feeling. I had a feeling of liberation, restored manhood; I had a natural high. And I truly felt almost invincible."

There was also power in the lunch counter. Sharing a meal signaled social equality in the Jim Crow South. Like sex, eating was perceived as a deeply intimate act. And no eating space was more intimate than the lunch counter, where diners stooped to take their seats and eat with neighbors and strangers alike.

Instead of integrating during the four-year-plus struggle that began in the winter of 1960, some lunch counters closed. Others removed their stools. Writing in the *Carolina Israelite* newspaper, Harry Golden unpacked the absurdity of the moment. "It is only when the Negro 'sets' that the fur begins to fly," he wrote, proposing a tongue-in-cheek solution. The Vertical Negro Plan called for refashioning segregated sit-down lunch counters into integrated stand-up restaurants.

Golden was being playful. But the stakes were high. And so was the drama. In Jackson, Mississippi, a 1963 Woolworth's sit-in escalated into one of the most violent of the era. When an integrated group led by college students attempted to gain service, a mob of white counterprotesters threw salt in their eyes, dumped mustard on their heads, and dragged one protester to the floor, where they kicked him repeatedly.

When President Johnson signed the Civil Rights Act of 1964 into law on July 2, he outlawed segregation in restaurants and other places of public accommodation. The law restored dignity to black patrons of white restaurants and set the stage for a modern restaurant industry that now thrives in the South.

After a long absence, Southerners have returned to communal dining. Large unbroken tables—introduced as class equalizers during the French Revolution, copied by American hotels in the nineteenth century, and interpreted as lunch counters in the twentieth—are regaining popularity. At the Beatty Street Grocery, a Jackson, Mississippi, café that abuts a scrap-metal yard, white construction workers in brogans and black government bureaucrats in cap-toes gather today at high-top counters to eat fried bologna sandwiches on toasted white bread. Fifty years after the South desegregated its restaurants, shared meals like these showcase the rapid pace of change in the region and the promise of the welcome table ideal.

LYNN, LORETTA

(1932–)

SHE WAS BORN A COAL MINER'S DAUGHTER IN Butcher Hollow, Kentucky, became a young wife and mother who turned her life with a philandering husband into country gold, and is now revered as the Queen of Country Music. Brash hits such as "Fist City," "The Pill," and "Rated X" were girl-power anthems in the 1960s and '70s, ones that conservative country radio programmers wouldn't touch.

"I was just singing about what was going on," Lynn once said. "They weren't used to hearing a woman talk like that. Well, they found out with me!" In later years, her fearless attitude attracted the likes of the rocker Jack White, who produced her 2004 Grammy-winning comeback album, *Van Lear Rose*, and her plainspoken, straight-shooting songs have inspired a legion of present-day female country music stars, from Miranda Lambert to Kacey Musgraves.

LYNYRD SKYNYRD

PIONEERS OF A DRIVING, POWERFUL, THREE-guitar Southern rock sound, the band was dismissed by early critics as boozy, sloppy, and self-indulgent. With thirty-five million records sold and indestructible hits—"Sweet Home Alabama," "Free Bird," and "Gimme Three Steps," perpetually in heavy rotation on classic rock radio—Lynyrd Skynyrd (named for a Gainesville, Florida, high-school phys-ed teacher who hated long hair) is having the last laugh. The band was discovered by the musician and producer Al Kooper in an Atlanta nightclub in 1972. Within a year, a debut album, *(Pronounced 'Lĕh-'nérd 'Skin-'nérd)*, had gone gold and the band was opening for the Who on a national tour. Between 1973 and 1977, they released five highly successful albums. Three days after the release of *Street Survivors* in 1977—with the album's cover presciently featuring the band members surrounded by flames—a chartered plane carrying band and crew crashed near Gillsburg, Mississippi, killing singer and main lyricist Ronnie Van Zant, guitarist Steve Gaines, and backup singer Cassie Gaines. Most of the survivors were seriously injured, and no band recorded under the name Lynyrd Skynyrd for ten years. The original band has remained controversial, some branding them racist rednecks, others defending them as misunderstood. "Sweet Home Alabama," for example, contains a famous swipe at Neil Young, although in fact the band and Young were friends and admirers of one another's work. In the cover shot of *Street Survivors*, you can just make out that Van Zant sports a Neil Young *Tonight's the Night* T-shirt beneath his jacket.

"Dinner not as elegant as when we dined before," wrote the Reverend Manasseh Cutler in 1802 after a meal at the White House. President Thomas Jefferson's unusual macaroni casserole, soused with flour and butter, had confused and displeased the representative from Massachusetts. Inspired by Jefferson's travels in France and Italy, that early dish may not have much resembled today's universally familiar comfort food—but in 1824, Mary Randolph (the wife of a cousin of Jefferson's) published a familiar recipe in *The Virginia Housewife*: boil pasta, layer with cheese and butter, and bake. Southerners have followed her lead ever since. Once an indicator of wealth and luxury made with imported noodles and cheese, mac and cheese is now enshrined as one of our most democratic sides. Velveeta and chopped hot dogs are as likely to cement the noodles at a barbecue joint or church fund-raiser as Parmesan, ham, and peas. Black and white, rich and poor, we've made this once-exotic recipe our own.

Madeira wine ranked among the most popular quaffs of the colonial era, owing to both geography and politics. It was produced on the Portuguese island of Madeira, off the coast of Morocco. Steered by favorable currents and winds, ships bound for the North American colonies from Europe often passed near Madeira, making it one of the last spots for provisioning and stockpiling trade goods before the crossing.

That was the geography. The island's wine industry was also abetted by politics: the British Parliament exempted the islands from the Navigation Acts, thanks to the marriage of King Charles II and Portugal's Catherine of Braganza. This essentially turned the island into a proto–duty-free zone and promoted commerce with the British colonies.

Madeira wine was not known for quality originally. It improved, however, through careful cultivation and blending as demand for more refined wines grew abroad. Like port, Madeira was eventually fortified with brandy or other high-proof distillate to stabilize it during the long months in transit, rocking in sweltering cargo bays. Many found the fortified taste agreeable, among them Thomas Jefferson, who frequently bought quantities of Madeira for his cellar. But then he was posted to France, discovered superior French wine, and thereafter spurned the stuff.

With the recent interest in beverages resuscitated from the past, Madeira has been making a low-key comeback in shops and bars around the South. It's worth sipping in a snifter or mixing sparingly in a cocktail.

MAGNOLIA

by Frances Mayes

W ELL, HOW ARE YOU, MAGNOLIA? LOOKING
pretty as ever," my uncle always greeted
a woman whose name he could not remember.
(Men were designated "Coach.") "Magnolia,"
of course, speaks metaphoric volumes: it her-
alds the woman as a flower of the South, as
mysterious and beautiful, her skin flawless; it
acknowledges her fragrant allure. And that
flower of the South knew full well that my
uncle had no idea what her name was.

Magnolia grandiflora, a true native. Does
any other flower have quite the mystique? The
California poppy, the Washington cherry, the
Texas bluebonnet? Not a chance. They lack
a perfume as strong as knockout drops, they
lack the magnitude of the creamy tight buds
that open into face-size blossoms of extravagant beauty, and they lack gravitas. At the first
funeral I ever attended, a full-open magnolia
blossom lay on top of the gleaming, dark wood
coffin. One was enough.

When I lived for many years in California,
the lost scents of the South haunted me most.
Anytime I returned, I'd find myself outside
after dinner, listening to the screeching cho-
rus of tree frogs and night birds, just breathing in the layers of sweet, dank, fecund air.
To me, moonlight smells like honeysuckle.
When I was small, my bicycle leaned behind
a big mother gardenia against the red barn.
Cycling reminds me of the cloying, decadent
presence of those flowers that bruised brown
when I touched the petals. I'm amazed when
my scraggly daphne bush sends out heavenly

blasts that no conjurer of scents ever came
close to capturing in a bottle. Jasmine spreading around the front steps may be home for
copperheads, but the narcotizing perfume
rising to the porch compensates for that
inconvenience.

I have all these scents and others in my
North Carolina garden. When I bought this
1806 house, I acquired an immense garden of
old roses. For a couple of late spring weeks,
these heritage roses send out delicate whiffs.
Maybe it's the names that transport me—
Comtesse de Murinais, Clotilde Soupert,
Albertine, Louise Odier. Here's the atmosphere of Proust's *À la recherche du temps perdu*
right smack in the Piedmont pinewoods.
All this fragrance of jasmine, honeysuckle,
daphne, gardenia, rose—our magical scents,
yes, but the truest Eau de South, I must insist,
remains the magnolia.

The big tree is as primitive as anything
in a rain forest: leaves with undersides like
suede riding chaps, tough cones, low limbs
grabbing the ground and sprouting, dense
roots that crowd out anything that's trying
to grow. We have two towering magnolias,
one far enough away from the house that the
shed piles of tough leaves don't bother me,
the other too close to my bedroom window.
Though it blocks light, I love the sunlight
glossing the leaves, especially when they're
dusted with snow. And on a summer night
when I raise the window, the soft, waxy
sweetness of the ethereal flowers suffuses the
room. That's when I think, "Why live anywhere else, ever?"

MANATEES

by Roy Blount, Jr.

IT IS EASY TO CHUCKLE AT THE ANCIENT sailors who mistook manatees for mermaids, not to mention the biologists who (with a wink?) classified the order of manatees as Sirenia, for the mythological sirens who lured sailors to their deaths. According to the messy secondhand version we have of Christopher Columbus's journal of his first journey to the Americas, he (translation from the fifteenth-century copier's Spanish) "quite distinctly saw three mermaids, which rose well out of the sea; but they are not so beautiful as they are said to be, for their faces had some masculine traits."

Masculine as in whiskery; but unmaidenly in more respects than that. Male or female, a manatee looks like an overstuffed duffel bag, a vegan walrus, a pacifist torpedo, a boneless moose, a cross between a seal and a shar-pei dog. And yet, gender aside, a manatee is a charmer.

They're *affable* animals. They are no threat to people, or even to fish. They are nuzzlers. They coexist uneventfully with alligators, except when a manatee tries to play with an alligator. Alligators don't play. Which is not to say that an alligator will turn around and kick a manatee's butt when a manatee does a couple of barrel rolls next to an alligator and then mouths the alligator's foot. No, the alligator just goes like give-me-a-break and swims away. Manatee meat is tasty according to many human accounts, but to an alligator, a manatee is—I'm guessing—too big, too hey-hey-buddy, and, literally, too thick-skinned.

Alligators have no sense of humor. And as far as we can tell, fine, they can live with that. Maybe it is more of a challenge to be a manatee, to live with having neither sentient prey nor natural enemies. Watch video of somebody swimming with manatees: they are like, "Uh, hello. Are you from some other planet? Well, then, let's nuzzle." Manatees tend to have scars from motorboat encounters. Conceivably, they would like to play with motorboats. But motorboats kill them, and so do carelessly discarded fishing line (maybe manatees think they can unsnarl backlashes, but now I'm just kidding) and plastic six-pack things (maybe they want a beer, and now I'm not kidding as much).

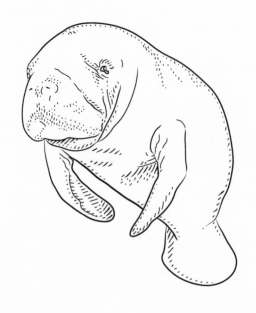

Manatees are called sea cows, because they are hefty, they mosey along, and they graze—on aquatic plants such as floating hyacinth, pickerelweed, alligator weed, musk grass, sea clover, and something called manatee grass, which is also grazed on by surgeonfish, sea urchins, and possibly pinfish but is particularly important to the manatee diet. It looks hard to digest.

So life for a manatee is not as easy as it looks. But manatees sleep for half the day, sinking to the bottom of the shallow, mostly fresh waters they inhabit (from Virginia to Texas), and bobbing up to the surface every twenty minutes or so, to breathe, *fbluh*, because they are mammals. They get pneumonia if the water is lower than sixty degrees, so they find their way to warm springs (which are dying out) and power stations. The manatee's teeth are way back behind its prehensile upper lip, which is divided into independent halves and is used to rustle up dinner and also to communicate with other manatees, and with human swimmers, by touch. But you shouldn't touch them anymore, because that makes them more vulnerable. They are said to show signs of complex associative learning, and to have good long-term memory.

They may weigh more than a ton. And the only reason a given manatee doesn't live for sixty years is something or other human.

MANGROVE

STILT-LIKE AND NEARLY SPECTRAL, MANgroves appear to walk on water. Their dense tangles of exposed roots prop up the evergreen foliage above, which attracts hordes of nesting terns, herons, and other birds. But the real magic occurs underwater. A dendritic webbing of mangrove roots slows tidal currents, traps nutrient-rich sediments, and forms its own ecosystem of oysters and muck, crabs and baitfish, and the tarpon and redfish and snook that lurk in the labyrinth, poised for ambush.

Worldwide, there are some eighty species of mangrove, none of which can tolerate freezing temperatures, so that limits them in the United States to subtropical shores such as Florida's Everglades and Ten Thousand Islands. There, three species of mangrove—red, black, and white—form smaller hummocks and larger islands and armor shorelines for mile after mile. They, in turn, attract a species that can't exist in the mangroves without the help of sunscreen, beer, and shallow-draft boats: anglers intent on pulling fish from their clutches.

MANNERS

IN HIS BOOK *Outside the Southern Myth*, the late Mississippi scholar Noel Polk made as shrewd and concise a definition of Southern manners as any: that they "operate as a general commitment to *niceness*; they anticipate and head off if possible any sort of rupture in the fabric of whatever interaction is taking place."

MARDI GRAS

by Guy Martin

IT'S NOT ENTIRELY CLEAR HOW THE MANY riotous, drunken pagan celebrations of fertility at the approach of the vernal equinox grew over the millennia to become riotous, drunken Christian blowouts prior to Lent. But it's fair to say that the party impulse is an organic one as the days lengthen and the planting season begins—fertility is on the brain because it is in the genome.

As it does with so many other excuses to party, the Deep South, along what we'll call the French Gulf coast, has honed its Fat Tuesday celebrations to a fine, hot dagger point over the last three centuries. Nosing his way up the Mississippi in March 1699, Pierre Le Moyne, Sieur d'Iberville, camped at the confluence of a small bayou and the river roughly sixty miles downstream from what would twenty years later become New Orleans. It's not recorded whether Iberville and his men got drunk or even had any wine with them on the evening of March 3—probably not. As emissaries of the king, Iberville and his brother Jean-Baptiste, Sieur de Bienville, were not enormously bibulous or extreme characters. But Iberville was enough of a churchman or enough of a pre-Lenten celebrant (we don't know which) to mark his little bivouac as the Pointe du Mardi Gras. It was a jolly name, or at least it conveys jollity three hundred years on, but it's a fair assumption that it wasn't all that damned jolly around the campfire on Iberville's expedition that evening. The French boys were roughing it in 1699 down on the Mississippi. So it's likely that the name Pointe du Mardi Gras contains more than a dollop of gallows irony. At any rate, it's thought that this is the first moment that the day was registered on the North American continent, if not exactly celebrated.

In 1703, one of Bienville's original troops, Nicholas Langlois, thought that Mardi Gras would help boost spirits at the garrison in the capital of French Louisiana, Mobile. We don't know quite how this "celebration" worked out, either. But nevertheless, Monsieur Langlois's Mardi Gras is still considered the founding moment of organized Mardi Gras celebrations on the continent—a dozen years before Bienville and his troops even found the bend in the river that would become New Orleans. Needless to say, this fact sticks in the craw of the historically minded latter-day proponents of the holiday there, for whom Mardi Gras has become an incendiary necessity of life itself.

The message of any bacchanal with a proscribed end—especially that of Mardi Gras—is one of tolerance. For those of us who know what Mardi Gras in Mobile or

New Orleans (or Galveston or Pensacola) can become, some words of wisdom from Ronal Serpas, a former New Orleans police chief, ring truest. The police are the soldiers of Mardi Gras—we celebrate, they serve. After noting that any one block on a parade route in New Orleans could hold ten thousand people, Serpas observed, with not a little understatement: "The thing about Mardi Gras is, we get the impression that quite a number of the people have been drinking."

MARDI GRAS INDIANS

Of all the colorful and curious sights that bombard the senses during New Orleans' Mardi Gras celebrations, none are more colorful and curious than the Mardi Gras Indians. Origins are murky, but just as white society formed parade "krewes" inspired by Roman and Greek mythology for carnival season, black neighborhoods developed social clubs named after imaginary Indian tribes—Yellow Pocahontas, Wild Tchoupitoulas, Red Hawk Hunters, and dozens more. They started parading in native-inspired costumes in the mid-nineteenth century, competing (and frequently rumbling) with other tribes. Today's processions are raucous but generally peaceful affairs, with rivalries channeled into ever-more-elaborate finery—a tribe's Big Chief can spend a year fashioning a feather-and-bead headdress and suit so massive (a hundred pounds or more) it suggests a walking parade float. His similarly bedecked retinue includes "spyboys" who scout for rival tribes, a "wildman" who wields a symbolic spear, and a second line of musicians and revelers. Meetings on the street with other tribes lead to prideful displays of costumes and dancing, and plenty of taunting insults. You won't spot Indians tossing beads to undergrads along St. Charles Avenue, though. Their processions mostly stick to the neighborhoods that spawned them, with starting times and places passed along by word of mouth. One could spend twenty carnivals in New Orleans and never once encounter a Mardi Gras Indian—and that would be a shame.

MARSH TACKY

The official South Carolina State Heritage Horses, Marsh Tackies were once common on the Sea Islands of South Carolina and Georgia. Around fourteen hands high and 750 pounds, they can be buckskins, bays, milkshake grullas, red roans, even blue roans. They have double manes, long tails to beat back the bugs, and hard, flinty hooves—sure-footed easy keepers, with a sixth sense of getting around in the woods.

Legend pegged them as descendants of horses that Spanish explorers loosed here in the 1500s. But experts rolled their eyes—pure horse pucky, they insisted. Tackies were just scrub horses, like the wild Chincoteague ponies of Virginia's Eastern Shore, stunted by centuries of poor diet, casual care, and indifferent breeding. It didn't matter. Tackies served their purpose as Indian ponies and Revolutionary and Rebel cavalry mounts, pulling wagons and plows, hauling the midwife and the mail, carrying high-rolling Northern quail hunters through thicket and briar, and finally the famed Pony Patrol, riding beaches looking for German saboteurs during World War II.

Eventually John Deere and Henry Ford put an end to their necessity. The tackies' numbers dwindled and the breed seemed on a fast track to extinction, until DNA testing finally confirmed their Spanish blood. Now there's a breed association, a registry, and a studbook, all DNA-confirmed. And their numbers are up—four hundred and counting.

MARTHA WHITE FLOUR

THUMB THROUGH CERTAIN SOUTHERN CHURCH cookbooks and you'll notice recipes that specify using Martha White flour. This is *not* an idle suggestion. If you make biscuits, piecrust, or fried chicken with something else—well, bless your heart. Still don't believe it? Try telling your mother-in-law you prefer the store brand. *See Flour.*

MASON-DIXON LINE

WHEN THE BRITISH ASTRONOMERS CHARLES Mason and Jeremiah Dixon completed their survey of the boundary between Maryland and Pennsylvania (latitude 39°43'26.3" N) in 1767, little could they have known that their names would one day become synonymous with the division between North and South. At the time they were only settling a land dispute. By the 1800s, though, the Mason-Dixon Line had been stretched westward along the northern borders of West Virginia, Kentucky, and Missouri, becoming the dividing line between free and slaveholding states. Offering the country a simple line drawn between North and South, a partition in every other way so complicated and confusing, the Mason-Dixon Line has since become shorthand for the point at which the nation's political, cultural, and social identities shift. Although the origins of the nickname Dixie for the South remain ambiguous, one theory holds that it is an adaptation of Jeremiah Dixon's name. Surely this would have come as a great surprise to Dixon, as he spent only a handful of years in the United States. At home in England, however, it was said Dixon was fond of wearing bright red and drinking to excess, which does suggest a deep affiliation with much of Alabama.

MASON JARS

ONE POPULAR ONLINE COOKWARE RETAILER offers a mason jar cocktail shaker for $29.95, with an exhortation to "pour on the Southern hospitality." Keep looking around, and you'll find every kind of mason jar barware for sale somewhere. How have we come to this? The use of these ubiquitous canning jars as a drinking vessel is as old as Prohibition moonshine. Just like putting up peaches or chowchow in the jars—which took their name from John Landis Mason, the New Jersey native who invented and patented them in 1858—home distillers put up their batches of homemade corn alcohol. While the peaches ended up in a serving dish, the jar of moonshine got passed around a circle, everyone taking a communal sip from its wide-mouth rim. Quart jars filled with iced tea or lemonade have never been a stranger to the Southern table either. Perhaps the occasional barman took it a step further

and added a splash of booze. But once the cool bar kids got their hands on quilted jelly jars (*quilted* is the word used by the longtime jar manufacturer Ball to describe the glass bevels), the fourteen-dollar old-fashioned got a makeover. Those of us with our vintage rocks glasses can only hope it's a passing fad.

THE MASTERS

PRESTIGIOUS, GREEN-JACKET-BEQUEATHING PRO-fessional golf tournament held each spring in Augusta, Georgia. *See Amen Corner.*

MAYHAW

NATIVE PEOPLES NEVER HAD MUCH USE FOR the tart and bitter mayhaw, which grows wild on thorny trees deep in the swamps of Alabama, Mississippi, Florida, Louisiana, and Texas. Only when sugar came into the picture did this cranberry-sized wild cousin to apples, pears, and crabapples become a sought-after Southern ingredient for jellies, jams, and syrups. During a roughly three-week period each spring, foragers don waders and take to canoes to skim fallen red, pink, and yellow mayhaws off the water's surface with nets and scoops. Elsewhere, commercial operations have domesticated the fruit. As development continues to decimate its wetland habitat, those farms may represent its future.

For a good number of Southerners, there's no such thing as mayonnaise. There is only Duke's Mayonnaise, made according to the sugarless recipe that Eugenia Duke of Greenville, South Carolina, devised in 1917. When Duke was toying with mayonnaise, it was the country's hottest condiment: Northern and Southern diners kept it close when making salads or preparing seafood. But the mayonnaise rage eventually subsided up north, where today it might go largely unsold if not for tuna fish and egg salad. In the South, though, it was impossible to extricate mayonnaise from the region's cuisine and Southerners' happy memories of it. Far removed from its classical French origins, it was devoured in the South every spring in the form of deviled eggs. Summertime brought tomatoes slathered with mayonnaise and sandwiched between white bread. In the fall, there were shrimp to fry and mayonnaise-based comeback sauce to serve with them. And in winter, holiday spreads of tomato aspic with mayonnaise and mayonnaise chocolate cakes. Mayonnaise is such a constant in Southern life that at least a few Southerners want it to be part of the hereafter, too: Duke's regularly hears from customers who want their remains forever kept in a Duke's jar. *See Duke's Mayonnaise.*

by Logan Ward

ROBERT FRANK "BOBBY" McALPINE is an Alabama-born residential architect with the sensibility of a poet. Working in a language of timber, stone, steel, and glass, he expresses the timeless qualities of Home with a capital *H*: sense of place, communion with nature, permanence, peacefulness, grace, hope, and fellowship. McAlpine is a great communicator who connects deeply with clients and designs to meet their emotional needs and desires. "The best house," he once said, "is the house that looks like how we feel inside."

McAlpine is beloved in the South because he is *of* the South. He cherishes history, tradition, the land, a welcoming energy, and the poignant beauty of shabbiness and decay. His work is at once rustic and tailored, nostalgic and modern. An admirer of the English architect Edwin Lutyens, who once described a home to a client as "a house you will love to live in," McAlpine prefers rambling romanticism to symmetrical classicism. He's less inspired by Southern architecture (Georgian town houses or Greek Revival plantation manors) than Southern people—"the way the isolation and rural context and heat of the South breed a different kind of character," he has said. "There is a willingness in Southerners to embrace eccentricity in people, and it's that kind of gladness and inclusion that I find most inspiring." His homes express that inspiration in a variety of ways—a graciousness of proportion, less-formal bleeding of rooms into rooms, or the unhurried pacing of a winding entry that allows guests to decompress and drink in their surroundings. The land is always important. McAlpine's houses—often narrow, linear, glass-filled—engage with the environment, delivering its inhabitants into the landscape.

The son of a sawmill boss, McAlpine grew up in the timber country of southwestern Alabama and eastern Mississippi. Blessed with a preternatural knack for architecture, he was sketching floor plans by age five. He was twelve when he received his first quasi-commission, to draft a set of plans for a ranch house for a family friend in Aliceville, Alabama. After graduating from Auburn University's College of Architecture, Design and Construction, McAlpine and partners set up shop in Montgomery. Known simply as McAlpine, the firm has designed hundreds of homes across the South and beyond, and later opened offices in Nashville, Atlanta, and New York. Several former McAlpine acolytes have branched out and opened their own firms. One is the Charlotte architect Ken Pursley, who says, "Bobby doesn't intellectualize his buildings. So many people who work in a traditional palette follow rules and regulations, reference books and maxims handed down from architects like Palladio. Bobby looks at things more from a human or emotional aspect. How a space feels is more important than if it's traditionally right or wrong. That comes from his being in touch with himself and the human condition."

McCARTYS POTTERY

USUALLY ADORNED WITH A WAVY BLACK line that represents the Mississippi River, these kiln-fired, Mississippi-made treasures in cobalt blue, jade, and nutmeg brown are made priceless by the hands that crafted them. Lee McCarty (1923–2015) and his wife, Pup (1926–2009), learned to throw clay while attending Ole Miss in the 1940s. When Pup enrolled in a pottery class, the full roster of football players intimidated her. So Lee joined her, and they cottoned to the craft. A few years later, William Faulkner even invited them onto his Rowan Oak property to dig clay. In the early 1950s, Lee's aunt gave the couple access to her old mule barn in Merigold, and the pair transformed its wooden frame into a home and studio, where visitors would stop by for a dish and leave with new friends and a piece of Mississippi history. Classically unadorned, with clean straight lines and glazed in hand-mixed custom pigments, the earthy delights are cherished by home cooks and the Smithsonian alike.

McCULLERS, CARSON

(1917–1967)

IF EUDORA WELTY, HARPER LEE, AND Flannery O'Connor make up the varsity squad of twentieth-century Southern female writers, then Carson McCullers is the one who didn't even try out for the team—she was too busy smoking cigarettes behind the gymnasium. Known for an emotional artistic intensity, McCullers was born in Columbus, Georgia, but moved almost constantly throughout her life, with multiple stops in France, Italy, North Carolina, and New York, among other places. The tumultuous relationship she shared with her husband, Reeves, included one divorce, one remarriage (to each other), numerous separations, and suicide attempts for both, including one in which Reeves tried to convince McCullers to kill herself with him. Before she was even thirty, McCullers suffered a series of strokes, only the start of a lifetime of poor health and physical pain. Throughout it all, though, she managed to produce some of the century's most sensitive and celebrated fiction while befriending and working with leading artists and thinkers of the time, including Tennessee Williams and Edward Albee, who adapted her work for the stage. McCullers's 1940 novel *The Heart Is a Lonely Hunter*, published when she was twenty-three, is often listed as among the twentieth century's finest, though *The Member of the Wedding*, published six years later, may be her defining masterpiece.

MEAT-AND-THREE

by John T. Edge

THE MEAT-AND-THREE IS A MID-TWENTIETH-century restaurant adaptation of the groaning-table dinner that fueled farm laborers at midday. A vegetable-driven meal, dependent on links between the farm and the table, it's a harbinger of country life, cooked and served by and for city folks.

As Southerners moved from farms to cities, entrepreneurs transformed the midday meal, moving service from kitchen tables and dinner tables to simple cafés where factory workers ate fried pork chops and hoecakes between shifts and office workers ate noontime plates of turnip greens, stewed squash, and field peas with snaps. Out of that rural-to-urban transition came the meat-and-three, which often translates as one meat and three vegetables, plus cornbread and iced tea.

The term describes a broad range of cooking. In and around Charleston, South Carolina, red rice and okra stew are common. On the western fringes of the South near Austin, Texas, country fried steak shows up often. In Louisiana, Cajun restaurants specialize in rice and gravy-based dishes. The name varies, too. In Louisiana and Mississippi, the term *plate lunch* is more common. Country-cooking restaurants, owned by whites, serve meat-and-threes. So do soul food restaurants, owned by blacks. Since the 1990s, the meal, although still called a meat-and-three, has frequently been rendered as a meat-and-two. Banana pudding, made with store-bought vanilla wafers, is a common meat-and-three dessert, served by the scoop in small melamine bowls.

Nashville is the capital of meat-and-three culture. Hap Townes, one of the progenitors, began selling lunches from a wagon there in 1921. At first he sold hot dogs and other quick-service foods. But his clientele of college students and factory workers soon clamored for a taste of the homes they'd left behind. By 1946, when his son, also known as Hap Townes, opened an eponymous café in the shadow of the local baseball stadium, the menu had shifted to the form we now recognize. Some credit the Townes men—who cooked excellent country fried steak, fried corn, stewed raisins, and stewed tomatoes—with coining the name and codifying the style of service.

Meat-and-three cafés (the term often applies to the restaurant as well as the meal) are democratic institutions. Today customers at Arnold's Country Kitchen, the Nashville inheritor of the Hap Townes legacy, include the homeless who crowd into a nearby shelter, lawyers who make the trek from downtown, and white-tablecloth chefs who see connections between what they attempt at night and the food Arnold's cooks each day. A cinder-block café with a steam-table line along the back wall, Arnold's simmers fat butter beans, bakes pan after pan of macaroni and cheese, and cooks cornbread to order on a flattop. Quick service from that steam table belies the long cooking time and deep knowledge required to execute many of the dishes.

In the contemporary South, meat-and-threes serve as places of communion, where customers dine on the foods their forebears cooked. Angelish Wilson, who ran Wilson's Soul Food in Athens, Georgia, explained her relationship to customers this way: "I'll cook like your grandmama and treat you like one of my own." Addie Williams, who once worked the U-shaped lunch counter at the downtown Atlanta Macy's department store, went a step further. She graded her regulars. If a customer

cleaned his plate, she marked his ticket with an A. Minor infractions, including unnecessary reaches for saltshakers and orders that didn't include sufficient green vegetables, could result in a C or D.

These humble cafés do more than satisfy cravings for nostalgia. Like barbecue joints and fried-chicken bunkers, meat-and-threes connect the South's past and present, linking the region's farmscapes and cityscapes.

MEMPHIS, TENNESSEE

by Hampton Sides

IT's HARD TO EXPLAIN WHY I LOVE Memphis so much. The traffic can be horrendous, the weather's muggy, and racial mistrust often hangs heavily on the air. And I have to admit, parts of town are rough on the eye. Out East, there's a thoughtless sprawl that goes on forever—a Redlobstered, Olivegardened, La Quintasized land where not very long ago there was nothing but cotton fields. When you survey the Bluff City's history, you see much heartache. Yellow fever epidemics, race riots, riverboat disasters, and that seismic event that still shapes the city's sense of itself, the flash point by which any understanding of Memphis must be gauged: the MLK assassination.

Still, I love the place. I love Memphis, I guess you could say, in the way that you love a brother even if he does sometimes puzzle and sadden and frustrate you. Say what you want about it, it's an authentic place. I was born and raised in Memphis, and no matter where I go, Memphis belongs to me, and I to it.

I love the way that wherever you are in Memphis, you hear the dirge of trains. I love the way in winter, the dead magnolia leaves, having lost their sheen, tumble and clatter in the wind. I love the tang of pit-house smoke, and the sound of blues that seems to ooze from the city's every pore. I love the rambling old houses in Central Gardens when the azaleas are in garish bloom, and the offbeat energy lately emanating from new-old haunts like the Cooper-Young neighborhood and the recently revitalized Overton Square.

I love the downtown skyline at night, as seen from Arkansas, with the old deco-Gothic towers silhouetted against the sweltering night, and the thirty-two-story glass and steel pyramid anchoring the north end. (Originally built as a sports arena in a shape meant to evoke the original Memphis on the Nile, the massive pyramid reopened as the mother of all Bubba tabernacles—a Bass Pro Shops superstore.)

And I love the way the Mississippi River looks beside the city, with the big steel bridge whose upper structure forms a mighty M over that great torrent of gravy, all brown snarls and snags and whirlpools, that river that is our river, *the* river—strongest, widest, swiftest. People from Memphis are known as Memphians, and that seems somehow right. Shades of amphibian, rubbery beings of the water and mud, life-forms that start out as one thing but morph into something else. We came from the river and to the river we shall return.

The thing about Memphis is that it's pleasingly off-kilter. It's a great big wack job of a city. You go there and you can't believe the things people will say, the way they think, the wobbling orbits of their lives. There's an essential *otherness*. When you look at an image by William Eggleston, a Memphian and one of history's greatest fine-art photographers, you get a sense of what I'm talking about: warped perspectives, angles that make you question your assumptions. Looming tricycles, screaming neon, beehive hairdos spun into high art. "I am at war with the obvious," Eggleston has said.

Or if you had hung out with the late Civil War historian Shelby Foote, another Memphian, and the first writer I ever met, you'd have caught a glimpse of the same thing. Here was a man of meticulously cultivated crotchets. He demanded Pet Evaporated Milk in his coffee. He was an avid watcher of *As the World Turns*. He spoke in a terrific accent, full of custardy lilts and Delta diphthongs, and wrote with antique writing implements in a cryptic hand all his own. For twenty years, he worked in a musty grotto-like study in the rear of his house on East Parkway, scratching away at his American *Iliad*, five hundred words every day for nearly twenty years, until he reached Appomattox. "Ah spec Ah'm bout thru now," he said, and the trilogy was done.

Memphis produces these people. It's like a factory for original souls. And those it does not produce, it pulls into its voracious tractor beam. Musicians, especially: Rufus Thomas, Johnny Cash, Jerry Lee Lewis, Isaac Hayes, Roy Orbison, Al Green. Skinny Elvis, and Fat Elvis, too.

It's always been that way. For two hundred years, all the pathos and pain of the Mississippi River, all the eccentricity and excess, seemed to splash upon the city's musky cobblestones. Steeped in the mean dreams of cotton, it was a place that celebrated a touch of insanity: high rollers, riverboat captains, mountebanks, snake oil salesmen, redneck wizards, roisterers, wrestlers, cotton brokers, Pentecostal preachers, inventors hopped up on some invisible vapor, some indigenous psycho-vibe, that could be sensed but whose existence could be neither measured nor proved. John Hiatt captured it just right in "Memphis in the Meantime," when he sang:

> Maybe there's nothin' happenin' there
> Maybe there's somethin' in the air
> Before our upper lips get stiff
> Maybe we need us a big ol' whiff.

It's a city of dreams and dreamers, many of them failed ones, but not always. A guy comes along and says, Let's take black music and white music and put 'em together. You're crazy, they say, and so Sam Phillips goes and does it. Genius. A guy comes along and says, Let's buy a fleet of airplanes and create a service that delivers packages overnight to anywhere in the world. Insane, they say, so Fred Smith goes and does it. Absolutely positively. A quixotic young doctor moves to Memphis in the early sixties with the idea of curing a nearly always fatal disease—childhood leukemia—and soon a research hospital opens in the slums north of downtown, named for the patron saint of lost causes. The breakthroughs that Dr. Donald Pinkel and his staff chart soon put St. Jude's

Children's Research Hospital on the world map as a place that attempts the impossible.

This thing about Memphis: Is there really a there there, or just a belief in the thereness? I can't precisely say, and I'm afraid if I delved any deeper, it would kill the very thing itself. That's how fragile it is. Like a frog on dry land, it can't stand too much direct light or desiccating heat. Like some of Eggleston's photos, it's unanalyzable. You can't define it or bottle it. You can't explain or parse it. You just have to go there and get a whiff for yourself.

MESS

EVEN IF THE FRIED CHICKEN ON THE FUNERAL-clean dining room table is just so, and the beans are tidily snapped, and the cornbread is sliced so there isn't a stray crumb on the serving dish, you're bound to have a big old mess of greens. From the Texas Gulf to coastal Carolina, mess doesn't imply disarray: it's a counting term, most commonly applied to meat and vegetables that defy easy quantifying. The expression apparently traveled across the Atlantic, since the *Dictionary of American Regional English* traces it back to 1697, when someone in Massachusetts wrote about enjoying "a Mess of English Beans." But it found its foothold in the South, where eaters got in the habit of serving up messes of peas, coon, and stewed catfish. So how much makes a mess? The late Florence King, an author and columnist whose people came from Virginia, wrote, "*Everybody* knew that it meant a dozen or a pound, unless, of course, it meant a bushel or a peck, or, in the country, a truckload." It's a slippery definition because, in most cases, a mess is what it takes to feed whoever's expecting to be fed.

MICHELADA

AN ICE-COLD BEER IS THE COOLING COUNTER-point to hot and spicy Southern cooking—but the beer cocktail called a Michelada turns that equation on its head. Invented in Mexico, the Michelada starts with an icy beer mug that's "dressed" (the sides coated with lime juice, the rim dipped in salt), with spicy condiments then dumped into the bottom of the mug before beer is added. Mexicans like celery salt, Maggi seasoning, and Cholula hot sauce, while some American imbibers prefer to mix the beer with a little Bloody Mary mix. Instead of cooling relief while you're eating spicy food, a Michelada adds zip when you're eating plain foods, like cold boiled shrimp or a dozen raw oysters on the half shell.

MIDNIGHT IN THE GARDEN OF GOOD AND EVIL

A MAN WALKING AN INVISIBLE DOG. A DRAG queen named the Lady Chablis. Minerva, the voodoo priestess. These are only a few of the unforgettable Savannah residents populating John Berendt's 1994 true-crime best-seller, *Midnight in the Garden of Good and Evil*. Recounting the eight years Berendt spent living in Savannah, much of it following the shooting of a male hustler named Danny Hansford by Jim Williams, a world-renowned antique dealer, "the Book," as it's known in Savannah, has sold more than five million copies and spent more time on the *New York Times* best-seller list than anything ever published (216 weeks). Williams was acquitted after four trials, providing more than enough drama for any narrative, but the real magic in *Midnight in the Garden of Good and Evil* lies in its beguiling depiction of Savannah itself. By evoking the city's charms so adroitly, Berendt unleashed an influx of attention on Savannah, not to mention hundreds of thousands of tourists. The *Times* noted, quite prophetically, that it "might be the first true-crime book that makes the reader want to call a travel agent and book a bed and breakfast for an extended weekend at the scene of the crime."

MILK PUNCH

NEW ORLEANS IS NOTABLE FOR HAVING A deeper bench than the average city when it comes to adult beverages. But the Crescent City also has entire phyla of cocktails generally unfamiliar to less enlightened precincts. So it is with the breakfast cocktail. While other cities make do with the overly garnished Bloody Mary or the anodyne mimosa on joyless Sundays, New Orleans has a long, inviting list of delicious drinks to accompany the Eggs Sardou any day of the week.

The milk punch stands at the head of this class. A colonial-era drink that sees a spike during the modern holiday season, it's really a class of drink rather than a specific tipple. It may be made with just about any spirit (rum, brandy, whiskey), which is shaken with milk or cream and brightened with a bit of sugar, vanilla, and nutmeg. It's distantly related to eggnog but more refreshing and gossamer, and will not menace anyone with the phlegmy consistency of its eggy cousin.

At some of the more ambitious cocktail bars of late, you may find on the cocktail list a clarified milk punch, which is nearly transparent. This is alarming to traditionalists, but delicious to all.

MINOR-LEAGUE BASEBALL

IT'S OKAY THAT YOUR MIND JUST AUTOMATI-cally flashed to *Bull Durham*. The Costner/Sarandon/Robbins classic remains the cultural gold standard of the thick, humid minors, an evocatively frozen-in-time world of bus transport, fetchingly goofy promotions, dollars-a-day paychecks, and the undying hopes and dreams that baseball unfailingly conjures. If anything, *Bull Durham* skewed a little flashy and fancy-pants; minor-league Southern ball is populated mostly by teams with chuckle-worthy names—Biloxi Shuckers! Montgomery Biscuits!—that fall somewhere between evocatively throwback and as cheesy as concession-cart nacho dip, and their stadiums are all boiled peanuts and paper beer cups and other details you imagine might not have changed all that much since the twenties. Technically speaking, games are played and somebody keeps score, but the action mostly lopes along lazily in the background of Sunday afternoons sweltering enough to slow down time. For fans, they aren't so much "games" as background bat cracks, ball-into-glove sound effects, sporadic cheers. Frankly, the home team could be playing the Shorebirds or Crawdads or Jumbo Shrimp or whomever out there; for most of us in the stands, that time-warp afternoon is the whole point.

MOBILE, ALABAMA

by John Sledge

ALABAMA'S ONLY SEAPORT HAS ALWAYS been a place apart—semitropical, exotic, graced with rich historical and architectural legacies. Indeed, one antebellum traveler declared Mobile the most distinctive American city he had seen, a sentiment echoed by the London *Times* reporter William Howard Russell in 1861, President Woodrow Wilson in 1913, John Dos Passos in 1943, and Henry Miller two years after that. "Mozart for the mandolin" was what *Tropic of Capricorn*'s author said exactly. That just about nails it, in my opinion. Mobile was founded by the French in 1702, sixteen years before that other city on the Mississippi. Mardi Gras started here in 1703, and it's still going strong. It's okay if most Americans don't realize that, though we will quickly let them in on the secret. As we like to say, we do Mardi Gras for ourselves, sans the raunch, whereas New Orleans does it for the tourists. Think of Mobile as New Orleans' better-behaved older sister. Less energetic, somewhat understated, and a little formal. But still intriguing, like a woman who has held her beauty, has seen a slice of life, and has some pretty colorful stories to tell. Better company at table than in a bar.

It is all too easy to misread Mobile, however—to see her as a bastion of conservatism in love with Old South traditions and embarrassing politics. Those elements are certainly present, mostly dating from World War II, when the city's booming shipyards attracted thousands of poor upcountry Protestant whites—"barbarous Baptists from the north," as one local writer put it. But to really know Mobile, you have to get down into her seams, smell the sweet earth, salt air, and gumbo, stroll down Dauphin Street from Broad to the river, take delight in a riot of white azaleas blooming in a yard or in the orange blaze of trumpet vine spilling down a courtyard's ancient brick wall. Mobile also has more than her share of characters mixed in with the scenery, smells, and God-fearing working folk, and always has. There's the statuesque tattooed woman with vivid dyed hair who gambols down Dauphin every morning no matter the temperature; the black transvestite who painted his house pink in the heart of a historic district; the Asian woman who shucked all her clothes when her restaurant kitchen got too hot and kept right on working in bamboo sandals; and the buttoned-up lawyer who once accepted Spanish pieces of eight as his legal fee from a hard-bitten Gulf shrimper. Mobile is all these things and more, including a battleship and a world-class garden and lots of shiny commercial endeavors the chamber of commerce likes to brag about. But fundamentally, she's an old soul, eminently worth knowing.

MONROE, BILL

(1911–1996)

The father of bluegrass music, William Smith Monroe was the youngest of eight children born on his family's farm near Rosine, Kentucky. He was fond of describing himself as "a farmer with a mandolin and a high tenor voice." This is like saying George S. Patton was an army officer who sometimes used bad language. Monroe was a peerless singer, songwriter, mandolin player, bandleader, and musical revolutionary. Although he didn't single-handedly invent bluegrass, he caught the baby when it came out, and he defined what remains the standard bluegrass lineup— mandolin, fiddle, banjo, guitar, and stand-up bass. He and incarnations of his band toured relentlessly for decades, often driving hundreds of miles to play, then driving hundreds more through the night to the next gig. And Lord help the musician who couldn't keep up onstage. Almost every player who spent time in the band—such as Earl Scruggs on banjo and Lester Flatt singing and playing guitar— not only was up to the task but went on to achieve stardom on his own. Monroe once described bluegrass this way: "It's got a hard drive to it. It's Scotch bagpipes and old-time fiddlin'. . . . It's blues and jazz and it has a high lonesome sound. It's plain music that tells a story." It was, of course, anything but plain. As early as the mid-1940s, Monroe's Bluegrass Boys were famous for their breakneck tempo, tight arrangements, and intricate, piercing vocal harmonies.

MONTICELLO

Thomas Jefferson's home outside Charlottesville, Virginia, is now a UNESCO World Heritage Site that draws 500,000 visitors a year. There may be no presidential pad that better reflects the restless intellect, quirky obsessions, and moral contradictions of its owner. *See Jefferson, Thomas.*

MOON PIES

Since 1917, the Chattanooga Bakery in Chattanooga, Tennessee, has been turning out daily supplies of this sweet convenience-store staple. As the story goes, the treat's inventor, Earl Mitchell, happened upon the idea for his chocolate-coated graham-cracker-and-marshmallow sandwich after asking a Kentucky coal miner to describe his ideal snack; the miner outlined what would become the Moon Pie in a portion "as big as the moon." (The standard size measures in a bit smaller at approximately four inches in diameter.) A century on, Moon Pies have become entrenched in Southern culture: there are Moon Pie festivals and eating contests from Bell Buckle, Tennessee, to Bessemer, Alabama; during Mardi Gras, parade krewes throughout the South have a penchant for tossing out miniature versions from their floats; and each New Year's Eve, the city of Mobile, Alabama, drops a twelve-foot-tall lit version as the clock strikes midnight.

MOONSHINE

Bootleg whiskey—also known as scrap iron, white corn, white moon, old tangle-foot, and a host of other aliases—has been a beloved nectar of Southern swamps, hills, and hollers since 1791, when the government put a steep tax on distillers large and small. Transforming corn and rye into a more portable, profitable product was deemed a God-given right. Several hundred hill folks loaded up their squirrel rifles and took after the revenue agents. After several dustups with the militia, the aggrieved reckoned discretion a better solution, and began brewing by the light of the moon, when wood smoke from the still was all but invisible; a guerrilla war ensued, and there is a steady market to this day. The boys who ran the loads down the mountain in souped-up jalopies became the first generation of NASCAR drivers.

As high as 190 proof, smooth shine is like liquid fire with an aftertaste of popcorn. Rough shine will eject glass eyes, snap suspenders, and stop your watch cold. You can help it some by throwing in sliced peaches, apples, or cherries. The government tells you it's all poison. Not so fast. As an Appalachian folk song from the 1920s and '30s puts it: "They call it that good old mountain dew, and them that refuse it is few. I'll shut up my mug, if you fill up my jug with that good old mountain dew."

MOSQUITOES

by Daniel Wallace

THE MOSQUITO IS THE DEVIL'S HOUSE PET. When Satan lost his footing and fell from heaven, God let him retain a few powers to better test our faith, and the mosquito was one of them. You won't find that in the Scriptures, specifically, but it's implied, the same way it's implied that having more than seven cats is a sin. The existence of the mosquito is proof of God's existence; it serves no other purpose. I've spoken to experts and they assure me that our ecosystem would do just fine without a mosquito in it, that it essentially has no function. And yet it's the most dangerous animal on the planet. Your chances of incurring death-by-mosquito are ten thousand times greater than getting trampled by a herd of stampeding possums. Many people assume the opposite is the case. Not so.

A mosquito is disease on wings. Malaria, yellow fever, West Nile, dengue fever, and most recently the Zika virus are all spread, generally and principally, by the mosquito. They've been around for about fifty million years, without really changing, like a Twinkie.

In the light of all this death and microscopic mayhem, the fact that they can also kill a backyard cookout may seem a small thing to the non-Southerner, but the truth is that in the South there are four seasons: fall, winter, spring, and mosquito. So small as to be almost invisible, so crafty and fast it is often unkillable by the human hand, it stalks us. It is inescapable.

Dangerous assassins, these weeds of the insect world. But insanity is also a mosquito by-product. This can be caused by the one mosquito—a single mosquito—that slips through a teeny tear in your window screen and, right after you turn off the light, finds the path to your ear. That's how it was for me on so many hot and humid summer nights in Alabama. I grew up poor. Our window screens were made of asbestos and the mercury we drained from old thermometers we found in the town dump. Mosquitoes flew in with impunity, and a mosquito with impunity is a scary thing. It feels empowered. It comes at you with an aggressive confidence—élan. How it finds the ear itself is a mystery; some scientists say it may remind them of the Jurassic caves they used to live in. Regardless, the mosquito (Spanish for "little fly") is drawn to the ear and in the dark of the night is virtually indistinguishable from the darkness. It's under these conditions that insanity occurs.

No one would be happier than my uncle Merle (who lost his right arm to the mosquito—such a long story) if we could rid ourselves of each and every one of the maleficent infidels. But we can't; it's literally impossible. So how do we protect ourselves? I own anti-mosquito bracelets; I spray myself with poison. I've purchased a flock of dragonflies and bought a huge outdoor fan of the kind normally used to cool down nuclear reactors. Everything helps but nothing works. Like Taylor Swift, mosquitoes are a fact of life.

A COLLOQUIAL TERM FOR CRAWFISH, AC-knowledging their propensity to burrow in swampy bottomlands and take on a silty taste when not properly cleaned before cooking. *See Crawfish.*

MUFFULETTA

GENERATIONS OF TOURISTS IN NEW ORLEANS have "discovered" Central Grocery & Deli, the old-world market just up the street from Café Du Monde. Taking a respite from the crowds and hustle of the French Quarter, they duck into this shop lined with jars of jam and boxes of tea, and they purchase a paper-wrapped muffuletta, the sandwich created here by a Sicilian immigrant named Salvatore Lupo in 1906. Rather, they buy a quarter wedge of one of the substantial round loaves of the same name filled with striated layers of deli meats and cheeses and topped with a punchy variation on giardiniera called olive salad. Then they find a bench in a quiet spot and dig in. Little do they know this impulse dates back to the creation of the muffuletta, when the city's central farmers' market stood nearby. Lupo noticed that the mostly Sicilian farmers would buy the meats, cheeses, olive salad, and bread, then sit down on a crate and spread these precarious picnics on their laps. How much easier to layer it all in a sandwich.

by Roy Blount, Jr.

FRANKLY, I HAVE NEVER ATTENDED A MULLET festival myself, and cannot know what passions such an event engenders. Still I find it troubling that someone at the 2014 Boggy Bayou Mullet Festival in Niceville, Florida, threw a full beer can that hit a featured attraction, the country singer Dustin Lynch, in the face. On YouTube you can watch Lynch, undaunted, peering into the crowd and saying, "I want to come to your workplace and throw [stuff] at you, man."

You can see where that could lead. "Mommy, Mommy, why is the man in the big hat throwing [stuff] at the Jiffy Lube man? Can I throw [stuff] at the Jiffy Lube man?"

And here's what people will be thinking: that's about the kind of trend you'd expect from a celebration of the mullet. The "lowly" mullet, as it is so often called, the "humble," the "much-maligned" mullet. Time for reassessment, folks.

Traditionally, of course, what people throw during a mullet festival is mullet, and not at anyone, but for distance, and charity, and an occasion to *drink* beer. Famously, the Flora-Bama Lounge, on the Florida-Alabama line, draws some thirty-five thousand people annually to its Interstate Mullet Toss. The all-time record, 179 feet, could be seen as a tribute to mullet aerodynamics.

But no, the preferred way to toss a mullet is to wad it up and throw it like a softball. Does anybody toss trout? No. Or tilapia, even? In recent years tilapia has become the fourth-most-popular fish in America, even though it is no less of a bottom feeder than mullet—and indeed many tilapia imported from China have been fattened up on chicken doody. Yet when I mention to people that I am writing about mullet, so many respond by saying, "Does anybody ever *eat* one?"

You damn right. A specialty of the very nice Spring Creek Restaurant in Crawfordville, Florida, is a very nice dinner of fried mullet, caught in local waters from the establishment's own boat. In St. Petersburg, Florida, Ted Peters Famous Smoked Fish has been largely mullet-based since 1951. And yet here is one of the first things I learned from elder relatives, fishing for croakers and whiting in North Florida. One of us accidentally caught a mullet (it can happen, although mullet, essentially vegetarian, aren't big biters). Can't eat that, I was told. Good only for bait.

It's not a pretty fish. Its face is too small. Where you can almost imagine a redfish breaking into a smile (not in a boat, though), a mullet's face amounts to big bug eyes and little squinched-up sucky lips. A mullet's body is sleek but also swarthy. Generally its colors (*mullet* comes from the same Indo-European root as *melanin*, dark pigment) resemble those of the old, piratical Oakland Raiders.

And we must not fail to mention the mullet hairstyle, short in front, long down the back—inspired, conceivably, by the little-face-long-body look of the fish. The *New York Times* a few years ago reported that the mullet coif had become fashionable, but come on: these are highly modified versions. The fish's image is never going to be improved by that of the 'do. At one point the state of Florida, which

officially changed the name of the dolphinfish to mahi-mahi so potential eaters wouldn't associate it with Flipper, tried to change mullet's name to the Spanish, *lisa*. Didn't catch on. A mullet doesn't look like a Lisa.

It doesn't need to. It is high in heart-healthy omega-3 fatty acids. Because it doesn't eat other fish, it is low in mercury content (and lots of game fish eat it, so it's good for them). It reproduces rapidly, so it's sustainable. A fish (a Mediterranean staple for thousands of years) for the twenty-first century!

And it inspired *Man and Mullet: An Elegy for a Lost Way of Life*, by Alan Ryle Frederiksen. Michael Swindle in his own good book *Mullet-heads* calls Frederiksen "the Melville of mullet." This vertiginous portrait of old-school gillnetters grappling with a school of running mullet—a great knot referred to collectively as *he*—indeed evokes *Moby-Dick*. To appreciate it is to dive in and get lost, but here is the knot:

Fish on the move; surface appeared
to come alive with escaping mullet . . .
fused into a mass . . . like acrobats
leapfrogging one another but with this
difference: now hundreds in the air
formed a solid wall of lunging bodies.
The conglomerate melded . . .

And here, inside one mullet: ". . . deftly one removes the black membrane covering the fatty belly, then greases hands and fingers in the oozy substance reborn of the leafy detritus—black mangrove (gopherwood)—ancient tree planking Noah's Ark . . ."

Try to find a copy. I also recommend Googling "mullet gizzard."

MUSCADINE

SOUTHERN ARISTOCRATS HAVE SPENT CENTU-
ries trying to coax fine wine out of fickle
grapes of foreign origin. Meanwhile, the rest
of us have settled for a few muscadine vines
in the backyard. Come rain, come snow, come
crushing heat and humidity, the South's native grape persists as it has for millennia.
Protected by a leathery hull, the antioxidant-
rich muscadine's sweet pulp makes superlative jams and jellies. Even its tough exterior is
good for something: simmered until tender, it
stars in old-fashioned hull pies and cobblers.
As for muscadine wine, for the most part it
tends toward cloying and unpleasantly strong.
Ask around, though, and you just might locate
one of those amateur vintners renowned in
his small town for taming the early-fall harvest. Imports will never have such hard-won
character.

MUSCLE SHOALS, ALABAMA

by Patterson Hood

FIRST LET'S GO BACK IN TIME. MAYBE
1977 or so. Upon driving into Muscle
Shoals, Alabama, on one of the country roads
that got you there, you would have passed a
sign welcoming you to THE HIT RECORDING
CAPITAL OF THE WORLD. An unlikely boast
for this little town nestled in a dry county on
the banks of the Tennessee River in Northwest

Alabama. The Muscle Shoals Area (as the region is generally referred to) is actually four
connected but separate small towns and their
surrounding areas. Sheffield, Tuscumbia, and
Florence each have their own unique flavor
(and separate governments), but as most locals
can scarcely tell where one ends and another
begins, it's understandable to clump them together. And unlikely as it might have seemed,
during Muscle Shoals's heyday in the sixties
and seventies, more million-selling records
did in fact come out of that little burg than
anywhere else on the planet.

Percy Sledge made "When a Man Loves
a Woman" there. It went on to become one
of the most successful singles of all time.
Classic soul records from Aretha Franklin,
Wilson Pickett, Etta James, Bobby Womack,
and Clarence Carter all came from the tiny
studios in town, especially Fame Studios
and Muscle Shoals Sound (which was actually in neighboring Sheffield). The Staple
Singers had number-one hits with "I'll Take
You There" and "Respect Yourself." Willie
Nelson, Paul Simon, Rod Stewart, Lynyrd
Skynyrd, and Bob Seger are just a few of the
other artists that made classic records there.
The Rolling Stones came down to record
"Brown Sugar" and "Wild Horses" right before flying to the West Coast to play a festival
at Altamont.

I grew up in Florence and came of age
during the lean times of the eighties. My
father is David Hood, who was one of the
founders of the Muscle Shoals Rhythm
Section, which played on many of the legendary hits. Unlike many of his peers, Dad stayed

and has made a living the best he could during the very tough years that followed. I played in and around the area for years before finding some success in Athens, Georgia, with my band Drive-By Truckers. My partner in that band, Mike Cooley, grew up in Tuscumbia, and through the years several other Shoals natives have contributed to our music. In 2004 we returned to the Shoals to record our album *The Dirty South*, and a couple of years later made a Grammy-nominated album there with the soul legend Bettye LaVette.

Times have changed in the years since that early heyday. But there has been a renaissance in the community that in many ways goes far beyond what was there before. Legal liquor was voted in a few decades ago. Downtown Florence has been revitalized and is actually a tourist destination, lined with prosperous restaurants and shops. The world-famous clothing designers Billy Reid and Alabama Chanin are based there, and their success has further bolstered the area. Hollywood came calling and made an acclaimed documentary about the music scene. Fame Studios is still in operation, and a nonprofit was recently formed to restore and reopen Muscle Shoals Sound Studio with the help of a generous grant from Dr. Dre and the music company Beats.

Local artists have revived the music scene, too. John Paul White had a number-one album with his former band Civil Wars and has since moved back home to start a successful recording studio and label, releasing hit records from St. Paul & the Broken Bones, Dylan LeBlanc, and his own acclaimed solo record. Grammy winner Jason Isbell, who grew up in the area and still retains deep roots there, is fast becoming one of the most successful artists in the world. The members of Alabama Shakes grew up just twenty-five miles or so down the road in neighboring Athens, Alabama, and have gone on to win Grammys and release a number-one album. They've ushered in a new chapter in the musical legacy of my hometown.

NABS

NABS ARE A LONGTIME STANDBY OF SOUTHERN gas-station cuisine: cracker sandwiches, usually orange cheese crackers with a filling of peanut butter or cheese, that come in plastic-wrapped packages of six or eight. The name came from the National Biscuit Company, aka Nabisco, which first marketed the peanut butter cheese crackers by that name in the 1920s. Although Nabisco was headquartered in the Northeast, the crackers became popular in the South, particularly in textile plants where the air was often kept warm and moist so cotton would spin better, and where the absence of labor unions meant long shifts with short breaks. A six-ounce glass bottle of soda was called a "dope," and the snack cart where people could grab a quick bite, the "dope wagon." A five-cent dope and a pack of Nabs provided a fast way to fuel up and keep going. Over the years, a "pack of Nabs," along with other portable snacks such as cans of Vienna sausage, also became popular with farmworkers and fishermen, who needed something easy to carry that didn't need to be kept cold.

Nabisco eventually stopped making Nabs, and its trademark for the name expired, but similar cracker packs are still made by Charlotte-based Lance (now Snyder's-Lance) and Tom's (originally made by the Tom Huston Peanut Company in Columbus, Georgia, itself now a Snyders-Lance subsidiary). While the original Nabs had peanut butter filling, Lance's Toast-Chee, a cheese cracker with a cheese filling, and umpteen other variations also picked up the now-generic Southern nickname—which explains why you can find a pack of nabs almost anywhere, even if there are no actual Nabs to be found.

NASCAR

THE SPECTACULARLY REDUNDANT ACRONYM stands for the National Association for Stock Car Auto Racing, founded in 1948, a lucrative family-owned business that governs and sanctions races. Bill France Sr.'s vision was that "common men in common cars could appeal to common folk en masse." The cars look like normal ("stock") cars, which they resemble in the same way F-16s resemble balsa-wood gliders. A NASCAR car's engine may produce 750 horsepower and has a life expectancy of a thousand miles or less. In a race, drivers make left turns around a track (usually oval-shaped) until they complete a certain number of laps, miles, or kilometers. NASCAR traces its roots to bootleggers who transported illegal whiskey from Appalachian stills to Southern cities. They modified their cars—boosting horsepower with extra carburetors and turbochargers, stiffening the suspension, adding

switches to turn off headlights and brake lights, and so on—to help them outrun the authorities. They also developed such driving maneuvers as the 180-degree "bootlegger's turn." Junior Johnson, famed as a bootlegger and NASCAR driver, was known for doing this and then driving straight at a pursuing police car, reasoning—correctly—that no cop wanted to catch a bootlegger badly enough to die. He started driving at fourteen, long before he could obtain a license. "I didn't need one," Johnson explained, "'cause I wasn't gonna stop!"

NASHVILLE, TENNESSEE

by Marshall Chapman

THERE ARE NINETEEN PLACES NAMED Nashville in the United States. But only one is an actual city, one that fires the imagination unlike any other. That Nashville sits on a bluff above the Cumberland River in Middle Tennessee. State capital and home to Vanderbilt University, it has inspired many nicknames over the years—Music City, U.S.A., Athens of the South, Home of the Grand Ole Opry, and so on. These days, it's known as an "it" city, the hot chicken capital of the world, and the setting for the popular TV series that bears its name. Oh, and a foodie's paradise; more chefs of international renown, I recently read, are moving there than to any other city in the world.

If you're a musician or songwriter, add another nickname to the list—Heaven. There's no better place you could live. Over the years, Nashville has attracted Hall of Fame songwriters like Dolly Parton, Kris Kristofferson, Roger Miller, John D. Loudermilk, Marijohn Wilkin, and Harlan Howard. Now rockers like the Black Keys, Kings of Leon, and Jack White call the city home, as do up-and-comers Aaron Lee Tasjan, Pujol, and Diarrhea Planet (yup, really).

When I first arrived here, in 1967, Nashville was an overgrown, sleepy Southern town whose metropolitan government had *just* legalized liquor sold by the drink. But still, there was something in the air, and if you were a musician, you could feel it. Bobby Bare (of "Detroit City" fame) said it best: "You'd get off that plane and immediately feel the vibe. It was like electricity. There was so much going on. You couldn't help but get caught up in it. You'd get very creative and want to *do* something. It was magic."

Today's Nashville is a far cry from that drowsy place I first encountered. Everywhere you look, high-rises are going up. Driving into town recently, I counted twelve cranes looming across the cityscape. If Nashville were a state, some joke, the crane would be the state bird. It's said that Nashville has replaced Atlanta as the most progressive city in the South, and Austin as the fastest-growing. A thousand people move here every month, most of them young. Boxlike, modern glass houses now dot the hills surrounding downtown. This growth and demographic shift have moved some to call Nashville a "landlocked San Francisco." But unlike other fast-growing cities, Nashville seems to be holding onto its uniqueness. As long as there's Prince's Hot Chicken, Brown's Diner, Arnold's Country Kitchen, Bluebird Cafe, Ryman Auditorium, and Tootsie's Orchid Lounge, Nashville will always be Nashville.

NASHVILLE HOT CHICKEN

THANK A SCORNED LOVER FOR THE PALATE-searing pleasure of Music City's now-famous take on fried chicken. During the Depression, Thornton Prince, a notorious ladies' man, came home from a night of tomcatting. His steady woman, none too pleased, fixed him a plate of fried chicken with every hot spice she could find, including peppers from her garden. *One bite should change his ways forever*, she thought. He chomped down . . . and loved it. From that first bite grew a business, and more than eighty years later, the rest of the country loves it, too. Imitators pop up regularly—even KFC came up with a knockoff—but none match the spirit and spice of the original: Prince's Hot Chicken Shack, still run by Thornton's extended family in a tiny strip mall on Nashville's eastern outskirts. Yardbird with attitude comes coated in a fat-and-cayenne sludge and straddled across cheap white bread topped with dill-pickle moons—the sides provided as comically inefficient antidotes to the pain. Prince's ranks its offerings from mild all the way up to XXXHOT, which should be ordered by devoted masochists only.

NATCHEZ TRACE

THE 444-MILE DRIVE FROM NATCHEZ, Mississippi, to Fairview, Tennessee, would be a scenic journey regardless of its historical significance. But it's the forested trail it commemorates, a route blazed by Native Americans and later trod by early Americans—from traders and soldiers to itinerant preachers and highwaymen—that lends it its special magic. Largely following a geographic line from the Mississippi River to the salt licks of central Tennessee, the present-day two-lane parkway contains some fifty points of access to the landmarks of old: the two-thousand-year-old Pharr Mounds near Tupelo, Mississippi; remnants of early inns and settlements; and a monument to the explorer Meriwether Lewis, who died near Grinder's Stand, at mile marker 385.9.

NEAL, BILL

(1950–1991)

by Bill Smith

I WAS A GUEST CHEF AT A FRIEND'S RESTAU-rant a couple of summers ago. I had sent recipes and instructions ahead, but they weren't really precise. When one of the cooks there asked me how to fine-tune something, I said, "Just make it taste good." That was Bill Neal talking. Despite his reputation for being somewhat imperial at times, Bill was a boss who invited collaboration. I worked with him not at Crook's Corner (the pioneering Chapel Hill, North Carolina, restaurant he later opened in 1982, where I am now the chef) but at his first restaurant, La Résidence, a cool French place that he and his wife, Moreton, started in Chapel Hill in the mid-seventies. Bill and Moreton had become enchanted with everyday French cooking on a trip to Provence. That restaurant resulted from their excursion.

It was an exciting place to be. We worked our way through *Mastering the Art of French Cooking*, then branched out to study Marcella Hazan, Simone Beck, Elizabeth David, and Diana Kennedy. We watched Julia Child on TV. We devoured cooking magazines and made excursions to big cities to eat at important restaurants and bring back ingredients we couldn't find in North Carolina. We read Flaubert. I am speculating here, but I suspect that it was dawning on Bill then that the delicious *cuisine bourgeoise* he was beginning to explore had a great deal in common with the good home cooking that he had grown up with in South Carolina.

Although La Résidence's food was French, we were viewed as a part of the wave of new American cooking that was showing up everywhere. Bill sought out farmers before we had a farmers' market. One of Moreton's family layer-cake recipes entered the dessert list. The menu was seasonal from day one. While we began with a traditional basic repertoire, Bill often reminded us to also think of the kitchen as a laboratory. To be open to new ingredients and new ideas. Things were not hidebound, either. Our cooking was home cooking, so if tarts weren't quite round or the mirepoix was irregular, that was fine. It was

okay if homemade looked homemade. Things just had to taste good.

In the early 1980s, Bill and Moreton divorced. She stayed at La Résidence while he started Crook's Corner with his friend Gene Hamer, taking over a beer-and-barbecue joint down the street. Bill jumped into Southern cooking with both feet. With the help of supportive local residents and some well-timed national publicity, he quickly showed the food world that Southern cuisine was not the cooking of *The Beverly Hillbillies*. He knew that the Southern dinner table is a treasure with countless splendid things to offer us.

Sadly, Bill died young, in 1991, my first friend to become a victim of the HIV epidemic. His legacy remains, though. It waxes and wanes from time to time, but it never goes away. Looking back now, I feel very lucky indeed to have worked in a kitchen that afforded me such creative luxury. Things learned there went way beyond recipes. *See Shrimp and grits.*

"NEKKID"

IT'S PROBABLY IMPOSSIBLE TO BEAT THE CLARification of this term offered by the late comedian, Georgia native, and *Atlanta Journal-Constitution* columnist Lewis Grizzard: "Naked means you ain't got no clothes on. Nekkid means you ain't got no clothes on and you're up to somethin'." In 2011, *nekkid* earned a measure of immortality: an entry in the *Oxford English Dictionary*.

NELSON, WILLIE

(1933–)

by Joe Nick Patoski

H E WAS RAISED BY HIS GRANDPARENTS TO do exactly what he does now, just like his "little sister" Bobbie, who is actually two years older than he is. The elder Nelsons, Alfred and Nancy, had emigrated from the hardscrabble hills of Northwest Arkansas to the blacklands of north-central Texas with their sixteen-year-old son, Ira, and his new sixteen-year-old wife, Myrle. Back in the Ozarks, Alfred was a blacksmith by trade, but he and Nancy were better known as singing schoolteachers who would take over a church or school and teach a community to sing, using the hand-sign shape-note method. Ira and Merle's marriage fell apart and they went their separate ways, leaving behind a daughter and a son. The grandparents taught Bobbie piano and took her to singing conventions. The younger Willie took to guitar and riding his bike across the county line to hang out around the jukeboxes in honky-tonks. The Nelson kids became the featured entertainment at school and at the Abbott Methodist Church. As teenagers, they were the core of a Bob Wills–style Western swing band that performed regularly on KHBR radio. Willie had his own all-female fan club that bought him stage wear and a graduation suit.

As adults, Willie and Bobbie headed in different directions. Willie struggled, working as a disc jockey, selling Bibles and vacuum cleaners, doing whatever he had to do to get by while pursuing a life in music. He finally achieved success as a songwriter with a burst of country hits in the early 1960s— "Hello, Walls," "Family Bible," "Crazy," "Funny How Time Slips Away," "Night Life." But Willie wanted to be the star, not just the writer, and his songwriting royalties underwrote his performing aspirations for the next ten years. Meanwhile Bobbie married, divorced, married again, and found satisfaction playing Hammond organs in restaurants and at trade shows, working her way down to Austin, where she worked piano bars as well as Hammond demo gigs. One of the regulars at her weekly gig at Mike & Charlie's was University of Texas football coach Darrell K. Royal, the most popular man in Texas, who was already hip to her brother's music.

Willie's run as a Nashville recording artist lasted a decade, including a couple of top-ten country hits, a stint on the Grand Ole Opry, frequent television appearances on *The Ernest Tubb Show*, two albums for Jerry Allison at Liberty Records, thirteen albums for Chet Atkins at RCA Records, and one outlier single, "I Never Cared for You," for Fred Foster at Monument Records. He did themes, like his album of all Texas songs. He did introspection, covering Beatles ballads, passing as country-folk and dressing like a lounge singer rather than a Nudie-suited hillbilly. He did twisted, as in "I Just Can't Let You Say Goodbye," based on a newspaper clipping about a romance that ended in murder, taking the killer's point of view. He could go deep and spiritual, as with the splendidly cosmic album *Yesterday's Wine*.

Nothing really stuck. He kept plugging away but seemed destined to eventually suffer the fate of most country talents: selling insurance or cars, or buying a nightclub. Instead, one Christmas Eve, his home in the hills north of Nashville burned down. His band and extended family found shelter at a bankrupt dude ranch outside of Bandera that his Texas booking agent knew about. They started playing Floore's Country Store honky-tonk in nearby Helotes every week and played golf at the dude ranch high on LSD. Within a year, Willie and his band discovered Austin, where little sister Bobbie had been hanging. Along the way to Willie Nelson and his Family band becoming a thing, a rocking, hard-driving jam band powered by two drummers and two bass players, Bobbie rejoined her brother to play piano.

That was more than forty-five years ago. Since then, Willie blew up into the one-name superstar, the voice of Texas, champion of the family farmer and of weed, and an icon of American music with enough tracks in the can to release new product into the twenty-second century. But Willie wouldn't have achieved what he did without that stealthy, slight woman in black with the long blond hair at the piano, by his side. Bobbie keeps it all balanced. Willie's bus doesn't pull out of the gig until she's on it. They're doing exactly what Alfred and Nancy taught them to do all those years ago.

NESHOBA COUNTY FAIR

For a hot and sticky week in July, visitors descend on Philadelphia, Mississippi, for the Neshoba County Fair's mash-up of quintessential Southern experiences. There, you can wager on a horse race from the bed of a pickup truck, hands wrapped around deep-fried corn dogs and fresh-squeezed lemonade. Democrats and Republicans alike turn up to kiss babies and do some good ole tree-stump politicking. Competitors cakewalk for layered caramel and chocolate masterpieces. And concertgoers rush across the red-clay track with their lawn chairs to beat one another for a front-row seat to the nightly shows. But the best part is the hospitality. Rural farmers first began meeting in 1889 on the site, which holds brightly colored family-owned row houses built to accommodate the kinfolk who would return year after year. Those visiting for the day (or staying outside the property) are made to feel like part of the conversation—literally. Don't be surprised if you're invited up to chat over a glass of tea on a porch swing or for a late-night sing-along.

NEW ORLEANS, LOUISIANA

by Wayne Curtis

NEW ORLEANS IS THE GALÁPAGOS OF American culture, which is to say that while the rest of the nation has come to look like much of the rest of the nation, New Orleans has not. Although its citizens may slurp as much Starbucks and scarf as many Subway sandwiches as other Americans, the city's identity remains connected to more historic staples, like coffee with chicory (a nineteenth-century favorite still available today) and po'boys (long sandwiches on crusty bread treasured as much for their audible crunch as for their taste). Much about the city has evolved and modernized in recent decades—architecture, music, cuisine—but change rarely occurs without someone first setting an anchor in the past.

New Orleans was colonized in 1718 by the French, who occupied a bend near the mouth of the Mississippi River on a natural levee where a band of Quinipissa Indians once lived. The French showed little aptitude for colonizing; following various colonial wars and geopolitical intrigue, in 1763 they signed the place over to the more efficient Spanish. Under Spanish rule the city nearly burned to the ground, twice—in 1788 and 1794—and its core, now called the French Quarter, assumed much of its present-day form in the rebuilding. In 1803, the United States acquired New Orleans along with a considerable backyard (the Louisiana Purchase, extending to present-day Canada). Americans set about

shaping the city in their image but faced a setback around 1809 when a massive influx of French-speaking refugees arrived from Cuba, forestalling Americanization by a generation or two.

All this is to explain why in large part the city is not like the rest of America—it was built not on English cultural bedrock, as so many other North American coastal cities were, but atop a Creole collage. What's more, geographic remoteness further enhanced the sense of remove from the continent. For decades, New Orleans was essentially an island, reached predominantly by ship from the Gulf of Mexico or flatboat down the Mississippi.

Although in the twentieth century it acquired the nickname the Big Easy, New Orleans has never been particularly easy. It suffered from periodic outbreaks of tropical diseases, including yellow fever in the nineteenth century. Levees would occasionally fail and flood the city. Hurricanes regularly blasted it. It was also a hub of a massive slave trade in the nineteenth century, and after emancipation, like much of the South, it embraced Jim Crow apartheid.

Despite it all, much of New Orleans' unique culture has persisted and thrived. It was the cradle of jazz around 1900, and many of the popular early songs are still played by young musicians in boisterous brass bands—albeit now with a funk or hip-hop overlay. Bands of African Americans still mask as flamboyantly feathered "Indians" in the spring, as their great-grandparents did, forming neighborhood tribes who take to the streets to enact arcane rituals of power and respect. Foodways that appear fleetingly in other communities have worn deep ruts here, like a mule cart that's traveled the same trail for three hundred years; residents speak the language of gumbo, and red beans and rice, and bread pudding. Any new permutations first pay respect to their forebears. New Orleans remains a city of rhythms and rituals, of call and response, a place where the audience is as integral to a performance as the act. It's not uncommon to come upon a parade with no spectators, because everyone decided it was more interesting to join in.

This is also a city where the unseen plays as important a role as the visible. Note that the French Quarter is bordered by Canal Street, on which no canal was ever built, Rampart Street, on which a rampart was never constructed, and Esplanade Avenue, along which few ever promenaded. (The remaining border is the Mississippi, which often expresses a desire to be elsewhere.) Among the most important of the invisibles is residents' profound connection to the city. When New Orleans flooded so painfully in the wake of Katrina and the levee failures in 2005, it was rebuilt despite cries from the hinterlands that this made no sense. More than a decade on, it's clear that the most important elements in the rebuilding have been New Orleanians' deep love for their city and their general disregard for those who don't understand that. When an interviewer in Los Angeles asked the jazz legend Terence Blanchard, who had evacuated there, if he planned to return to his flooded hometown, Blanchard replied, "Sure. Because I can't stand your music and I hate your food."

This could serve as a motto for the ages.

NICKNAMES

Some of the South's claims to unfettered greatness are debatable—for example, it is theoretically possible, if unlikely, that there is solid college football in the Midwest. But few would argue that anyone is better than Southerners at coming up with nicknames. Research has proved that only 25 percent of Southern-born adults go by their given Christian names (editor's note: no, it hasn't, but it's probably close). As evidence, we've assembled a short list of Southern nicknames that includes, but is not limited to, Bunny, Porkchop, Bubba, Butterbean, Toot, Pip, Jude Rose, Vivi, Petty, Willow, Bow Legs, Ace, Gidget, Kitty, Cookie, Sissy, Scooter, Lady Bird, Kay Kay, Ty Cobb, Hoof, Chick, Doodle, Coach, Ladybug, Jug, Doc, Sweetness, 'Toine, Benmont, Bear, Hoke, Sweetie Pie, Shug, Skeeter, Gator, Hawg, Snake, Cricket, Nugget, Chunk, Sugar Pie, Sugar Cake, Cake Sugar, Cake Pie, Dink, Peanut, Boss, Rocky, Topsy, Daisy, Bailey, Sonny, and Dale Jr.

WHEN AN ILLUSTRATION OF A NOISETTE ROSE by the French botanical artist Pierre-Joseph Redouté began circulating around Europe in 1824, the American-bred bloom, you might say, went viral. "Perhaps no new rose was ever so much admired as this," wrote Thomas Rivers in the 1877 edition of *The Rose Amateur's Guide*. ". . . Parisian amateurs were quite enraptured with it." The first class of rose the United States ever introduced, the Noisette blossomed from a friendship between a Charleston, South Carolina, planter named John Champney and Philippe Noisette, a French-born botanist. Sometime between 1800 and 1814, Noisette gave Champney, his Charleston neighbor, an ancient Chinese variety of rose called Old Blush. Champney crossed that with a *Rosa moschata* (or musk rose), christening the result Champney's Pink Cluster. He presented one of those back to Noisette, who then hybridized it to create the first Blush Noisette and sent a seedling to his brother in France. Parisian rapture ensued. The fragrant climbing flowers—now with more than a dozen variations—remain popular worldwide, but especially in the South for their resistance to disease and tolerance for summer swelter.

UKRAINIAN IMMIGRANT NUTA KOTLYARENKO never hung his cowboy hat in the South. He began his career in the 1930s by making G-strings for burlesque performers in New York City. In the forties he changed his name to the easier-to-pronounce (and market) Nudie Cohn and opened Nudie's Rodeo Tailors in Hollywood, California. But when he started fashioning Western-style suits of neon fabrics adorned with flamboyant swirls of embroidery and rhinestones, Nashville's top country-music acts quickly became his biggest and flashiest customers. George Jones, Marty Robbins, and Glen Campbell were fans, and Porter Wagoner's entire performing persona became synonymous with the suits. The unapologetically outrageous style became a rare sartorial bridge between traditional country and sixties counterculture—Nudie's custom suit for the Georgia-raised rocker Gram Parsons, featuring embroidered marijuana leaves, a naked woman, and a cross, ranks among his most iconic. Not long after Nudie died, in 1984, his longtime former head tailor, Manuel Cuevas, set up his own shop in Nashville, where stars from Marty Stuart to Jack White have made sure that there will forever be a place in Southern style for expertly tailored excess.

NUTRIA

THE NUTRIA IS A COMMON WATER-LOVING mammal of the South whose known aliases are coypu, river rat, and swamp rat. The formal designation is *Myocastor coypus*, from the Greek for "mouse-beaver," although "mouse" is probably being kind. It looks more like a rat. A rat the size of a pit bull.

The rodents are native to South America, and penned nutria were introduced in Louisiana for their fur in the 1930s. But they soon went walkabout and thrived in the marshlands. The nutria is today common along much of the Gulf coast and has moved much farther inland. It dislikes freezing weather—its sad, scraggly tail is easily frostbit—but in milder winters will push north and extend its range. It's also found in North Carolina, Tennessee, and the Delmarva region.

The nutria is rarely beloved, for several reasons: its unlovable snakelike tail; its disconcertingly large orange-yellow incisors; and its habit of chewing up marshes and burrowing into and weakening embankments, including man-made levees. People have launched many efforts to control them, including attempts to rebrand nutria fur as socially acceptable for the fashion conscious, and designers such as Billy Reid and Michael Kors dabbled with it. Big-time chefs have been recruited to popularize dishes made with its high-protein and low-cholesterol meat, but with limited success. In both cases, consumers remained largely unpersuaded that they would not, in fact, be wearing or eating rat. Louisiana's statewide bounty program has shown some success, however. Hunters get paid five dollars per tail, and in 2016 some 349,235 tails were cashed in, notably reducing, for the moment at least, the acreage impacted.

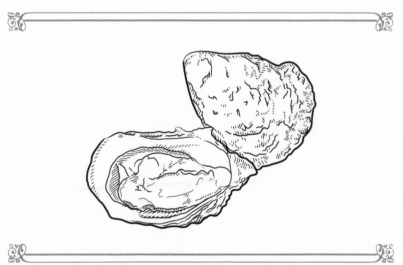

O'CONNOR, FLANNERY

(1925–1964)

In near-perfect prose, Flannery O'Connor wrote about some very odd people doing some very odd things—in other words, real life in the American South. Marked by dark humor and infused with her deep Catholic faith, O'Connor's short stories are widely considered some of the finest ever written. *The Complete Stories*, published posthumously, won the 1972 National Book Award and included such classics as "A Good Man Is Hard to Find," "Good Country People," and "The Life You Save May Be Your Own." O'Connor also published two novels—*Wise Blood* (1952) and *The Violent Bear It Away* (1960)—but she is best known for her stories. Born in Savannah, O'Connor moved to Milledgeville, Georgia, where she lived on her family farm, Andalusia. She studied at the famed Iowa Writers' Workshop, where, because of her strong Southern accent and intense bashfulness, the legendary director Paul Engle reportedly read her stories aloud to the class for her. Lupus killed her father when she was fifteen, and in 1951 O'Connor was stricken by it, too. She returned to Andalusia, where she lived the rest of her short life with her mother and several peacocks, the descendants of which still roam the grounds today.

OFFAL

Wherever you find the kind of culinary repertoire Italians call *la cucina povera* (cooking of the poor), there will be a local taste for offal—the organ meats and other squidgy bits that typically count as a by-product of butchery. Slaves of the antebellum South and then the poor country folk, both black and white, knew that the lower you ate on the hog, the tastier things got. Southern foodways encompass a vast tradition of offal cookery, from fried pig ears, to chitlins stewed with vinegar and hot sauce, to head cheese. Traditionally, the best time to eat variety meats was right after the annual hog killing on a farm. Kidneys, lungs, liver, and hog maws were perishable and needed to be processed and cooked quickly. Other offcuts could then be preserved—the feet pickled, the skins and fat cured. Organ meats have lately become a hallmark of Southern revivalist cookery, and rare is the badass chef who does not try his or her hand at fried pig tails and souse. The regional taste for offal doesn't limit itself to pork: throughout the South, diners display a prodigious appetite for chicken gizzards, livers, and hearts. *See Gizzards.*

OKEFENOKEE SWAMP

It's been said that it was once possible for a man to hike the entire way across North America's largest swamp—thirty-eight miles north to south, twenty-five miles east-west—by stepping on the backs of alligators. A Southern whopper, granted, but it's a lively one. Long a refuge for those seeking to disappear, Okefenokee sprawls seven hundred square miles, straddling the Georgia-Florida border. Early Native Americans called it the Land of the Trembling Earth, and it's not hard to grasp why the swamp became a fortress for the followed. It's inhospitably stunning. A deafening hum of cicadas fills the air, and the black-water current hardly moves. Bald cypress and swamp tupelo branches haunted with Spanish moss frame the sky of this wonderland of old-growth timber stands, spongy islands, flooded prairies, and other habitat niches that shelter hundreds of species: Florida black bears, endangered red-cockaded woodpeckers and wood storks,

sandhill cranes, ospreys, otters, bobcats, and more than twenty species of frogs and toads serenading swamp visitors. While some areas allow motorboats, the primary mode of transportation remains as it was when native tribes navigated its dark waterways, the paddled canoe—some 120 miles of canoe trails crisscross the refuge—and conservationists aim to keep it that way. In 1937, President Franklin D. Roosevelt issued Executive Order 7593, legally protecting and creating the Okefenokee National Wildlife Refuge, setting aside the swamp as an intriguing place to vanish, however temporarily, for many adventurers and fugitives to come.

OKRA

by Jessica B. Harris

The story of okra is a long one. A quintessentially Southern food, as the chef and author Virginia Willis describes it in her eponymous cookbook on the subject, it seems as Southern as field peas and collard greens. It has long been demeaned for its sliminess, and at times marginalized as one of those "Southern things." But cooks knew it far outside the South, and most likely for thousands of years, before a single green pod ever reached these parts.

A relative of both cotton and hibiscus, as its delicate flower suggests, okra had its beginnings, scholars believe, in equatorial Africa, in the Sahel region south of the Sahara, ranging from Mali eastward to Ethiopia. Cooks there prize it as a thickener as well as a vegetable, and it appears in a continent-wide array of dishes, among them Egypt's *bamia* (an okra stew that can be prepared with lamb or beef or served as a vegetarian side dish) and Senegal's *soupikandia*, a soupy stew that is an ancestor of gumbo. Indeed, the word *gumbo* is a corruption of the words for the vegetable in the Bantu languages of Central Africa, *tchingombo* and *ochingombo*. (To this day, anyone who wants okra in any French-speaking region need only ask for *gombo*.) From the continent's midsection, the plant made its way to Mediterranean shores—first cultivated in Egypt perhaps as long ago as 2000 BC—before winning hearts and stomachs in the Middle East and beyond. It is prized as *bhindi*, or lady's fingers, in India.

No one is sure exactly where, when, or how okra made its way to the Western Hemisphere, although enslaved Africans generally get credit. There is evidence of the plant in Brazil in 1658, and it most likely arrived in the southern United States via the Caribbean. It reached Louisiana in the early 1700s, and also appeared in Charleston, South Carolina, early on. Thomas Jefferson noted its cultivation in Virginia before 1781 (and planted it in his own gardens at Monticello in 1809, after his presidency). By 1824, it was well known enough to appear in several recipes in Mary Randolph's *The Virginia Housewife*, the most notable of them entitled simply "Gumbs: A West India Dish"—steamed okra pods served with melted butter, which Randolph deemed "very nutritious and easy of digestion." Jefferson's family had okra recipes that were soupy stews containing ingredients such as potatoes, squash,

onions, lima beans, parsley, and occasionally tomatoes. Bacon was used for seasoning, and chicken was added later, as were veal, corn, and green peppers. The results probably resembled a Charleston gumbo more than a Louisiana one.

It seems that no one lacks an opinion about okra. Admirers praise its thickening abilities and versatile flavor; detractors cannot get past its mucilaginous properties. The vegetable can be fried, steamed, stewed, boiled, pickled, and even eaten raw or blanched in a salad. It is especially prized, though, as the thickener for soups and rich gumbo of the type served in South Louisiana. These days, okra is also gaining acceptance beyond the South, as chefs and cooks throughout the country discover its versatility through myriad international and Southern recipes and find new uses for the pod that is one of Africa's gifts to the cooking of the New World.

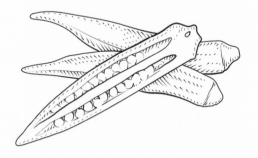

LONG KNOWN BY COOKS AND CONSUMERS alike in the Chesapeake Bay region as the "third spice" (right after salt and pepper), this popular crab seasoning has expanded across the country and beyond, particularly in the South. It's used to flavor everything from pasta to pumpkin seeds, beer to Bloody Marys, chocolate to Cheetos. Most of these pairings should be avoided like bad oysters, but the stuff *is* surprisingly addictive on shellfish, french fries, Tater Tots, corn on the cob, boiled peanuts, hard-boiled eggs, and even—in moderation—cantaloupe. A German immigrant spice merchant named Gustav Brunn first marketed his invention in 1939, under a name that sounds as if it were calculated to arouse suspicion: Delicious Brand Shrimp and Crab Seasoning. He couldn't give the stuff away. Before long he changed the name to Old Bay, after the Old Bay Line of steamboats that operated on the Chesapeake between 1840 and 1962. It took off and never looked back. The cult of Old Bay defies rational explanation. There are T-shirts displaying the iconic yellow, blue, and red tin with captions like "'Tis the Seasoning," "Old Bay Picking Team," and "I Put Old Bay on My Old Bay." There are Old Bay tattoos and Old Bay–flavored ice cream. In 2013, the company released a commemorative can featuring six players from the Baltimore Ravens to celebrate the team's Super Bowl victory. In 2014, Maryland's Flying Dog Brewery released the seasonal Dead Rise Old Bay Summer Ale, featuring citrus hop notes, a crisp, sharp finish, and a dash of Old Bay. It withstood initial skeptics and is still available May through September in the mid-Atlantic.

THE OLD-FASHIONED IS A WHISKEY COCKTAIL that has been old-fashioned since the late nineteenth century. H. L. Mencken once rightly called it "the grandfather of them all." It's essentially the original cocktail. Early topers found that the taste of spirit—whiskey, brandy, rum, whatever—slightly adulterated with a bit of sugar and a few dashes of bitters (which were originally dispensed as medicine) made for a fine way to begin the day and ward off various forms of unpleasantness: disease, dry mouth, foul mood.

As with many drinks, the old-fashioned grew to become an evening libation. When drinkers in the latter half of the nineteenth century started ordering blasphemous cocktails that mixed wine and spirits (e.g., the martini, the Manhattan), purists were aghast and insisted on ordering an "old-fashioned whiskey cocktail."

Over time, the drink has suffered from gradual debasement. It went from being a simple, austere, and elegant cocktail, perfectly balanced, to one that became a vector for various and sundry fruits—oranges and overly red maraschino cherries, in particular, have been pulverized in the bottoms of glasses and abandoned there as if in a tableau of pomicultural carnage. James Beard once aptly said that he liked his "old-fashioned without any refuse in the way of fruit."

Also, some believe a splash of club soda will always improve an old-fashioned. These people are no doubt wrong in many other life choices as well.

OSSABAW HOGS

AFTER EITHER BEING RELEASED OR ESCAPING their captors in the sixteenth century, hogs on Georgia's Ossabaw Island got smaller and smaller and smaller. Their significance, though, has only increased. Because the feral hogs couldn't roam beyond the boundaries of the 25,000-acre Sea Island to which Spanish explorers brought them, they retain most of the characteristics of colonial pigs, even if they weigh a relatively dainty two hundred pounds. That's made them hugely popular with Southern historic sites such as Colonial Williamsburg, Charleston, South Carolina's Middleton Place, and Mount Vernon, which are reluctant to confuse visitors by exhibiting the pink, vaguely rectangular pigs that are standard on American farms today. Ossabaw hogs, by contrast, are black and round, with thick coats and long snouts. What visitors can't see is how Ossabaws taste: the hogs have dark, fatty flesh that's been likened to *jamón ibérico*, although it performs just as well in the Southern context when roasted or smoked whole. Although the hogs continue to thrive on Ossabaw, only about two hundred of them live on the mainland, earning them endangered status. *See Wild hogs.*

OUTLAW COUNTRY

IN THE EARLY 1970S, POWER PLAYERS ON Nashville's Music Row began insisting on a more radio-friendly country-music sound, one featuring pop melodies and lush, sweeping string arrangements from artists like Charley Pride and Conway Twitty. Other musicians, such as Kris Kristofferson, Willie Nelson, and Waylon Jennings, could barely hide their disgust, with Jennings famously saying that he "couldn't go pop with a mouthful of firecrackers." But as much as outlaw country meant a rawer sound, it was just as applicable to the artists' way of doing business. Nelson and Jennings, along with cult figures such as Tompall Glaser and Bobby Bare, insisted on complete control of their recordings, something unheard-of in the Music Row

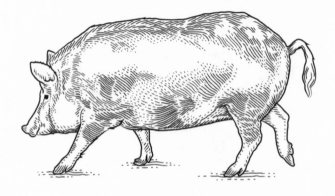

hit-making machine. And they backed up their chutzpah: the 1976 album *Wanted! The Outlaws*, a compilation that featured songs from Glaser, Nelson, Jennings, and his wife, Jessi Colter, became the first country album to go platinum, selling more than a million copies. Four decades on, the outlaw spirit is alive and well. Sirius XM satellite radio has a catchall Outlaw Country channel, and renegade artists such as Chris Stapleton, Jason Isbell, Sturgill Simpson, and Margo Price continue to carry the torch.

OXFORD, MISSISSIPPI

by Ace Atkins

SOMETHING DRAWS US HERE, WHETHER IT'S the connection to Faulkner, a nationally known bookstore, or the many bars that surround the town square. Mention Oxford, Mississippi, and people ask about the literary scene. *Can you throw a stone in any direction and hit a writer? Do y'all talk about writing at the bars? How tall is John Grisham?*

We actually have so many professional novelists, screenwriters, poets, and essayists living and working in Oxford that trying to name them all would be a disservice to those I might forget. And while I see several writer pals around town nearly every day, we seem to talk everything else but shop. Mostly, we go to movies. As far as John Grisham's height, I've never met or seen him, as he left

town nearly twenty years ago, a little before I arrived.

For me, most of the draw comes from Oxford's past. The famous four—Faulkner, Willie Morris, Larry Brown, and Barry Hannah—have all passed on. Those guys, two of them great pals, were what brought me here. I had the honor of drinking many beers with Larry, the master of Southern grit, sometimes with a shot of god-awful Rumple Minze, and hanging out and shooting pistols and rifles with Barry, a master of short stories who wrote in wild and rhythmic ways. Barry loved guns, motorcycles, and noir. He also loved telling tall tales. He once introduced me as "the best goddamn fighter pilot I've ever seen."

Neither one of us could fly a plane.

When the late Dean Faulkner Wells released her memoir, *Every Day by the Sun*, the story of growing up as Faulkner's favorite niece, she drew on the strength of Oxford's literary friends. Famously shy, she was terrified of reading from her book at the big release. So a handful of writers sat onstage with her, and we read her words while she listened with everyone else. Everyone loved Dean. She and her husband, the novelist Larry Wells, often hosted literary salons at their house, especially when visiting authors came through town (Faulkner had edited *Absalom, Absalom!* on their dining room table, a fact that caused most visitors to swoon). For many of us, Dean made "Pappy" more than just a statue and a face on a postage stamp. Through her, he was the real person who told ghost stories to the kids at Rowan Oak and refused to take phone calls during dinner. She didn't even realize he was famous until she walked down the street with him in Paris, drawing stares and whispers.

To my great regret, I missed Willie Morris by one year. He moved just before I arrived in town. But the stories Dean, Larry, and his many other friends told about Willie were legendary. I can't drive past the city cemetery without thinking about the night he covertly buried his beloved Lab, Pete, somewhere not far from Faulkner's grave.

As for the living, you can find most of us at local watering holes, bourbon being our common denominator from Faulkner on. We're bonded by the beauty and grit of this place—which makes for great material—and its sense of noir. From Faulkner's *Sanctuary* to Larry's *Father and Son* to Barry's *Yonder Stands Your Orphan*, there's a darkness in most of our work, fueled by bourbon and the hardscrabble landscape outside the oasis of the quaint square, with the old white courthouse surrounded by brick storefronts.

I don't believe anyone would dispute that the heart of the literary scene is Square Books, a storied shop that's brought an endless lineup of all-stars since Richard and Lisa Howorth opened it in 1979. Most Thursdays you can find a nationally known writer speaking during the weekly *Thacker Mountain Radio Hour*, an hour of literature and music with roots in the traditional Southern medicine show. Afterward, you can usually find the local writers welcoming the visitor. Drinks flow freely.

I once heard a visiting writer ask Richard Howorth what brings so many different voices here to work. *Is it Faulkner? Or has it grown into something more?* Howorth thought about it for a moment, then paraphrased a line from *Casablanca*: "I think they come here for the waters."

OYSTERS

AMERICA'S OYSTER, *CRASSOSTREA VIRGINICA*, used to live in such abundance in the Chesapeake Bay, Atlantic estuaries, and the Gulf of Mexico that it could feed a nation. During decades of railroad expansion, the oysters traveled across the country, packed in ice and sawdust, bound for upscale bars and taverns. Prohibition put an end to this trade, and oyster bars faded from every region except the South. New Orleans oyster houses, with their nimble and fast-talking shuckers, never went anywhere. Nor did the seafood shacks of the coastal South, which kept a kind of raucous American oyster bar culture alive. Recent years have seen both a decimation of wild oyster populations, due to overharvesting and environmental degradation, and a resurgence of oyster bars throughout the country, thanks to advances in "off-bottom" shellfish cultivation. Southern oystermen—particularly those around the Chesapeake and Mobile Bays—have lately joined the boutique oyster party. Their hand-harvested product may not have the mouthful-of-pennies brininess of Northern cold-water oysters, but they have a soft sweetness all their own.

OZARKS

COME AUTUMN, THE DECIDUOUS FORESTS that blanket the central United States' Ozark highlands explode in a crimson-yellow-orange riot to rival the most vibrant Vermont tableau. Encompassing forty-seven thousand square miles spread over four states—Arkansas, Kansas, Missouri, and Oklahoma—the region (technically, a large plateau rather than a mountain range) is awash in clear, bubbling streams and breathtaking vistas. Rainbows appear almost daily. Early arrivals, mostly explorers and the Scotch-Irish immigrants who settled here during early-nineteenth-century land grabs, were daunted by the high, rugged ridges, steep hillsides, and treacherous passes. But later travelers sought out the Ozarks' tamer features, such as the "healing waters and springs" that made Eureka Springs, Arkansas, a fashionable turn-of-the-century spa destination. As a result, the region lays claim to an eclectic mix of people and cultures, from Native Americans and New Age spiritualists, to back-to-the-land types and sustainability-minded developers, to an impressively mismatched range of high-profile figures: George Washington Carver, Paul Harvey, Langston Hughes, and Brad Pitt are all native sons.

P

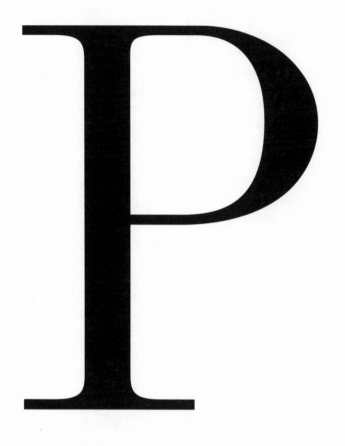

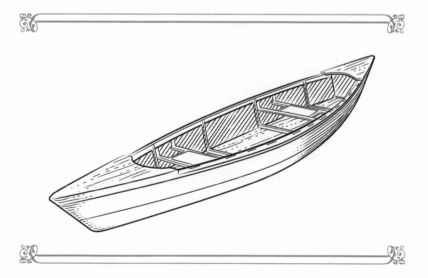

(1929–2016)

THE PAINKILLER IS A REFRESHING MIXED drink (phylum: Tiki) consisting of rum, pineapple juice, cream of coconut, and orange juice. It originated, circa 1971, at the Soggy Dollar Bar in the British Virgin Islands, where the recipe was long regarded with the sort of secrecy applied to the classified ingredient in your grandmother's pimento cheese. In 1989, Charles Tobias, founder of Pusser's Rum (distilled from a formula for blending the rum once rationed out to British navy sailors) and a fan of both bar and drink, sought the recipe but got repeatedly rebuffed. He later claimed to have reverse-engineered the drink after extensive experimentation, and he then trademarked the name. The company's website now refers to it as the Iconic Pusser's Painkiller®. The site, somewhat confusingly, also divulges the cocktail's "secret formula": two parts Pusser's, four parts pineapple juice, one part cream of coconut, and one part orange juice, served on the rocks and garnished with nutmeg.

Like its distant island cousin the Dark 'n Stormy, the Painkiller is one of the rare cocktails trademarked and defended with some vigor by a liquor brand. If you decide to open a bar and call it Painkiller (as some ill-fated entrepreneurs did not long ago on Manhattan's Lower East Side), you will be called out to the sidewalk and flogged with lawyers. *See Dark 'n Stormy.*

ARNOLD PALMER'S SUCCESS ON THE GOLF course may have earned him the nickname "the King," but in many ways, Palmer was golf's everyman. Born in working-class Latrobe, Pennsylvania, he attended Wake Forest College on a golf scholarship, turned pro at twenty-five, and went on to collect sixty-two PGA tour titles over a six-decade career, with spectators flocking to witness Palmer's emotional, charismatic playing style. His Southern legacies include his record of fifty consecutive starts at the Masters (including four wins at Augusta National), and a tradition that extends beyond the green. After ordering a blend of unsweetened tea and lemonade at the 1960 U.S. Open, Palmer unwittingly ignited a trend known far and wide across the South. The drink—originally two parts unsweetened tea to one part lemonade—became an instant classic as requests for "Arnold Palmers" spread throughout the country, earning the golfer a splash of immortality in beverage history as well.

PALMETTO

THERE'S SOMETHING BOTH NOBLE AND MYTH-ical about this camel of trees. A drought-tolerant, frond-topped tower undaunted by seawater, the palmetto is also an unlikely hero of the American Revolution, during which South Carolina Patriots relied on its elastic-ity to absorb the shock of incoming British cannonballs. In 1776, sheltered behind make-shift walls of palmetto logs at Fort Moultrie (on Charleston Harbor), soldiers were able not only to fend off attacks but also to steadily return fire, eventually forcing the British ar-mada to retreat in defeat. Today the tree's spiky silhouette continues to punctuate the coastal landscape from the Lowcountry to Florida and is, of course, the predominant symbol on the South Carolina flag.

PALMETTO BUGS

EXTERMINATORS WILL TELL YOU THERE'S A difference between species, but in the South, you can confidently call any cockroach longer than your thumb joint (knuckle to nail) a pal-metto bug. Or, more likely, scream, *"Palmetto bugggg!"* as it scuttles at up to twenty miles per hour across the floor like the winged spawn of Satan that it is. Technically speaking, though, the culprit is an American cockroach, *Periplaneta americana*—also known in certain circles as the state bird of Florida, the Bombay canary, and other aliases—and, honestly, you'd rather see one of them in your home than a small cockroach, which is a harbinger of infestation. A palmetto bug, on the other hand, most likely just wandered—or flew—in from some damp place like your mulch bed. In any case, feel free to flail away and bat at the reddish-brown beast like a banshee. A flip-flop is as effective a weapon as any.

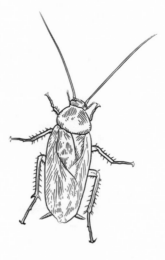

PAPPY VAN WINKLE

Here's a fun little project: stroll into your local liquor store and ask the clerk for a bottle of Pappy Van Winkle's Family Reserve—then time how long he laughs at your folly. This most coveted of bourbons has humble roots: the Van Winkle family has been making bourbon for more than a century, spanning Prohibition, iconic brands such as Old Fitzgerald and Rebel Yell, and all the convolutions inherent to the industry in Kentucky. The Pappy label wasn't introduced until the 1990s, as a means of marketing some "old" bourbon (aged for fifteen, twenty, even twenty-three years), and for a while one could find it perched on retailers' shelves next to the Wild Turkey and Jim Beam. Then, at the same time the craft liquor boom hit, the Beverage Tasting Institute gave Pappy 20-Year an unprecedented 99 rating—and a cult was born. Production is still frustratingly limited, leading to annual "Pappy Days" on which fans pray to get their hands on newly released bottles, and a resale market where those same fifths fetch $2,000 apiece or more. So will this be your year to finally score some Pappy? Sure. And you can ride home from the liquor store on your trusty unicorn.

PARKS, ROSA

(1913–2005)

Rosa Parks Day comes around twice a year, as states from Ohio to Oregon honor the Alabama-born activist who got "tired of giving in" to racist laws and abusive authority figures. The granddaughter of black nationalists, she was born Rosa McCauley in 1913; as a child, she was so headstrong that her grandmother fretted about young Rosa "talking biggity to white folks." In 1932, she married Raymond Parks, a barber who was then involved in the defense of the Scottsboro Boys. Rosa Parks assumed a prominent role in the local civil rights struggle, too: after learning that women could join the NAACP, she was elected secretary at the first chapter meeting she attended. Parks had spent more than a decade registering voters and protesting segregation before she boarded a Montgomery City Line bus in 1955, taking a seat in the first row of the section designated for black passengers. When the driver ordered her to give her seat to a white passenger, she refused. Parks's arrest for her defiance sparked a bus boycott that lasted for more than a year. The boycott was successful, and Parks kept agitating for an end to substandard housing, job discrimination, and wrongful imprisonment. Sometime in the decade before her death at ninety-two, she scribbled on a paper bag that is now housed at the Library of Congress, "The struggle continues . . . the struggle continues . . . the struggle continues."

PARTON, DOLLY

(1946–)

by Allison Glock

I MARRIED MY HUSBAND BECAUSE HE LOVES Dolly Parton. (That wasn't the only reason, but I'd be lying if I said it wasn't up there with "incredibly smart" and "kind to children.") Dolly is a litmus test. People who love Dolly tend to understand that life is a huge mess of contradiction and struggle but that is no reason not to have a great time while you're here. Dolly is nothing if not pure inspiration. Sprung from Tennessee mountain dirt, one of a dozen children living ankle by cheek in a single-room cabin, Dolly rose to become the most important female songwriter in the world. She is also an uncommonly generous philanthropist, an actress, an award-winning film producer, a pop-culture icon, a canny businesswoman, a gifted musician, and most famously, a singer, blessed with an idiosyncratic soprano so twangy-sweet it brings grown men (see above) to their knees.

Unlike other country music legends, Dolly has never gotten tangled up with drugs, or fallen drunk out of a limo, or married a no-good man who treated her like a needy cur, or posed topless. Dolly doesn't play tragic. She smiles! She laughs! And by laughing loudly and often, she—amazingly, magically, in her saucer-plate sequins and vaudevillian makeup—embodies dignity. Also, good sense.

Back when she was just starting out, Elvis himself asked to record her song "I Will Always Love You." Catch was, he wanted half the rights. Dolly turned him down. That ballsy decision ended up earning her millions of dollars years later. Not to mention admission into a club of what surely must contain only one member: women who said no to Elvis Presley.

Dolly has always said no to the right things. (With the exception of *Rhinestone*.) No, I won't sell my songs. No, I won't tone down my look, or my ambition, or my intelligence. As a result, her list of accomplishments is as massive as her, um, assets, but what makes it unique is less length than breadth. What other woman has garnered a *Ms.* magazine Woman of the Year Award, a Kennedy Center Honor, forty-seven Grammy nominations (eight wins), a Good Housekeeping Seal of Approval (the first ever awarded to a *person*), and a recurring role on *Hannah Montana*? Dolly reaches the high and low, feels Jesus and gravity, and through it all radiates humility and graciousness. She is the anti-Madonna. And the antidote to the reflexive cynicism and weariness of our world.

"Dolly is an angel," my husband says, only half joking. Okay, not joking at all. I see her more as a role model. WWDD? Well, work harder than a lumberjack, for one. And do it in high heels and a push-up bra with a grin on her face. Dolly bleeds optimism, which is not the same as naïveté. As she sings in a 2008 song, "I'm just a backwoods Barbie, too much makeup, too much hair. Don't be fooled by thinking that the goods are not all there."

When she is given grief (or death threats) from folks who, say, can't reconcile her Christian faith with her inclusive personal politics, Dolly punctures their bigotry without rancor. "God and I have a great relationship," she explains with a wink, "but we both see other people."

Which is the true genius of Dolly. Brains as big as hers, used only for the power of good.

At seventy-some years old, with more than sixty indelible years in show business, Dolly has integrity and bone-dry honesty that remain as unassailable as her wigs. "If I have one more facelift, I'll have a beard," she jokes.

She has lived her life on her terms; killed the whole country with kindness; showed women the green, golden ground between doormat and tiger lady. Dolly is a walking self-help book, an animate example of the classy way to get it done. It all starts, she says, with owning your crazy. WWDD?

"Find out who you are," she advises. "And do it on purpose."

PATTON, CHARLEY

(1891–1934)

BORN IN 1891, CHARLEY PATTON WAS THE blues' first big star, traveling all over the Mississippi Delta and drawing huge crowds at plantation parties and juke joints, with a woman on each arm and a gravel-coated but booming voice—legend has it that you could hear him from five hundred yards away without amplification—that influenced other players such as Howlin' Wolf. He could also jam out on the guitar, giving the blues a shot of boogie and groove. His recorded output

is minimal—just sixty-odd songs cut from 1929 until his death five years later—but they solidify Patton as one of the blues' great entertainers.

PAWPAW

by Bill Heavey

THE PAWPAW IS THE LARGEST, MOST DELIcious, and least-known fruit in the New World, found throughout the southern, eastern, and midwestern United States. The green, kidney-shaped berries ripen in September and October. They are big. While most mature pawpaws weigh between five and fourteen ounces, they can go two pounds. For this reason, the pawpaw harvester both glories and fears when, gently shaking the fragile tree, he hears the heavy thud of ripe fruit hitting the ground around him after falling twenty-five feet. (You have to shake the trees this way to get the delicious fruit. Coons and possums seek them out on the tree, while deer, foxes, and just about every other mammal eat them off the ground.) I once filled a backpack and two garbage bags with sixty pounds of them in an afternoon along the Potomac in Washington, D.C., then drove and sold them to a tony restaurant in Baltimore for five bucks a pound. On the way home at 2:00 a.m., I was so exhausted and starved that I stopped for two Big Macs. I've since vowed never to repeat that foolishness.

The fruit is yellow and fleshy and tastes tropical, as if it couldn't possibly have come from North America. The flavor hints at mango and banana but isn't quite either. Pawpaws were far more important in earlier times than today. Proof of this lingers on in the many rivers, creeks, counties, streets, and towns named Pawpaw. Chilled pawpaw was a favorite of George Washington's. Thomas Jefferson planted trees at Monticello and had seeds shipped to France when he was there, to give to friends. Lewis and Clark were fans. On September 18, 1806, their journal reads: "Our party entirely out of provisions subsisting on poppaws. We divide[d] the buiskit which amount[ed] to nearly one buiskit per man, this in addition to the poppaws is to last [us] down to the Settlement's which is 150 miles. The party appear perfectly contented and tell us they can live very well on the pappaws."

The trees like moist but well-drained, fertile bottomland, which often means the banks of streams and rivers. They grow in stands that are actually a single organism. The flowers are protogynous, which in practical terms means the trees require pollen from a completely unrelated tree to pollinate. Otherwise, incest would take place. They are usually pollinated by blowflies, the same kind that eat carrion, which is probably why pawpaw flowers smell—I'm not making this up—like roadkill.

Why didn't pawpaws catch on? It's simple. They bruise easily, don't travel well, and have the shelf life of soap bubbles. The web is full of cheery exhortations to make delicious pawpaw breads, pies, cookies, and custards. This is bullshit, because many components of the fruit's flavor turn out to be highly volatile. So cook or freeze away, but don't expect the finished product to taste of pawpaw. I prefer to eat them raw, the moment I find them. Pawpaws are a sacrament to the eternal cycle of the earth and the ephemeral tyranny of ripeness. Stand there with insects buzzing around you and spiderwebs brushing your face, eat, and savor the fact of your existence on this particular planet. But don't forget to take some home and mash them into really good vanilla ice cream. They're amazing that way.

PEABODY HOTEL DUCKS

No, you have not been imbibing a bit too freely at the grand old bar in the even grander lobby of the Peabody hotel in downtown Memphis. Five mallard ducks did indeed just exit the elevator, waddle down a long red carpet, and happily plop into the lobby's antique central fountain. This it-could-happen-only-in-the-South institution dates back to the 1930s, when a Peabody manager and his equally tipsy hunting buddy thought it would be a gas to sneak a few live decoys (legal back then) into the fountain. Guests loved it, and by 1940, a bellman named Edward Pembroke had assumed the role of "duckmaster"—escorting trained ducks to and from the lobby each day, a role he fulfilled for the next fifty years. (He even took them to visit Johnny Carson on *The Tonight Show*.) When off duty, the world-famous waterfowl continue to preen in the Peabody's sole penthouse, a $200,000 marble-and-glass rooftop suite with sweeping views of the city. Another of their perks worth quacking about: duck never appears on any

Peabody menu—making the hotel's occasion-worthy Chez Philippe quite possibly the only *canard*-free French restaurant in the world.

to their peachy supremacy being questioned. Bite into one of each—not such a hardship—and decide for yourself.

PEACH WARS

Georgia might have co-opted the stone fruit's image—Atlanta alone has more than seventy streets named Peachtree-something-or-other, and every license plate bears its likeness. But numbers don't lie, and since all the way back in the 1950s, South Carolina has actually shipped more peaches annually, currently more than doubling Georgia's total. So is South Carolina the *real* Peach State? As with any number of entrenched Southern rivalries—Coke and Pepsi, Auburn/Alabama, cornbread with sugar or without—it depends entirely on whom you ask. Both states have rich commercial peach-farming traditions that trace back to the mid-1800s. It's a Georgia grower named Samuel Henry Rumph, though, who gets credit for the Southern peach boom; he both introduced the Elberta, an easier-to-ship variety that he christened with his wife's middle name in 1875, and hatched the idea of a refrigerated train car to ship the produce north. South Carolina's crop experienced slower growth but began to dominate the market in the mid-twentieth century and hasn't let up since. Each group of farmers touts superior taste, which is determined largely by weather—factors such as rain and heat—and also soil condition. Partisans of each state are fiercely loyal, naturally, and don't take kindly

PEA CRAB

You're shucking your way through a cluster at an oyster roast when you pry open a shell and find a creepy-looking, spider-sized orange crab inside. Don't panic. Some people would be jealous. Take our pea crab–loving first president, who supposedly enjoyed the crunchy creatures sprinkled over his soup. Or the author of a 1907 *New York Times* piece that attributed to the kleptoparasites "all the sweetness and delicate salt flavors of the entire crab family." Pea crabs are tiny crustaceans that wash into oysters with seawater and nestle in their gills, where they make themselves at home and siphon off a bit of the plankton that oysters feed on for themselves—a harmless habit as long as there's enough food to go around. They're the oysterman's caviar, raw or cooked, and you may not see one again for a long time. Close your eyes and go for it.

PEANUT BUTTER AND MAYONNAISE SANDWICH

ELVIS LOVED PEANUT BUTTER AND BANANA, but other country boys his age went for a different combination of crunchy and creamy. If you didn't eat a PB & mayo, your parents or grandparents probably did. Two affordable and calorie-rich spreads on standard-issue white bread, the sandwich most likely gained popularity in the 1930s and '40s. Distasteful as it may sound to the uninitiated, the mayonnaise is mostly there for texture—which might be why it fell out of favor. Today's supermarket peanut butter is creamier than the rustic spreads of days gone by, so it doesn't need the extra boost. Southerners of a certain age, though, still wouldn't have it any other way. Sliced banana makes a nice addition, too.

PEANUTS

GEORGE WASHINGTON CARVER MAY HAVE been more taken with peanuts than any other Southerner. Born to slaves in Missouri in the 1860s, the pioneering scientist came up with hundreds of applications for the plant in the wake of boll weevils wrecking the region's cotton crop. Carver invented peanut hand cleanser, peanut charcoal, peanut margarine, and peanut mock oysters. Yet in his enthusiasm for the subterranean legume, he just barely outpaced his regional cohorts, who had been snacking on peanuts since the eighteenth century. Peanuts are native to South

America, but Spanish explorers introduced them to Africa, their last stop before reaching the Southern colonies. Initially eaten only by enslaved people, they quickly found favor with white elites, who turned them into soup and candy. Later, Confederate soldiers sang dreamily about the end of the war, when they would "kiss our wives and sweethearts and gobble goober peas!" By the 1920s, peanuts' popularity was soaring in ballparks, at movie theaters, and under circus tents beyond the South, gladdening strapped cotton farmers who weren't sure what else to plant in their sandy soil. Nowadays, approximately one out of every seven nuts consumed in this country is a peanut, and almost half of U.S.-grown peanuts hail from Georgia.

PECANS

ANYONE WHO HAS TAKEN A DRIVE THROUGH the South has seen the roadside signs hawking paper-shell pecans. The distinction feels atavistic, since nearly all pecans these days have soft shells. Unlike walnuts, which require a nutcracker to open, and black walnuts that require nothing short of a jackhammer, paper-shell pecans can be rolled open between your fingers like peanuts. The shells splinter and the sweet nut meats slip right out. Horticulturists developed paper-shell varieties in the late 1800s, which spurred an increase in both ornamental plantings and commercial production of this native American variety of hickory. Not coincidentally, old-fashioned molasses and chess pies laid the foundation for pecan pie, a dessert that didn't become popular until after World War II but now is so ubiquitous it serves as the South's edible mascot.

PERCY, WALKER

(1916–1990)

by Jon Meacham

TRAGEDY—OR, MORE PRECISELY, A PAIR OF tragedies—gave him a home of his own. Born in 1916, as a teenager Walker Percy lost his father, a lawyer in Birmingham, Alabama, to suicide and his mother to an automobile accident. By the summer of 1932, Percy and his two brothers had taken up permanent residence in the Greenville, Mississippi, house of their cousin, the planter-poet William Alexander Percy. It was "Uncle Will," as he was known, who gave young Walker a Renaissance sense of the world that included a love of literature, an appreciation of the role of mystery in the created order, and an insatiable thirst for knowledge. Will Percy, Walker would later write, was the most remarkable man he had ever known—a man to whom he owed a debt that could never be repaid.

Readers thus owe Uncle Will, too, for Walker Percy left a lasting mark on American literature and letters. Trained as a physician—he attended the University of North Carolina at Chapel Hill and medical school at Columbia—Percy, who would in time convert to Roman Catholicism, soon came to realize that his central concerns were spiritual rather than clinical. "What began to interest me," he wrote of his great shift from medicine to literature, "was not the physiological and pathological processes within man's body but the problem of man himself, the nature and destiny of man; specifically and more immediately, the predicament of man in a modern technological society."

In a series of novels (*The Moviegoer, The Last Gentleman, Love in the Ruins, Lancelot, The Second Coming, The Thanatos Syndrome*) and in nonfiction work such as *Lost in the Cosmos*, Percy explored themes of alienation, faith, redemption, and the nature of language itself.

Reacting to a glowing 1978 assessment of his work by Harvard's Robert Coles, Percy was wry. "I am having the uncomfortable feeling of having at last been stuck in my slot—as a 'Christian existentialist,'" he wrote his friend Shelby Foote in 1979. "I hear sighs of relief all over: now that they know what I am, they don't have to worry about me."

Always a Southerner—he spent his working life in Louisiana—Percy nevertheless resisted the label of "Southern" writer on the grounds that his concerns, like those of other artists, were universal, not local. "Yes," Percy, who died in 1990, wrote Foote late in life, "God bless us for doing what we did and even surviving." To which grateful readers might say: amen to that.

(1932–1998)

SOME MUSICIANS' SOUNDS EVOLVE OVER TIME, their styles molded by changes in the greater culture, business pressures, the drive in their makers' minds. Not so with Carl Perkins, whose scorching, exhaust-tinged rockabilly sound, delivered most notably via Sun Records, lasted his entire career. Many probably know Perkins through 1956's "Blue Suede Shoes." The track's inspiration, it was said, came when Perkins overheard a young man admonishing his girlfriend for her clumsy footwork on the dance floor; Perkins wrote the lyrics that night on a paper bag. "Blue Suede Shoes" crossed over to country, R&B, and pop radio, reaching No. 2 on the Billboard Hot 100 singles chart. As it happened, a horrific truck accident left Perkins stranded in the hospital while his song burned up the charts. After the success of Elvis Presley's version—its release postponed until Perkins's version had faded—Perkins moved more into songwriting, a slight chip on his shoulder. But his music and fame would endure. His "Matchbox" is a rockabilly touchstone. He was part of the Million Dollar Quartet (along with Presley, Jerry Lee Lewis, and Johnny Cash) that recorded an hour of ad hoc music in 1955. And his sound particularly influenced a group from Liverpool. "If there was no Carl Perkins," Paul McCartney once said, "there would be no Beatles."

WHEN SUMMER FEELS NEVER-ENDING AND the season's abundance of fruit and veggies is wilting and wrinkling in the refrigerator, Southerners have long turned to pickling. Thomas Jefferson waxed poetic about it: "On a hot day in Virginia," he wrote, "I know nothing more comforting than a fine spiced pickle, brought up trout-like from the sparkling depths of the aromatic jar below the stairs of Aunt Sally's cellar." The tradition of brining food to preserve it dates back four thousand years as a way to continue eating foods out of season and on long sea voyages. Today pickling enthusiasts in the South and beyond have mason jars of strawberries, greens, tomatoes, okra, cauliflower, peppers, beets— you name it—lining pantry shelves. Chef Andrea Reusing, owner of Lantern restaurant in Chapel Hill, North Carolina, grew up seeing her grandmother's Ping-Pong table laden with canning equipment. It clearly made an impression. Reusing once stocked her toddler daughter's bedroom with crocks of fermenting cabbage—the room's temperature was ideal for storage. The process doesn't require twenty pounds of produce and special equipment; you can pickle for short-term storage using just a mason jar and a basic brine recipe (combining vinegar, water, sugar, salt, and whatever spices you want to add for a freelance twist). The results will keep in the fridge for up to a month.

PIGGLY WIGGLY

In 1916, when Clarence Saunders came up with the then-novel concept for a self-service grocery store, his contemporaries laughed. When he named it Piggly Wiggly, they questioned whether he was of sound mind. A century later, the joke is on the naysayers. Far from fading into obscurity, the pioneering Memphis chain thrived and launched a food-shopping transformation that endures today. Though Saunders's descendants are no longer associated with the company, Piggly Wiggly remains a Southern icon, with more than five hundred stores still open in seventeen states, and a symbol of the power of ingenuity. And the name? All part of Saunders's original knack for stirring up buzz. According to company lore, when someone asked him why he'd chosen such an unusual name for his store, Saunders looked at him for a beat before replying simply, "So people will ask that very question."

PIGS' FEET

At a Depression-era juke joint, many customers could be found eating fish sandwiches, or a pickled egg. But odds are someone in the tiny room was eating a barbecued pig's foot, the lowest-on-the-hog part that became emblematic of the blues' grit and make-do spirit. In 1933, Jacksonville, Florida's Wesley Wilson wrote "Gimme a Pigfoot (and a Bottle of Beer)"; even though the lyrics begin "Up in

Harlem every Saturday night," Bessie Smith, a native of Chattanooga, may well have been thinking back to the South when she recorded the song and made it famous. Or maybe not: pig foot was prevalent in upper Manhattan, a reminder of transplanted black Southerners' rural roots. It was also salty, which helps explain why club owners with liquor to sell were so keen to serve it. But the snack's simplicity, affordability, and celebratory connotations widened its appeal: convenience stores across the South uphold the general-store tradition of keeping a jar of pickled pigs' feet on the counter. Whether pickled, boiled, or grilled, pigs' feet still make appearances in dive bars, though in the contemporary South they're most frequently seen in posole and other stews that Latino immigrants brought to the region. *See Soul food.*

PILAU

No matter how you spell it, pilau is Southern through and through: the Charleston, South Carolina, food writers Matt and Ted Lee describe the one-pot rice meal as "the definitive Southern dish." But it's also a product of the world, with a family tree rooted in ancient India. Pulao, a simmered mix of meat and rice, made its way to Persia, and eventually popped up everywhere from Bukhara to Brazil: both paella and pilaf are descendants of the recipe first recorded in Sanskrit. Seasonings and cooking methods vary from one culture to another, but the distinguishing element is rice, long the culinary lifeblood of the Lowcountry. "Few foods seem to be so at home in South Carolina," Helen Woodward wrote of pilau in her introduction to the 1930 book, *200 Years of Charleston Cooking*. The late food historian John Egerton found sixteen accepted spellings for the dish, ranging from *plaw* to *perleau*, and nearly as many pronunciations. There's no single right way to make it, either, although the rice is typically fluffy and the adorning ingredients—whether shrimp, oysters, chicken, sausage, bacon, bell peppers, or tomatoes—are totally combined with the grains.

PIMENTO CHEESE

LOOKING FOR A PRIME EXAMPLE OF SOUTHERN hospitality? Look no further than pimento cheese, the beloved mayonnaise-based sharp cheddar spread that's smeared on burgers, stirred into grits, and snapped up at cocktail parties across the region. The "caviar of the South" is a New Yorker by birth, but Southerners warmly welcomed it in the early twentieth century without conflict (unless you count squabbles over the spelling of *pimento* and precisely what consistency is best). Originally, pimento cheese was a celebration of two foods made possible by the Industrial Revolution: commercially produced cream cheese and canned pimentos. Cooking-school teachers instructed their students to combine the two, which they did dutifully until food manufacturers started selling premade pimento cheese. It was a nationwide hit. After World War II, though, pimento cheese's popularity slipped in the North. Around the same time, Southern home cooks started concocting their own versions with Worcestershire sauce, hot sauce, and paprika, homing in on the basic template for Southern pimento cheese; the preparation is so esteemed that it's served every spring on sandwiches at the Masters Tournament.

PIRATES

DURING THEIR LUCRATIVE HEYDAY, ROUGHLY from the mid-1600s to the mid-1700s, around two thousand armed entrepreneurs terrorized the Southeastern seaboard and the Caribbean, seeking gold, silver, spices, medicine, and artillery traveling between Europe and the New World. Most pirate ships functioned as democracies, with voting rights and equal shares of the booty. The names of a few of the outlaws live on in infamy (and plenty of mythology): Blackbeard, terrorizing North Carolina with his *Queen Anne's Revenge*. Black Caesar, raiding the Florida Keys. Stede Bonnet, the "Gentleman Pirate," swashbuckling in the Bahamas. Anne Bonny and her lover, "Calico Jack," pilfering off Jamaica. Once caught, pirates were given no quarter, and often "danced the hempen jig" (met the noose) in public places such as White Point Gardens in Charleston, South Carolina—where Bonnet was hanged—to serve as a deterrent to others. Eventually, the fledgling Continental navy turned to privateers—state-sanctioned pirates who plundered in the name of patriotism—to help fend off the British, from the American Revolution to the War of 1812. These days, Southern pirates are mostly relegated to putt-putt courses in Myrtle Beach. *See Blackbeard.*

PIROGUE

A PIROGUE IS A SMALL SHALLOW-DRAFT BOAT popularized in this country by Cajuns. Early pirogues were cypress dugouts, while modern ones are fiberglass or, if you're inclined to spend $3,500 for a custom job, cypress planks. The boats are pointed at both ends and "hard chined," which means that the sides and bottom meet at a sharp angle, which increases cargo capacity in terms of both space and displacement. Pirogues are also quiet, nimble, and light enough for one person to carry. These characteristics have made them ideal and iconic swamp boats for centuries.

It is possible that more people have sung about pirogues than paddled or push-poled them. Hank Williams famously sang, "Me gotta go pole the pirogue down the bayou," in his 1952 hit "Jambalaya." Hank Jr. followed suit in 1969, singing, "ride around in my old pirogue" in "Cajun Baby." In Johnny Horton's 1956 rockabilly song "I Got a Hole in My Pirogue," the boat damage grievously interferes with his social life: "Yeah I'm here on the bayou, sittin' all alone / With a busted bottom and I cain't pole it home." Some of these dudes were just name-checking pirogues. One who definitely was not was the great Doug Kershaw, whose

1961 "Louisiana Man" is about a boy growing up on a houseboat in a family of swampers. He mentions his father jumping into his pirogue at 3:30 a.m. But it's the song's refrain that most aptly captures the spirit of both pirogues and bayou life. "Setting traps in the swamp catching anything he can / Gotta make a living, he's a Louisiana Man."

PIT MASTER

FROM THE CAROLINAS TO MEMPHIS TO THE Texas Hill Country, behind every authentic Southern barbecue joint is a real live pit master. A savant of slow cooking; a Beethoven of basting; a maestro of meat. And we do mean *behind.* Follow the smoke back there, past piles of split hickory, and you'll find the pit master at work, usually in a separate structure even more ramshackle than the restaurant. Even the stars—men and women like Rodney Scott of Scott's Bar-B-Que in Hemingway (and now Charleston), South Carolina; Sam Jones of Skylight Inn BBQ in Ayden, North Carolina; and Helen Turner of Helen's Bar-B-Q in Brownsville, Tennessee—have to keep the pits burning. They're strong from splitting logs, shoveling coals, and hefting sides of pork or beef. They're smudgy from spending their lives at the center of an omnipresent haze. And they're tired, because a whole hog or a Boston butt on its way to becoming pulled pork requires roughly the same round-the-clock care as a newborn. They'll be gratified to hear that their hard work brought you to your knees. Just don't ask them to spill any secrets. Their craft is fairly straightforward, but there in the basting jug and spice rub they've got a few arcane ingredients and techniques only they know, which they'll either take to the grave or pass along to their children—if they prove worthy. Long after you depart and the sun sets, they'll still be at it, because great barbecue has never made itself. Being a pit master is a calling, not something you can claim with a certificate from the Internet.

PLUFF MUD

by Jack Hitt

FILLING UP AN OLD HELLMANN'S JAR WITH some of Charleston, South Carolina's unique marsh mud before leaving town has always been a pretty common thing among Lowcountry teens. I was shipped off to a Tennessee reform school when I was fifteen, and after my daily beatings, I typically retreated to my dorm room to twist open the lid to take in the peculiar aroma. I wasn't just relieved. I was transported.

Locals call it pluff mud, possibly for the sound it makes when its uncanny suction slurps the shoe right off your foot. Or maybe pluff mud is a folksy spelling of "plough mud," since early farmers used the nutrient-rich ooze to fertilize their fields. No one really knows the origin, although most of the crackpots in town are pretty sure they do.

Still, nothing calls a Charlestonian back home—not a whiff of grits on the stove or peanuts boiling in a pot—quite like pluff mud's mildly acrid, slightly sweet stank. Agronomists can explain it scientifically, and it is miraculous. Pluff mud begins with lots of death—little sea critters, the local cordgrass, other plants, and decaying sea life mixed with the briny spoor of all those birds and critters sucked downward, like your tennis shoe, into an anaerobic sludge and then occasionally washed over by the descending fresh waters and silts to create a cassoulet of muds that, in angled light at low tide, glistens with the iridescence of certain bird feathers, or a bubble in the sun.

To step in it is a pure B-movie quicksand experience. The more you wiggle to get out, as with a Chinese finger trap, the deeper you go (and forget the damn shoe). Veterans can crazy-walk through it but only by surrendering to its power. The only sure exit strategy is the water bug's. You need lots of surface tension, which for big fleshy humans means hurling yourself spread eagle onto the mud and snow-angeling your hulk to shore. No matter how one gets in or out of pluff mud, it's vaudeville comedy.

The most controversial aspect of pluff mud is its earthy bouquet, which no one has adequately described. Most will tell you that it stinks, like rotten eggs. But that's like saying wine smells like grape juice. You're missing all the complexity and nuance; besides, it's not really a sulfury stink. The old well water on Sullivan's Island (before they hooked up to the city supply)—that was rotten eggs, okay? The paper mill in North Charleston—know what I'm saying? But the High Battery at low tide— not even close.

Pluff mud has a funk, true, but it's half-pleasing to take in, almost human really. There's a bit of grassiness in there, of course, something that feels very right now—alive—but also something minty and fresh like a newborn, but the odor also feels dank and cold, a cellar smell reminiscent of death, but in the cosmic sense, the death of eons and millennia, a sense of death on a tectonic scale.

It's so fabulously complicated it would really require one of those elegant elites who live by their extraordinary talent to smell—those perfumers and flavorists—who can deconstruct any waft into its legions of constituents. Pluff mud is complex because it summons olfactory memories of all who've lived there, primordial in that way, but also just you, a mud that elicits your own private nostalgia, a backseat somewhere, a gnarly odor to anybody except you, calling you back to that time, a surrender really—whenever, wherever. The funk of the best night of your life.

PO'BOY

The po'boy is an oversize regional sandwich native to New Orleans. It is not unlike a submarine sandwich or hoagie sold elsewhere in the nation, except for the fact that it's nothing like those others, as any New Orleanian will tell you, often vehemently, and sometimes adopting the knuckle-raised stance of a prizefighter. Po'boy lore traces the sandwich's origins back to a 1929 transit strike. Sandwich shop owners and former streetcar conductors Benny and Clovis Martin offered their former colleagues free sandwiches during the long strike. When one walked in, they'd shout, "Here comes another poor boy," and the name migrated to the sandwich, from which it could not be dislodged.

Po'boys come in many varieties, with roast beef, shrimp, and fried oyster among the more popular. When you're ordering, the clerk will ask if you want it "dressed," which means made with lettuce, tomato, and mayonnaise. The traditional answer is yes. Aficionados of po'boys insist that they cannot be legitimately found outside greater New Orleans. A po'boy must be made with a certain type of long, crusty bread, which is produced by several bakers in the region who typically resupply po'boy shops several times daily to ensure freshness. The sound of the first bite into a po'boy is often as prized as the taste—the fleeting crunchiness of the crust gives way to the muffled softness of the doughy interior.

Most in the New Orleans region refer to it as a po'boy, although some insist on the more patrician "poor boy." In general, the latter sort of people should be avoided.

POKE

by Bill Heavey

AN HERBACEOUS PERENNIAL PLANT FOUND across the United States, except for the northern plains and mountain states, that prefers recently disturbed areas, grows to eight feet, and produces purple berries whose crimson juice people formerly used both as a substitute for red ink and to enhance the color of pale wines. It has long been a traditional food in the Southern Appalachians, and for years the Arkansas-based Allens Canning Company canned it and sold it to the public as "poke sallet greens." Poke can also kill you dead, since all parts of the plant are poisonous—root, berry, leaf, and stem. There are at least four deadly toxins in poke, including an alkaloid (phytolaccine), a resin (phytolaccatoxin), and a saponin (phytolaccigenin), all of which sound like ingredients in Roundup Shiva, Destroyer of Weeds. The most serious hazard apparently comes from a supertoxic plant protein called lectin, which is also found in the world's deadliest plants, such as the castor bean (*Ricinus communis*) and the prayer bead (*Abrus precatorius*). Plant lectins are the active ingredient in ricin, the biochemical warfare agent. Yum.

And yet people still eat it, and celebrate it. There is an annual Poke Salad Festival in Blanchard, Louisiana, and at least three other states. The singer-songwriter Tony Joe White (who also wrote "Rainy Night in Georgia") had a hit with his 1969 song "Polk Salad Annie," a gravel-voiced talking blues that includes the immortal lines "Everybody said it was a shame / 'Cause her mama was working on a chain gang / A wretched, spiteful, straight-razor totin' woman / Lord have mercy, pick a mess of it." The song has been covered by everyone from Elvis Presley to Tom Jones to Conan O'Brien. But Tony Joe's version is untouchable. He grew up on the stuff.

So what's the deal? The young green shoots and leaves of pokeweed—less than six inches long—make delicious greens when boiled until tender in at least two changes of water. Avoid any red parts. The shoots taste similar to asparagus; the leaves are like spinach. I once fed my own mother both fresh poke and freshly picked wild asparagus. She tasted and pronounced the poke markedly superior. "It has such a *green* taste," she said. She died later that day. Actually, she's eighty-six and doing fine. But she has since learned more about poke and vowed never to eat it again.

PO' MONKEY'S

ONE OF THE ONLY TRUE-BLUES MISSISSIPPI juke joints to endure into the twenty-first century, this one-room shack in the cotton fields of Bolivar County is the building-sized extension of the late Willie "Po' Monkey" Seaberry, a farmer who, in 1963, augmented his day job by opening a juke joint, donning a bright suit, and inviting the world in. Po' Monkey's evolved from a functional operating center for Delta blues into a required tourist stop for modern-day pilgrims. The house's evocatively ramshackle decor—stapled posters, Christmas lights, disco balls, stuffed monkeys, and of course a jukebox—came to serve as visual shorthand for the music, and the clientele, predominantly African American at first, soon gave way to crowds of all stripes. Seaberry, who lived at the club, would change into a rainbow-colored series of suits that became legend (he's said to have had more than a hundred); his posted rules of etiquette were unbreakable ("No Loud Music, No Dope Smoking, No Rap Music"); and his Thursday "Family Night" welcomed comers from whatever corner of the globe the music had reached. In 2009, the Mississippi Blues Commission erected a historic marker, immortalizing the club as an official site on the Mississippi Blues Trail. Seaberry died in 2016; the future of the venue is unclear.

PORK

EVER SINCE THE SPANISH CONQUISTADOR Hernando de Soto brought his thirteen pigs to Tampa Bay in 1539, pork has been the hands-down favorite meat of the South. Consider the traditional dishes and ingredients that rely on the humble hog: country ham, boudin, barbecue—whether whole hogs, shoulders, or just ribs. Many of us wouldn't dare cook peas or greens without a hunk of salt pork, and some purists still refuse to make biscuits or piecrusts without lard. Pork also sneaks into supporting roles in dishes like jambalaya, as smoked sausage, and shrimp and grits, as bacon. Even fried chicken tastes better when it's fried in pork fat. Whether we're eating high

on the hog or low, pork is equally at home in soul-food stew pots on the coast and lonely mountain smokehouses. *See Bacon; Country ham; Cure masters.*

POTLIKKER

THE LOUISIANA GOVERNOR HUEY P. LONG was not generally regarded as a paragon of morality. But on March 1, 1931, he wrote a column that ran in newspapers across the country, entitled "The Ethics of Potlikker." In the piece, Long suggested that crumbling corn pone into potlikker instead of dunking it reflected a lack of scruples—indeed, as Long put it, "horrible manners." (This was a salvo in a months-long fight with an editor of the *Atlanta Constitution* who was a crumbler.) Clearly, potlikker is serious stuff in the South. It's described, most simply, as the water left in the pot after boiling greens, but as Long might have said, that doesn't do the elixir justice. As with chicken broth in Eastern European culture, cooks have credited greens broth with curative properties. It's nutritious, as enslaved kitchen workers no doubt realized when plantation owners rejected it as unfit for their tables. A mainstay of black Southern cuisine, potlikker has recently surfaced on upscale menus compiled by chefs loath to toss delicious greens juice. They've been known to reduce it with shallots and clams and transform it into a fancy sauce. But you can also just eat it with a spoon, like soup, or crumble—er, make that *dunk*—your cornbread in it.

PRESLEY, ELVIS

(1935–1977)

FROM GRAFFITI ON THE GATES OF GRACELAND to stacks of doctoral dissertations, what hasn't been written about Elvis by now? His bio reads like Southern Shakespeare, born in Tupelo, Mississippi, riding a rebellious sound and style up from abject poverty to a level of international superstardom that hadn't even been invented before, only to fall victim to destructive appetites and the peculiar isolation of the famous. Nobody had ever created as many hit records. Nobody had ever transferred recording industry domination to Hollywood with such ease. Nobody had ever attracted fans who so strongly identified with their idol, even as he traveled in private planes, rented out entire theme parks, and performed in rhinestone-studded jumpsuits. And yes, Elvis also ate fried peanut butter and banana sandwiches, shot televisions, and carpeted his ceiling with lime-green shag. Four decades after his untimely death, legions of admirers still hold him in special reverence, while detractors claim his fame was built upon the backs of less-lauded black artists. So how does one contend with the legacy, the icon, the enigma that is the King of Rock and Roll? It's complicated. But if nothing else, consider one indisputable fact: Elvis cut his very first record as a small gift for the person he loved most in the world—his mama.

PRIDE, CHARLEY

(1934–)

by Randall Kenan

IN SOME ALTERNATE UNIVERSE, THERE'S A bust of Charley Pride in the Baseball Hall of Fame. This is not as far-fetched as it may sound. Though many know the best-selling, Grammy-winning recording artist as the only African American country music star of the late sixties and seventies—with record sales that rivaled Elvis's—he also played for years on Negro American League and minor-league teams, pitching for such squads as the Memphis Red Sox, the Birmingham Black Barons, the El Paso Kings, and a semi-pro Montana team called the East Helena Smelterites. A native Mississippian and son of a cotton sharecropper, Pride began singing publicly while living—and actually working at a smelting company—in Helena, initially getting paid ten dollars to sing for fifteen-minute sets at games. In Montana he sang solo, made demo tapes, and joined a four-piece combo called the Night Hawks.

I remember, as a country boy growing up in the 1970s, how ubiquitous Pride's hits were on the radio: "Kiss an Angel Good Mornin'," "Is Anybody Goin' to San Antone," "I'm Just Me." He was a mainstay on *Hee Haw* and *The Lawrence Welk Show*, and on Bob Hope specials. Black folk certainly knew who he was, and respected him after a fashion, though I'm not sure he drew their affection the same as James Brown, or Al Green, or Diana Ross. There was something Nixonian about his success, something peculiar, irregular. Southern white folk seemed to accept him in a color-blind way, though jokes I heard from my white grade-school classmates made it clear they could see the man singing on their TV screen. In truth, Ray Charles had previously broken down walls between what was then known as country and western and other genres—rhythm and blues, soul. Charles's 1962 album *Modern Sounds in Country and Western Music* and its follow-up made a strong case that those forms all sprang from the same American roots.

Pride's career break came in 1966, when the legendary Chet Atkins took an interest in his song "The Snakes Crawl at Night" and signed him to RCA Victor. Pride was not an instant hit. Although he played the Grand Ole Opry as a guest in 1967—the first black player there since a harmonica player in the 1940s—the Opry and its audience were not a progressive lot at the time, and he didn't become a member until twenty-six years later. But radio soon turned out to be very, very good to him. Between 1967 and 1987, he scored fifty-two Top 10 hits on *Billboard*'s country charts, won two Grammy awards for gospel, and in the early seventies was named the CMA's best male performer twice. All in an era when the face of country was overwhelmingly white.

Comparisons to Jackie Robinson are too easy; some club owners refused to book Pride at first, and he was denied some opportunities readily available to other country performers. He forged on, not exactly silent about the slights, but not making much of a fuss either. "No one had ever told me that whites were supposed to sing one kind of music and blacks another," he wrote in his autobiography. "I sang what I liked in the only voice I had."

By now, still performing in his eighties, and part owner of the Texas Rangers, Pride has become an old-school country grandee, inducted into the Country Music Hall of Fame in 2000. After him would come Darius Rucker, Mickey Guyton, Linda Martell, the Pointer Sisters, Rhonda Towns, Rissi Palmer, Valerie June. All underscoring a lasting and powerful black presence in country. But Charley Pride was the pioneer—the country airwaves' first dark balladeer.

(1940–2015)

EVERYTHING ABOUT GENE AUTRY PRUDHOMME—
a farmer's son from Opelousas, Louisiana,
the youngest of thirteen children, and a dead
ringer for the actor Dom DeLuise—was
outsize. Exceeding five hundred pounds at
his heaviest, he left a lasting mark on New
Orleans food culture as executive chef at the
venerable Commander's Palace and his own
K-Paul's Louisiana Kitchen, and in numerous TV appearances that made him a national
celebrity—South Louisiana's answer to Julia
Child. "That genial genius of massive girth,"
the *New York Times* restaurant critic Craig
Claiborne once called him. Prudhomme got
Americans so excited about blackened redfish,
during the Cajun-cuisine craze he ignited
during the 1980s, that the species, reportedly, nearly vanished, prompting restrictions
on commercial fishing. He emphasized local
produce and right-off-the-boat seafood decades before "fresh" and "local" became menu
boilerplate. He even helped popularize tur-
ducken, the gluttonous, Frankenstein's mon-
ster of a roast amalgamating deboned chicken,
duck, and turkey. When he passed away at
age seventy-five, he left behind nearly a dozen
cookbooks—most famously 1984's *Chef Paul
Prudhomme's Louisiana Kitchen*—and an enormous culinary legacy. The world now knows
about gumbo, jambalaya, boudin, crawfish,
andouille, hot sauce, and red beans and rice,
and Chef Paul is much of the reason why.

by Wayne Curtis

PUNCH IS A CLASS OF ALCOHOLIC BEVER-
age that for more than three centuries has
been embraced, reviled, celebrated, scourged,
and ridiculed. It has proved resilient, especially in the South, where it has never fallen
fully out of fashion. Broadly speaking, punch
has enjoyed three golden ages. The early 2000s
to the present day mark the third, which so far
shows no signs of flagging.

When and where punch first arose is a
matter of fractious opinion, some of it informed, much of it not. The esteemed drink
historian David Wondrich, author of the
definitive history *Punch: The Delights (and
Dangers) of the Flowing Bowl*, believes it arose
among seventeenth-century British sailors
cruising the Indian Ocean. The British had
a well-documented history of adding things
to things (for instance, wormwood to ale to
make something called "purl"), and it seems
likely that a seaman or two mixed local arrack
(distilled from palm sap) with sugar and spices
and the squeezings of something, anything, to
make it palatable. And so punch was born.

Even the name has stirred up controversy. Long-standing tradition claims that it
comes from the Hindustani word for "five,"
the number of ingredients early punch contained (spirits, citrus, sugar, water, and spices).
This perfectly serviceable explanation has the
added ballast of history—it appears in a letter
written in 1632 by an official of the East India
Company—but is not universally embraced.

Wondrich, for instance, believes it refers to the container in which it was mixed.

Whatever its origins, punch followed sailors on a leisurely voyage around the globe—to Europe (where brandy or gin replaced arrack), and eventually to the West Indies, where punch met rum and formed a lasting dalliance. From there it moved north to North American colonial ports. Punch dominated the drinking life in the South through the eighteenth and early nineteenth centuries— aristocrats, commoners, planters, and city tavern-goers all enjoyed a nice bowl of it. It was a communal drink, shared by nearly all, and thus admirably democratic.

It first fell out of favor in the nineteenth century, due in part to the rise of the cocktail. It was the "have it your way" era of drink. People stashed away their punch bowls, bringing them out only for holiday gatherings. After a modest revival, the second fall of punch took place in the twentieth century. It became associated with card parties hosted by the elderly and uncool, and with lurid drinks served in plastic garbage cans by university students. By the midcentury, punch had more or less slipped into a coma.

Its demise was not as pronounced in the South as elsewhere, though; renegades held out with their ladles, like infantrymen with their field pieces who had never been told the war was over. At least a handful of noted Southern punches never fell entirely out of favor. One of the best known of the genre, the Chatham Artillery Punch, had first been concocted in the 1850s in Savannah to celebrate the return of a militia unit from a training exercise. In Charleston, South Carolina, the St. Cecilia Society Punch initially appeared in the 1800s to lubricate the annual gathering of the elite St. Cecilia Society. Both have remained in high repute ever since.

How is punch defined? It is almost universally served communally in a bowl, yet a bowl alone is not enough to define it. Punch must contain at least these three ingredients: spirits, sugar, and citrus. The original formula, circa 1700, specified one part of sour (typically lemon or lime juice), two parts of sugar, three parts of liquor, four parts of water or something likewise diluting, such as tea. (The mnemonic jingle: one of sour, two of sweet, three of strong, four of weak.) You could try this, but you'll end up with a drink that appeals to those whose vocabulary lacks the phrase "too sweet," which is to say everyone around 1700. A ratio for more modern tastes, per David Wondrich: one of sour, one of sweet, four of strong, and six of weak.

This ratio is all you really need to succeed at entertaining. At a minimum it produces a serviceable punch, and possibly something truly outstanding. Punch is very forgiving. It need not be measured in drops and drams. It's made with whole bottles poured freehand. You can tinker and tweak as you go along, bringing up the sweetness if necessary, or adding a bit of brandy if the rum base seems too thin. The only ironclad rule: punch is never consumed alone.

Q-R

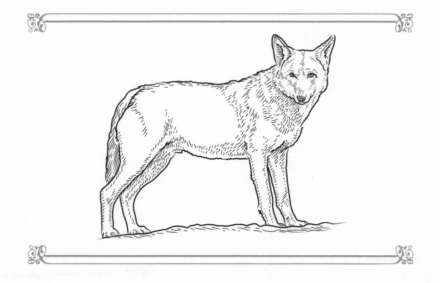

QUAIL

by Roger Pinckney

Talk about birds to your average Northerner and you'll be talking backyard jays and thrushes. Talk about birds to a scientist and you'll be talking bipedal, endothermic egg-laying vertebrates, flighted and flightless, all feathered, hummingbirds to condors, some ten thousand distinct species. Talk about birds to a hunter and you'll be talking *game* birds: ducks, brant, coots, gallinules, grouse, geese, scoters, turkeys, pheasant, doves, and in some locales, cranes, and even bustards. Bustards? Bustards!

But if you're talking birds to a Southern sportsman, it's like no other bird exists. You're talking the king, the northern bobwhite quail, Gentleman Bob, Sir *Colinus virginianus*. There is more flavor in a four-ounce quail than in an entire factory-farm frying chicken. Stuff a dozen with short sticks of andouille sausage, wrap 'em with pepper-cured bacon, pin them tight with toothpicks, and throw them on the charcoal. Done when the andouille bubbles. Make your tongue beat your brains out.

Bob is a gentleman and a sport, but he keeps himself close to home. Quail covey up in extended family groups and skitter here and there, scratching and scrabbling among the underbrush, but they whistle one another home each sunset, *bob-white, bob-white*.

A covey needs everything—food, water, and an owl-proof blackberry bramble—within a quarter mile, and small farms across the South provided perfect habitat. Quail populations exploded after the Civil War, when several million of the freshly emancipated hacked out farmsteads in the pinelands. But farmers got fewer and farms got bigger until six hundred, eight hundred, a thousand acres was a middling field, monocultures of cotton, peanuts, corn, and beans. Throw in a plague of fire ants, insecticides, and herbicides, and statutory protection of hawks and owls, and quail numbers plummeted. Isolated populations remained in the Red Hills of Southwest Georgia, the Alabama Black Belt, and West Texas, but throughout most of the South, the explosive whir of a covey rise was just a sweet memory.

Quail hunters, though, were not about to watch their birds go the way of the dodo. And the love of a four-ounce bird drove them crazy: habitat recreated; land leased, bought, and sold; crops planted and left unharvested; birds hatched, raised, and released. Entire fortunes squandered, wives and mistresses estranged, bitches bred and pups whelped, horses and mules bred. University courses in quail management, master's degrees and PhDs. Britches and shotguns ordered custom fit, bourbon by the barrel, vets by the battalion, hay and cedar-chip dog bedding by the ton. Ten billion dollars and counting.

Forget Cape buffalo, old *nyati*, "the Black Death." He may tread upon you, gore you, hook you, and throw you into the mopane bushes, but he will leave your wallet alone. The diminutive bobwhite quail is the most dangerous game animal on earth. Bernard Baruch, "the Lone Wolf of Wall Street," had a quail plantation. Henry Ford and R. J. Reynolds Jr. did, too. Ditto Robert Woodruff, president of Coca-Cola. An invitation to shoot with any of them was like an invitation to the royal box at Ascot. But most of us have to pay, and pay dearly, at venues across the South. Walk behind stalwart pointers? You can do that. Ride in a bird buggy behind a Jeep? Sure. A yellow-wheeled, rubber-tired wagon pulled by a matched team of redbone mules, with a gentleman at the reins? Priced accordingly. Maybe two grand?

Beware, quail might drive you crazy, too.

RAINEY, MA

(1886–1939)

NOW REMEMBERED AS THE MOTHER OF THE Blues, Ma Rainey was known in her time as the Gold-Neck Woman of the Blues and the Paramount Wildcat, nicknames that reveal how she became one of the South's most popular songstresses. Generations of blues fans forgot that in her time, contemporaries of Rainey swore that she outperformed her fellow African American blueswoman Bessie Smith (whom, contrary to legend, Rainey did not kidnap and force to join her vaudeville revue). Rainey was born Gertrude Pridgett in 1886 in Columbus, Georgia, a port town with a busy calendar of traveling minstrel shows. She joined the circuit in 1904, touring with the Rabbit Foot Minstrels. A decade later, she and her husband created their own act, Rainey and Rainey, Assassinators of the Blues. She started taking the stage solo after signing with the Paramount label in 1923. Audience members were bewitched by her down-home patter and distinctive look: Rainey wore an untamed horsehair wig, gold caps on her teeth, chains of gold coins around her neck, and so much skin lightener that she had a golden glow. But Paramount did a disservice to her strong voice: notorious for its frugality, the studio made its artists sing into amplifying horns, and then released their music on cheap shellac. The surviving records' poor quality long subdued the blues world's respect for Rainey.

APPALACHIAN PEOPLE DON'T SEE MUCH green in the woods between the fall avalanche of orange and the spring emergence of ramps, which helps explain why they get so excited about these garlicky wild leeks each year. Ramp festivals have drawn crowds for generations: West Virginia's Feast of the Ramson dates back to 1937, seven years after North Carolina's first Ramp Convention. Mountain cooks sauté ramps with scrambled eggs and potatoes, and pickle them to prolong their short season. Generally, they know better than to eat the pungent alliums raw. (Stories abound of children being sent home from school for stinking up their classrooms.) Chefs around the country look forward to ramp season now, too, cooking the newly trendy ingredient just about every way you can imagine, which is putting pressure on a limited natural resource. Do your part by harvesting only the greens, leaving behind the bulbs and roots to regenerate—both for the old-timers and for the next umpteen waves of foragers about to "discover" them.

ALTHOUGH HER RURAL ROOTS WERE OBscured by the circumstances of her birth in 1896 in Washington, D.C., the foremost chronicler of Florida's backwoods came from a farming family. Rawlings's father, a patent examiner, pined for his parents' Maryland farm, while her mother spoke longingly of the southern Michigan homestead where she had grown up. "We cannot live without the earth or apart from it, and something is shriveled in a man's heart when he turns away from it," Rawlings wrote in *Cross Creek*, a memoir of her years spent as an orange grove keeper. Rawlings described the writing process as "agony" but had enough confidence in her craft to retire from the *Louisville Courier-Journal* at age thirty-two. Two years later, Scribner's published her literary sketches of the nature and neighbors she encountered in marshy central Florida, marking the start of Rawlings's lifetime professional relationship with the editor Maxwell Perkins. He helped nurture a string of novels populated by palmetto trees and alligator hunters, culminating in *The Yearling*, which in 1939 won the Pulitzer Prize. Rawlings's career faltered after a friend she had described in *Cross Creek* as an "ageless spinster" sued her for invasion of privacy.

RED BEANS AND RICE

by *John Currence*

No Monday ever passes for me without the thought of red beans and rice floating through the transom of the day's culinary opportunities. I love it like few other dishes. There is little, probably nothing, I cook more frequently, and there's absolutely nothing I crave more deeply (this from a man who has opened more than one restaurant inspired by a craving or two).

Red beans and rice seems to have become the New Orleans Monday house favorite at least a century and a half ago, for a couple of reasons. Sundays there have always been days for festive eating. Families cooked big meals after church or dined at old-line French Quarter restaurants. Neighborhood mom-and-pop places did a brisk business as well. As a result, Monday became the food-service day of rest.

For house servants, Monday was also the traditional laundry day. The chore of handling a big family's week of laundry, washing, drying, folding, and pressing could be a Herculean task. So something like red beans—requiring little more than Sunday's leftover ham bone, minimal chopping and dicing of vegetables, and a very low flame that could be left for hours without much tending—would be the perfect dish for a cook plugging away at a lengthy task away from the stove.

As restaurants blossomed, laundry days got less complicated and our lives became more so. Red-bean Mondays became a citywide restaurant theme. Everyplace from Commander's Palace to Fat Harry's offered a plate of red beans that day. No two versions are the same, and the pride a New Orleans cook takes in his red beans is as serious as in his or her bordelaise, *grillades*, or daube glacé. It's a badge of honor. But pride doesn't prevent plenty of cooks I know from admitting without remorse that Popeyes, as corporate a chain as there is, has a formidable recipe. (A quick web search brings up dozens of copycat versions. I've attempted several, and none approach the original.)

I have spent decades refining my own recipe. I've altered techniques, soaking beans overnight, giving them a quick boil, and letting them sit for an hour before cooking. I've gravitated back and forth between neck bones/hocks and andouille sausage for flavoring. I've added sugar or cane syrup or both, and alternated between fresh and powdered garlic. Next Monday, I will most likely have a slightly different take, if only to perpetuate my twisted pursuit of something I'm not sure even exists: the perfect bowl of red beans and rice.

The closest to that I've experienced was served around a table every Monday, once New Orleans reopened after Katrina, in late 2005. The food writer Pableaux Johnson gathered a group of folks weekly around his table. His door was open to all. Most of the same few people would arrive in early evening. Often, friends of friends drifted in, the smell of red beans and andouille in the air. In those dark months of despair and confusion, Monday-night red beans were a weekly beacon of hope, the finish line of another week of recovery, a moment of joy with friends.

In the years since, Pableaux and I have

taken to debating the merits of different techniques and recipes. His Southwest country recipe is in direct opposition to my citified take. I know, however, that it never really comes down to whose is better than whose, but rather that the tradition remains—a tradition never more important than on those Mondays after the storm, when everyone needed comfort, my friend's door was always open, and there was a bowl and a spoon for whoever crossed his threshold.

REDDING, OTIS

(1941–1967)

A GEORGIA NATIVE WHO GOT HIS START AS A member of Little Richard's backup band, Otis Redding was soul music's beast. Built like a linebacker, he refined "deep soul," a sound that married frenetic, greased-lightning party numbers with raw, scarred ballads. In the process, he became the cash king for Memphis's Stax Records, recording hits such as "I've Been Loving You Too Long" and "Mr. Pitiful." Redding's initial audiences were almost exclusively black until 1967, when he headlined the Monterey Pop Festival, performing a short but career-defining set that won over the mostly white audience and made fans of groups like Jefferson Airplane and the Rolling Stones (whose "Satisfaction" Redding covered during his performance). Poised for a commercial breakthrough, Redding quickly went back into the studio and recorded the single "(Sittin' on) The Dock of the Bay," showcasing

his softer, more reflective side. Then, a tragedy: on the early morning of December 10, 1967, Redding was killed in an airplane crash in Wisconsin that also took the lives of four members of his backing band, the Bar-Kays. His single, released posthumously a month later, would become not only Redding's sole number-one hit but arguably one of the greatest songs in music history.

REDEYE GRAVY

SLAP A SLAB OF COUNTRY HAM IN A HOT cast-iron skillet, remove it when both sides are browned and curling, and repeat with as many slices as you have mouths to feed. Then pour in half a cup of hot coffee, scraping up all the orange-colored ham bits left behind on the bottom of the pan and stirring until an oily red-tinged "eye" forms in the center, and you'll have redeye gravy. With no flour to thicken the mix, it's technically less a gravy than a pan sauce. But regardless, the combination of two potent flavors—the intense saltiness of country ham and the bitterness of black coffee—is a stroke of Southern genius and an excellent accompaniment to buttermilk biscuits.

REDFISH

THE RISE OF THE REDFISH TO ICONIC HEIGHTS links directly to Paul Prudhomme, the late, beloved Cajun chef whose rightfully revered signature dish, blackened redfish, shone a floodlight on the saltwater species in the 1980s. In turn, commercial fishing took a harsh toll on redfish populations. But staunch conservation measures fueled their recovery, and these days the fish's brawny attitude and everyman appeal has given rise to redfish mania among anglers. The fish prowl nearshore breakers, marsh creeks, and inlets, and can be caught with utilitarian curly-tailed jigs, chunks of dead bait, and highfalutin hand-tied flies alike. In varying parts of the South they're known as red drum, channel bass, and occasionally spottail, but "redfish" is slowly becoming ubiquitous. Regardless of what you call them, these fish, which can grow to ninety pounds, support a massive recreational fishery from Texas to Florida to Virginia. *See Prudhomme, Paul.*

RED'S

CLARKSDALE, MISSISSIPPI, HELPED BIRTH THE blues—it's where Robert Johnson supposedly cut his fabled deal with the devil. But to capture true Delta magic, head to Red's Lounge, one of the few remaining clubs with a genuine juke-joint vibe. Crimson lights. No frills. Odds-and-ends chairs so close to the "stage" (actually just a carpet on the floor) that you can reach out and touch such ax icons as R. L. Boyce and Leo "Bud" Welch when local talent lays it down on Wednesday, Friday, Saturday, and Sunday nights. Strike up a conversation with some of the Brits or Germans who've made the pilgrimage, too, while pulling on a Budweiser tall boy dispensed by the owner, Red Paden. When the lovable curmudgeon isn't behind the tiny bar, he's tending the chicken and ribs he has going on a smoker out front. But the real sizzle is inside.

RED WOLF

EVERYBODY KNOWS ABOUT THE GRAY WOLF—that thing howling against the moon on airbrushed T-shirts at the county fair. Gray wolves are even nicknamed "common wolves." But there's another wolf in North America, native only to the South: *Canis rufus*, the red wolf. Once populating a stretch from the mid-Atlantic to Florida, red wolves—derided for years as "the devil's dogs"—were hunted feverishly. Because of that, along with drastic loss of habitat, they were declared extinct in the wild in 1980, when seventeen of them were captured for breeding. To conservationists' pleasant surprise, those captured wolves bred successfully, and before long biologists reintroduced them to North Carolina's Alligator River National Wildlife Refuge, where about a hundred red wolves roam today. Sized somewhere between gray wolves and coyotes, red wolves are the shade of dried pine straw lit by sunset, a helpful camouflage in the Southeast's piney forests. Now listed as an endangered species, red wolves rely on that camouflage—as well as federal protection—as they struggle to reestablish a viable foothold in the Southern wilds.

REID, BILLY

(1964–)

BILLY REID HAS A KNACK FOR MAKING clothes that basically look as appropriate in Florence, Alabama—where his company is headquartered—as they would in Florence, Italy. Reid started his fashion career as a child in his grandmother's house in Amite City, Louisiana, where his mother ran a clothing boutique. In 2010, he exploded onto the international scene by winning both the CFDA/Vogue Fashion Fund Award and the GQ/CFDA Best New Menswear Designer in America Award, a shocking achievement for a designer from anywhere, let alone Alabama. Embodying genteel Southern traditions and global sophistication, Reid is now a star in the constellation of the Deep South's cultural elite. His annual Shindig in Florence celebrates the region's wider cultural riches, featuring music from the likes of Alabama Shakes, and his boutiques, decorated with antiques, worn rugs, and mounted animal heads, also sport decanters of whiskey, ready for shoppers to sip while perusing the racks.

R.E.M.

IT SAYS SOMETHING ABOUT THE DUALITY OF the South that one of its most prominent musical exports in the eighties and nineties was a group of aggressively liberal college-town activists from Athens, Georgia, known for mandolins, candy-colored melodies, and a song called "Shiny Happy People." Formed in 1980 and saddled with the "alternative" label ascribed to pretty much anyone who wasn't Bon Jovi, the foursome of Michael Stipe, Mike Mills, Peter Buck, and Bill Berry produced several underground-rattling, adored-by-undergrads albums in the Reagan era (among them *Murmur*, *Reckoning*, and *Lifes Rich Pageant*) before launching into the commercial stratosphere with 1992's *Out of Time*. The rich, homey album—including "Losing My Religion," its biggest moment—served as a sunny counterpoint to the band's follow-up, the impossibly strong *Automatic for the People*, which included the universal heartbreaker "Everybody Hurts" and the Andy Kaufman tribute "Man on the Moon." R.E.M.'s left-leaning activism encompassed everything from voters' rights to LGBT issues to animal rights; Stipe once attended MTV's Video Music Awards ceremony wearing a series of white T-shirts trumpeting assorted pet causes (RAINFOREST; HANDGUN CONTROL NOW). Though *Automatic* marked R.E.M.'s airplay pinnacle, the band produced albums of consistent highlights (including *New Adventures in Hi-Fi* and *Up*) before they called it quits in 2011, having sold eighty-five million records and secured a spot in the Rock and Roll Hall of Fame. *See Athens, Georgia.*

RICE SPOON

HERE'S THE QUICKEST WAY TO TELL IF A COU-
ple have roots in Charleston, South Carolina:
check their wedding registry for a rice spoon.
To the eighteenth-century English, the long-
handled utensil with its oversize bowl served as
a stuffing spoon. But well-to-do colonists in the
South Carolina Lowcountry—the New World's
leading rice producer—used it to dish out the
lucrative grain at the city's traditional two-
o'clock dinners (not to be confused with anything as pedestrian as lunch or supper). Today
most of us can't often find time for leisurely afternoon repasts, but the spoon remains a cherished totem of Southern hospitality.

ROADKILL

by Daniel Wallace

ROADKILL IS WHERE NATURE AND MAN
meet in a way neither of them hoped to.
It is the literal crossroads between the natural
and the man-made world, perhaps the best example of our uncomfortable cohabitation with
the other living things with which we share the
planet. Not including insects, approximately
one million animals in the United States start
the day as whatever they are and end it splayed
across the pavement. It's a sad and messy state
of affairs, and only one good thing can possibly come from it: dinner. Vultures, crows,
foxes, possums, and some humans love to eat
roadkill. It becomes part of the food chain. It
may be a stretch to call this a happy ending,
but it's as close to one as roadkill allows.

Cultures are defined and exposed by roadkill. For instance, penguins are common victims in New Zealand; in Australia, wombats
and kangaroos; in Montana, elk, moose, and
bear. In the southern United States, the road
is littered with possums and raccoon and deer
and squirrels—a mishmash, a hodgepodge,
real variety. As a nation we kill almost fifty
million squirrels a year, and that's just the tip
of the roadkill iceberg. I live in North Carolina
now, but on trips back to my home state,
Alabama, I have noticed a lot of dead armadillos on the road. They weren't there when I was
a kid. Armadillos used to seem exotic to me,
remnants of our Triassic past, extra-large roly-
polies. Now they are just another squashable
thing, and, incidentally, are dispatched by vehicles more than any other animal in America.

Under certain conditions, a small family could live off of roadkill for a while, but only if the family really wanted to. More than a million deer become casualties every year, so that's a lot of dinner for some lucky scavengers. Precautions would need to be taken, of course. If this is something you're interested in trying out, first remember this handy ditty: *How fresh is it? How flat is it?* The flatter it is, the less likely you'll want it in the stew. Worms are also a concern, so you'll want to cook the living hell out of it. The pros: roadkill is lean, high in protein, free of additives, and free of charge. The cons: you yourself could get run over while picking up the roadkill; you become Vulture Enemy No. 1; and you also become "the guy who eats roadkill," a con that may also be a pro, depending on your address. Imagine finding a fresh deer carcass near a cornfield and a ditch where wild blackberries are growing. That adds up to one swanky delight, an entire meal. You could have a dinner party. Just don't mention where you shop.

ROBERT'S WESTERN WORLD

LOCATED ON A CHEEZ WHIZ STRETCH OF Lower Broadway in Nashville, Robert's is the only honky-tonk that locals deem worth visiting. It occupies what was long the home of the Sho-Bud Steel Guitar Company, and then a liquor store during the dark days of the eighties after the Grand Ole Opry ditched the neighboring Ryman Auditorium for the suburbs. The business's original owner, Robert Wayne Moore, jump-started the resurrection of downtown in the early 1990s when he augmented his Western wear and boot shop with live music. The stage is to your left as you walk in, the walls cluttered with all sorts of Nashville memorabilia. If it's the weekend, saddle up at the bar and order a fried bologna sandwich and a drink and revel in the sounds of the house band, Brazilbilly—fronted by the current owner, Jesse Lee Jones—or the Don Kelley Band, some of Music City's finest bar musicians. Upstairs, there's a nondescript second entrance just steps from the Ryman, and many a legend has slipped through that door for a surprise set at Robert's.

LIKE MOUNT OLYMPUS AND VALHALLA, Rock City sits atop a great mountain and looks down on much of the world. What makes Rock City different from the other two is that you can go to Rock City—you can actually *see* it. This is the idea, anyway, that Clark Byers tried to implant in the minds of every station wagon–ful of families traveling in, across, or through the South: SEE ROCK CITY! THE EIGHTH WONDER OF THE WORLD! These signs and similar ones were everywhere, many of them on the sides of barns. Byers painted them himself. At one time, there were over nine hundred of them, in nineteen states. Only a handful remain today.

Rock City, perched on Lookout Mountain near the Georgia-Tennessee border, does not disappoint if what you are looking to see are a lot of rocks, because Rock City is, in fact, a city of rocks. Trails snake through the many different formations, including the politically incorrect Fat Man's Squeeze, where two big rocks are situated so closely together that only the wispiest member of your family could get through. There are also the Fairyland Caverns, and Mother Goose Village. But the real selling point, the big deal that brings thousands of visitors a year to Rock City, is this: if you stand on the very highest rock on Lookout Mountain, you can see seven states just by turning your head.

"FIRST, MAKE A ROUX." THAT, OR SOME variation on it, is the lead sentence of almost every Cajun recipe you'll ever encounter. The French word *roux* (pronounced "roo") describes a cooked and seasoned thickening mixture of oil and flour that's at the heart of gumbo, étouffée, and many soups, stews, and gravies. Stirring the mixture in a heavy pot on a hot stove colors the roux as the flour cooks—producing variations that include lightly cooked brown roux, medium copper penny–colored roux, and long-cooked black roux. The Louisiana chef Paul Prudhomme once warned home cooks to stir roux carefully, as just a little splash of this "Cajun napalm" on bare skin can cause severe burns. It's also possible to purchase premade roux sold in glass jars. If you must.

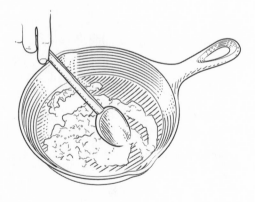

ROWAN OAK

The primitive Greek Revival antebellum mansion in Oxford, Mississippi, built in 1844, where the writer William Faulkner lived for more than thirty years, until his death from a heart attack in 1962, and wrote most of his novels. Surrounded by twenty-nine forested acres, the renovated two-story home is now owned by the University of Mississippi and open to visitors, who come from all fifty states and dozens of foreign countries. *See Faulkner, William; Oxford, Mississippi.*

RUM

by Wayne Curtis

First, you must let bygones be bygones. Rum was not wholly responsible for that unfortunate episode after your high-school prom, involving the neighbor's shrubberies and two weeks of being grounded. Most of that resulted from your lack of self-discipline. Admit it.

If you've avoided rum ever since, you should consider how unfortunate that is. In our lifetime it has progressed from a spirit featured in trash-can fraternity-house punches to something approaching (in some cases exceeding) the best cognac: to be sipped gently and with momentary awe. Rum's recent revival is a heartening tale. It merits revisiting and reacquaintance.

But let's begin at the beginning. Rum is an ardent spirit made of sugarcane or its by-products. It's historically linked with the sugar islands of the Caribbean, and thus with slavery. Rum was the cornerstone liquor of the American colonies, consumed in prodigious quantity in the seventeenth and early eighteenth centuries up and down the Eastern Seaboard, especially in Charleston, South Carolina, which had a direct pipeline to Barbados, where rum flowed like water. After American independence, trade complications with the rum-producing islands, combined with a surfeit of grains in the ridiculously fertile trans-Appalachian interior, led to the rise of American whiskey in general and bourbon in particular. Let us by all means salute the development of bourbon. Still, a deep-grained allegiance to whiskey does not preclude you from enjoying rum, nor admitting it was America's original spirit.

Rum was rediscovered during Prohibition, when Havana essentially became the corner bar for much of the South. Thirsty travelers in Cuba found that the rank rum of their forefathers had been much improved—thanks in large part to the Bacardi family, which had started to tend to its product with a diligence unaccustomed among other distillers. This notwithstanding, rum failed to regain a spirit plurality during the cocktail craze of the 1930s to 1950s, largely because it labors under regrettable misconceptions. Foremost among these is the belief that, because rum comes from sugar, it must be sweet and therefore a drink for the callow and unsophisticated. This is not true.

Much of rum's appeal today lies in its broad diversity. It's made on scattered islands, each with its own cultural traditions and techniques. Thanks to time and technology, rum production is no longer as easily pigeonholed, geographically, as it once was, but three essential styles of it cover the general taste topography of today's market: Jamaican-style pot-still rum (which is funky and dense), Spanish-style column-still rums (clean and light), and Martinique-style *agricole* rums (which tend toward vegetal and grassy). Most rum made today begins as molasses, a by-product of sugar production. But Martinican rum stands out: it's made from freshly pressed sugarcane juice. This creates a distinctive flavor, especially in the younger white rums, which some insist require repeated tasting before one's palate becomes sufficiently educated. This may be true.

Rum's devil-may-care diversity may also serve as a hindrance to its wider embrace. Since each island has its own regulations on rum production, the tastes can vary such that it's hard to predict what a new-to-you bottle will deliver. Bourbon, cognac, and Scotch are all more closely regulated at their points of origin. So basically, it comes down to a matter of personal preference: Would you like the sixty-four-color pack of Crayolas to make your drinks? Or are you perfectly content with the eight-pack?

In the past decade or two, rum has resurfaced in the South and beyond as a gentleman's drink. Premium rums have made their way onto the shelf, many of them quite delectable; if you spend twenty-five dollars or more on a bottle, odds are you can sip it neat and not feel the need to drown it in Coca-Cola. Another encouraging trend is the return of

craft rum distilling on the North American mainland, especially in areas where sugarcane grows. St. Augustine Distillery in Florida, High Wire Distilling and Red Harbor Rum in Charleston, and Old New Orleans Rum produce notable quaffs. Richland Rum, in Georgia, started in 1999 and today makes rum from four different strains of sugarcane it tends on its own farm. It's tasty, and would make colonials promptly reach for another.

RURAL STUDIO

AN UNDERGRADUATE DESIGN-BUILD PROGRAM of Auburn University's School of Architecture, Planning and Landscape Architecture, Rural Studio represents a radical departure from the theoretical "paper architecture" taught in most schools. Based in the Hale County, Alabama, hamlet of Newbern (population 186), it was cofounded in 1993 by the late Samuel "Sambo" Mockbee and Dennis K. Ruth, and emphasizes socially conscious architecture and hands-on learning. Instructors and students design functional structures for the residents of Hale and surrounding counties, all part of the Black Belt, an impoverished western Alabama region known for its dark, fertile soil. Some of the best-known projects are in Mason's Bend on the Black Warrior River.

Mockbee, a fifth-generation Mississippian, was a partner in a successful architecture firm when he decided to quit and start the Rural Studio with Ruth, his longtime friend and an Auburn architecture professor. What drove them was a belief that everyone—regardless of color, socioeconomic status, or education—deserves access to good design. Architects, they believed, have an ethical imperative to drive meaningful social and environmental change. They promoted the use of local materials and the arts of reusing, refurbishing, and recycling—especially if those kept costs down.

By 2017, the Rural Studio had completed more than 170 projects, including scores of houses, a public library, a community center, a Boys and Girls Club, a county bridge, public restrooms, and a new town hall for Newbern. Many of the program's hundreds of alumni continue the work, creating a Rural Studio ripple effect across the South and beyond. "Architecture, more than any other art form, is a social art and must rest on the social and cultural base of its time and place," Mockbee once said. And also: "Everyone, rich or poor, deserves a shelter for the soul."

RUSSIAN TEA

RUSSIAN TEA IS NOT FROM RUSSIA. At least, not Russian Tea as Southerners know it. The giftable mixture of supermarket drink powders, the stuff of countless midcentury community cookbooks, dates back to the late 1800s and early 1900s, when American urbanites sipped black tea with lemon and sugar in imitation of upper-class Russians. ("Russian tea is not a special brand, but is the ordinary tea served with lemon instead of cream," reported the Kinston, North Carolina, *Daily*

Free Press in 1902. "Two lumps of sugar and a quarter of a lemon are placed on the saucer.") Within decades, so-called Russian Tea, often doctored with clove and cinnamon, washed down chicken salad and mixed nuts at meetings of bridge clubs and church groups across the South. After World War II, the basic formula of hot tea with citrus evolved into a showcase for a bounty of space-age convenience foods: Tang, powdered lemonade, instant tea. And there, at last, is the Russian Tea many Southerners know and love—layered lovingly in a mason jar tastefully tied with grosgrain or gingham.

RUTLEDGE, ARCHIBALD

(1883–1973)

IF YOU COULD SET SOUTH CAROLINA'S Lowcountry to a spoken-word score, this would be the music: Archibald Rutledge's deeply affecting stories of hounds and hunting, his rich poems about the icons of marsh and coastal wilderness, of Spanish moss and mourning whip-poor-wills and longleaf pine. Born in 1883 in McClellanville, Rutledge grew up at the famed Hampton Plantation, built in 1730, hangout of both George Washington and Francis "Swamp Fox" Marion. Steeped in the lore of the Lowcountry, he spent more than thirty years as a professor of English at a small Pennsylvania academy, then returned to his natal swamp woods in 1937 to reign for nearly four decades as the South's most accomplished outdoor writer. He was South Carolina's first poet laureate, publishing books of prose and poetry and even recording scores of poems for the Library of Congress. *Deep River*, published in 1960, was a Pulitzer finalist. Despite wide acclaim, Rutledge never shook loose of the ties to his childhood home. He died in 1973, in the little log cabin near Hampton Plantation where he was born.

RYE WHISKEY

RYE WHISKEY IS ONE OF THE FOUNDATIONAL American spirits. It was made chiefly from ryegrass, which distinguished it from liquor made from corn, wheat, or barley. It's thought that the rise of rye followed the influx of immigrants from Ireland and Scotland who brought distilling techniques with them. Rather than using barley, which was common in their homelands, they chose rye, a hardier grass that provided good alcohol yields when fermented. Rye was produced in many frontier settlements, notably in western Pennsylvania and Maryland's panhandle, and then all down the Appalachian Mountains. Production and consumption of it spread widely enough that when one comes upon references to whiskey in an early-nineteenth-century account in the South, the odds are it was rye. (Unless the account took place in Kentucky, which early on evinced a predilection for corn liquor.) It remained popular throughout the nineteenth century, but the Eastern rye industry never really recovered from the shutterings of Prohibition.

In the recent craft-spirits revival, though, rye has made a notable comeback. It's now distilled everywhere from Mount Vernon—at a replica of George Washington's distillery—to small distilleries throughout the South, including Catoctin Creek (Virginia), Corsair Distillery (Tennessee), and Thirteenth Colony Distilleries (Georgia). Major producers like Bulleit and Jim Beam have also stepped up their rye game.

RYMAN AUDITORIUM

by Marshall Chapman

I'VE LIVED IN NASHVILLE FOR MORE THAN forty-eight years, and I have had more religious experiences at the Ryman Auditorium than in all the churches in town combined. Which is saying a lot, since Nashville (so I'm told) has more churches per capita than any city on the planet.

My first Ryman experience happened my first night in Nashville. I had just turned eighteen and had come to town to look at Vanderbilt University. My parents had wanted me to go to Sweet Briar, Agnes Scott, or Hollins. They couldn't understand my interest in Vanderbilt. But for me, it was simple. This was *Nashville*—Music City, U.S.A. When my student escort asked where I wanted to go that first night, I didn't hesitate.

"I'd like to go to the Grand Ole Opry," I said.

So off we went downtown, to the Ryman,

where the Opry was based in those days. I remember this like it was yesterday: sitting in those hard pews, a large woman in front of us nursing a baby at her bare breast, somebody's spilled Coke dripping from the balcony above, and Bobby Bare singing "Detroit City" while women flocked down the aisles flashing their Instamatics.

Ryman Auditorium is often hailed as one of America's most historically significant music venues. Built in 1892 by a riverboat captain and businessman named Thomas G. Ryman, the late-Victorian Gothic Revival structure has served Nashville in several different capacities over the years. First, as the Union Gospel Tabernacle, it was a revival hall where people went to get "saved." But after 1904, the year Thomas Ryman died, it became known forevermore as the Ryman Auditorium. With a seating capacity of over two thousand, it was for many years the largest indoor venue in Middle Tennessee. From 1904 to 1943, it became known as the Carnegie Hall of the South, a showcase for all sorts of attractions: the Metropolitan Opera, Enrico Caruso, Harry Houdini, Roy Rogers (*with* Trigger), Mae West, even Teddy Roosevelt. Meanwhile, a Nashville radio show featuring hillbilly music had become so popular that by 1943, it needed a larger venue. So from 1943 to 1974, the Ryman was home to the Grand Ole Opry. With its wooden pews and stained-glassed windows still intact, it became known as the Mother Church of Country Music.

During my freshman and sophomore years at Vanderbilt, a classmate named Woody Chrisman (aka Woody Paul, of the musical group Riders in the Sky) and I often hitch-hiked downtown on weekend nights to the Ryman, where we invariably ended up in Roy Acuff's dressing room. I remember scrambling up those steep backstage steps, carrying our instruments. Woody and Mr. Acuff would swap fiddle tunes, while Charlie Collins and I strummed along on our Martin guitars.

After the Opry moved to its new home in Opryland in 1974, the Ryman pretty much remained empty for the next two decades. Every now and then, I'd hear rumors that this landmark might succumb to the wrecking ball. But then, in 1994, an $8.5 million restoration saved the day. Since then, the Ryman has become a favorite stop for touring artists from all musical genres. Lucinda Williams, Lyle Lovett, Kris Kristofferson, Jerry Lee Lewis, John Hiatt, Bruce Springsteen (solo), the Reverend Al Green, Aretha Franklin, ZZ Top, and Dolly Parton are but a few of the acts I've caught there over the years. Religious experiences indeed.

And then, something happened that was bound to, sooner or later. In 1999, the Grand Ole Opry returned to the Ryman for its winter broadcasts. Fourteen years later—on November 26, 2013, to be exact—I played the Opry at the Ryman as a guest performer. I had played it a couple of times at the newer Grand Ole Opry House, but this was my first time to play it at the *Ryman*. As soon as I stepped on that stage, I felt the vibe. I couldn't help it. It was surreal. All the ghosts of the ones who'd come before, I *felt* their presence. Johnny Cash kicking out the footlights. Hank Williams returning for a record six encores at his Opry debut in 1949. Minnie Pearl trembling with stage fright in the wings, Emmylou Harris dancing with Bill Monroe, and so on.

As I stood there soaking it all in, I looked out at the spot where I'd sat as a starry-eyed high-school senior watching Bobby Bare. I glanced up at the Confederate Gallery, where in 1971 I'd sat watching Neil Young and James Taylor during a live taping of *The Johnny Cash Show*. And the whole experience of what was and what had come before somehow *lifted me up*.

The Ryman is where souls get saved. Sometimes without their even knowing it.

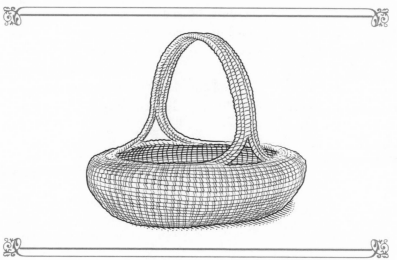

SANTEE DELTA

WHAT DEFIES BELIEF ABOUT SOUTH CAROLINA'S Santee River Delta isn't that it is the largest river delta on the Eastern Seaboard of North America, or that it hosts the longest stretch of undeveloped shoreline on the Atlantic, or that nearly a half million acres of wild marsh, forest, and coastal islands have been set apart for conservation. It's that so few people are aware of this semiwild treasure right under their Southern noses.

On the ocean side of U.S. 17, the river's north and south branches unspool across a vast wedge-shaped expanse of tidal forest and marsh. By the early 1700s, maps were already showing checkerboarded rice fields dug into the Lowcountry by slave labor. By 1776, Charleston was the center of an empire built on rice. Then, after the Civil War, as rice exports dwindled, wealthy Northern industrialists turned the old plantations into private duck-hunting estates, locking hundreds of thousands of acres behind their ivy-trellised gates. Today those twentieth-century enclaves are a twenty-first-century beachhead against development. Some have been transferred to state or federal game agencies, others to conservation organizations. And many of the private properties that remain lead a vanguard of habitat conservation and management that pumps ducks into skies across the region— and shapes the delta's future as surely as rice shaped its past.

SAVANNAH, GEORGIA

by Jeff Vrabel

HOTTER THAN YOU REMEMBER, MORE HU-mid than should be allowed by the current laws of physics, and home to moss-dripping squares, sprawling oaks, one iconic murder-mystery book, ghastly souvenir shops, a major Atlantic container-cargo seaport, Forsyth Park, uneasy urban planning, and the country's fiercest St. Patrick's Day parade, the Hostess City of the South (established 1733) remains one of the region's touchstones, a place where an elegant past and present dance under permeating charm and steamy weather and usually seem to get along. For the tourists, there's River Street, a cobblestoned pathway of drinks and boiled seafood and saltwater taffy joints that lines the Savannah River, down which roar container ships large enough to block out the sun. For classic Southern charm, pretty much any of the city's squares will do, blocks of oak and Spanish moss and street performers and old people on benches and kids running where they shouldn't be. For foodies and creative types, a host of new restaurants and art galleries have sprung up in recent years, while for butter people, there's that Paula Deen place. It's the oldest city in Georgia, so lots of archetypes jostle for space here.

Yet to my mind Savannah's highlight might be Historic Grayson Stadium, a funky, oft-damp minor-league jewel formerly home to the Sand Gnats and now home to Savannah's entry into the summer-collegiate Coastal Plain League. That would be the Savannah

Bananas, so named thanks to an online contest, always a dicey proposition in a town with such liberal open-container laws. It's easy to make jokes about the Bananas—we've made a bunch, wondering if public opinion is split, asking what time the game is on sundae—but the stadium is Savannah in baseball form: delightfully old-timey, aged, sweet, funky, in love with its past but making inroads toward the present. The bathrooms are cramped and the floors usually wet and the peanuts forever boiled. It's slathered in aesthetically stressful ads for off-brand colas, local banks, and insane lawyers. VIPs are treated to seats on four La-Z-Boys set up at the top of the grandstands behind home plate. Sometimes they let the kids run the bases after the game. And like its home city, the stadium is, in its own obliquely charming way, temporarily perfect.

SAWMILL GRAVY

IF REDEYE GRAVY IS A STUDY IN ECONOMY, sawmill gravy seems the polar opposite—so luxurious it's almost ostentatious: finely milled flour whisked into the fat rendered from pork sausage, thickened with whole milk and spiked with black pepper. But it wasn't always that way. "Even the name suggests poverty," wrote John Egerton in his classic *Southern Food* of the original, which grew out of late-nineteenth-century logging camps in the Southern Appalachians. Cornmeal, not flour, helped give it thickness—and a good bit of sawdust-like grit. The gravy helped stretch the

flavor of a small amount of meat, most likely salt pork, to fortify men whose work involved felling virgin twenty-foot-diameter poplars with handsaws. Over time, it's gone from breakfast make-do to must-have.

SAZERAC

IF NEW ORLEANS IS EVENTUALLY SWEPT BE-neath the waves like a modern Atlantis (as many hydrologists and climatologists predict), future generations will remember the city for three things: As the birthplace of jazz. As a city where food was second only to Catholicism as official religion. And where the Sazerac cocktail was invented.

The Sazerac is a sublime drink by any measure. It is essentially an early-nineteenth-century "cocktail"—defined in 1806 as consisting of spirit, sugar, and bitters, and *only those three ingredients*—but pimped out with later-nineteenth-century adornments.

In the 1840s, the company of Sazerac *et fils* began importing its brandy to New Orleans. Somewhat later, the name migrated to a coffeehouse. It was here that the brandy and Peychaud's bitters (originally made by a New Orleans pharmacist) became acquainted, and the name then attached itself to the drink. When French brandy became hard to come by owing to the decimation of French vineyards by an aphid in the late 1800s, rye whiskey was substituted.

What distinguishes the Sazerac from the old-fashioned is the addition of absinthe (only a light rinse of the glass, please, not a full dollop) and lemon zest—again, only a faint spritz of citrus oils, not a wedge. The lemon and anise serve as a light overture to bass-heavy melodies of cognac or rye (or equal measures of each, which is recommended).

Like the martini, the Sazerac lays claim to a proprietary glass: a faceted rocks glass with a graceful taper, which looks like a flawed diamond. You can drink a Sazerac in other types of glasses, but it will always taste better when served in a proper one.

SCOTCH-IRISH

AROUND 90 PERCENT OF THE FIRST SETTLERS in Appalachia arrived here directly from Ireland—only they weren't exactly Irish. In fact, that's the whole reason they were coming here. They'd originally moved to the Ulster region of Ireland from Scotland in the seventeenth century, but soon found themselves unwelcome there (read: they were Presbyterian), so they just kept moving westward until they hit American shores. Primarily settling in the mountains of North Carolina and Tennessee, the Scotch-Irish (an Americanism by which they became known) prided themselves on hardscrabble values and built their communities in rough mountain terrain that often resulted in isolation; this in turn helped preserve their distinctive traditions, including the music, language, and storytelling that still define much of the region's culture. It is estimated that perhaps 10 percent of the nation shares some Scotch-Irish ancestry today, so if you ever happen upon a man in a kilt hurling an entire tree into a field on North Carolina's Grandfather Mountain, rest assured he's only "turning the caber"—an event in the yearly Scottish-themed Highland Games there—and there's a chance one of your relatives might have once done the very same thing.

SCUPPERNONGS

THOMAS JEFFERSON ONCE WROTE THAT WINE made from the scuppernong grape, a bronze-skinned variety of muscadine hailing from North Carolina, "would be distinguished on the best tables of Europe, for its fine aroma and crystalline transparence." A couple of centuries on, it hasn't quite taken off the way Jefferson predicted, but we still appreciate the sweet, hardy scuppernong and its wine below the Mason-Dixon. *See Muscadine.*

SEA ISLANDS

WHEN YOU VIEW THEM ON A MAP, IT LOOKS like you could skip along the Sea Islands, the name for a string of a hundred or so barrier islands that hug the coastline from the mouth of the Santee River in South Carolina down along Georgia to just past the Florida border. What a trip it would be. There are the famous resort islands Hilton Head, Jekyll, and Amelia, where vacationers flock to go yachting and play golf. There are nature preserves with stunning beaches and tidal salt marshes, including Hunting Island and Wassaw Island. There's Morgan Island, inhabited (we swear this is true) only by a colony of 3,500 free-range rhesus monkeys transplanted there in 1979. Don't forget Parris Island, where 17,000 Marine recruits undergo basic training each year. And through the range of South Carolina and Georgia islands, there are pockets of the

most authentic Gullah and Geechee culture to be found anywhere in the Lowcountry. Oh, and history buffs wouldn't want to miss the lighthouses and Civil War fortifications. Come to think of it, skipping across the Sea Islands could not possibly do them justice. That would take a lifetime.

SEA TURTLES

THE SOUTH TAKES ITS SEA TURTLES SERI-ously. Of the seven recognized sea turtle species, five nest along the southern Atlantic and Gulf coasts—the loggerhead, hawksbill, Kemp's ridley, green, and leatherback—though the loggerhead is by far the most common. Along certain beaches in South Carolina, where some of the most pristine nesting areas are found, bright orange signs dot the sand reading, LOGGERHEAD TURTLE NESTING AREA—EGGS, HATCHLINGS, ADULTS, AND CARCASSES PROTECTED BY FEDERAL & STATE LAWS. Turtle Patrol officers stand guard beside females as they bury their eggs in the sand. South Carolina even named the loggerhead the official state reptile in 1988. Averaging around three hundred pounds and three feet in length, loggerheads, like all sea turtles, are distinct for their flipper-like forearms and large heads that they cannot withdraw into their shells. Sea turtles come ashore only to lay their eggs, and, if all goes right, some sixty days later those nests erupt with dozens of babies. Almost all endangered or threatened, sea turtle populations face high risks. If you're lucky, though, a friendly Turtle Patrol officer might just let you watch one bury her eggs—as long as you stay behind the line.

the story behind it is wholly fictional. In 2016, feeling guilty, Seger admitted to the *New York Times* that he'd invented the drink and fabricated the story. Why? Because a classic cocktail consists of about 50 percent liquor and 50 percent plausible tale, and if you want to sell a drink, it should come with a good story. Few in the cocktail community became exercised about Seger's revelation. Most agree that a fine story makes a good drink taste better, and no one suffers much harm if the taffy is pulled a bit longer than one is normally accustomed to.

SEELBACH COCKTAIL

THE SEELBACH WAS A CLASSIC HISTORIC cocktail until 2016, when suddenly it wasn't.

The origin story went as follows: a bartender at the Seelbach Hotel in Louisville was making drinks for a couple in 1912. One wanted a Manhattan, the other a champagne cocktail. The champagne inadvertently spilled over from the bottle into the Manhattan, and the bartender set the mess aside to make it anew. But he sampled it later, decided it was quite tasty, and it became popular, at least until Prohibition, when it was lost.

The drink was "rediscovered" in 1995 by the Seelbach restaurant director, Adam Seger, who decided to return it to the menu. Cocktail writers came upon it, and its fame spread. Made with bourbon, triple sec, and Angostura and Peychaud's bitters, then topped with champagne, it is indeed quite delicious. Also,

SEERSUCKER

THE CLASSIC SUIT IS STILL LOVINGLY WORN BY grandees along the Gulf and in other equally hot and wet parts of the South, quite often with bucks and a bow tie or four-in-hand, and yet, sadly, without a shred of irony or much awareness of history. Pukka and bright and energetic as this fashion is when we encounter it in the better Mobile law firms or peppering the tables in the main dining room at Galatoire's on Fridays, seersucker did not begin life atop the socioeconomic ladder. The magical milk-and-sugar weave, which causes the stripes to pucker slightly to keep the fabric off the skin, thus keeping its wearer cool, was first used by stevedores and locomotive engineers—men in extremely hot, manual-labor circumstances. It was only in the F. Scott and Zelda Fitzgerald era of the pre-Crash twenties that some university snots with not enough to do decided to make suits out of the stuff as a spoof of the working classes. The boys didn't expect that the suits would work so well, pre-air-conditioning, or become so madly popular.

All that history leads to the current Southerner's duty regarding seersucker: distressing the icy perfection of the suit by wearing it in every circumstance, not just at summer board meetings or old-line restaurants. Gentlemen of the North typically wear it only once or twice a year. Gentlemen of the South, whose region truly owns and champions the fabric, should endeavor to look as if they've had it in the family since the Fitzgeralds were visiting Zelda's relatives in Montgomery.

SEGREGATION

WHETHER DE JURE (BY LAW) OR DE FACTO (IN fact), segregation—the discriminatory separation of the races in order to oppress African Americans—permeated all aspects of Southern life throughout much of the twentieth century, from education to transportation to places of worship to housing to entertainment. *See Jim Crow.*

SEWANEE

by Jon Meacham

A SYNONYM FOR THE UNIVERSITY OF THE South and the town the Episcopal institution inhabits, Sewanee is geographically found on a thirteen-thousand-acre domain atop the Cumberland Plateau in southeastern Tennessee. Yet as generations of alumni, professors, trustees, regents, and bishops will tell you—eagerly, for passion for the place is a characteristic of the tribe—Sewanee is also an imaginative reality, a kind of real-life Barchester of winter fog and Gothic chapels, of undergraduates and faculty in tattered gowns, of great books, enduring symphonies, and endless forests. "It's a long way away, even from Chattanooga, in the middle of woods, on top of a bastion of mountains crenellated with blue coves," wrote the poet-planter William Alexander Percy. "It is so beautiful that people who have once been there always, one way or another, come back. For such as can detect apple green in an evening sky, it is Arcadia—not the one that never used to be, but the one that many people always live in; only this one can be shared."

Derived from a Shawnee word meaning "south" or "southern," Sewanee, at its founding in 1857, represented the culmination of a nearly three-decade-old vision of James Hervey Otey, an educator and Episcopal priest, to build a church-owned university to serve the Southern states. In the context of antebellum politics and culture, the school was neither wholly nationalist nor wholly sectionalist. Otey saw the university as an undertaking in keeping with the Union; another important founder, the Louisiana bishop Leonidas Polk, would die under arms as a Confederate general.

The creation of the university was fraught. The board of trustees first met on Lookout Mountain on July 4, 1857; the school was chartered in 1858 and a cornerstone was laid on the plateau in 1860. Then, of course, the war came, and everything was lost. Sewanee, as has been often noted, lay in ruins; skirmishes and Union incursions had destroyed what little there was. The subsequent resurrection of the university, in idea and in fact, owed much not to any single Southerner but to a native of New Hampshire: Charles Todd Quintard, who had succeeded Otey as bishop of Tennessee. Quintard toured England in search of funds—there were precious few resources to tap in the post-Appomattox South—and the university was refounded, opening for students in 1868.

Long known for a fine literary tradition (embodied in the *Sewanee Review*, the oldest continuously published quarterly in America) and for its ecclesiastical connection, Sewanee has been a stronghold for the liberal arts through turmoil and tumult. The university is devoted to introducing students to what Matthew Arnold described as the best that has been thought and said in the world, in intimate classes taught only by professors. There are no teaching assistants; the only extant graduate school is an Episcopal seminary. Life in the tiny environs of Sewanee is itself an element of one's education. As Mark Twain once remarked, if you want to know a man truly, get to know him in a village, not a city, and Sewanee

is a crucible for enduring friendships not only among students themselves but across generations. Edward McCrady, vice-chancellor and president for two decades in the middle of the twentieth century, believed Sewanee's mission was to shape a student's "manners and morals, as well as his information."

Such close-knit networks of kith and kin risk breeding provincialism, but Sewanee has long transcended the geographic confines of its official name—the University of the South—to include not only the particular but the universal. You can see more from a mountain, and Sewanee's global focus, ranging from questions of the soul to our stewardship of the physical environment, belies its physical isolation. There is something irresistible about the place and its people—for, as Mr. Percy noted, we always, one way or another, come back.

SHAG

BEFORE GOLF COURSES, OUTLET MALLS, AND high-rise condos enveloped Myrtle Beach, South Carolina, like kudzu, the male-led swing-style dance known as the shag, also called the Carolina shag, sprang forth from the town's open-air beachfront dance halls. The dance's origins are murky, but there on the sand, beginning in the late 1940s, a regional variation of R&B called beach music began showing up on jukeboxes at the still-segregated clubs (the best known of which included the Pad, the Pavilion, and the Arcade). A descendant of the Carolina jitterbug, the shag developed as recognition for beach music grew in the fifties and sixties and bands such as the Drifters, the Tams, the Dominoes, and the Temptations became popular. The footwork timing is the same as East Coast swing: triple step, triple step, rock step. Unlike the jitterbug, dancers don't bounce and rarely hold both hands. A Grand Strand old-timer will tell you that a proper shag should be danced from the waist down—smooth footwork sliding across polished hardwoods, with the Embers playing in the background.

traditional crab and rice soup served prior to the main course. Deas left out the rice, thickened the soup with a few tablespoons of flour, then added orange crab roe for color and its exquisitely delicate taste. A Charleston classic, and a staple on downtown menus to this day, was born.

Alas for gourmands, it is now illegal to take "sponge crabs," females with mature egg sacs. Many chefs now substitute crumbled or grated egg yolks in place of the crab roe.

SHE-CRAB SOUP

A BISQUE, OR CREAM-BASED SOUP, GARNISHED with thin-chopped chives and livened up just before serving with a half jigger of dry sherry. Legend says it was invented by Rhett's butler, who obviously gave a damn. To elucidate the specifics: R. Goodwyn Rhett was the mayor of Charleston, South Carolina. The butler was William Deas, who was also a singer in a gospel quartet. And the occasion was the 1910 visit of President William Howard Taft, a notorious gourmand (a polite term for a glutton with extremely good taste) who weighed more than three hundred pounds. Wherever Taft traveled, each community tried to outdo the last with culinary extravagance: stuffed flounder, stuffed trout, custom cured hams, beefsteaks, quail by the dozens, desserts with French names few could pronounce.

During the visit, Mayor Rhett pulled Deas aside and asked him to "dress up" the

SHRIMP AND GRITS

by Matt Lee and Ted Lee

HERE'S THE KEY TO WHY SHRIMP AND grits became such a successful ambassador of Lowcountry cooking: utter brilliance on the palate. The amiable pairing of gently sweet native shrimp from the creeks and marshes with savory, starchy corn grits from farther inland seems perfectly balanced. Whether served for breakfast, lunch, or—more commonly nowadays—dinner, it's the rare comfort food that whispers of the sea. So "shrimp and grits" appears nightly on the menus of ambitious restaurants far beyond the dish's native region. It has earned a place of honor alongside other Southern icons: cornbread, she-crab soup, fried chicken, burgoo, pecan pie.

Ironically, while most associate shrimp and grits with Charleston, South Carolina, in particular—the way gumbo is always New Orleans' calling card—until the mid-1980s you would never actually hear a native Charlestonian utter the phrase "shrimp and grits," even if he had just served you a bowl of it. Until a cluster of modern restaurants changed the lexicon of grits in the 1990s, most Charleston home cooks confusingly referred to cooked grits as "hominy"—a word the rest of the world uses to describe nixtamalized corn, of the sort used for tortillas and tamales. Not here. Stephen Colbert, who grew up on East Bay Street, has on numerous occasions defended the archaic "hominy" of his parents' generation on national television.

There may also be some promotional magic at work in shrimp and grits' current prominence, arising out of an encounter that took place in 1985 in, of all places, Chapel Hill, North Carolina. Bill Neal, a chef and cookbook author raised on a farm in Gaffney, South Carolina (upstate, peach-growing country), had in 1982 opened Crook's Corner, serving the kind of honest and refined farm cooking he had grown up with to University of North Carolina students and professors. Neal had spent time in Charleston, so she-crab soup and shrimp and grits were always on the menu at Crook's. In 1985, after the legendary *New York Times* food writer and editor Craig Claiborne, a native of Mississippi, raved about the dish (and published the recipe) following a visit to Neal's kitchen, shrimp and grits broke out to a national audience.

To be sure, the structure of the dish had already been around a long time: a recipe for "Shrimps with Hominy" appears in the 1930 book *200 Years of Charleston Cooking*, and it couldn't be more basic—shrimp sautéed in butter with salt and pepper, served with "hominy." By comparison, the "Breakfast Shrimp" in *Charleston Receipts* (1951) is amplified with diced onion and green pepper, bacon grease, Worcestershire, ketchup, and flour to create a thick gravy. In Neal's 1985 recipe, the one the *Times* published, the shrimp are cooked in smoky bacon fat, then dressed with lemon juice, sautéed mushrooms, and green onion—minimalist, compared with midcentury examples.

The flavor profile of Neal's version—piquant, smoky flavored, with the slightest amount of gravy—would dominate restaurant practice for most of the next three decades. Though Neal died in 1991, his influence lives on at Crook's Corner, now helmed by Bill Smith, and also in the kitchens of many other superb Southern chefs, who worked under Neal's tutelage and continue to spread the shrimp and grits gospel (Robert Stehling of Charleston's Hominy Grill; John Currence of City Grocery, in Oxford, Mississippi; and Amy Tornquist of Watts Grocery, in Durham, North Carolina, to name a few). Today, in the hands of new generations of cooks, interpretations of the classic combination are breaking out in exciting new directions. Don't expect its popularity to dwindle anytime soon. *See Neal, Bill.*

SIDEBOARD

A SIDEBOARD IS MORE THAN A PIECE OF DIN-
ing room furniture; it's a party host. Its very
use signifies an *occasion*, with enough company
to warrant auxiliary surface area beyond the
dining room table. Even when it's not loaded
down with platters of food or dessert—and
maybe a punch bowl or pitcher of iced tea—it's
usually (and patiently) displaying the serving
pieces and storing the silver and linens that
will be deployed for the next big event. In the
South, table-height sideboards are often called
"huntboards" or simply "slabs."

SIMMONS, PHILIP

(1912–2009)

CHARLESTON, SOUTH CAROLINA, HAS EARNED
an international reputation for hospitality by
throwing open its house gates, and none of
those gates are more distinctive than those
created by Philip Simmons, perhaps the best-
known Southern blacksmith of the twentieth
century. Born on Daniel Island (now a part of
Charleston) in 1912, Simmons was schooled
across the Cooper River in the city, where he
was drawn to the creative clamor emanating
from smithies crafting boat parts and wagon
wheels. He completed his apprenticeship
with the formerly enslaved (and unrelated)
Peter Simmons just before Charleston enacted
the nation's first historic preservation ordi-
nance, which sent homeowners scrambling
for artisans to repair their decorative window
grilles, stair rails, and balcony fencing. Philip
Simmons ultimately forged more than five
hundred ornamental pieces, and his wrought-
iron curves and curls still stretch across the
city. Such eloquent metalwork prompted
the Smithsonian Institution in 1976 to invite Simmons to participate in the American
Folklife Festival; six years later, he received
the National Endowment for the Arts' highest honor for traditional artists. "I drive by and
see them still standing, and it makes me feel
good," Simmons told *Charleston* magazine in
2006, three years before his death. "[D]on't
make no difference if it's on the Battery or for
people with not so much money. As long as
the customer was satisfied, then I'm feeling
very satisfied." *See Wrought iron.*

SIMONE, NINA

(1933–2003)

"She is loved or feared, adored or disliked, but few who have met her music or glimpsed her soul react with moderation," Maya Angelou wrote of this complex North Carolina native. Simone was born Eunice Waymon in 1933 in Tryon. A talented pianist, she dreamed of playing Bach in concert halls, but Philadelphia's Curtis Institute of Music (for which she auditioned) apparently wasn't keen to enroll an African American woman. After changing her name to throw her mother off her career path—the Methodist preacher would not have approved—Simone started singing a blend of jazz and blues in East Coast bars. In 1958, she recorded "I Loves You, Porgy," which shot up the Billboard chart and won Simone a recording contract. Within a few years, though, she identified more as an activist than an artist, a shift hurried along by white backlash to 1964's "Mississippi Goddam," a sardonically melodic protest anthem that, as the story goes, took Simone just twenty minutes to write. Radio stations returned copies of the single broken in two. Over the next decade, Simone was personally devastated by failures of the civil rights movement, financially ruined, and increasingly tormented by undiagnosed bipolar disorder. She died in 2003, leaving a musical legacy that has popped up in Elton John's bridges and Talib Kweli's samples.

SLAW

Slaw takes many forms in the South. At Lexington Barbecue in Lexington, North Carolina, it's minced cabbage in a tangy, ketchup-based dressing; in West Virginia, you'll get a mayonnaise-bound mixture on your slaw dogs at old-school joints like Skeenies. Then there's hot slaw, a cousin to kil't greens wilted with a mixture of warm bacon grease and vinegar. You can get that at Greyhound Tavern in Fort Mitchell, Kentucky. Nowadays you need to add broccoli, carrot, and brussels sprout slaws to the list. But traditional slaws all have at least one element in common: raw cabbage. Depending on where you're eating and whom you ask, they're either a side-dish staple or an essential part of a barbecue sandwich.

SLEEPING PORCHES

The sleeping porch occupies a cherished place in the hearts of Southerners old enough to recall a time before central air-conditioning. Typically screened to keep out bugs, sleeping porches often open on two or three sides to increase air flow. They're often found on the second story of a home, away from odors and noise.

Sleeping porches took off during the early twentieth century in response to the rise of tuberculosis, a leading cause of death at the time. Also known as "tubercular cure porches," they were part of an open-air movement. Builders across the South and other parts of the country retrofitted existing homes with screened rooms and, starting around 1910, incorporated them into new homes, allowing consumptives and others to benefit from the cool night air. The porches became so popular that a 1917 *House Beautiful* article included them among a home's "essentials of health and comfort." Because of its mountain altitude and climate, Asheville, North Carolina, became a hub for tuberculosis patients. Scores of sanatoriums and boarding-houses bristling with sleeping porches opened for the care of "White Plague" sufferers. The sleeping porches—and consumptive lodgers—Thomas Wolfe encountered growing up in an Asheville boardinghouse feature promi-nently in his 1929 autobiographical novel, *Look Homeward, Angel*.

Eventually, the threat of TB faded and so did the curative associations. But sleep-ing porches remained popular until cen-tral air-conditioning arrived in the 1950s. Recalling her Mississippi youth in a 1996 in-terview, Eudora Welty said, "Of course, every house . . . had a sleeping porch, for the whole family. There would just be a row of beds on it. It was like a dormitory almost. Everybody searched for the cool of the night breezes. You could hear owls, and there were mockingbirds who sang all night in the moonlight."

As an architectural form, the sleeping porch may be an endangered species, but it's not yet extinct. You'll find the porches in older homes, beach houses, hunting and fishing camps, and even newly built "green" homes designed by some of the most important ar-chitects working today.

SMART-GROSVENOR, VERTAMAE

(1937–2016)

by Jessica B. Harris

O N SEPTEMBER 3, 2016, THE WORLD LOST its "culinary griot," as Vertamae Smart-Grosvenor liked to call herself. If she had lived in the 1920s, she'd have been a madcap flapper. If she'd lived in the early 1800s, her adventures as a self-created African princess could have made her the prototype for Princess Caraboo. As it happened, she lived in the twentieth and twenty-first centuries, and she grabbed them with both hands and made them her own. Vertamae crammed many lifetimes into one. She was a mistress of creative self-reinvention.

She was born in the Lowcountry of South Carolina, and that region would always in-fluence her thought and her way of being in the world. At around age ten, she moved to Philadelphia with her parents and dreamed of a life of travel and adventure. That dream became reality when she turned nineteen and bought a ticket on an ocean liner headed to Europe—destination, Paris. The move was a formative experience. In the City of Light, she met a group of expatriate artists and writers, includ-ing Allen Ginsberg, William Burroughs, and James Baldwin, who became a lifelong friend. She also met Robert Grosvenor, a New York–born sculptor who became her husband.

In the 1960s and 1970s, after her return to the United States, Smart-Grosvenor was a neighborhood fixture in the nascent years of the Black Arts Movement in New York's East Village. She performed improvisational theater in Tompkins Square Park and became a "moon goddess," a backup singer, in Sun Ra's avant-garde music collective, the Solar-Myth Arkestra. Most important, she cooked for her fellow artists. Her dinners were legendary, both for the meals served and for who might turn up at her table. James Baldwin, Maya Angelou, Yoko Ono, the scholar and cultural critic Larry Neal, the poets Felipe Luciano and Quincy Troupe, and other luminaries all feasted there.

Her career as a culinary anthropologist began in 1970, with her groundbreaking cookbook *Vibration Cooking: or, the Travel Notes of a Geechee Girl*. Proudly reclaiming the word *Geechee*, previously considered pejorative, the work established her as a Lowcountry cultural force. The book's recipes did not conform to traditional methodology—a cup of this, a tablespoon of that. Instead, she rendered them in vignettes about their origins—who created them, where the recipes came from—as well as about how to prepare them. She followed the cookbook with *Thursdays and Every Other Sunday Off: A Domestic Rap,* a mordantly humorous look at her experiences in the world of domestic work. She also wrote columns and cultural commentary for *Essence* and *Elan* magazines.

In 1980, Smart-Grosvenor began a career at National Public Radio that would span three decades and earn her many accolades, including Peabody, James Beard, and National Association of Black Journalists awards. Her commentary covered social, political, and cultural issues as well as food. Her expertise with food also spawned a musical, *Nyam: A Food Opera*, a compilation of traditional and original music and commentary that she performed around the country. In the nineties, she acted in films, appearing in the Lowcountry-set classic *Daughters of the Dust* (1991) and *Beloved* (1998), based on the Toni Morrison novel. She also starred on the small screen, with a public-TV show called *The Americas' Family Kitchen with Vertamae Grosvenor*. The show, one of very few with an African American host, prompted two more cookbooks (*Vertamae Cooks* and *Vertamae Cooks Again*) and brought her wider acclaim. By the end of the decade, New Hampshire's Franklin Pierce University awarded her an honorary Doctorate of Humane Letters.

At the time of her death, Smart-Grosvenor was a full-fledged culinary icon—her list of awards lengthy, her life and work the subject of two documentaries, *Travel Notes of a Geechee Girl* and *Vertamae: Always, Already*. But it's impossible to catch the whirlwind. The remnants she left behind are only a pale shadow of this vibrant, opinionated, amazing woman, who saw the world, savored it, and made it her own.

(1894–1937)

BLESSED WITH A POWERFUL, SOULFUL con-tralto that made her the most popular female blues singer of the 1920s and '30s, Bessie Smith, the "Empress of the Blues," makes Courtney Love seem puritanical. She famously sang, "I need a little sugar in my bowl/I need a little hot dog on my roll," once sought out a ri-val and beat her unconscious, and slept with her musical director and many of her female backup singers.

Orphaned at age nine, Smith busked in her native Chattanooga, singing and dancing out-side the White Elephant Saloon at Thirteenth and Elm while her brother played guitar. She began recording in 1923. Her first single, "Downhearted Blues," sold almost 800,000 copies in six months. When the Depression cut her blues career short, she tried Broadway. When that didn't work, she sang swing. Smith was killed in a car crash outside Clarksdale, Mississippi, in 1937. Her funeral drew seven thousand people, but her grave went unmarked because her manager/husband kept pocketing the money. In 1970, Janis Joplin bought her a proper marker. Prince Charles once said, "I believe there are only two truly regal women in this world, my mother and Bessie Smith."

ACCORDING TO SCIENTISTS, OF THE SOUTH'S six million species of native snakes, seven million are venomous. No, of course that's not right, but to most folks, when it comes to snakes, there's not a lot of wiggle room between love and hate. What's true is that the South's varied landscapes—from cottonmouth-friendly swamps to coral snake–worthy sand hills—are a sort of Noah's ark for Mr. No Shoulders. Florida alone is home to forty-six species of snakes. There are at least seventy-five in Texas. Compare that to, say, Maine, whose residents can boast of only a single species of legless reptile.

In the South, snake myths abound. To wit: Heck, yeah, a copperhead can bite you even after you've chopped that sucker into eighteen pieces. Heck, yeah, snakes will drop into your boat every chance they get—the same ones that will bite you if you water-ski through a nest of 'em. And you're telling me your cousin was bitten all to pieces by baby moccasins he thought were earthworms when he was put-ting them on the hooks? Mine, too! What are the chances?

"OTHER PEOPLE GO HAVE COFFEE, PEOPLE IN New Orleans go have sno-balls," says Ashley Hansen. Granted, as the proprietor of the iconic Hansen's Sno-Bliz stand her family has operated uptown on Tchoupitoulas Street since 1944, she has a vested interest in saying so. But to be clear, the Big Easy's sno-balls are vastly superior to pedestrian snow cones, thanks to the finely shaved ice that forms a fluffier base for a thorough soaking of flavored cane syrup. (Hansen's grandfather Ernest actually invented the first motor-driven ice-shaving machine that made this possible.) Typically open from March to October, neighborhood sno-ball stands across the New Orleans area now all seem to hawk their own special flavors; from quenching kid pleasers like grape and watermelon to I-dare-you options such as dill pickle and jalapeño, one could try a new one every day and never repeat through the entire season. (Yes, you may consider that a challenge.) "A sno-ball keeps you cool when days here keep getting hotter and hotter," Hansen says. "And when you walk into a sno-ball stand with all the syrup bottles lined up, it just smells so sweet—it smells like summer."

THERE ARE MANY STRIKING SIMILARITIES BE-tween actual migratory waterfowl and their human counterparts, nicknamed "snowbirds." Much like ducks, human snowbirds flee their Northern habitats as soon as the weather up there takes on a hint of chill. They descend in massive numbers (is anyone even left in New Jersey?) and follow predictable routes on their annual southbound journey. And they spend the ensuing winter months waddling around the sunnier, more hospitable environs of Florida, Texas, or just about anywhere else they can stick a beach umbrella.

SOFT-SHELL CRABS

A SANDWICH WITH LEGS HANGING OUT OF the roll would not typically be considered drool-worthy. But when said legs are attached to a soft-shell crab, Southern foodies come running. Softies generally arrive in late April or May, and chefs in the South scramble to get the delicacy on the menu. These coveted coastal crawlers are blue crabs that have shed their exoskeletons. Left undisturbed, they quickly generate a new shell to accommo-date their growing body. If they're harvested, however, the soft, shell-less exterior remains and the entire crab—body, legs, and claws—becomes edible. Because searching the ocean for crabs that happen to be in this transitional phase is nearly impossible, fishermen try to capture the crabs before they molt and then hold them in saltwater tanks. Once the crabs shed their shells, they're pulled from the water and delivered, alive and fresh, to clamoring chefs eager to serve softie fanatics who've been stalking social media for clues of the rock star crustacean's arrival. Restaurants serve them fried, grilled, or sautéed, complete with appetizing appendages.

SONG OF THE SOUTH

"WHATEVER YOU DO, PLEASE, PLEASE DON'T stick me in that briar patch!" begs Brer Rabbit, the troublemaking bunny at the center of Disney's 1946 film *Song of the South*. But while Brer Rabbit makes quick work of escaping his prickly thicket, Disney itself has never quite wriggled free of the thorny bramble it found itself in after making this controversial film. A combination of live action and animation, *Song of the South* was based on the classic Uncle Remus stories, adaptations of African American folktales first published in 1881 that featured trickster animals imparting a variety of life lessons via such indelible scenes as that of "the tar baby" and "the laughing place." The stories' narrator, Uncle Remus (portrayed in the film by the vaudeville actor James Baskett), is a preternaturally happy sharecropping former slave whose cartoonish dialect and overt racial stereotyping struck some twentieth-century audiences (at least late-century ones) as racist and patronizing. Though bits of the film—like its classic song "Zip-a-Dee-Doo-Dah"—still drift potently through the currents of American culture, Disney has ensured that the film, last released theatrically in 1986, is no longer available to U.S. audiences. *See Uncle Remus.*

SORGHUM

IN HER 1942 BOOK *SOUTHERN HARVEST*, THE author and engraver Clare Leighton wrote that attending an Appalachian sorghum boil was like being a participant at a sacrament. "This year's sorghum, essence of sun and rain and light and earth, was poured, hot still from the evaporators, upon biscuits," she reported. "We ate, and tongues were burned by the heated syrup. But over everything, man and woman and child, and stretching black shadow, hung this sacramental feeling, like a mist of holiness." Maybe it's the biscuits talking, but anyone who has tasted the dark, twangy sweetness of just-boiled syrup agrees there is nothing like it. The sweet sorghum cane must be pressed (often still in a horse-drawn mill) immediately after harvest. The pale green juice flows into an evaporating pan heated by wood fire, where it throws off vigorous eruptions of foam before reducing to a dark treacle. Sorghum has defied industrial production, perhaps because an acre of reed won't yield even a hundred gallons of syrup. It became nearly impossible to find until chefs resurrected a steady artisanal supply from producers such as Tennessee's Muddy Pond Sorghum Mill. Now anyone with Internet access and a good biscuit recipe can take this particular sacrament.

SOUL FOOD

by Adrian Miller

"SOUL FOOD" IS A TRADITIONAL AFRICAN American cuisine that fuses the culinary techniques and foods of West Africa, Western Europe, and the Americas. Conventional wisdom holds that the term *soul food* was coined in the 1960s, but it floated around in black culture at least a decade earlier. The "soul" concept originated in the music world, when jazz artists tapped the sounds of the black church in the rural South to create a sound white musicians could not mimic. That unique gospel sound was nicknamed "soul," and soon the term was slapped onto every aspect of African American culture, including food, as a sharp contrast to the majority white culture. *Soul food* has become shorthand for all African American cooking, but in actuality this cuisine should be distinguished from Southern cuisine, the Lowcountry cooking of the coastal Carolinas and Georgia, and the Creole cooking of the lower Mississippi.

A typical soul food meal consists of an entree of fried chicken, fried catfish, or chitlins (pig intestines); side dishes such as black-eyed peas, macaroni and cheese, mixed greens (cabbage, collards, and kale, mustard, and turnip greens being the most popular), and candied yams (sweet potatoes); some type of cornbread; a red-colored beverage; a bottle of hot sauce; and for dessert, banana pudding, peach cobbler, pound cake, or sweet potato pie. That sounds a lot like "Southern food," and it's easy to see how that and "soul food" are used interchangeably. The differences lie in the preparation. Soul food tends to be more intense in flavor (it's saltier, spicier, and sweeter and has more fat), blurs the line between savory and sweet (sugar in cornbread, for instance), and extensively uses variety meats like ham hocks and oxtails.

Despite its gloriousness, soul food has a lot of haters. Within the African American community, it gets dissed as "slavery food" or "the master's leftovers." Thus, to eat such food is to literally digest white supremacy. This is an enduring, and unfortunate, critique because it overlooks soul food's complexity. A closer examination of its history reveals that soul food is an interesting mix of poverty and prestige dishes that move up and down the social ladder over time. Even chitlins (yes, chitlins) were once savored by the European gentry.

Many people, African Americans and others, also feel that soul food needs a warning label because it's inherently unhealthy. This, too, calls for nuanced thinking. In the past, people ate rich foods such as fried chicken, barbecue, and sweet potato pie only on special occasions. Now many consume them several times a week, or every day. Without regular exercise and a balanced diet, that eating will not do your body good. Yet, think about what foods nutritionists now recommend: dark leafy greens, sweet potatoes, legumes, okra, more fish, hibiscus (as a beverage). These are the building blocks of soul food. It's not so much the food itself, but how it is prepared and its proportion of one's overall diet.

Today there are diverse ways to make soul food. Besides the traditional methods, cooks may put a health-conscious spin on it by flavoring dishes with something besides pork, decreasing the amount of fat, salt, and sugar, or avoiding animal products entirely. Some head in the opposite direction, using exotic ingredients like duck fat, goat cheese, and saffron, or experimenting with molecular gastronomy techniques. (Sweet potato spheres with collard green dust and chitlin foam, anyone?) Whatever form it takes, soul food deserves to be celebrated as one of America's greatest and most enduring cuisines. It doesn't need a warning label. It just needs more love.

SOUR ORANGE

THIS HARDY VARIETY OF CITRUS DOESN'T play well in fruit salads. Floridians balance the tart fruits with sugar to make marmalade and sour orange pie, a cousin to key lime that harks back to days gone by like a cranky conquistador at a beach barbecue. Spanish explorers in fact planted the first sour oranges in St. Augustine in the 1700s. *Citrus aurantium* has since put down roots all over the state. You'll find it growing wild and in backyards, where it can endure and even prosper in poor soil and freezing weather that would wither its tropical kin. Sweet orange growers, though they peddle the crowd-pleasing fruit of continental breakfast buffets, often graft their branches onto rugged sour orange stock.

SOUTHERN COLLEGE FOOTBALL

by Ace Atkins

I'VE HEARD WAY TOO MUCH TALK ABOUT why Southern college football is the best, corny pieces on ESPN or the new SEC Network about football being in our people's blood, akin to religion, and causing rivalries not unlike those of the Civil War.

I don't need to be lectured about college football in the South. I played on Auburn's undefeated team in 1993, and my dad was the MVP of Auburn's undefeated national championship team of 1957. I've been around college football my whole life. I get it.

What outsiders don't know is that Southern football isn't about dominance and winning, it's about conversation. Football is our common currency. Whether you're black or white, rich or poor, a transplant from Ohio or a native of Mobile, you can walk into any bar, sit down at any burger joint, and start talking football. Want to kill time while getting an oil change? Lament a recent bowl loss to someone you've just met.

A Southerner's love of football transcends the usual cultural conventions at play in the rest of the country. The biggest Southern football fan I know is a writer pal in New Orleans who happens to be gay. I'd put his knowledge up against any tobacco-chewing truck driver's in West Alabama. I know other states have their favorite programs, too. But in the South, our fandom is not spread out among different sports. Nor does it matter if you actually attended the school you're cheering for. The team you follow on Saturdays—hell, every day of the week—matters as much as what church you attend (or don't attend) and whether you hunt deer, turkeys, ducks, or antiques. It's your tribe, and that helps you relate to other tribe members, whether or not you have a single other thing in common.

I can strike up an instant friendship with someone on a bus by saying, "War Eagle." I would not get the same reaction if I wanted to talk amazing gourmet cheeses, indie film, or the year's best pinot noir. Football crosses all ethnic, socioeconomic, and religious borders in the South. It doesn't matter if you're not rooting for the same team—sometimes, that gives you even more to talk about.

A lot has been made about the rivalry of Alabama and Auburn. And things do get awfully heated, even poisonous. But I've never met an Alabama fan not willing to sit down and talk football with someone from Auburn. Even after writing twenty-one novels, I invariably encounter people at my Alabama book events with a ragged old copy of the *Sports Illustrated* cover I was on more than twenty years ago—and that's what they want me to sign.

They may not give a damn about the themes in my latest stories. But they're willing to talk about the 1993 team and the tense moments we all shared. It's a familiar and old conversation. And a way I know I'm home.

SOUTHERN COMFORT

FOR PLENTY OF PEOPLE, THE FIRST SWIG OF whiskey ever to pass their lips came from a communal bottle of Southern Comfort. Or so they thought—because until the brand's new owner, the Sazerac Company, recently reformulated the recipe, good ol' SoCo contained not a drop of whiskey. True, the brand got its start in 1874 when an enterprising New Orleans bartender named Martin Wilkes Heron spruced up some barrels of skunky whiskey with his own secret blend of fruits and spices. The stuff caught on, and Southern Comfort has been a field-party staple ever since, though long ago the base liquor got switched to a neutral grain spirit (like vodka)—technically making it a liqueur. Love it or hate it, the apricot-and-cinnamon-spiked flavor has stayed true, even as the iconic label received a makeover and a bit of real whiskey was reintroduced.

SOUTHERN GOTHIC

IMAGINE A MANSION, MAYBE IN SAVANNAH or Charleston, South Carolina, maybe a bit farther-flung, but out of place and time regardless. It is not hard to imagine the parties once held there: hoopskirted Scarletts fanning themselves on a broad wraparound porch behind white columns as thick as a person, making eyes at men sipping mint juleps and smoking fat cigars, music in the air. Whenever these parties happened, it was far in the past. The mansion is still standing, but vines now creep up those same columns and into broken second-story windows, the shine on the paint faded untold years ago, and the wood has begun to warp and crack from forces natural and otherwise. An ancient live oak grows nearby, Spanish moss heavy with thick swamp air dripping down onto a peaked roof. A woman sits in a rocking chair, dressed in a faded ball gown, slowly creaking back and forth. Never faster, never slower. *Creak, creak, creak*, eyes out to an overgrown field off in the distance, where ghosts of slaves toil and bleed over imagined crops. She looks as though she has not moved in decades. Maybe a witch, maybe a vampire, maybe just a lost soul who no longer understands which world she lives in. One thing is clear: Something is wrong there. Something is lost.

That's Southern Gothic.

SOUTHERNISMS

by Daniel Wallace

SOUTHERN COLLOQUIALISMS ARE MULTI-farious and, in fact, possibly infinite. That's what Pee-paw used to say, anyway. These colloquialisms are sometimes called Southernisms, but that word—*Southernism*—is itself somewhat colloquial. Anyway, there are a ton of them. Animals appear in a lot of them, but most concern dogs in some form or fashion. For example:

"That dog won't hunt."

"That's a hard dog to keep on the porch."

"You ain't nothin' but a hound dog."

"Run with the big dogs or stay on the porch."

"Happy as a tick on a fat dog."

Et cetera. Expressions like these don't come out of nowhere; they're most often reflections of the culture from which they arise. In the case of dogs, it's clear that dogs are integral to the South and the character of its people. Is it even possible to be Southern and *not* have a dog—or many dogs, probably? Not really. If you don't have dogs, if you don't *love* dogs, you're either deathly allergic or you've come from somewhere else and are just pretending to be Southern, probably to meet women or get out of the cold.

There are other animals commonly referred to in Southernisms as well, though, including but not limited to cats, turtles, gators, birds, possums, and skunks. "If you see a turtle sitting on a fence post, you know it didn't get there all by itself." President Clinton said that once and I've been saying it ever since. There are no wombats, kookaburras, or marmosets in any Southernism, period. Nature—trees, for instance—is important and makes a number of appearances, as in "lit up like a Christmas tree." And then there are those that mention both dogs *and* trees in a single Southernism. "It's so hot I saw two trees fighting over a dog," for instance.

Language evolves. Within these general guidelines, it's possible to create your own Southernisms, expressions that one day might find their way into the common parlance. Here are a few I've made up myself:

"Lonely as a pine tree in a parking lot."

"Funny as a three-legged dog in a horse race."

"Sweeter than a lollipop at an ant convention."

Try it yourself. There's an art to it, and it helps to have a Pee-paw who knows whereof he speaks. Regardless, start slowly, and be sensitive to meaning and cultural appropriateness. For instance, an expression like "That cat won't hunt"—just. Won't. Hunt.

SOUTHERN ROCK

WHEN A JACKSONVILLE, FLORIDA, GYM TEACHER named Leonard Skinner sent Gary Rossington to the high-school principal's office sometime in the late 1960s, little did he know that his name—with its spelling tweaked—would go on to epitomize a revolution of sorts in Southern music. Lynyrd Skynyrd was hardly the first or the only force to fuse a little twang into rock and roll's riff-heavy, guitar-driven sound. Beginning in the 1950s with trailblazers like Elvis, Bo Diddley, Buddy Holly, and Little Richard—not to mention the deep and lasting impact blues legends like Robert Johnson and Muddy Waters had on everyone from Eric Clapton to the Rolling Stones to Led Zeppelin—rock music has rarely strayed more than a few degrees of separation away from its Southern roots. As the genre matured and evolved, though, Southern artists began to reclaim that heritage and put an unapologetically Southern stamp on their records.

Think of the Allman Brothers Band (out of Macon, Georgia, and Jacksonville) with their guitar-heavy melodies, blues-inflected vocal drawls, and long improvisational jams. The Outlaws, the Marshall Tucker Band, and Elvin Bishop also personified Southern rock in its 1970s commercial heyday. But the subgenre and its influence expanded beyond actual Southerners, making "Southern rock" a fuzzy categorization at best. From the Band (all Canadians, other than Levon Helm) to Creedence Clearwater Revival (who despite their classics laden with images of bayous and riverboats came from the Bay Area) to current torchbearers like Blackberry Smoke, Southern rock at its best has reflected what Southern culture does best: pluck ingredients from all over and cook them up into something that, every so often, rises to the level of transcendent.

SOUTHERN SODAS

by Steve Russell

THE COLLECTIVE SOUTHERN SWEET TOOTH has launched scores of soft-drink brands. Everyone knows the big players that have fizzed their way to global dominance. But there are other, lesser-known regional brands that claim their own fiercely loyal local fans. Recognize any of these?

Ale-8-One

HOME: Winchester, Kentucky.

DISTRIBUTION: Core territory Middle Kentucky; reaches into Illinois, southern Ohio and Indiana, and eastern Tennessee. (Also now appearing in Harris Teeter supermarkets across the South.)

HISTORY: Winchester entrepreneur G. L. Wainscott tinkered with multiple flavored drinks before unveiling this ginger-centric recipe at the 1926 Clark County Fair. A slogan contest produced the name, a play on "a late one"—slang for being the latest thing. Fourth-generation descendant Fielding Rogers still blends (and protects) the recipe today.

TASTING NOTES: Supremely crisp and quenching, with a good balance of citrus and real ginger.

PAIRS BEST WITH: A steaming bowl of Kentucky burgoo at any well-stocked Derby party.

Big Red

HOME: San Antonio.

DISTRIBUTION: Southern and central Texas; reaches into other Southern and Midwestern states.

HISTORY: Debuted in Waco in 1937 with the fanciful moniker Sun Tang Red Cream Soda. Legend has it that a San Antonio bottling-plant boss overheard his golf caddies calling the neon-hued drink "Big Red," prompting an official name change in 1969. The iconic Texas musician Doug Sahm holds a Big Red longneck on a 1971 album cover.

TASTING NOTES: Like syrupy-sweet orange soda, spiked with even sweeter red Jolly Ranchers and a big squirt of vanilla cream. Big Red's own promo materials admit the taste is "indiscernible."

PAIRS BEST WITH: Barbecued brisket and hot links at Smitty's Market in Lockhart . . . followed by a visit to the dentist.

Blenheim Ginger Ale

HOME: Dillon, South Carolina.

DISTRIBUTION: About a hundred markets in its Carolinas stronghold, and a somewhat clandestine smattering of specialty shops in twenty-one other states.

HISTORY: When Dr. C. R. May's patients balked at the taste of the mineral water he prescribed they drink from an artesian spring in Blenheim, South Carolina, in the late 1800s, he and partner A. J. Matheson added Jamaican ginger and started selling the stuff. In 1993 the cult brand was acquired by the family that owns the iconically sprawling South of the Border rest stop in Dillon, where Blenheim is now bottled—in glass only.

TASTING NOTES: Medium body and carbonation, with a tingle of real ginger at the back of the throat. Want it even spicier? Look for the "hot" version with the pink cap.

PAIRS BEST WITH: Dark rum, for the best Dark 'n Stormy this side of Bermuda.

Cheerwine

HOME: Salisbury, North Carolina.

DISTRIBUTION: Widely available from Florida to Maryland, spottier as you move inland. If you're really jonesing, seek out your nearest Cracker Barrel from coast to coast.

HISTORY: In 1917, businessman L. D. Peeler moved a bankrupt syrup company from Kentucky to North Carolina, purchased a wild-cherry syrup from a St. Louis flavor salesman (yes, that was an actual job)—and the burgundy-hued Cheerwine was born. Peeler's great-grandson runs the company today.

TASTING NOTES: Maraschino cherry with a strong cola foundation and a hint of vanilla; less carbonation than typical sodas makes for easy drinking.

PAIRS BEST WITH: A fresh yeast doughnut from fellow North Carolina icon Krispy Kreme—the two even joined forces for a Cheerwine-infused doughnut in 2010.

Dr. Enuf

HOME: Johnson City, Tennessee.

DISTRIBUTION: About a one-hundred-mile radius of Johnson City.

HISTORY: In 1949, Chicago chemist Bill Swartz developed the formula for a B-vitamin-packed soft drink and struck a deal with East Tennessee's Tri-City Beverage to bottle it. Among the bottler's innovative promo ideas: affixing DR. ENUF IS HERE! bumper stickers on physicians' cars at the local hospital.

TASTING NOTES: Light-bodied, bubbly tonic, and just enuf (get it?) lemon-lime flavor to be refreshing. Less detectable is the 220 percent of the recommended daily allowance of vitamin B_1, good for curbing beriberi, nerve inflammation, motion sickness, and apparently just about every other ailment.

PAIRS BEST WITH: A three-day NASCAR tailgate blowout at Bristol Motor Speedway.

Grapico

HOME: Birmingham, Alabama.

DISTRIBUTION: Alabama, Georgia, and the Florida Panhandle.

HISTORY: First sold in New Orleans in 1916, Grapico earned its firmest foothold in Alabama after a Birmingham bottler bought the rights to make it in 1917. Another Birmingham bottler, Buffalo Rock, kept the brand going in 1981 and has proudly promoted it as a Southern soda with slogans like "Until we figure out how to batter and fry it, we suggest you enjoy it over ice."

TASTING NOTES: Sweet and super grapey. Really, really grapey. The kind of bursting-with-grape taste that can only come from . . . artificial grape flavoring.

PAIRS BEST WITH: Hauling in a ten-pound largemouth bass on the Coosa River on a muggy summer day.

Red Rock Cola

HOME: Atlanta.

DISTRIBUTION: Georgia; reaches into some bordering states.

HISTORY: Despite being introduced in 1935 in the long shadow of that *other* Atlanta soft drink, Coca-Cola, Red Rock quickly became popular enough to be bottled in forty-seven states. (An endorsement by Babe Ruth didn't hurt.) But high sugar prices and an outmoded distribution network pushed it back to its home turf, where a loyal local following has been revived.

TASTING NOTES: A cola for grown-ups—less fizz and cloying sweetness than your average omnipresent brand, which lets a hint of caramel through, too.

PAIRS BEST WITH: We would say a smile, but we're pretty sure that combination is trademarked.

SPANISH MOSS

DESPITE ITS REPUTATION FOR BRINGING heavy dolor, fright, horror, and/or loss to what we might diplomatically call overwrought song, story, and filmmaking alike—the art form doesn't matter to the plant—Spanish moss is neither a moss, nor a lichen, nor Spanish, nor is it parasitic. Rather, *Tillandsia usneoides* is a stand-alone comic pretender of grand proportions. Think of it as the skinny rapscallion joker of the plant world, giving off its supersaccharine staid aura while actually being a rather rakish prancer-dancer when you're not looking.

Tendrils of Spanish moss, some of which can reach twenty feet or so in length, can fly, and not just in the Deep South's frequent hurricanes, although our heaviest coastal tillandsia concentrations do coincide with our various hurricane alleyways, on both the Gulf and the Atlantic Seaboard. It isn't strictly parasitic, but it does use the trees in which it grows as architectural support to gather the dust and moisture from which it lives. Poetically, it lives on what it gathers, like an aboveground sea sponge. Its qualities of retention have allowed it to become an ingredient in everything from birds' nests to an ancient addition to wattle architecture, beloved by the eighteenth-century French on the Gulf for the tensile strength it brought to their half-timbered *bousillage* chinking, when added to mortar. In short, we shouldn't romanticize Spanish moss. Its reality is far stranger and ultimately more romantic than any bit of treacly scene setting.

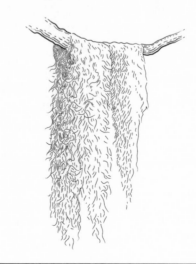

SPARTINA

Spartina alterniflora, or saltwater cord-grass, is the most prominent saltwater plant in Atlantic tidal marshes from here to Argentina. It comes in two varieties, tall and short, depending on the sand content in the mud—more sand equals shorter spartina. (If you're bogged down and fixing to drown, head for shorter grass and you might make it.) Together with brackish-water-tolerant *Spartina patens* (salt marsh hay) and *Juncus gerardii* (black needle rush), spartina creates an ecosystem that is the foundation for all Atlantic coast inshore sea life, from mud minnows to mullet to shrimp and blue crabs, to speckled sea trout and redfish, prey species for larger species, up to cobia and blacktip and even tiger sharks. It has often been noted that an acre of healthy spartina produces more food than an acre of the best Iowa corn ground.

Spartina dies off each winter, replaced by fresh green canes each spring. Great ricks of dead canes float out of the marsh on full- and new-moon tides, shuttled by wind and waves, creating trash lines offshore—shelter for pelagic fish. Pushed onto beaches by an offshore wind, dead spartina provides perfect natural erosion control.

STACK CAKE

A staple of Appalachia, stack cake rewards patience. For generations, mountain cooks have assembled its parts over months. They've picked the apples, then dried them or reduced them to apple butter. They've simmered the dusky sorghum syrup that sweetens the batter. In the dead of winter or the sweltering summer, they've used those prizes from their pantries to build a towering dessert for a wedding party or a holiday crowd. Finally they've waited just a few days more, for the preserved apple filling to soften a half dozen or more dense, cookie-like layers. Lacking in rich buttercream frosting or exotic coconut flakes, this dessert earns its centerpiece status over time. If you've ever had one made the old-fashioned way, you know it's worth the wait.

STANLEY, RALPH

(1927–2016)

He sounded like a ghost. That voice—a high, spooky tenor—seemed the distillation of all things Appalachian. Considered by most of the world to be one of the founding fathers of bluegrass, Ralph Stanley didn't much care for the term. "Old-time mountain style," he preferred to call his music, and he liked it pure, traditional, and very, very country. With his brother, Carter, Stanley formed the Clinch Mountain Boys in Norton, Virginia, in 1946, playing clawhammer banjo and singing harmony until taking over lead duties after

Carter's death, in 1966. In 2000, with more than five decades of celebrated work behind him, Stanley was startled to find his greatest mainstream success yet after an appearance on the multiplatinum soundtrack to the film *O Brother, Where Art Thou?*, singing the haunting a cappella ode "O Death." Featuring a voice so crackled with wear that it indeed sounded like a man personally well acquainted with death, the song won a Grammy in 2002 for Best Male Country Vocal Performance. "I never wanted to branch out," Stanley once said, and it was that unwavering focus on the past that helped him push old-time music light-years ahead.

STATION INN

by Marshall Chapman

I DON'T GO TO BARS, PER SE. BUT BEING A musician, I often find myself in music clubs that have bars. My favorite such room in Nashville is the Station Inn. Open since 1974, the Station Inn is known worldwide for presenting the best in bluegrass and roots music. It seats 175—mostly at tables and chairs. But back against the wall, patrons comfortably settle into seats salvaged from Lester Flatt's tour bus.

Like a relic from the Stone Age, the unassuming one-story flat-roofed stone building sits in the middle of a rapidly gentrifying area downtown called the Gulch, surrounded by sleek high-rises. The decor is vintage honky-tonk. Original Hatch Show Print posters and neon signs advertising beer (mostly Budweiser) adorn the windowless walls. At the far end of the room stands the bar, which offers beer (draft or bottled), soft drinks, popcorn, nachos, and pizza. John Prine once proclaimed the Station Inn had the best pizza in town. That may be debatable, but whenever I'm there, I nearly always order the small pizza with Italian sausage, green pepper, and onion, with a bottle of pale ale or Dos Perros beer (brewed locally at the Yazoo Brewing Company).

Booze is booze and beer is beer. But atmosphere and people are what make a bar great. And the Station Inn has long attracted characters. Take, for instance, the two women who for many years kept the place humming. One, Lin Barber, can still sometimes be found behind the bar, while the other, the late Ann Soyars, was usually out front, often working the door on busy nights. Ann referred to herself as "short bitch," Lin referred to herself as "tall bitch," and they both referred to the owner, J. T. Gray, as "son of a bitch." To label these no-nonsense country women "feisty" would be an understatement. They often said things that made me blush. But most important, they made me feel at home.

STAX RECORDS

STARTED IN 1957 IN A HUMBLE MEMPHIS GArage by the brother-sister duo Jim Stewart and Estelle Axton, Stax Records would become synonymous with Southern soul music, churning out hits from Sam and Dave, Carla Thomas, and Otis Redding as well as serving as a Southern outpost for Atlantic Records stars such as Wilson Pickett. *Stax* was also an adjective, with the "Stax sound" signaling tight horn parts and the funky sounds of the studio house band, Booker T. and the M.G.s. Redding's death in 1967 brought about the end of the first Stax era—an especially brutal blow as Stewart realized he'd signed over ownership of Redding's material to Atlantic because he hadn't bothered to read the contract. In a time of great upheaval and distress, Stax became home to socially conscious artists such as Isaac Hayes and the Staple Singers and a studio where collaboration between blacks and whites was second nature. But in 1975, after years of mismanagement and bad luck, Stax was forced into bankruptcy and shuttered its doors in early 1976. In the eighties on past the turn of the century, the label was revived and continued on purely to reissue releases from its catalogue, before being resurrected in earnest in 2012. In 2015, Stax issued the debut record from Nathaniel Rateliff & the Night Sweats, as well as a new album from one of its original artists, William Bell.

STEEL MAGNOLIAS

by Robert Harling

BEFORE THE PLAY OR THE MOVIE EXISTED, "steel magnolias" was simply a description of Southern women. I've heard it all my life. It means something that appears delicate and fragile but wields unexpected strength. When I wrote the play, in 1987, it seemed the fitting title. The story of *Steel Magnolias* is entirely true, inspired by family tragedy. My sister, Susan, had recently died of complications of diabetes, and I desperately needed to celebrate her, my mother, and the loving community of neighborhood ladies that had supported them through good times and bad.

The sublime Margo Martindale, the actress for whom I wrote the role of Truvy, reminds me that when we were in rehearsal for the play's New York opening, we all thought I had written a drama. We had no idea there would be "laughter through tears," or that these characters—wise and witty women in a small-town Southern beauty shop—would capture the imagination of New York theatergoers. The play caught on, and soon Hollywood came a-callin'. Every actress you could think of attended the show. They had to close off the street because of the crowds when Elizabeth Taylor showed up. Cher was there. Lucille Ball. I had tea with Bette Davis! I could write a play about that experience alone. Then the director of the film adaptation, Herbert Ross, assembled the cast of any playwright's dreams: Sally Field, Shirley MacLaine, Dolly Parton, Olympia Dukakis, Daryl Hannah, and an incandescent newcomer, Julia Roberts, who would play my sister.

When I started work on the screenplay, fashioning the simple, one-set, beauty-parlor play to fit the big screen was a challenge I loved. The audience would now get to see all the events and eccentricities that, in the theater, the clients of Truvy's Beauty Spot had only discussed. My daddy, whom Tom Skerritt would now play, really did shoot at birds in the trees. My sister's wedding did indeed have a bleeding armadillo groom's cake. (Years later, the *New York Times* credited *Steel Magnolias* with reviving the popularity of red velvet cake.)

The producer, Ray Stark, decided to film in my hometown of Natchitoches, Louisiana, where the story all took place: instant authenticity. It was surreal to see Dolly, Shirley, Sally, and the rest of the cast in the homes, grocery stores, and churches where their real-life character inspirations led their daily lives. All agreed that the experience enhanced their portrayals. Sam Shepard, who came through town to play Dolly's husband, pointed out what a singular experience this was; writing a play about one's family's experience in one's hometown, then having a movie made in that very town, with that cast, was a very lucky thing. Shirley MacLaine did not attribute it to luck. She was quite certain it all happened because Susan wanted her story told. Shirley's always right.

After the film's release in 1989, life became a whirlwind. Heady stuff. We had a royal premiere in London for Prince Charles and Princess Diana. We opened the Berlin Film Festival when the wall was coming down. After the festival's opening night, Ray Stark arranged an additional screening in East Berlin. It was the first time a Western film, with paid admission, was shown in East Germany since the wall had gone up, and the line of East Berliners waiting to buy tickets stretched as far as I could see. It was incredibly moving to sit and watch the film with them. It had been dubbed into German, and the audience had no idea who any of the actors were, except Dolly. But they laughed in all the places American audiences had. And they cried. It blew me away. After decades of the Iron Curtain and Communist government, their first glimpse of a Western movie was about life in a Southern town. *That* was the true heady stuff.

In the wake of the film, awareness of the play hurtled around the world. It's been translated into umpteen languages. It's a crazy trip to hear one's dialogue spoken in Chinese. It's a thrill to know that my sister's story moves theatergoers in Croatia, and makes Egyptian audiences laugh. As I write this, a tour of an Indian production is under way in Bombay. The Southern show goes on.

People keep asking, "Why is *Steel Magnolias* still so popular after thirty years?" I can't take any real credit. I just wrote down what happened. It's ultimately my sister's story, with quintessentially Southern characters full of wit, warmth, and intelligence. I guess a tale about people overcoming adversity together with love, support, courage, and respect never gets old.

STEEPLECHASE

There's more to Southern horse racing than the Derby. The region also lays claim to a different kind of Thoroughbred scene with a smaller but equally rabid following: steeplechase, an English style of racing with a grass or turf course studded with ditch obstacles and hedged fences over which horse and rider must jump. From March to November, the calendar is packed with events across the region—from the Carolina Cup (in Camden, South Carolina) to the Foxfield Spring Races (Charlottesville, Virginia) to the Tryon Block House Races (Columbus, North Carolina) to a slew of other events from Georgia to Maryland, plus a couple of outliers just above the Mason-Dixon. Just as steeplechase differs from flat-track racing, so too should your betting style. Whereas dry, temperate weather is advantageous on the track, in steeplechase it's all about gender. More often than not, fillies tend to outperform geldings on the jumps.

STETSON HATS

In the 1860s, John Batterson Stetson was diagnosed with tuberculosis. He was living in New Jersey at the time but thought the climate out West might help improve his health. By the time he found himself panning for gold in Colorado a few years later, suffering from exposure, high winds, and cold rain, Stetson realized perhaps Western weather

wasn't better after all. So he made himself a hat. Taught hat making by his father, Stetson knew that a large pocket of air between the top of the head and a hat's crown kept the head warm; he knew a wide brim would protect against the elements; and he understood that a cowboy's life could depend on hauling water. Guided by these principles, he created the Stetson hat, featuring a six-inch-high crown, a seven-inch-wide brim, and a waterproof lining that doubled as a makeshift bucket. Within a few years, the Stetson Hat Company was cranking out millions of them, and they've been enshrined as classics of Southern style ever since. Now headquartered in Garland, Texas, Stetson Hat Company still makes millions of hats a year, mostly for non-cowboys, and is the foremost hat brand on the planet.

STONE CRABS

When the Miami Beach establishment that would eventually become known as Joe's Stone Crab first put the odd crustacean on its menu, in 1921, at the behest of a marine biologist, nobody else in Miami was serving it. The body of this compact brown crab contains very little meat (and frankly isn't worth eating), but the claws are enormous and delicious. So began the crab fisherman's practice (now enforced by regulation) of releasing any stone crab captured, after removing its largest claw. The released stone crab will survive and grow another claw. The crabs were an immediate success at Joe's and have been ever since; stone crab claws are served there with a sturdy wooden mallet, for breaking them open, and a variety of dipping sauces.

STONEWALL JACKSON'S ARM

In the spring of 1863, near Chancellorsville, Virginia, doctors amputated the left arm of Confederate general Thomas "Stonewall" Jackson, wounded by musket balls errantly fired by his own soldiers. The next morning Jackson's chaplain came upon the limb outside the surgical tent, deemed it worthy of a dignified burial, and laid it in the family cemetery behind Ellwood, his brother's nearby plantation home. After Jackson died a week later, most of him got buried many miles away in Lexington. But a gravestone in Locust Grove, Virginia, marks the vicinity of his arm's final resting place—now overseen by the National Park Service and open to visitors—with a ghoulishly deadpan inscription: "Arm of Stonewall Jackson, May 3, 1863."

SUN STUDIO

As the home of blues, soul, and rock and roll, Memphis is the cradle of modern music. And one of its musical titans is Sam Phillips, a radio engineer who dreamed about starting his own recording studio, which he did in 1950. After years of Phillips's pounding the pavement to bring in artists—B. B. King and Howlin' Wolf were some of the first to cut songs there—a young man fresh out of high school named Elvis Presley walked in the door of Phillips's Sun Studio. Following a few start-stop sessions, in the summer of 1954, Presley picked up his guitar and as a goof launched into Arthur Crudup's "That's All Right." Phillips promptly got the song to a Memphis radio station, and the King's career was on its way. Known as an architect of rock and roll, Phillips would go on to record the likes of Johnny Cash, Carl Perkins, and Roy Orbison, releasing the tracks on his Sun Records label. But it was a happy accident that led to Sun's most storied moment. Riding high on the success of "Blue Suede Shoes," Perkins came in to cut new material. Phillips introduced Perkins to his latest prodigy, Jerry Lee Lewis. Cash was already in the control room, as he wanted to check out Perkins's stuff, and Presley—now the biggest star in music—dropped in for a visit. Soon the foursome began riffing on gospel and bluegrass numbers, launching the Million Dollar Quartet session into music history. Today Sun offers tours during the day and remains an active recording studio at night, hosting the likes of rock veterans U2 and up-and-coming artists looking to be the next big thing.

SURCEE

Your husband goes to the market, and when he returns, he surprises you with a pint of fresh blueberries, or a bunch of just-picked posies, or a sweet-smelling candle in a scent he knows you like. This serendipitous treat is called a "surcee"—a small, unexpected, typically inexpensive gift given . . . just because. Depending on whom you ask, the word, used mainly in the Carolinas and Georgia, can also be spelled *sercy*, *surcy*, or *sirsee*. Its origins are as murky as its spelling. According to the *Dictionary of American Regional English*, the etymology of *surcee* is uncertain, but some have speculated that it stems from the Scottish verb *sussie*, meaning "to take trouble, to take care, to bother oneself." But you don't really need to know any of that to appreciate a surcee. A simple thank-you will do.

SWEETGRASS BASKETS

Rows of coiled sweetgrass baskets stretch out across the tables in Charleston, South Carolina's historic City Market, basket weaver beside basket weaver, fingers ticking away over sweetgrass and palmetto. So it has been for decades, today's weavers only the latest practitioners of this Gullah tradition, one of the oldest surviving African art forms in the United States. First brought to these shores in the seventeenth century by West African slaves who had crafted baskets from similar grasses in their homeland, sweetgrass basket weaving has its roots in utilitarian purposes but has, over time, come to be seen as a form of high art. Today these baskets serve as containers for much more than grain or chaff, holding within their grass coils generations of knowledge, spanning continents and oceans and time. With most practitioners centered in and around Mount Pleasant, South Carolina, it's said that only two hundred families continue the tradition. Woven from the basic materials of sweetgrass, bulrush, pine needle, and palm leaf, Gullah sweetgrass baskets made today still look almost identical to those from West Africa.

SWEET POTATOES

WITH ALL DUE RESPECT TO APPLE PIE, SWEET potato pie really should be the edible symbol of America. When Columbus made landfall, Native Americans were already growing the nutrient-packed root veggie, and the tater (actually a member of the morning-glory family) took off in the Southeast in the mid-1600s. Today two Southern states claim sweet potatoes as their vegetal mascot: North Carolina, the top U.S. producer since the 1970s, and Mississippi, where the town of Vardaman has crowned itself the "sweet potato capital of the world." Of course, the sweet potato is a fixture of the Thanksgiving table—recipes for holiday casseroles are handed down like family heirlooms. Sweet potatoes get dotted with the traditional mini-marshmallows, spiked with bourbon, souped up with secret ingredients such as sorghum (a surprising substitute for maple syrup). If you're lucky enough to find sweet potatoes with their greens still attached and lively, scoop them up. Southern chefs are wild about the roughage. More tender than collards, less astringent than spinach or chard, they work well in stir-fries, stews, omelets, and pasta. They can also stand alone, sautéed in a bit of fat or plated raw in a fall salad. To quote Grandmother: they'll have you grinning like a possum eating a sweet potato.

SWEET TEA

DOLLY PARTON'S CHARACTER IN *Steel Magnolias* calls sweet tea the "house wine of the South," but the beverage got its start as something considerably stronger. Nineteenth-century Southerners liked a little tea with their bourbon, pouring it into punches to make staggering doses of alcohol more palatable. But once ice became readily available and temperance came into fashion, drinking tea with sugar became a regional pastime and preoccupation. Honestly, it's hardly fair to classify sweet tea as a drink: in the eyes of Southerners, it's a magical brew; a liquid symbol of culture; the region's lifeblood. The recipe is simple: dissolve more sugar than seems prudent in hot tea, and then add ice. (Stirring sugar into already-iced tea produces sweetened tea, a decidedly lesser drink.) Yet the drink has a knack for evoking complex emotions, ranging from nostalgia to intimacy to pride. Twice as sugary as cola, sweet tea inspires people to get tattoos of mason jars garnished with lemon wheels and drive forty miles out of their way for perfect pours. In 2003, a Georgia legislator jokingly filed an April Fools' bill to criminalize restaurants serving tea with sugar on the side. When pressed, he admitted he wouldn't have minded if it had been voted into law.

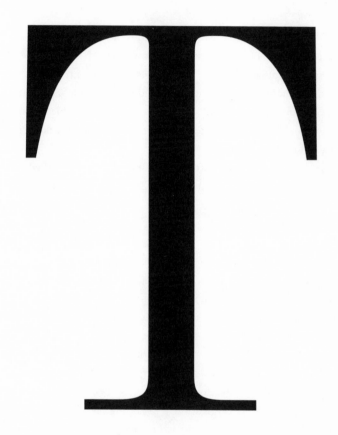

SOUTHERNERS TAKE TABASCO FOR GRANTED—until one day we find ourselves in front of a plate of fried eggs in an airport coffee shop in the Maple Syrup Belt with none to be had. Since its invention by Edmund McIlhenny, in 1868, the Louisiana hot sauce made from fermented Tabasco peppers has become a worldwide phenomenon. In the heyday of nineteenth-century American and British oyster culture, devotees considered it the ultimate condiment for oysters on the half shell—an early advertisement, in fact, featured an illustration of a Tabasco bottle emerging Venus-like from an oyster shell. In 1885, British soldiers carried bottles of it at the Battle of Khartoum, in Sudan. Tabasco sauce is so central to Southern eating that some of us carry tiny bottles of the stuff in our luggage for fear it won't be available in foreign locales. And, not to cause alarm, but some scientists believe Tabasco is verifiably addictive—something to do with the flood of endorphins released as you ingest hot peppers. Once you're accustomed to natural painkillers coursing through your brain, eating without that comforting burn just isn't the same. *See Avery Island; Hot sauce.*

THE FORMULA FOR THIS "CONCRETE OF THE Lowcountry" dates back to the late 1500s: blend equal parts lime, sand, oyster shells, and water, and let dry until the mixture is just set but still pliable. Construction of building components made from tabby—walls, wedges, bricks, roofs, foundations, and floors, to name a few—peaked during the first half of the nineteenth century. By 1824, a range of domestic, industrial, civic, and religious structures using tabby were commonplace between Charleston, South Carolina, and St. Augustine, Florida, both along the coast and inland. In addition to being convenient, affordable to produce, and fireproof, tabby was extremely adaptable, allowing builders to get creative; in Woodbine, Georgia, workers poured a plantation house in the shape of a large anchor. One proponent of the material, the Georgia planter and statesman Thomas Spalding, recommended making it only between February and September to avoid winter freeze-thaw cycles and hurricane-prone autumn months, and to take advantage of high humidity, which shortened the setting time. Palmetto branches were used to protect batches of tabby from rainfall while it dried. For an up-close view of the sand-and-shell wonder, visit the Chapel of Ease on South Carolina's St. Helena Island, Gamble Mansion in Ellenton, Florida, or the aptly named Tabby Manse, a circa 1786 spread near Beaufort, South Carolina.

TAILGATING

THE SOUTH TAKES ITS FOOTBALL SERIOUSLY, and that dedication extends to the prelude known as the tailgate. Historians debate the first true instance of what is essentially a glorified, gussied-up cookout. Some point to the First Battle of Bull Run, in 1861, when spectators hitched up carriages, packed picnics, and traveled the thirty-odd miles southwest from Washington, D.C., to Manassas, Virginia, to witness—mind-boggling as it may seem—the first major encounter of the Civil War. Others cite the 1869 gridiron matchup between Rutgers and Princeton, which many consider the first intercollegiate football game. Wherever the tradition started, it is generally acknowledged that the South has elevated it, whether the spread of fried chicken, deviled eggs, burgers, brats, barbecue sandwiches, and, yes, booze takes place underneath the chandeliers of the tents dotting the Grove at Ole Miss; aboard the flotilla known as the Volunteer Army bobbing outside Neyland Stadium at the University of Tennessee; inside the tricked-out railroad car Cockabooses at the University of South Carolina; or on Jacksonville Landing for the infamous World's Largest Outdoor Cocktail Party—the annual neutral-site Florida-Georgia grudge match. Of course, people tailgate before other events—NASCAR races, concerts, and the like. But pigskin pregaming sets the standard.

TAMALES

IF YOU'VE SPENT TIME IN THE MISSISSIPPI Delta, chances are you know about the "tamale trail." As a rule, that unofficial connect-the-dots collection of gas stations, drive-throughs, and roadside vendors is first stumbled upon, then hunted down obsessively with maps and guidebooks. Unlike their heftier Mexican brethren, the Delta's corn-husk-wrapped packages of tender masa and ground meat are often no bigger than a stubby finger. They arrive tied up in bundles of four or six and stained red with their spicy cooking juices. Locals eat them sandwiched between saltine crackers with a dab of ketchup, but in the early stages of obsession you'll want to consume as many as possible in their plain state, singeing your fingers on the hot husks. A number of the region's best-known restaurants offer their own versions, as well. Food historians suspect that Mexican migrant workers brought tamales to Mississippi in the early part of the last century, and they caught on as an easy-to-pack lunch for day laborers. Now they're as much a part of Delta culture as the blues.

THINK OF THE MOST FEARSOME NFL running back you've ever seen. Remove his appendages, cover him in big platelike scales, color his sides and belly in brilliant silver and his back a dark greenish or bluish black, and give him a forked tail. Oh, and increase his strength fourfold. That is *Megalops atlanticus*, the tarpon, aka the silver king, one of the world's premier game fish and one that American anglers eagerly seek worldwide—the current world record is a 286-pounder caught in 2003 off West Africa; the U.S. record, a 243-pounder caught in 1975 off Key West. It's regularly caught by conventional and fly tackle off the coast of Florida, where tarpon often cruise shallow waters in schools. While tarpon are extremely bony and close to inedible, unless you're *really* hungry, they are in all other respects a near-perfect game fish: big, powerful, spectacularly acrobatic, and challenging to hook and land. Upon being hooked, they often leap completely out of the water, at which time it's advisable to "bow to the king"—that is, lower your rod tip so you have more slack line to absorb the impending shock. You must play the fish until it's tired—this can take fifteen minutes or three hours—before bringing it alongside to remove the hook and release it. A "green" fish may pull a guide overboard or, worse, leap into the boat, where its thrashing has been known to break legs and railings. Biologists have been unable to detect in tarpon any sense of remorse.

SOME NATIVES OF CHARLESTON, SOUTH Carolina, might call John Martin Taylor, known fondly in the culinary world as Hoppin' John, a "come 'yar," because he was not born in the Lowcountry that he has written about so lovingly. Quite a few might not recognize his name at all—a pity, since Taylor's books and advocacy of Charleston's foodways heritage helped lay the groundwork for the resurgence of the city and its cuisine into the darlings of food lovers that they are today. Years before the likes of Sean Brock (of McCrady's and Husk) and Mike Lata (FIG, The Ordinary) became Lowcountry food luminaries, Taylor was championing heirloom ingredients—Carolina Gold rice, benne seeds, sorghum—and all-but-forgotten recipes.

In 1986, after years working as a photographer and painter, Taylor (who grew up inland in Orangeburg) broke into the culinary field when he opened Hoppin' John's, a Charleston bookstore and mecca for chefs, overflowing with thousands of cookbook titles, one of the nation's first to specialize in culinaria. His 1992 scholarly cookbook, *Hoppin' John's Lowcountry Cooking*, quickly became a classic, followed by *The New Southern Cook*, *The Fearless Frying Cookbook*, and *Hoppin' John's Charleston, Beaufort & Savannah: Dining at Home in the Lowcountry* (most of them, sadly, now out of print, though you can ferret out copies online). Each took a deep dive into the region's history and its distinctive culinary style. Although Taylor closed his store in 1999, he still markets heirloom stone-ground grits and cornmeal, both to consumers and to restaurants scattered around the country. Now in his sixties and residing in Savannah, he is both a local legend and a worthy doyen and guardian of the history and scholarship of Lowcountry cooking.

TENNESSEE WALKING HORSE

THE GAIT OF A TENNESSEE WALKING HORSE IS a thing of beauty. As the breed's name implies, that beauty resides in its unique style of walking, with legs lifting higher and advancing faster than other breeds' while still delivering a smooth, steady ride. A well-trained walker can do so in a basic "flatfoot walk" and a more pronounced "running walk," in which the horse's head bobs in sync with the gait. The breed was developed in the late 1800s as a cross between pacer breeds and Spanish mustangs, and given its characteristics became a popular show horse. Even the Lone Ranger and Roy Rogers rode walkers. Unfortunately, controversy also surrounds them. To exaggerate the walker's high-legged gait even further in the arena, some trainers shoe the horses with weighted "performance" stacks that can cause pain. The United States Equestrian Federation prohibits that practice, which has led to acrimony among breeders and sanctioning organizations that stand on both sides of the debate. The breed's biggest annual showcase, the Tennessee Walking Horse National Celebration in Shelbyville, Tennessee, allows the so-called action devices, attracting fans and animal-rights protesters alike.

TENNESSEE WHISKEY

TO BE CALLED BOURBON, WHISKEY MUST BE made from a mash of at least 51 percent corn; it must be aged in new charred oak barrels; and it can't be bottled at less than 80 proof. But contrary to the near-religious conviction of many fans, it does *not* have to be produced in Kentucky to be called bourbon (though it must be produced in the United States). So why don't bottles of Tennessee-made whiskey that meet all the requirements, namely, George Dickel and Jack Daniel's, have the word *bourbon* anywhere on them? By tradition and choice, actually. Perhaps because they can't match the output of Kentucky distilleries (from where 95 percent of the country's bourbon flows), Tennessee distilleries have carved out their own brand identity. In fact, state law now restricts the term *Tennessee whiskey* to the stuff actually produced in the Volunteer State (take that, Kentucky!), and further requires (with rare exceptions) that it be made with a charcoal-filtering step known as the Lincoln County Process. Of course, many Kentucky bourbons are also charcoal filtered, further muddling any cross-border distinctions.

TEX-MEX

by Robb Walsh

Tex-Mex IS A TERM THAT, WHEN USED BY Mexican nationals and much of this nation's food elite, often translates to "Mexican food that's been bastardized by a bunch of Texas rednecks." The term was first applied to Americanized Mexican food, to distinguish it from authentic food of interior Mexico, after the 1972 publication of Diana Kennedy's cookbook *The Cuisines of Mexico*. The English-born Mexican-food authority trashed the "so-called Mexican food" north of the border, with its messy combination platters and revolting appetizers such as "greasy chips and mouth-searing salsa." Though originally intended as a pejorative, "Tex-Mex" now simply describes the bicultural regional cuisine of the Texas-Mexico border. Familiar Tex-Mex inventions include chili, nachos, Frito Pie, frozen margaritas, fajitas, breakfast tacos, and yellow cheese enchiladas.

The cuisine's signature dish, chili con carne, was created by Spanish-speaking native peoples known as Tejanos in the late 1700s, during the era of the Spanish missions. They simmered minced meat and beef fat with ancho chiles for hours to make the tough longhorn beef raised on mission cattle ranches palatable. About a century later, from the 1860s into the 1930s, chili con carne grew in popularity thanks to the Chili Queens, flirtatious cooks who sold chili, enchiladas, and tamales in open-air food stalls in the squares of San Antonio, and became famous in the process. Writers such as O. Henry and

Ambrose Bierce helped immortalize them, and newspaper travel correspondents penned romanticized coverage of them and the exotic Texas-Mexican culture they represented, once railroads enabled Midwestern tourists to visit Texas. The Chicago World's Fair of 1893—attended by more than twenty-seven million people, a quarter of the U.S. population at the time—had a re-created San Antonio Chili Stand on its midway, serving legions of fairgoers the first "Mexican" food they'd ever tasted and sparking the spread of the dish far and wide. In 1895, what would become Wolf Brand chili debuted, initially sold by the bowl in Corsicana, Texas, by a former chuckwagon cook. By the end of the St. Louis World's Fair in 1904, chili parlors that sold chili con carne and tamales had opened in St. Louis and Carlinsville, Illinois. Grocery stores around the country soon began to sell Gebhardt's and other bottled chili powders.

Around the turn of the century, a Chicagoan named Otis Farnsworth pioneered the Tex-Mex restaurant genre. While visiting San Antonio's chili stands, he was shocked to see Anglos in fancy clothes lining up in the barrio to eat street food. So in 1899, Farnsworth built the Original Mexican Restaurant in San Antonio's fashionable commercial district. The menu included the "Regular Supper," which combined enchiladas, tamales, chili con carne, Spanish rice, and refried beans on a single plate; the "Deluxe Supper" added tacos and more. Cooks and waitstaff were Hispanic, but the customers were Anglos. Gentlemen were required to wear jackets.

Tex-Mex thrived in the early twentieth century, but the rise of the automobile led to a new kind of Americanized Mexican food. The Cal-Mex of Southern California featured cheap tacos in preformed taco shells sold in drive-in restaurants such as Taco Bell that began to dot the interstate highways. Burritos are another Cal-Mex standard that became a favorite across the country. Nowadays, few new Tex-Mex restaurants are opening; instead, hip taquerias like Torchy's Tacos, Velvet Taco, and Tacos A Go Go carry on the bicultural food tradition.

Still, Tex-Mex has had a profound impact on American eating habits. Chili con carne endures as a classic one-pot meal, as well as a topping for hot dogs, burgers, and french fries. The Tex-Mex tradition of dipping tortilla chips in salsa, a spin on the potato chips and sour cream dips of 1960s suburbia, spawned a multibillion-dollar snack food category (Fritos, Doritos, Tostitos, et al.). And thanks in large part to San Antonio's David Pace, inventor of Pace Picante Sauce, in the early 1990s salsa passed ketchup as America's top-selling condiment.

THOROUGHBREDS

EVEN IF YOUR ENTIRE EXPOSURE TO HORSE racing is watching the Kentucky Derby telecast once a year, you surely understand that all the excitement, all the mint juleps, all the *hats*, spring from the simple question of which Thoroughbred horse is the fastest. Thoroughbreds, though also prominent in show jumping, dressage, and polo, are synonymous with racing. The breed—tall, lean, muscled—came to the American colonies from England and matched our national character well with its hot-blooded spirit and speed. Today the horses are the center of a $34 billion industry (at Keeneland, the prestigious Thoroughbred auction house in Kentucky, promising yearlings regularly fetch north of a million dollars) and a worldwide culture that operates with its own language, customs, and scandals. A very precious few of these horses earn quirky names such as Seattle Slew and American Pharoah and win the Triple Crown. Most don't, of course. But even an anonymous Thoroughbred racing nothing but its own shadow across a morning pasture is a sight as thrilling as any high-stakes photo finish. *See Keeneland; Kentucky Derby.*

TIDEWATER

GEOLOGISTS, ESPECIALLY NON-SOUTHERN ONES, define *tidewater* as a region where freshwater meets salt, and rivers rise and fall with the tides. There are tidewaters up and down the East Coast. But there's only one Tidewater with a capital *T*, and it belongs to Virginia, much as the Lowcountry belongs to South Carolina and Georgia. Four great rivers—the Potomac, Rappahannock, York, and James—slice through Virginia on their way from the Appalachians to the Atlantic. They spill into Chesapeake Bay, the largest estuary in the Lower 48. Tidewater Virginia, called "a blend of romance and fact" in a 1929 book by the same name, starts east of the rocky fall line, where these and other rivers meet the coastal plain and curl back on themselves in lazy oxbows.

For many historians, Tidewater Virginia is the cradle of America. Jamestown, the first permanent settlement among the original thirteen British colonies, is there, as are the former colonial capital Williamsburg and Yorktown, site of George Washington's decisive victory over the British in 1781. Five U.S. presidents were born in the Tidewater, among them Washington and James Madison, father of the Constitution.

In *A Tidewater Morning,* the writer William Styron, a native of Newport News, wrote: "I came to absorb the history of the Virginia Tidewater—that primordial American demesne where the land was sucked dry by tobacco, laid waste and destroyed a whole century before golden California became an idea, much less a hope or a westward dream." He recalled the "scores of shrunken, abandoned 'plantations' scattered for a hundred miles across the tidelands between the Potomac and the James." And he reflected on the changes wrought during the 1930s in the lead-up to World War II. "[The Tidewater] was not the drowsy old Virginia of legend but part of a busy New South, where heavy industry and the presence of the military had begun to encroach on a pastoral way of life."

Since then, Newport News, Norfolk, Portsmouth, Chesapeake, and Virginia Beach have fused into a Tidewater megalopolis. Nevertheless, sportsmen, boaters, and weekend warriors from Richmond and other cities cherish the region, sometimes known simply as "the Rivah." They flock to homes and marinas nestled among the filigree of spits, sloughs, creeks, and bluffs lining the great estuary.

TIPITINA'S

A NIGHTCLUB IN NEW ORLEANS' UPTOWN neighborhood, Tipitina's is one of the chief stops on a musical pilgrimage to the Crescent City. While it does not have the ancient lineage of other clubs that served as nurseries of American jazz and rock (many since shuttered), for four decades Tipitina's has been a greenhouse extending the longevity of traditional New Orleans music.

The club was founded in 1977 by a group of music fans dismayed to discover the legendary blues singer and pianist Professor Longhair (also known as "Fess," born Henry Roeland Byrd), then nearly sixty years old, was playing in obscurity at sketchy venues. They established a neighborhood club on Napoleon Avenue, naming it after one of his best-known songs. Fess often played at the club until his death, in 1980. The club underwent a major remodeling in 1984, when the upstairs apartments of the 1912 building were converted into a mezzanine overlooking the stage and club floor. Tipitina's Foundation, the club's nonprofit arm, has long supported local musicians both in deed and financially, and it was especially active in replacing instruments lost by school bands during Hurricane Katrina.

The club's logo includes, somewhat inscrutably, a partially peeled banana. This is an artifact of Tipitina's original incarnation as a juice bar; bananas are no longer available there.

TO KILL A MOCKINGBIRD

IT IS REMARKABLE THAT GEORGE W. BUSH awarded Harper Lee the Presidential Medal of Freedom in 2007 for her contributions to literature despite the fact that she had published only one book. Published in 1960 (and winner of a Pulitzer Prize the following year), *To Kill a Mockingbird* is the still-powerful, much-beloved story of a lawyer who defends a black man accused of raping a white woman in Depression-era Alabama, of his children and a mysterious neighbor, and of a small town infected with calcified racism. It's a vision of Lee's South both lovely and terrible. A little like an *Uncle Tom's Cabin* for the twentieth century, *Mockingbird* quickly burrowed into the American consciousness as a kind of definitive portrait of race and region in a particular moment in time, spawning a popular 1962 film adaptation starring Gregory Peck. Lee insisted that the novel was not autobiographical, despite the fact that she, like her heroine Scout Finch, grew up during the Depression in small-town Alabama, where her father, also a lawyer, had defended two black men in a murder trial. *See Lee, Harper.*

TOMATO PIE

EVERYBODY MAKES TOMATO PIE A LITTLE BIT differently, but the basic ingredients remain pretty much the same: garden-fresh summer tomatoes, cheese, and plenty of mayonnaise, all baked in a pastry crust, something like a Southern answer to a deep-dish pizza. Although the use of mayonnaise most likely dates the savory pie to the mid-twentieth century, today it's as entrenched a seasonal tradition as holiday ham. Though occasionally fancied up with chopped herbs or goat cheese, tomato pie generally hews to the same boy-is-it-hot simplicity as its close cousin, the tomato-and-mayonnaise sandwich on white bread. Here, too, every ingredient matters. Don't even bother trying to make a pie out of mealy supermarket 'maters.

TOOLE, JOHN KENNEDY

(1937–1969)

IN 1976, THE CELEBRATED NOVELIST WALKER Percy received a phone call from a woman he did not know. What she suggested over the line was, as Percy put it, "preposterous." Her son, John Kennedy Toole, who had taken his own life seven years earlier, had written a very long novel in the 1960s and never gotten it published, but now she wanted Percy to read it. When Percy asked why, Toole's mother said, "Because it is a great novel." Percy obligingly and politely skimmed the first few pages, keeping his eye out for any reason to stop. He never found one. What he found instead was Ignatius Reilly—perhaps the finest comedic personage ever to appear in American letters—tearing across New Orleans in a succession of lunatic escapades. Within this Falstaffian farce, entitled *A Confederacy of Dunces*, Toole somehow managed to create a story at once hilarious, sad, and profound. It is said that Toole's suicide was prompted in part by depression brought on by the novel's multiple rejections; with Percy's help, though, the book was finally published in 1980. The next year Toole posthumously won the Pulitzer Prize for Fiction.

TOUPS, ALZINA

(1928–)

IN A FORMER WELDING SHOP ON THE BANK OF Louisiana's Lafourche Bayou, Alzina Toups has been cooking and serving transcendent Cajun food for forty years: gumbo, lima beans, black-eyed pea jambalaya, and countless shrimp and crabmeat dishes spiked with garden herbs. Toups lives and works in Galliano, a short drive from the Gulf of Mexico, where she was born to a Cajun fisherman and a Portuguese mother. She learned to debone a fish on her father's boat and inherited her mother's appreciation for the simple but deep flavors of Cajun cuisine and the region's bountiful produce and seafood. Her talent is legendary among townsfolk and the local Catholic clergy, who know her from Mass. And, increasingly, she's

appreciated around the world. She has fed New Yorkers and Frenchmen and a party of twenty German chefs at the unadorned table in her kitchen. Everybody eats family-style beneath an image of the Virgin Mary. It may sound humble, but the food certainly isn't, and that's why Alzina's is harder to get into than most Michelin-starred restaurants. She only takes reservations, and she's usually booked four months out.

TRETHEWEY, NATASHA

(1966–)

"IN THE PORTRAIT OF JEFFERSON THAT HANGS at Monticello, he is rendered two-toned" is how Natasha Trethewey begins "Enlightenment," one of her many Southern-steeped poems that probe the region's dualities: celebrated and condemned; spiritual and sensual; black and white. Born in 1966 to a black mother and a white father in Gulfport, Mississippi, Trethewey split her childhood between their homes after their divorce, an arrangement that introduced her to the intricacies of skin tone and passing. She was a nineteen-year-old cheerleader at the University of Georgia when her ex-stepfather murdered her mother; Trethewey first started writing poems as a way to manage her grief. In 2000, she published her first book, *Domestic Work*, a collection of poems about black Southerners' labor. The poet Rita Dove praised Trethewey for pressing beyond descriptive scenes to wrestle with fears and desire, awarding Trethewey the first of many prestigious prizes she would claim. She received the Pulitzer Prize in 2007 for a set of ten sonnets, elegies, and autobiographical poems devoted to an African American regiment that guarded a Confederate prison. She was named the poet laureate of Mississippi in 2012 and the poet laureate of the United States in 2012 and 2014.

TRIGGER

IT'S REALLY JUST AN OLD, BATTERED MARTIN N-20 classical acoustic, nylon-stringed, with a Prismatone stereo electric pickup salvaged from a busted Baldwin guitar. But put the weathered instrument in the hands of its owner and it magically becomes Trigger, storied accompanist to one Willie Hugh Nelson, Texas musician. There's a second oblong hole worn above the bridge and below the circular sound hole, carved by millions of hand strokes, picked single notes, and chord strums over the course of tens of thousands of songs. The faded scribbles of Leon Russell, Kris Kristofferson, Ray Price, Merle Haggard, and scores of other close personal music friends adorn the Brazilian rosewood.

The look may be distinctive, but the tone is wholly unique. Two notes picked on those six strings is all it takes to know it's Willie playing. The fluid strings allow him to channel one of his greatest inspirations, the Romany guitarist Django Reinhardt, and bend and sustain notes in a manner steel strings cannot replicate.

It has been like that since 1969, when Shot Jackson installed the pickup, giving Willie the sound he was looking for to complement his behind-the-beat jazz-styled vocals. Starting with *My Own Peculiar Way*, the RCA album released in 1969 toward the end of Nelson's Nashville residency, up to the here and now, Trigger has been a constant—sonically, physically, and spiritually. The guitar is stewarded, shepherded, and babied by the longtime instrument technician Tunin' Tom Hawkins, who fiercely protects his charge and skillfully telegraphs "Don't even *think* about it" with his stage scowl. Tunin' Tom knows: Without Trigger, Willie would be naked. *With* Trigger, anything can happen. *See Nelson, Willie.*

TROTTERS

Through iron-pot alchemy, enslaved cooks in antebellum times transformed humble pigs' feet—aka trotters—into dishes that persist today. Rich in gelatinous cartilage, they add rib-sticking heft to pots of greens and peas. Braised and smoked, they stand alone at soul-food joints across the turnip-green and neck-bone diaspora. Pickled, they're a gas-station standby. *See Pigs' feet.*

TUBMAN, HARRIET

(c. 1820–1913)

Harriet Tubman didn't care if you were frightened—she was going to get your ass free. Known to pull a loaded revolver on timid slaves in an effort to urge them along the Underground Railroad, Tubman was one of the Railroad's most effective conductors, leading more than three hundred slaves to freedom. Along the way she earned the nicknames Moses and General Tubman. A fierce and righteous abolitionist who had escaped slavery herself in 1849, Tubman worked for Union forces in South Carolina during the Civil War, serving as, among other things, a spy. Using knowledge gathered on her reconnaissance missions, she guided Union troops on the Combahee River Raid, which led to the emancipation of seven hundred South Carolina slaves. In doing so, Tubman became the first woman to lead an armed mission in the Civil War. In April 2016, 103 years after her death, it was announced that Tubman would achieve another first for an American woman: she would take the place of Andrew Jackson on the twenty-dollar bill, becoming the first woman featured on American paper currency.

TUPELO HONEY

We're talking about the edible variety, not the Van Morrison ballad (although both are classics). Sometimes called the champagne of honeys, tupelo honey comes from a small area of northwestern Florida and southern Georgia, where bees tap ogeechee trees growing along the Apalachicola, Chipola, Ochlocknee, and Choctahatchee Rivers. Some have described its taste as buttery and mildly floral, without the cloying sweetness of other honeys. And because it has low levels of glucose, it's the only honey that some diabetics can safely eat. Bees produce the honey in springtime—typically May—when the starburst blossoms are dripping nectar. Beekeepers then harvest it from hives they've placed along the riverbanks on floats (often they need boats to access them in swampy precincts). If that sounds like a lot of work, it is. But you'll understand what the buzz is about when you drizzle some over a warm hunk of cornbread.

TURKEY HUNTING

by Bill Heavey

THE WAY TO HUNT TURKEYS IS TO RISE about the time you would otherwise be going to bed, and dress yourself in camouflage from head to toe, including hat, gloves, face mask, and snake boots. Some guys wear sunglasses with camo frames and even lenses (violating all sorts of laws of optics and nature). Arm yourself with a shotgun that shoots watermelon-sized patterns at sixty yards. This can only be achieved by using a special "turkey choke," such as the BlackOut, UnderTaker, or Jelly Head. Ideally, you will have roosted birds the night before. This means you'll have scouted the area and actually seen the tree into which the birds flew to spend the night. Ideally, you will also have identified where they're most likely to head—usually an open space like a meadow or a field—and can set up to intercept them there. Since you failed to do either of these, simply slip through the woods until you hear gobbling or stumble across an area that "feels" like it might attract turkeys. Choose a broad-trunked tree and take a seat at its base. The tree breaks up your outline to the

sharp-eyed wild turkey and keeps you from falling over backward when you doze off. Turkey hunting doesn't have to involve long periods of inactivity, but it tends to.

Sit there for hours or until all feeling has left your lower body, whichever takes longer. If you wish, select from the wide variety of turkey calls—box calls, friction calls, diaphragms originally made of condom latex, gobble tubes, etc.—and make any of the dozen or so of the bird's known vocalizations. I've never found this to make the slightest difference, but it passes the time. It's also a good way to attract the attention of other hunters, who may think you're a real turkey and come try to shoot you. Some turkey hunters contend that this increased danger keeps them alert. (Incidentally, if you *do* see another turkey hunter, shout to him but do not move. Moving is a good way to get mistaken for a

turkey.) Around noon, attempt to stand up and restore blood flow to your lower extremities. Make your way back to camp. When your friends ask how you did, say, "Well, I was all covered up in 'em. I mean, thick as ticks on a dog's back. Gobblers in front, behind, left, and right. They had me pinned down, but they were all henned up and wouldn't come in." Your friends will nod, express sympathy, and say they've had the exact same experience. This is complete bullshit.

I've actually killed quite a few turkeys, but always while being guided by someone who knew the area, understood how turkeys will most likely react in a given situation, and knew how to call to them and get them to approach. Basically, all I did in any successful turkey hunt I've taken part in was pull the trigger when told to and then pose heroically with the bird. I call this "baby-in-the-car-seat hunting," for the approximate skill level it required of me.

I shot my first turkey from a pop-up blind, sitting on a small folding chair with my gun barrel sticking out of one of its shooting ports. I had to lean slightly uphill, I remember, because the blind wasn't pitched on flat ground. About an hour after sunup, my guide successfully called in two toms. "Shoot the one on the left," he said. "Aim halfway up his neck." I did, but in the excitement of the moment, I'd forgotten about the recoil of a three-inch 12-gauge turkey load. Before the pellets had left my gun barrel, I had left the chair and was flying backward inside the blind, fully horizontal, like a camo flying carpet. And thinking, "Wow! I just killed my first turkey!"

TURNER, TED

(1938–)

IN A REGION FULL OF COLORFUL CHARACTERS, consider the self-made billionaire Robert Edward Turner III a double rainbow. The near-bottomless résumé of the man who personifies "crazy like a fox" reads like Renaissance Man Mad Libs: America's Cup winner; former owner of the Atlanta Braves and the Atlanta Hawks; bombastic genius behind the first cable "superstation"; founder of the first twenty-four-hour news network, CNN, as well as TBS, TNT, Turner Classic Movies, and Cartoon Network; creator of the Goodwill Games; erstwhile owner of World Championship Wrestling; ex-husband of three women, including Jane Fonda; owner of the world's largest private herd of bison, an animal he helped bring back from the brink of extinction (its meat now served at more than forty Ted's Montana Grills around the country); champion of environmental causes, from clean energy to sustainable land management; second-largest landowner in America, with more than two million acres; benefactor of the United Nations Foundation he helped form to the tune of $1 billion; cohead of the Nuclear Threat Initiative, which encourages global disarmament; consummate outdoorsman, fisherman, hunter, horseman, you name it. Although the freewheeling media mogul was born in Ohio, he made his fortune in Atlanta, a place he helped shape into the city you see today. In the years following the disastrous merger of his Time Warner with AOL in 2000—a deal that ultimately cost him *billions*—Turner may have slowed a little. But don't feel too sorry for "Captain Outrageous": he still has twenty-eight homes and, at last count, four girlfriends.

TWAIN, MARK

(1835–1910)

by Roy Blount, Jr.

MARK TWAIN DIDN'T HAVE DEEP SOUTHERN roots. His parents were from Virginia and Kentucky, which may be Southern enough for most people, but not for anybody who comes from farther down. He was born and grew up in the border state of Missouri. As for the territory between there and New Orleans, he made its acquaintance mostly in passing, from Mississippi riverboats. He lived and worked in Pennsylvania, Ohio, California, Nevada, Connecticut, New York, and Europe.

So why do we call him a Southern writer?

He cherished Southern cooking: "Perhaps no bread in the world is quite as good as Southern cornbread, and perhaps no bread in the world is quite so bad as the Northern imitation of it."

He cherished Southern talk. "A Southerner talks music," he wrote, but his appreciation of that music was not limited to the melodious. Several regional dialects, black and white, smooth and scabrous, went into the voice of Huckleberry Finn, which (thanks to Twain's easy command of formal syntax and literary language as well) became the template of modern American narration.

He turned his two weeks or so with a jackleg attachment to the Confederate army, which culminated in the killing of a hapless lad like him, into a darkly comic tour de force. Most important, he faced up to something he had not realized the evil of during his all-American boyhood. He had to account for growing up surrounded by slavery (and related "windy humbuggeries"), and therein lies the soul of his work.

Twain was certainly good at what most people may think of when it comes to Southern humor: hyperbole, flamboyant characters, animal noises. But he also had a great touch for a quieter, more elliptical sort of joke, which adds a Zen-like spin to something that would appear to be stupid. When he was born in the town of Florida, Missouri, he tells us in his *Autobiography*, the town "contained a hundred people and I increased the population by one per cent. It is more than the best man in history ever did for any other town." This, I submit, is in the same crisp suprascientific vein as the joke I have called the quintessential Southern one: Old boy is asked whether he believes in infant baptism. "*Believe* in it?" he says. "Hell, I've seen it *done.*"

Here's another. A house comes floating down the Mississippi after a flood. Huck and Jim board it, to see what they can scavenge. Huck gives us a long list of conceivably useful odds and ends, of which this is the last item: "Jim he found . . . a wooden leg. The straps was broke off of it, but, barring that, it was a good enough leg, though it was too long for me and not long enough for Jim, and we couldn't find the other one, though we hunted all around."

If there were a Museum of Classic Southern Humor, it would feature a large monument—an obelisk, say—to that other leg. But the joke runs deeper. The flood-borne house also contains a pile of stuff that Jim checks out. He sees that it's a dead body. Don't look at the face, he tells Huck, "it's too gashly." So they go about gathering a fine miscellany of stuff that might come in handy—"a tolerable good currycomb," "a ratty old fiddle-bow," and so on. So much for the dead man, for now. But that body, we will come to find out, is all that's left of what really could have been valuable to Huck, if this one had not, in life, been such a sorry excuse: his father.

See Faulkner, see Flannery O'Connor, see Cormac McCarthy: it is truly Deep Southern for humor to border on the horrible.

TYBEE BOMB

On February 5, 1958, high over South Carolina's Daufuskie Island, an Air Force B-47 was in trouble. The bomber, under the command of Colonel Howard Richardson, was heading back to Homestead Air Force Base in Florida, from a simulated bombing of Reston, Virginia. It was carrying a hydrogen bomb.

Colonel Richardson thought the exercise was over, when an F-86 fighter clipped his aircraft in midair, shearing away its number-six engine. The F-86 spun out of control, and its pilot ejected. The B-47 plummeted more than three miles before Richardson regained control. The crew requested permission to jettison the bomb, a precaution in case of a crash or an emergency landing. Permission was granted, and the bomb was dropped while the plane limped along at 200 knots and 7,200 feet of altitude, barely airborne. The crew noted no explosion when the bomb struck the sea. They managed to land the B-47 safely at an airfield outside Savannah.

The next day, February 6, a recovery effort began for what came to be known as the Tybee Bomb. The Mark 15 bomb weighed 7,600 pounds, and contained 400 pounds of high explosive and enriched uranium. Some sources describe it as a fully functional nuclear weapon; others claim it's disabled. If a nuclear detonation ever occurred, it would cause a fireball with a radius of 1.2 miles, and severe structural damage and third-degree burns for ten times that distance.

On April 16, 1958, the military announced that search efforts had been unsuccessful, and the bomb was presumed lost.

U-V

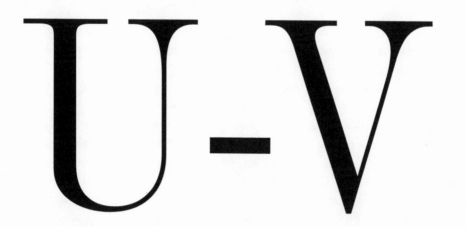

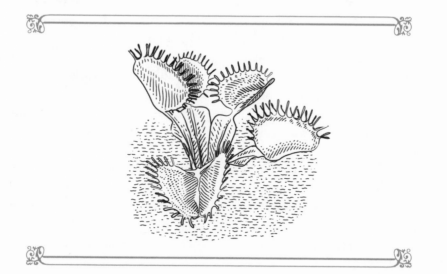

UGA IS THE MOST FAMOUS MASCOT IN COL-lege athletics and probably the most pampered dog in the world. Pronounced *uh-guh* (not *you-juh*), the name is a portmanteau of "University of Georgia," where the dog has been the mascot for the university's sports teams for more than six decades, since then law student Sonny Seiler received a bulldog as a gift in 1956. He has owned every Uga since. A solid white English bulldog, the tenth and current dog in the Uga line is nicknamed Que. He is driven to Georgia football games in the back of his very own SUV, its thermostat set at sixty degrees to prevent him from overheating. Que wears a Nike football jersey and a red collar decorated with spikes. Like Ugas that preceded him, he sleeps on a bag of ice in his red doghouse on the home sideline of Sanford Stadium. He is the four-footed galoot of football, a big pink tongue hanging out of his mouth.

The dog has always been the consistent star of Georgia games—fans line up by his doghouse for photos and visit the stadium's Uga mausoleum, where past mascots were laid to eternal rest. Though one Uga or another has, er, desecrated the end zones of both the University of South Carolina's and Vanderbilt's home fields, and stuck his nose in a pan of roast beef tenderloin with demi-glace sauce in a Sanford Stadium suite, he is known, invariably, as a *damn good dawg*.

As THE FICTIONAL NARRATOR OF THE At-lanta newspaper editor Joel Chandler Harris's popular folktales starring the trickster Brer Rabbit and his foils—Brer Bear, Brer Fox, and other "creeturs"—the former slave Uncle Remus has prompted no small amount of debate. As a teenager, Harris spent four years working on a plantation outside his hometown of Eatonton, Georgia, and he credited a few of the slaves he befriended, including George Terrell and Old Harbert, with both telling him the African fables that he interpreted in his collections and serving as inspiration for Remus. Harris considered Remus—named in part after one of the mythological twin founders of Rome—his alter ego, the "other fellow" that took him over when he wrote. He first introduced Remus—complete with a thick regional dialect inspired by what Harris heard during his time on the plantation—as a city dweller who would pop up in Harris's *Atlanta Constitution* column to opine on life in the burgeoning metropolis; inspired to preserve the Brer Rabbit stories, traditionally passed down mouth to ear, he then began having Remus chronicle those tales in the paper. Harris published the first of seven collections, *Uncle Remus: His Songs and His Sayings*, in 1881; the stories spread worldwide, making him one of the most famous writers of the day—fans included Rudyard Kipling, Mark Twain, and T. S. Eliot.

In recent decades, some critics have labeled Harris's contribution as nothing more than nostalgic "plantation romance," perpetuating the myth of the "kindly darky," and cultural appropriation—later abetted by Walt Disney's 1946 animated adaptation, *Song of the South*. (The acclaimed author and fellow Eatontonian Alice Walker has espoused this viewpoint.) Other scholars point to Remus's slyly subversive teachings to the white plantation master's son, from endorsing mixed-race couples to his claiming a knowledge superior to "Mars John," as an effort by the relatively racially progressive Harris to both critique and alter the opinions of his post-Reconstruction audience in a way they would find palatable—not unlike tricking a child into eating spinach. In any case, by committing the stories to paper, Harris preserved them for generations to come. As the *New York Times Book Review* noted after Harris's death in 1908, "Uncle Remus cannot die." *See Song of the South.*

THE VARSITY

THERE IS NEVER A QUESTION OF *whether* TO have a chili dog at the Varsity, the world's largest drive-in restaurant, which opened in 1928 in Midtown Atlanta—but only how many of them to order, and how to decorate them. *What'll ya have?* echo the servers behind the counter to patrons who've elected to leave their cars and stand inside. Some choose onions, mustard, slaw—or, naively, nothing, which the menu disparagingly refers to as "naked." In keeping with the parlance of the restaurant, it is a sin not to also order an "FO"—a Frosted Orange, a cold, thick drink the color of a Creamsicle.

The Varsity sits off North Avenue near the infamous I-75/I-85 Connector, its spinning "V" sign as constant a presence as the traffic. On football game days when Georgia plays Georgia Tech, the restaurant—now too small physically for the number of customers it typically draws—might feed up to thirty thousand. The food is served, to go, in rectangular cardboard boxes and is a memorable cure for hangovers and also ideal for graduations and family reunions, the onion rings and chili cheese dogs perennials on any Southern bucket list. There are now seven Georgia locations, including one in Athens and two at the Atlanta airport.

VENUS FLYTRAP

THE SCIENTIFIC NAME *Dionaea muscipula* does little to convey how terrifyingly ghastly this plant is to unsuspecting flies. Tiny hairs on the inside of its leaves trigger a clamp-down before enzymes slowly digest the flytrap's prey, which also includes ants, spiders, and beetles. With bright red inch-long Mick Jagger lips, these meat eaters grow naturally in clusters in just one area of the entire world—a crescent of boggy land along the North and South Carolina coasts, primarily within sixty miles of Wilmington, North Carolina, in an area called the Green Swamp. Around that preserve, two forces stalk the plants—poachers seeking profit on the botanical black market, and state biologists who tag the plants with dye that glows under a black light. The tagging helps track plants that turn up for sale.

In 2014, the conservationists won one battle in the ongoing war—flytrap pilfering went from a misdemeanor citation with a fifty-dollar fine to a full-on felony. These plants don't mess around, and neither do their protectors.

VERANDA

by Logan Ward

A VERANDA IS A GROUND-LEVEL COVERED porch enclosed by a balustrade and stretching across one or more sides of a house. Some consider *veranda* a ten-dollar word, preferring "wraparound porch" for its sturdiness, familiarity, and polite understatement. Like *bungalow*, *cummerbund*, *toddy*, and *punch*, *veranda* is an English word imported from the Indian subcontinent. After centuries of assimilation, it still echoes a faint exoticism, and it's that lyrical echo—the slow unfurling in the mouth—that conveys the cultural significance embodied by this beloved architectural cornerstone.

That cultural significance runs deep. The veranda is and always has been equal measures practical and romantic. Existing neither fully indoors nor outdoors, it symbolizes the Good Life—domestic freedom, leisure time, family togetherness, hospitality, a love of nature. The veranda keeps you cool in summer and fills your lungs with fresh air. On the veranda, you knock mud from your boots and brush your dog. You eat—and dine—there, sip juleps and iced tea, smoke cigars, slurp Popsicles without anyone fretting over sticky drips. You greet passing neighbors from the veranda. You string lights below the open eaves and throw magical outdoor parties.

Verandas—exterior porches of any kind—were not a European architectural convention during the colonization of the Americas. The first houses along the Virginia coast were slab-sided boxes built to keep out Atlantic storms, bears, Indians, and other New World dangers. Porches evolved as a way to adapt to the region's heat and humidity. Some of the first showed up in the eighteenth century in what is today Louisiana. Enslaved Africans and poor white farmers improvised covered, wraparound *galeries* using concepts brought from the West Indies. During the 1800s, columned verandas showed up on Greek Revival houses. As the frontier melted away and the South grew more hospitable and prosperous, verandas of all styles—front porches on more modest homes—became de rigueur. The arrival of central air-conditioning in the mid-twentieth century altered the equation but only slightly. We Southerners still put them on houses today, not as a bonus feature, like a swimming pool, but rather as an integral part of the home.

A veranda invites you to sit, rock, swing, and joggle, to read and nap and marvel at an afternoon thunderstorm. A veranda begs conversation—news, gossip, confessions, tall tales. A veranda "is like a room in your house that's really part of the world," Eudora Welty once told a reporter. In his memoir, *The Lost Room*, Reynolds Price, recounting a day spent on a porch, wrote, "I'll never be gladder than this on Earth."

Call it a ten-dollar notion, but maybe this liminal space is an integral part of the Southern spirit.

VIDALIA ONIONS

It started in Toombs County, Georgia, west of Savannah, with a farmer named Moses Coleman. In 1931, he unintentionally grew a crop of sweet onions, which mild weather, high rainfall, and low-sulfur soil had conspired to mellow. After Coleman fetched a respectable $3.50 per fifty-pound bag, his neighbors began growing sweet onions, too. In the 1940s, the state of Georgia built a farmers' market at the intersection of two highways in nearby Vidalia. From there, the onions' reputation spread. Several decades later, the variety had become so popular that the Georgia General Assembly was compelled to stave off competition, in a majestic flourish, with the Vidalia Onion Act of 1986. Since then, only twenty Georgia counties have been legally allowed to produce the famous onions, sold all over the country and the world.

VIEUX CARRÉ

The Vieux Carré is the second-most-famous cocktail in New Orleans. Or possibly the third, or fourth. Let's just say it's definitely in the top half dozen. Named after a once-common term for the French Quarter (French for "old square"), the drink was invented in 1938 by Walter Bergeron, head bartender of the city's Hotel Monteleone. That's according to the writer Stanley Clisby Arthur. Cocktail lore further asserts that Bergeron concocted it so the Monteleone could compete with the popular Sazerac, the city's most famous drink, which was closely associated with the Sazerac Bar at the Roosevelt Hotel. Like the Sazerac, the Vieux Carré is not a drink for callow youth, nor for those who have otherwise failed to acquire a taste for hard liquor. It's made with equal parts brandy, rye whiskey, and sweet vermouth, further enlivened with one-third part Benedictine liqueur and a few dashes each of Peychaud's and Angostura bitters.

It is an excellent drink, deserving of wider renown outside the city of its conception. To this day the hotel's Carousel Bar serves it frequently, often with lots of ice. But many prefer it served as an "up" drink, chilled fleetingly with ice and strained, then garnished with a twist of lemon peel.

HISTORIANS HAVE PRETTY MUCH GIVEN UP on determining when people first started consuming vinegar: Roman soldiers probably slurped it on the march, and Greek physicians prescribed it for a variety of ailments. Anyone who's fooled with making wine has accidentally made vinegar at some point, meaning the liquid was extremely well known when America was colonized: in the 1700s, Southerners could produce vinegar at home or purchase premade varieties. Either way, they used the stuff for just about everything: halitosis sufferers were advised to sip vinegar after eating onions, housemaids were urged to scrub the floors of sickrooms with it, and nurses applied it to burns. Early Southerners who didn't have access to lemons or limes found vinegar was a fine acidic substitute for citrus in desserts such as chess pie. But vinegar's most valuable use, in a hot climate prior to refrigeration, was as a preservative, and Southerners quickly acclimated to the taste of it in their vegetables, relishes, and sauces. Even today, restaurants keep cruets of pepper vinegar on their tables so diners can perk up their greens, and vinegar looms in the forefront of the South's most revered barbecue.

by James Conaway

MORE THAN TWO CENTURIES AGO, THOMAS Jefferson dreamed of Virginia as prime terroir for fine wine. The author of the Declaration of Independence hoped that vines would provide an alternative to tobacco plants, which wore out the Commonwealth's soil, and that affordable wine made from the grapes would wean the yeoman farmer from hard cider and whiskey and help civilize him. "No nation is drunken," Jefferson wrote plaintively in *Notes on Virginia* in 1781, "where wine is cheap; and none sober" where spirits are the common beverage.

Some of this vision has come true in Virginia. Jefferson himself imported two dozen varieties of *Vitis vinifera*—wine grapes—from Europe for planting on an acre on the south slope of Monticello, and an Italian, Filippo Mazzei, to do it. The vineyard was to serve as an incubator and an example, but Mazzei planted the vines on overlays of clay that didn't drain well, and animals often ate the grapes instead. Lacking the knowledge and the science available today, in this endeavor Jefferson failed. However, the dream hung on, nourished by Jefferson's musings over expensive, imported Lafites and Haut-Brions. Though these wines have no equals in Virginia today, some Commonwealth cuvées are creeping up on the interlopers like old Mosby's Raiders. (There's even a very creditable Gray Ghost Vineyards in Rappahannock County.) The most exciting Virginia wines tend to be red and are made in the Piedmont, which runs from the Maryland line south to Monticello and beyond, along the foothills of the Blue Ridge.

The vinous pilgrim can do worse than to start at Monticello, where the vineyard has been restored by the man who could be called the living father of Virginia viticulture, Gabriele Rausse, another Italian (this one successful) who has an eponymous winery nearby that offers very good quality. A bit north of Charlottesville is Barboursville Vineyards, where yet another fine, long-serving Italian vintner, Luca Paschina, nurtures both Italian and Bordelais blends.

Farther north and about an hour west of Washington, D.C., is Linden Vineyards, founded by Jim Law, an incubator of apprentice winemakers. Some have gone on to achieve distinction on their own, such as Jeff White, at Glen Manor Vineyards on the west slope of the Blue Ridge overlooking the Shenandoah River, and Rutger de Vink, of RdV Vineyards near Delaplane. De Vink's winemaking adviser is from France's Médoc,

where he receives RdV wine regularly by jet-liner, a nice turnabout since the wines of the Médoc so inspired Jefferson in his time that he had some shipped to Monticello. To have such a representative in the Piedmont completes a historic connection that no doubt would have pleased the third president greatly.

Other notables include the Bordeaux varietals of Boxwood Estate Winery, outside Middleburg, and Afton Mountain Vineyards, high on the Blue Ridge. Ox-Eye Vineyards over in the Shendandoah Valley, on the steppes of the Alleghenies, makes an excellent Riesling grown in limestone soils.

Beware pop-ups and vanity operations in various parts of the state that invite you to bring your dog, your pony, or your swingers to the equivalent of modern-day circuses. Such blatant tourism plays could undermine Virginia's promise as a worldwide contender just as it's getting off the ground. But the postponed vision of the sipping sage of Monticello has definitely come to pass, and sorting the good from the less so has become an industry in its own right.

W

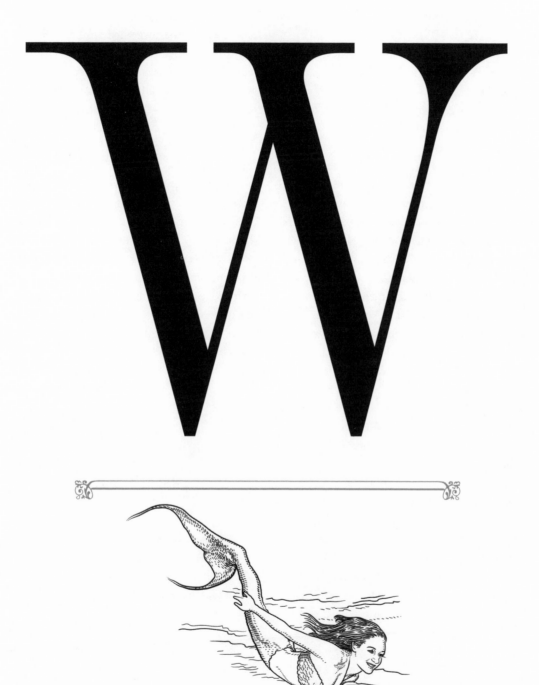

WAFFLE HOUSE

UNLIKE ALMOST ANY RESTAURANT ON EARTH, Waffle House meets Robert Frost's famous depiction of home as "the place where, when you have to go there, they have to take you in." It's open 24 hours a day, 365 days a year. Waffle House is even better than your real home because they never get huffy about taking you in. The franchise's commitment to staying open is legendary, to the point that the Federal Emergency Management Agency actually has an unofficial Waffle House Index. Green means that a given location is serving a full menu. Yellow means it's open but has been forced to offer a limited menu. Red means that location has had to close. People who pay FEMA no mind whatsoever get scared at the news of a shuttered Waffle House, instantly tweeting that their local one is closed, meaning—actual quote here from a Floridian in the path of a hurricane—"shit's about to get real." The franchise was founded in 1955 by Joe Rogers Sr. and Tom Forkner in Avondale Estates, Georgia (the original store is now a museum where you can make your own waffle). The idea—a winner then, a winner still—was to combine the speed of fast food with sit-down service and twenty-four-hour availability. There is some debate about the name. Some say waffles were chosen because they were the most commonly ordered item. Others claim that they were the most profitable. We may never know. We do know and take comfort in the more than 1,500 stores in twenty-five states, the overwhelming majority in the South, where WH is a cultural icon. The layout—counter seats, booths, an open kitchen, and a jukebox—has remained constant, as has the two-sided laminated menu, featuring waffles, omelets, hash browns, biscuits, burgers, steaks, and pork chops. Its appeal cuts across all distinctions of race and class. There are people who've never been there sober or before 3:00 a.m. and people who've never been there for any meal but breakfast. There are meth heads and judges, families and tradesmen, travelers and locals. Our democracy should be so inclusive. The menu explains Waffle House shorthand, but regulars don't need the menu to ask for what they want. "Covered" refers to cheese, "chunked" to ham, "smothered" to onions, "diced" to tomatoes, "peppered" to jalapeños, "capped" to mushrooms, "scattered" to spread and cooked crisply on the grill (this chiefly applies to the hash browns, which should always be ordered "scattered" and "well done"), and "all the way" means you want absolutely everything.

WALKER, ALICE

(1944–)

BORN IN 1944 AS THE EIGHTH AND LAST child of African American sharecroppers in Eatonton, Georgia, Alice Walker had an early life in the rural Jim Crow South that has fueled her books, short stories, and poetry—most notably her now-iconic 1982 novel, *The Color Purple*, which spawned an Oscar-nominated movie and a Tony Award–winning Broadway musical. Told in a series of letters by the main character, Celie, to God, and then to her sister, Nettie, the book weaves themes of sexism, racism, classism, violence, and sisterhood to illuminate the experience of black women, securing Walker the first Pulitzer Prize to go to a woman of color. In fact, Walker coined *womanism*—inspired by the Southern folk idiom "you acting womanish"—to describe feminists of color, a term still in use today. A longtime activist, from the civil rights movement to, controversially, her criticism of the Israeli government, Walker has also brought attention to important issues such as female genital mutilation, and almost single-handedly revived interest in Zora Neale Hurston by editing a 1979 anthology of the Florida-raised writer's work. Walker's own papers are now lodged with Emory University's Manuscript, Archives, and Rare Book Library in Atlanta, including a rare look at the budding talent of the writer as a precocious fifteen-year-old: a scrapbook of verse she titled *Poems of a Childhood Poetess.*

WASHINGTON, D.C.

by James Conaway

JOHN F. KENNEDY FAMOUSLY SAID THAT Washington, D.C., has all the efficiency of the South and all the charm of the hard-edged industrial Northeast. He meant it ironically, of course, but half a century later Washington is a thoroughly modern American city, with a functional subway system and a relatively well-heeled, youthful citizenry propelling its watering holes and music to new heights. Manners may not be exactly honeyed Georgian, but Washington is civil, and the vast, ambulatory bureaucracy better dressed than in Kennedy's day.

Much of it is mounted on hybrid bikes or upholstered stools next to Gucci'ed lobbyists in craft cocktail bars, microbreweries, and José Andrés's latest culinary invention. "D.C." is now one of the country's best cities for eats, as well as one of the wealthiest, its collective gaze directed upward not at faceless office buildings but at blue sky preserved by legal height limits and fringed with a cadre of mature trees that give the city a lovely, sylvan mien.

This habit of mixing nature with urban succor goes back to July 16, 1790, when the city was founded, with a unique 146-acre manicured lawn known simply as "the Mall," gorgeous open space on some of the most valuable real estate on earth, lovingly cared for by the National Park Service. Here the world's best collection of museums, like a prize dairy herd, feeds culture to twenty-five million tourists annually. The Mall set the historical precedent for physical openness and all-American optimism, and this endures.

Even though Washington's eternally on the make—what national capital isn't?—it manages to accommodate the ambitions of the world with remarkable ease and grace, regardless of who's in the White House. The city's designer, Pierre L'Enfant, a Parisian, daringly imposed upon the usual grid system of streets an overlay of diagonal avenues like the spokes of wheels that give Washington a touch of European sophistication. It also contributes to another Washington superlative: best walking city in America, in which the ambulatorily inclined can without too much effort find their happy way from the brick sidewalks of Georgetown to the apex of Mount St. Alban, where stands, in the midst of Frederick Law Olmsted's commons, the inspiring National Cathedral, one of its steeples bristling with surveillance gear, for that, too, is Washington.

Likewise, Rock Creek Park, one of the nation's oldest, splits the city north to south like a vernal wedge, affording endless trails and some old-growth oaks and beeches. Again the keeper of this vast natural preserve is the Park Service, unsung hero of the capital's subtle blend of urban and wild, as all-American as the city itself.

WATERS, MUDDY

(1913–1983)

THOUGH HE'S ACCURATELY CHRISTENED "THE father of modern Chicago blues," Muddy Waters was born McKinley Morganfield in Issaquena County, Mississippi, earning his geographically evocative name from his grandmother because he, well, played in the mud all the time. In his non-puddle time, he began to play the harmonica by age five and spent the bulk of his childhood swimming in the sea of Son House, Robert Johnson, and Charley Patton, when he wasn't working as a sharecropper and/or running a juke joint out of his house, which he usually was. He recorded with the musicologist Alan Lomax for

the Library of Congress in 1941, and in 1943, the fire of his talents drove him to Chicago. From there, Waters went about burning up the city's iconic South Side clubs and, with Chess Records, knocked the world off its axis with songs like "I'm Your Hoochie Coochie Man," "Mannish Boy," "Got My Mojo Working," and "Rollin' Stone," which made a big enough bang to inspire a band and a magazine. Before long, his electrified Muddy Waters Blues Band was setting the pace for Chicago blues and all subsequent rock and roll, blues-influenced or not; the basic noisy storm and thump of the style he crafted in the South Side remains a blueprint for any band with a guitar and a song about a lost woman (Eric Clapton, Jimmy Page, Jeff Beck, and AC/DC all claimed Waters as a powerful influence). Waters died in 1983 with six Grammys to his name, as well as a claim to an immutable bedrock sound in American music.

WATSON, DOC

(1923–2012)

by Seth Avett

I STEPPED OUT OF THE COLD AND INTO DOC Watson's living room. It was a sunny day in the Blue Ridge Mountains, and there was still snow on the ground from a recent storm. I was thirteen years old—a kid with braces, skate shoes, and a limited appreciation of music. I knew of this legendary North Carolina folksinger and guitarist, who had played for presidents and won every award they give for making music. I had even begun learning one of his songs from my guitar teacher, but up until that point, my musical interests seldom reached beyond the artistic ventures of Kurt Cobain or Jimmy Page. So how did a kid still relatively oblivious to the history of American roots music find himself in the home of one of its most celebrated masters?

Wayne Hayes was a man who lived in my hometown of Concord, North Carolina. He was a local guy, a music lover, a songwriter, and a social studies teacher at the high school I would eventually attend. Around 1988, he wrote a song in honor of Doc's famed son, Merle, who had recently passed away. He sent the song to Doc, a gesture that would prove to be the beginning of an enduring friendship. Wayne was also a friend of my father's (it seems that in a small town, guys who play guitars and sing old country songs are bound to become friends sooner or later). They got together often in my dad's wood shop or in whatever garage was available to talk, play songs, tell stories, and maybe have a cold beer.

Around 1993, Wayne asked my father if he'd like to visit Doc at his home in Deep Gap, North Carolina. Thankfully, Dad passed the invitation on to me. He figured this extraordinary opportunity would be more valuable for a young person, especially one with a few years of guitar lessons under his belt (or maybe he just saw an obvious advantage in the possibility of hearing something other than Nirvana's *Bleach* blasting from the speakers in my bedroom). Doc was scheduled to play in Winston-Salem in a few weeks, and Wayne set it up for me to meet him during the day at his home, and to go to the performance with them that night.

I remember the experience of going to Doc Watson's house in the same way one might remember a first day at a new school, or a first breakup, or the first time driving a car with no one else in it: an event when you know things will not be the same after this. My mind was about to be opened musically, and by someone esteemed and respected the world over, no less.

The nature of the visit and the surroundings were in no way glamorous. He appeared to live the relatively simple rural life that one might expect from his music. He lived in a modest home in a beautiful part of the state, in a friendly and uncrowded neighborhood near the Blue Ridge Parkway. We sat in his living room and talked about music. I remember Rosa Lee, his wife of forty-six years at the time, making something in the kitchen. She talked with me about their garden, about which vegetables had done well that year and which hadn't. His daughter, Nancy, showed me around the house; I saw a hammer dulcimer for the first time, sitting in a small room that also happened to have six or seven Grammys on one wooden shelf. They had a couple of cats. I remember that when Doc opened the door by the carport, he somehow knew if they were there, despite his blindness. It was incredible. I recall thinking his hearing must be very different and clearly more advanced than mine. He let me play his guitar, and I showed him what little I had learned so far. He gave me some pointers. He gave me a pick. I remember feeling very calm, very at ease sitting and talking with him. So much of his character was right there, at the forefront of casual interaction: humility, knowledge, care, humor.

The performance that evening was at Salem College. Doc would be playing solo, and Wayne drove the three of us to the venue. We stopped and had supper at a K&W Cafeteria. I remember a swell of pride as Doc asked me to guide him into the restaurant. We walked slowly through the cafeteria line, his hand on my shoulder. I was nervous because I thought I might mess up somehow.

During the show, he played the song I was trying to learn at the time and, much to my amazement, mentioned me in his introduction—something about how there's a young fellow in the audience trying to learn this one and that he's doing a good job with it. I remember how clear his voice was, and how melodic his picking was, and how I, along with the rest of the audience, was completely rapt. I had never experienced a performance like it: simple in presentation, technically complex at times, highly professional, engaging, relatable, and vastly entertaining. He was funny and friendly and human and powerful but not in a way that I had ever seen before. In my mind at the time, "power" in musical performance was often synonymous with "volume" or even "aggression." The power Doc had as a musician, and as a person, was not of the variety that required loudness. On the stage his ability to tell a story and to interpret a song so fully and with such a natural feel for melody was enough to draw the undivided attention of everyone in the room, no matter the size. Millions would have this experience firsthand

throughout his eighty-nine years. His was a voice of unparalleled temperament, even and strong, graceful yet gloriously matter-of-fact. It truly was, and will remain, one of our classic American voices, rightfully in the company of Louis Armstrong, Hank Williams, Sr., Elvis Presley, Ella Fitzgerald.

In life, Doc was friendly and respectful to strangers, friends, family members, and fans. He exemplified patience, and brought joy and laughter to those with whom he came in contact. In conversation, he spoke and listened with interest, even to a thirteen-year-old kid from Concord.

Doc Watson changed the way I saw the acoustic guitar. He changed my understanding of how a song could be presented in sound and mood, and helped lead me to a uniquely rich tradition of music, a path of research and inspiration that continues for me daily. I am eternally grateful to this man who spent so much of his life sharing songs, and who was kind enough to share some with me all those years ago, on a clear day in the Blue Ridge Mountains.

WEEKI WACHEE MERMAIDS

by *Roy Blount, Jr.*

I'M TOLD ONE OF THE PIRATES OF THE Caribbean movies involves ferocious killer mermaids, one of whom, for some reason, falls in love with a clergyman. I don't think so, Hollywood. Mermaids have been set in stone for me ever since, as a boy, I saw a certain picture postcard: two beautiful women in tails, yes, and also in old-fashioned swimsuit tops, and their eyes have an unearthly gleam, and their lips are a brazen red, and their long fine hair floats filmily, driftily, spookily, above and behind.

And one of the mermaids is drinking what I took to be a Coca-Cola, and the other mermaid is eating a banana.

Underwater.

Ah, Florida! I grew up in Georgia, and I often tell people that Lady Gaga stands for that state twice. But Florida was the first state where I saw things that I knew were supposed to be exotic, and those underwater Flaflas still resonate with me. The postcard was from one of Florida's earliest roadside attractions: Weeki Wachee Springs, off of U.S. 19 an hour or so north of Tampa. My parents took us to similar Florida destinations, such as Silver Springs, where we looked at fish and so on through a glass-bottom boat, and Sulphur Springs, where my grandfather soaked his rheumatism in murky water, but somehow we never made it to Weeki Wachee. Recently, at last, I did.

"Dancin' and singin' fish-tail women!" the loudspeaker blares, and there they are, moving and beaming, in crystal-clear emerald-tinted iridescent waters. We mermaid fanciers watch from a four-hundred-seat theater embedded in the spring's limestone bank. We look face-to-face through glass at mermaids sixteen to twenty feet deep in seventy-two-degree water. When Weeki Wachee first opened, in 1947, there wasn't much traffic on the highway. At the sound of an approaching car, mermaids would run out (taillessly) and lure it in with their siren calls. Weeki Wachee's fortunes have waxed and waned since then. The Mouse, as Floridians often characterize Disney World, may have made actual human-scale mermaids seem small potatoes. To some people. Not to me.

"Mermaids go with bubbles like fairies go with wings," says the promotional material from Weeki Wachee. Okay, it should be "as fairies go," but who quibbles over grammar with mermaids? When a Weeki Wachee mermaid takes a sip of compressed air from a handy hose, she rises. When she exhales a bit, she subsides. "Gobs of bubbles" are produced either way. Fish are attracted to the bubbles. Mermaids interact with the fish. (I believe alligators are screened out, somehow or other, but there are photos of manatees swimming with the mermaids. Some people have speculated that the myth of mermaids arose from sailors' sightings of manatees. If you've ever seen a picture of manatees and mermaids side by side—hey, who doesn't love manatees, but come on.)

But now the bubbles are getting smaller, and smaller, and smaller. We have reached the point in the show when a single mermaid has headed down, down, way out of sight, into this bottomless spring, and the pressure is mounting, on her and on her bubbles, so we know it's true, how deep she's going. The air hose comes up, without the mermaid. They're tiny now, her bubbles. She's shooting for a descent of 117 feet, *in ballet slippers*. You try doing that without using your tail.

Seems like she's been down there forever—two minutes and twenty-three seconds, by the clock. Time to reflect that more than 117 million gallons of water spring daily from the subterranean caverns whose bottom, if it exists, has never been touched. At last, she's back! Just as chipper as you please. And boom: the whole view is all bubbles. Underwater, of course, there are no curtains, so when a Weeki Wachee show segues from scene to scene, stagehands set off a wall of bubbles. I'll bet that if you have never been to Weeki Wachee, you have never seen so many bubbles at once.

And now we're getting down to the iconic scene. Sure, fish eat underwater, but pretty girls? How can such things be? And yet it is happening, before our eyes. One mermaid is drinking from a bottle. It's not Coke, I have learned from the Weeki Wachee souvenir booklet, because that drink's carbonation "causes mermaid bloat" and throws off the bubble-balancing precision that dancin' and swimmin' at a given level in a five-mile-an-hour current requires. It's Grapette, which is less bubbly. Okay. I go way back with Grapette.

And another mermaid is eating an apple.

I expected a banana.

WELLS, IDA B.

(1862–1931)

First, this native of Holly Springs, Mississippi, took on a railroad conductor. Orphaned by a yellow fever epidemic, Ida B. Wells had in 1883 moved to Memphis to support her siblings by teaching school. While there, she ended up in a crowded train car where the conductor ordered her to give up her seat for a white man. Wells refused and bit the conductor's hand before he and a porter dragged her out of her seat. Then, after becoming part owner of a black newspaper, Wells took on Memphis. After her friend Tom Moss was lynched in 1892 for defending his grocery store from a white mob, she wrote editorials urging blacks to leave the city. Her journalism so outraged white residents that they burned down her newspaper office. Wells relocated to Chicago, where she met and married Ferdinand Barnett on the third try: she twice postponed the ceremony because she was scheduled to give anti-lynching speeches. "I decided to continue to work as a journalist, for this was my first love," she wrote. "And might be said, my only love." Wells went on to help organize the National Association of Colored Women's Clubs, cocreate the NAACP, and run for the Illinois legislature.

WELTY, EUDORA

(1909–2001)

by Frances Mayes

READ EUDORA WELTY. START WITH THE short stories. They're sharp, funny, and deeply humane. I especially love her novel *The Optimist's Daughter*, a meditation on memory and place, Southern style. Read every word she wrote—the experience will bring you to the taproot of the region.

Welty wrote in Jackson, Mississippi. After her education in the North and the Midwest, she returned to 1119 Pinehurst Street, where she spent her time gardening, participating in the intense social life of a Southern city, reviewing books, roaming the countryside photographing people. And writing from the heart of a place. She knew that *where* something happens *is* what happens. Her ear was fine-tuned to the local idiom. I love coming upon "a hold" and "I swan!" "I can just hear that," we say as we read.

Southerners can small talk each other to death without a trace of boredom crossing anyone's face. Welty captures cadence, the lulling storyteller voice, loops of lyric, then brings them up short by sharp declarative sentences—she used the tone of conversation without succumbing to talking, talking, talking.

Here's what most of us never admit: Southerners are the most private people on the globe. Within tight interconnections of family, the real caring for one another, the incessant stories, the visiting, she's onto the truth that all these rituals offer an elaborate continuity for solitary figures.

You can tour her Tudor Revival house and garden. When I visited, the word that came to mind was *plain*. Her desk and typewriter stand along the window wall of a bedroom. The house is colorless but full of books. Books everywhere, even stacked on the sofa. Walking through, I recognized: this was liberation.

Years ago, I happened to stand behind Eudora Welty in line at an airport shop. She was buying mints. Elderly and hunched, she counted out the change. As she turned, I said, "Miss Welty, I just have to say how much I admire your work."

She snapped her purse and put her hand on my arm. "Well, thank you. You are just so sweet to say so."

Her Southern grace abides in all her work.

Of the monumental twentieth-century writers—note that I do not limit my claim to Southern writers—she had the biggest heart. I insist: take a trip to your nearest bookstore.

WESTERN SWING

WESTERN SWING MUSIC WAS BORN TO AC-complish one task: make the people dance. It grew up in Texas and Oklahoma as a rural answer to urban jazz and big-band tunes. The genre's fathers—Bob Wills and His Texas Playboys, the Light Crust Doughboys, and the Musical Brownies chief among them—drew on the quick tempos of swing bands, jazzy freewheeling improvisation, and the inclusion of decidedly country instruments (steel guitar, banjo, fiddle). At the dawn of the 1930s, dance halls across the lower Great Plains began to fill up, and by the late '30s and into the '40s, songs such as Bob Wills's "New San Antonio Rose" had feet stomping across the country. Then, in 1944, during the heat of U.S. involvement in World War II, the federal government demanded a 30 percent tax be placed on "dancing" nightclubs around the country, and Western swing saw its popularity wane. It would be wrong, however, to say its influence saw the same fate. The sounds echo through rockabilly, honky-tonk, Southern rock, and modern country. *See Wills, Bob.*

WHERE THE RED FERN GROWS

IF ANY REQUIRED READING MADE YOU CRY your innocent guts out as a middle schooler, chances are *Where the Red Fern Grows* was involved. The book, which is set deep in the Ozark Mountains of Oklahoma, tells the tale of Billy Colman, a young boy determined to own and train a pair of coonhounds. Those hounds turn out to be Little Ann and Old Dan, arguably the most famous pair of hunting dogs in all of literature. Hard to imagine that if not for some good old-fashioned nudging, Billy, Little Ann, and Old Dan might never have graced the written page. The author, Wilson Rawls, set fire to his first draft of the novel, but, at the urging of his wife, rewrote the story. At last count *Where the Red Fern Grows* had sold more than six million copies—and engendered a river of tears—since it was first published in 1961.

WHITE LILY FLOUR

AFTER THE ORRVILLE, OHIO–BASED J. M. Smucker Company bought the White Lily brand and closed its 125-year-old plant in Knoxville, Tennessee, in 2008, bakers were apoplectic. Southerners attribute near-mystical powers to the soft winter wheat flour. Biscuits would never be the same, they said. Milling White Lily in the Midwest? Might as well be distilling bourbon in the Napa Valley. Really, though, White Lily's wheat has always come primarily from Indiana, Michigan, and Ohio. If anything, the flour is fresher than ever—and still deserving of its status as a household name in the South. *See Flour.*

WHITE SAUCE

SINCE IT BECAME TRENDY A FEW YEARS BACK, white sauce—a barbecue sauce firmly rooted in Alabama—has been featured in all manner of national magazines, which feel compelled to explain to readers just what they might do with the mayonnaise and vinegar blend. The diversity of suggestions conveys not just the versatility of white sauce, but also its overriding deliciousness: there is apparently no food too good for white sauce. It flatters french fries. It betters bluefish. It enhances eggs. And it cajoles chicken into tasting better than anyone thought chicken could taste. That's the original application of the sauce, which is credited to Decatur's Bob Gibson. Like his contemporary Duke's Mayonnaise founder Eugenia Duke up in Greenville, South Carolina, Gibson had mayo on the mind in the 1920s; he debuted his sauce in 1925. It's still served at Big Bob Gibson Bar-B-Q, although you're likely to see it just about anywhere these days. And chefs across the region acknowledge Gibson's visionary wisdom when they pair it with smoked chicken wings.

WHOLE-HOG BARBECUE

WHOLE-HOG BARBECUE HAS LONG BEEN THE house specialty at such revered joints as Skylight Inn BBQ in Ayden, North Carolina, and Scott's Bar-B-Que in Hemingway, South Carolina. Its native range spans along the North and South Carolina coasts, where the practice of cooking entire pigs over coals dates back to colonial times. But a new appreciation for the endangered art has been taking it beyond its traditional boundaries. Whole hog is gaining ground at such new-guard spots as Buxton Hall Barbecue in Asheville, North Carolina, Martin's Bar-B-Que Joint in Nashville, and way up north at Arrogant Swine in Brooklyn. Requiring wood coals, a pig-sized pit, and up to twenty-four hours of cooking, monitoring, and coal shoveling, it isn't easy. But fans will tell you that the incomparable mix of white meat, dark meat, and crisp skin is worth the trouble. *See Barbecue.*

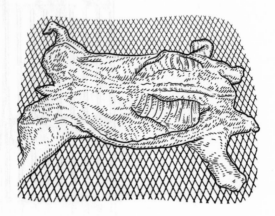

WHEN HERNANDO DE SOTO MADE LANDFALL on Florida's southwest coast in 1539, he had in a ship's hold thirteen sows he'd picked up in Cuba. (Those swine were most likely related to the pigs Columbus had released in the West Indies a few years earlier.) In a year, de Soto's herd had grown to a reported three hundred pigs. And thus the die was cast. *Sus scrofa*'s unhindered embrace of the South has resembled nothing less than a bristly hide pulled across the region, wreaking havoc on crops, property, and native species. Wild pigs are now found in every Southern state, and in states such as Texas and Florida, seemingly behind every prickly pear and palmetto. In 1901, the nation's uninvited pig herd was bolstered with an infusion of Eurasian wild boars when imported tuskers broke down a fence in the North Carolina mountains. Most of the pigs swarming swamps, timberlands, and even subdivisions are the progeny of animals free-ranged throughout the colonial period, and trapped and transplanted by hunters in more recent years. Given a reproductive rate that makes bunnies look practically chaste, wild pigs can be marginally controlled—and barbecued and grilled with tasty results—but they will never be vanquished. *See Ossabaw hogs.*

THE MOST INFLUENTIAL COUNTRY SINGER who ever lived—fans range from U2 to Bob Dylan to every budding musician in Nashville—Hank Williams (1923–1953) was a consummate storyteller, perfecting the tear-in-my-beer theme for generations to come. His thirty-five Top 10 hits include "Cold, Cold Heart," "I'm So Lonesome I Could Cry," "Hey, Good Lookin'," and "Your Cheatin' Heart," each of which populate jukeboxes all over the world. But Williams also suffered from crippling back pain, which caused him to drink heavily and take copious amounts of painkillers. His performances became uneven, and he made a habit of getting too far gone to play a show, which infuriated the Grand Ole Opry, leading to its revoking his membership in August 1952 after one too many slipups. Later that year, Williams died at age twenty-nine in the backseat of a car on his way to a performance in Charleston, West Virginia, with the cause of death determined to be heart failure.

Though his career was cut short, his legacy loomed large, especially to his son, Hank Williams Jr. Junior started his career by mimicking his father's sound, but in the wake of the Outlaw movement began to incorporate Southern rock and blues, often collaborating with his good friend Waylon Jennings. Williams Jr.'s daughter Holly has recorded three well-received albums and has opened a clothing boutique, H. Audrey (named after her grandmother), in Nashville, and his son Shelton Hank Williams III is also a musician, having added to the family legend with marathon live shows that veer from classic country to thrash metal. A dead ringer for Hank Sr., Williams III has also led the charge for the Grand Ole Opry to reinstate his grandfather's membership, releasing the song "The Grand Ole Opry (Ain't So Grand)" in 2008.

WILLIAMS, TENNESSEE

(1911–1983)

"AMERICA ONLY HAS THREE CITIES: New York, San Francisco, and New Orleans. Everything else is Cleveland." Contrary to popular opinion, Mark Twain did not say that: credit goes to Tennessee Williams. Thomas Lanier Williams III was born in Columbus, Mississippi, and moved to New Orleans when he was twenty-eight, taking on the name "Tennessee" by way of a fresh start. He forged himself in the licentious and bohemian French Quarter before becoming one of the most famous playwrights in American history with classics such as *Cat on a Hot Tin Roof*, *The Glass Menagerie*, and *A Streetcar Named Desire*. His plays are not happy places but rather are consumed by deep-rooted strife and repression, no doubt colored by his own unhappy family and the struggle of being a gay man in the early-twentieth-century South (he spent years in and out of mental institutions and wrestling with drug addiction before his death, in 1983). Still, there's a certain image of him that endures, captivating in its own

right—a man with a clean mustache and an immaculate tuxedo, sitting at some corner table at Brennan's on Royal Street, pouring from a pitcher of martinis—and he's become an indispensable part of New Orleans' lore, with a literary festival held each spring in his honor.

WILLS, BOB

(1905–1975)

JAMES ROBERT WILLS HAD A KNACK FOR getting folks on the dance floor. Born to a farm family just outside Kosse, Texas, Wills grew up on ranch-dance fiddling, a steady dose of blues (Bessie Smith was his idol), and jazz-style improvisation and solo play. He took that hodgepodge of influences and channeled it into a high-flying fusion that took over dance halls and jukeboxes from Georgia to California during the 1930s and '40s. Bob Wills and His Texas Playboys commanded the stage with winding fiddle and steel guitar solos, an ever-present drumbeat, and Wills's wisecracking brand of showmanship. The band didn't take long to become the most popular Western swing act in the country, attracting crowds of dancers eager for a chance to move to the tunes of the King of Western Swing. *See Western swing.*

WILTED GREENS

Southerners have historically preferred cooked-to-death cabbage and collards, but a quick toss in a hot pan makes for a faster, more nutritious route to cooked greens. *See Kil't greens.*

WISTERIA

You know spring has arrived in full force in the South when the tendrils of American wisteria—twisting counterclockwise up and around garden pergolas and wrought-iron fences—burst into cascading purple bloom. With varieties including the light-purple-flowering Kentucky wisteria and blue-flowering Texas wisteria, this beautiful backdrop for sipping sweet tea (or a julep) is native to the Southeast, growing well from Virginia to Florida over to Texas. Although American wisteria can spread up to fifty feet, it's not as invasive as Chinese wisteria, which if left unchecked can, like in-laws at Christmas, quickly overtake your space, choking out the natives.

WONDER BREAD

White bread, pickles, and onions. In brisket country, those freebies cost popular barbecue joints hundreds of dollars each week. Elsewhere, pit masters aren't so generous. But you can usually at least count on a slice or two of Wonder Bread. Why don't some of the country's best barbecue masters pair their labor-intensive meats with the likes of skillet cornbread or hot buttered biscuits? For the same reason they serve canned beans and bagged slaw. They cook meat. Working without kitchen staffs, they're already spending valuable time away from their main course when they drive down to the grocery store to load their sooty arms with the spongiest, moppingest white bread they can find. It's a blank sheet for their fat-and-vinegar symphonies.

WROUGHT IRON

What does the Eiffel Tower have in common with the ornamental gates, fences, railings, and window grilles that decorate buildings throughout the South? The answer is all in the material: wrought iron, a low-carbon alloy prized by blacksmiths for its durability, malleability, and resistance to corrosion that lends cities such as Charleston, South Carolina, and New Orleans part of their charm. As the name implies, the metal is worked by hand (hence wrought) until its shape and form have been sufficiently manipulated to suit the metalworker's, or his client's, taste. During its heyday in the late 1800s and 1900s, when blacksmiths such as Charleston's talented and prolific Philip Simmons produced works that would later find homes in national museums, wrought iron was a symbol of prosperity. Alas, the material's labor-intensive nature would eventually be its downfall, and by 1969, the last commercial wrought-iron plant closed its doors. Some wrought iron is still being produced today for heritage restoration purposes, but only by recycling scrap. *See Simmons, Philip.*

X-Z

XXX

A universal symbol for moonshine, derived from its makers' practice of marking an X on a jug for each distillation of their liquor. By the third distillation, you had a potent hooch indeed. *See Moonshine.*

YA-KA-MEIN

Around 1900, New Orleans had a bustling Chinatown, all but vanished today. Its legacy lives on in a favorite street food: ya-ka-mein, aka "ya-ka-meat." A soy-spiked broth brimming with noodles, green onions, meat, and wedges of hard-boiled egg, it's an effective palliative for hangovers (some refer to it as Old Sober). But it's more than that for African American cooks like Linda Green, a vendor at Crescent City parades and festivals who calls herself the Ya-Ka-Mein Lady—it's a family tradition. Green remembers watching her great-grandmother make ya-ka-mein. And among the many families who've kept it alive over the years, there's no one recipe. Creole seasoning, ketchup, and hot sauce are all popular additions.

Y'ALL

Americans from parts other than the South have, like Southerners, universally embraced the slippery lyrical convenience of the word *y'all*. In the mouths of Northerners or Westerners, however, it brings an ungainly lack of rhythm to the sentence structure, because the South's complex social architecture has created its deeper tones and shadings. Herewith, four basic templates of Southern use:

Hey y'all! An exclamatory form of motivational address used to encourage larger participation in drudge-like outings: fund-raisers, family reunions, and flower-, golf-, or hunt-club functions. Every Southerner hearing this phrase knows: a bad idea will follow.

We don't wanna inconvenience y'all. Because the second-person singular pronoun and the second-person plural are identical in English, using the contraction generally avoids confusion. In addition, when the speaker makes a socially delicate request of the addressees, the contraction softens the blow of the hard objects, the *you,* and scales back whatever unpalatable thing he or she might hope to get from the listeners into a neighborly possibility.

Y'all don't really wanna do that. The contraction's presence is rhetorically effective when intentionally used incorrectly, as above, when addressing a single person, a possible bad actor, with the Southern version of the British royal family's plural. It flatters—as if the addressee had serried knights on horseback at his or her command.

I don't think that bar is open, y'all. Useful with a large group of Southerners who have been overserved. On a long bar crawl, an SEC-playoff mentality takes hold, and the word is often forcefully attached after a (clearly implied) comma, punching the preceding information through the evening's haze. Whether it then helps the group rally to the next open watering hole remains up for grabs.

YARDBIRD

A SLANG TERM FOR CHICKEN, GOING BACK TO antebellum times in the South, which African Americans evidently took with them as they migrated to other parts of the country. During the Harlem Renaissance of the 1920s and '30s, some restaurant diners would order "yardbird and strings"—fried chicken and spaghetti. Fellow jazz musicians took to calling the saxophonist Charlie Parker (born in Kansas City) Yardbird, or just Bird, some said because of his fondness for eating fowl. *See Fried chicken.*

YARN

by Daniel Wallace

WHAT'S A SOUTHERN YARN? GOOD QUEStion. I wish my uncle Merle were here to tell you, because he could tell a yarn, could he ever, but he died in the salt mines. He was the foreman of one of the biggest salt mines in Birmingham, Alabama, in the early part of the last century, when salt mines dotted the landscape of Birmingham the way steel mills would later. A lot of people don't know about the Birmingham salt mines, but they rivaled the salt marshes of Venice and the salt mountains of Dubai for a time. The first salt deposit was discovered in Birmingham in 1876 by a stray cow. Birmingham is also where modern saltshakers were invented, not far from the house I would be born in many decades later. Fact: salt from the Birmingham salt mines filled up to fifteen thousand shakers a day, filled mostly by the very young and the very old, preschoolers and retirees. Yes, Birmingham was synonymous with salt. It was called the Salty City. Some say the salt mines were a mile deep, and some thought they went even deeper, that they were the mythical tunnels to China. There are even some who say a Chinese man was found at the bottom of one of the mines, digging *up* from his home in Beijing, and that when he came out he became principal of the high school. Principal Kwan, his name was. But that's another story. Uncle Merle wasn't interested in China. What had happened was he'd just bought a ring for the woman he hoped would become his wife—Lucille Endicott—and he dropped it one day, and it fell deep into the mine at least a mile or so and he went down for it, even though the bottom of the mine was not too far from the earth's molten core. What he didn't know is at the bottom of the mine there was a great big salt pool filled with piranhas, *salt* piranhas—which as everyone knows are the worst kind. They ate him until he was nothing but little bits of whatever he used to be.

And *that* is what a yarn is.

ZAPP'S POTATO CHIPS

LEAVE IT TO CAJUN COUNTRY TO INVENT chips this wild, wonderful, and worthy of their obsessive fans. When his equipment business failed in the oil bust of the 1980s, Ron Zappe did the only logical thing—he started making kettle-style potato chips in a defunct Chevy dealership in Gramercy, Louisiana. The early days were lean, with Zappe sometimes standing in the middle of busy intersections to hand out samples to passing motorists. Soon his Spicy Cajun Crawtator flavor caught on with locals who didn't mind if a potato chip lit a swamp fire in their mouths. The chip cult swelled exponentially with other smashup flavors such as Hotter 'N Hot Jalapeño, Cajun Dill Gator-tators, and Voodoo Gumbo, all fried in delicious peanut oil (instead of the industry-standard vegetable oil). Alas, Zappe ascended to snack-food heaven in 2010. So when Utz Foods bought Zapp's the following year, loyalists fretted if a Pennsylvania company could leave well enough alone. Well, Zapp's are still proudly produced in Gramercy,

and if the latest special-edition flavor—Sweet Pimento Cream Cheese—is any indication, their Cajun soul has been saved.

ZATARAIN'S

EMILE ZATARAIN DIDN'T ENVISION AN EM-pire when in 1886 he opened an Uptown New Orleans grocery store and prepared to ring up purchases on the state's first cash register. For Zatarain, buying a horse and buggy for deliveries counted as success. But then he came up with Zat-So Root Beer for the Louisiana Purchase Exposition and realized his future might lie with fine-tuning flavors. People went nuts for Zatarain's root beer extract, and his Creole mustard after that. Eventually, Zatarain created a seafood boil that perfectly crystallized how the Crescent City liked to season its food; during crawfish season, it still tops the company's list of best-sellers. But Zatarain's, which the family sold off back in 1963, keeps eaters in mustard seeds and red pepper all year long: its white boxes of jambalaya, dirty rice, gumbo base, and shrimp Creole mix sit on supermarket shelves across the country, wooing shoppers with the promise of a vicarious visit to New Orleans. "Every city had a manufacturer that was probably packing spices, extracts, and pickles, because those are hard to ship," the company's Dudley Passman told the *Times-Picayune*. "The difference was, we were based here in New Orleans, where our food tasted better than everyone else's."

ZOMBIE COCKTAIL

THE ZOMBIE RANKS AMONG THE MOST FAmous and fearsome of tiki drinks. It was invented by Don the Beachcomber, a Louisiana native who single-handedly launched the original tiki trend when he opened his bar in Los Angeles in 1934. The oft-repeated origin tale says that Don himself mixed the first zombie for a woefully hungover customer who lamented that he felt like "the living dead." (A less common variant involves Don serving a customer en route to the airport; the customer was later discovered sitting on a pier along San Francisco Bay, uncertain of how he arrived and unable to feel anything.) The epicurean writer Lucius Beebe noted that at the 1964 New York World's Fair, the zombie was a hit, costing a dollar each, and that customers were limited to one "by a management at once thrifty and mindful of municipal ordinances."

The tiki historian Jeff Berry, owner of the New Orleans restaurant and bar Latitude 29, spent a decade tracking down what went into a zombie. In his book *Sippin' Safari*, he published three versions of the recipe—dated to 1934, 1950, and 1956—with the 1934 zombie punch by general consensus coming closest to the original. The punch consists of three rums (light, dark, and overproof), lime juice, falernum, grenadine, Pernod, Angostura bitters, grapefruit juice, and cinnamon-infused sugar syrup. When consuming, be mindful of municipal ordinances.

ZYDECO

THE WORD *ZYDECO*, THE STORY GOES, ORIGInates from the French saying "*Les haricots ne sont pas salés*," meaning "The green beans are not salty." (This sounds a lot more like it contains "zydeco" when spoken in Creole French.) Consider that if you had more money, you might be able to afford some ham to add flavor to your beans, and you start to figure out what zydeco is: a rowdy, French-infused kind of blues that Creole African Americans developed in western Louisiana. It's dance music raucous and loud, closely related to Cajun music but marked by African singing and rhythms. Expect to hear accordion, expect to hear washboard, expect to dance. Zydeco's history is intermingled with that of the black experience in Louisiana, going back centuries, but it found itself an excellent match once rock and roll arrived, quickly adopting electric guitars and basses, drum kits, and other tricks. Pioneers such as Clifton Chenier brought zydeco to the rest of the country and the world, starting in the mid-1950s; the persistence of zydeco festivals in Germany and other far-flung places gives some indication of their success. Next time you hear a pop song with that in-and-out accordion driving in the background, take note: that's a bit of zydeco in there.

ACKNOWLEDGMENTS

A BOOK OF THIS SCOPE REQUIRES A CAPABLE and seasoned captain at the helm, and I owe huge thanks to Mike Grudowski for steering this project through every phase since the initial brainstorming session in February 2016. I'm grateful for his dedication and talent. Around the *Garden & Gun* offices, everyone pitched in. Deputy Editor Dave Mezz put in weekends and late nights, bringing the same exacting attention to detail that he does to the pages of the magazine. Design Director Marshall McKinney and former associate art director Braxton Crim helped guide the work of Dahl Taylor, who created the cover illustration, and Harry Bates, who drew the interior illustrations. Speaking of design, Shubhani Sarkar effortlessly brought *G&G*'s aesthetic to the pages of the book.

We all sleep better when we know Donna Levine, the magazine's copy chief, is on the job. I'm also grateful for *G&G* staffers Jed Portman, Elizabeth Hutchison, CJ Lotz, Amanda Heckert, Phillip Rhodes, and Dacey Orr, who all contributed entries, and for the diligent work of intern Caroline Sanders.

As they have done with the previous three *Garden & Gun* books, Karen Rinaldi, the publisher at Harper Wave, and Julie Will, the editorial director, inspire us to reach for new heights, and the book is much better because of it. Their insights are evident on every page. Along with Julie and Karen, our team at Harper—Brian Perrin, Leah Carlson-Stanisic, and Milan Bozic—are a true joy to work with.

Our literary agent, Amy Hughes of Dunow, Carlson & Lerner, is a tireless champion of the *G&G* brand and, more important, a good friend.

There are too many contributors to these pages to thank them all in this space. But I hope you'll read through their bios to see the breadth of their experience and accomplishments. There's certainly no book without their expertise. They make my job a delight.

At *G&G* we are fortunate to have three outstanding owners in Rebecca Wesson Darwin, our leader and CEO; Pierre Manigault; and Edward Bell III. They have believed in this magazine through thick and thin, and have always allowed us creative freedom and editorial independence.

Finally, nobody lived the ups, downs, and deadlines of this project more than my wife, Jenny. From the day I met her, she has been my most trusted sounding board and counselor. Thank you.

ABOUT THE CONTRIBUTORS

Ace Atkins

ACE ATKINS is the *New York Times* best-selling author of twenty-one novels, including *The Fallen* and *Robert B. Parker's Little White Lies*. Atkins has been nominated for every major award in crime fiction, including the Edgar three times and twice for novels about former U.S. Army Ranger Quinn Colson. A former newspaper reporter and SEC football player, Atkins also writes essays and investigative pieces for several national magazines, including *Outside* and *Garden & Gun*. He lives in Oxford, Mississippi, with his family, where he's friend to many dogs and several bartenders.

Seth Avett

Musician TIMOTHY SETH AVETT is a founding member, along with his brother Scott, of the Avett Brothers. He grew up in Concord, North Carolina.

John M. Barry

JOHN M. BARRY is a prize-winning and *New York Times* best-selling author of books including *Rising Tide*, *The Great Influenza*, and *Roger Williams and the Creation of the American Soul*. He lives in New Orleans.

Roy Blount, Jr.

ROY BLOUNT, JR.'s most recent books are *Save Room for Pie* and *Alphabetter Juice: Or, The Joy of Text*. He writes the End of the Line column for *Garden & Gun* and is a panelist on NPR's *Wait Wait . . . Don't Tell Me!*

Rick Bragg

RICK BRAGG is a best-selling author, which is a good thing, since if he fished for a living, he would starve to death. He lives in Alabama and teaches nonfiction writing at the University of Alabama. His most recent books are an award-winning biography of Jerry Lee Lewis and a collection of essays called *My Southern Journey*.

Nic Brown

NIC BROWN is the author of the novels *In Every Way*, *Doubles*, and *Floodmarkers*. Formerly the John and Renée Grisham writer in residence at the University of Mississippi, he is currently an assistant professor at Clemson University.

Monte Burke

MONTE BURKE is the *New York Times* best-selling author of *Saban: The Making of a Coach*; *4th and Goal: One Man's Quest to Recapture His Dream*; and *Sowbelly: The Obsessive Quest for the World Record Largemouth Bass*. He is also a contributing editor at *Garden & Gun* and *Forbes*.

Marshall Chapman

MARSHALL CHAPMAN is a Nashville-based singer-songwriter, author, and actress. She has written for *Garden & Gun*, *Oxford American*, *W*, *Southern Living*, *Performing Songwriter*, *The Bob Edwards Show*, and *Nashville Arts Magazine*.

Jennifer V. Cole

Mississippi-born JENNIFER V. COLE is a writer and editor based in New Orleans. After thirteen years on staff at *Travel + Leisure* and *Southern Living*, she embraced the gypsy ways of freelance life. Her work has appeared in *Garden & Gun*, *Esquire*, *Fast Company*, *Eater*, *Gravy*, and more, including *Bake from Scratch*, a magazine she launched in 2015.

James Conaway

JAMES CONAWAY is the author of *Memphis Afternoons* and other books. His latest, *Napa at Last Light*, will be published in early 2018.

John Currence

CHEF JOHN CURRENCE drinks whiskey, tells stories, and loves Popeyes fried chicken. He lives in Oxford, Mississippi, with his delightful wife, Bess, and insanely bossy daughter, Mamie.

Wayne Curtis

WAYNE CURTIS is the author of *And a Bottle of Rum: A History of the New World in Ten Cocktails* and has written frequently about cocktails, spirits, travel, and history for many publications, including the *Atlantic*, the *New York Times*, *Imbibe*, *Punch*, the *Daily Beast*, *Sunset*, the *Wall Street Journal*, and *Garden & Gun*. He lives in New Orleans.

David DiBenedetto

DAVID DIBENEDETTO is the editor in chief of *Garden & Gun*, where he oversees all of the magazine's media platforms. He is the editor of *G&G*'s *New York Times* best-selling books *The Southerner's Handbook*, *Good Dog*, and *The Southerner's Cookbook*, and also the author of *On the Run: An Angler's Journey Down the Striper Coast*.

John T. Edge

JOHN T. EDGE, founding director of the Southern Foodways Alliance at the University of Mississippi, began contributing to *Garden & Gun* in its first year of publication. He is the author of, among other books, *The Potlikker Papers: A Food History of the Modern South*.

Jenny Everett

JENNY EVERETT is a Charleston, South Carolina–based journalist covering food, health, fitness, and parenting. She writes the What's in Season column for *Garden & Gun* and inspires parents to cook with their children at her website, mylilsous.com.

Tom Foster

A longtime magazine editor and writer, TOM FOSTER is editor at large of *Texas Monthly* and *Inc.* magazines, and a frequent contributor to *Garden & Gun*. He lives in Austin, Texas, with his wife, son, and dog.

Allison Glock

ALLISON GLOCK has been a magazine journalist and author for twenty-plus years. Her writing has appeared in the *New York Times*, the *New York Times Magazine*, *Esquire*, *Rolling Stone*, *Men's Journal*, *Marie Claire*, *GQ*, the *New Yorker*, and many other publications. Her poetry has appeared in the *New Yorker* and the *Portland Review*. She is currently a senior staff writer for *ESPN the Magazine* and ESPNW. She has written seven books, including the acclaimed Young Adult novel series Changers, and received the Whiting Award for her book *Beauty Before Comfort*, a memoir of her grandmother's life in West Virginia and a *New York Times* Notable Book of the Year.

Vanessa Gregory

VANESSA GREGORY is a frequent *Garden & Gun* contributor who has also written for *Harper's* and the *New York Times*. She was a Mississippi Arts Commission fellow in literary nonfiction and is an assistant professor of journalism at the University of Mississippi. She lives in Oxford, Mississippi, with her husband, daughter, and dog.

Mike Grudowski

MIKE GRUDOWSKI is the project editor for *S Is for Southern* and a contributing editor at *Garden & Gun*. He has worked as a senior editor and written for *Outside*, *Caribbean Travel & Life*, *Rocky Mountain*, and *New England Monthly*. His writing has also appeared in *Men's Journal*, the *New York Times Magazine*, *Smithsonian*, *Sunset*, *Fortune*, and other magazines.

Robert Harling

ROBERT HARLING is a playwright and screenwriter. His plays and films include *Steel Magnolias*, *Soapdish*, *The First Wives Club*, *Laws of Attraction*, and *The Evening Star*. He is a graduate of Tulane University Law School and lives in Natchitoches, Louisiana.

Jessica B. Harris

JESSICA B. HARRIS is a professor, lecturer, and consultant, and the author, editor, or translator of sixteen books. Her most recent book is *My Soul Looks Back: A Memoir*.

Bill Heavey

BILL HEAVEY was born in Birmingham because his mother, who had married a naval aviator from the North, couldn't abide the thought of having a Yankee child. Heavey is a "generalist," a polite way of saying that while he is not particularly skilled at anything, he is adept at glossing over that and directing your attention elsewhere.

Amanda Heckert

AMANDA HECKERT is a deputy editor at *Garden & Gun*. A native of Inman, South Carolina, she previously served as the editor in chief of *Indianapolis Monthly* and as a senior editor at *Atlanta* magazine. She lives in Charleston with her husband, Justin, and their dog, Cooper.

Justin Heckert

JUSTIN HECKERT's nonfiction stories have appeared in *Garden & Gun*, *GQ*, *ESPN the Magazine*, *Esquire*, the *New York Times Magazine*, *Grantland*, *Oxford American*, *Atlanta*, and elsewhere. He has twice been named Writer of the Year by the City and Regional Magazine Association.

Matt Hendrickson

MATT HENDRICKSON is a contributing editor at *Garden & Gun*, where he handles much of the magazine's music coverage. He was formerly a staff writer at *Rolling Stone*, and his writing has also appeared in *Details*, *Entertainment Weekly*, and *Parade*. He lives in Athens, Ohio, but prefers Athens, Georgia, where his ideal night is spent eating the Frogmore stew at Five & Ten before hitting a show at the 40 Watt Club.

Jack Hitt

JACK HITT began his journalism career as the editor of Porter-Gaud School's sixth-grade literary magazine, the *Paperclip*, where he edited some of the finest haiku, penned by louche preteen sons of long-ago fallen gentry, in all of South Carolina's Lowcountry. That pretty much finished him off as an editor, and he now sticks to writing occasional magazine articles and, if food is scarce, a book.

Patterson Hood

Musician and writer PATTERSON HOOD is a member of Drive-By Truckers, whose most recent album is *American Band*. He was born and raised in the Muscle Shoals area of Alabama.

John Huey

JOHN HUEY, a native of Atlanta, has worked as a journalist for forty-five years, twenty-four of them at Time Inc., where he retired as editor in chief in 2012. He and his wife, Kate, live on Wadmalaw Island outside Charleston, South Carolina.

Elizabeth Hutchison

ELIZABETH HUTCHISON is an associate editor at *Garden & Gun*. A native of Charleston, South Carolina, and graduate of Clemson University, she also contributed to *The Southerner's Handbook* and produces the magazine's annual Made in the South Awards.

Jason Isbell

JASON ISBELL is a Nashville-based singer-songwriter from Green Hill, Alabama, and a Grammy Award winner. His most recent album is called *The Nashville Sound*. He's also a lifelong Braves fan.

Randall Kenan

RANDALL KENAN is the author of *A Visitation of Spirits*; *Let the Dead Bury Their Dead*; *Walking on Water: Black American Lives at the Turn of the Twenty-First Century*; and other works. He is a professor of creative writing at the University of North Carolina at Chapel Hill.

John Kessler

JOHN KESSLER was the longtime dining critic at the *Atlanta Journal-Constitution*. He writes frequently for *Garden & Gun* and other publications, and he is working on a book with the Giving Kitchen, Atlanta's resource for hospitality workers in need. He has also worked as a line cook and a chef.

Matt Lee and Ted Lee

Charleston, South Carolina–bred siblings MATT LEE and TED LEE first channeled their passion for Southern food into *The Lee Bros. Boiled Peanuts Catalogue*, a mail-order source for Southern pantry staples, and later into writing about food and travel. They have published three award-winning cookbooks and written hundreds of features for magazines and newspapers, and they are the hosts of *Southern Uncovered*, an exclusively Southern travel show, on the Ovation network.

CJ Lotz

CJ LOTZ is the research editor at *Garden & Gun*. A native of Eureka, Missouri, and a graduate of Indiana University, she has also worked in Haiti as a stringer for the Associated Press.

Josh MacIvor-Andersen

JOSH MACIVOR-ANDERSEN is the author of *On Heights & Hunger* and the editor of *Rooted: The Best New Arboreal Nonfiction*. A onetime Chattanooga resident, he currently lives and writes in Marquette, Michigan.

Guy Martin

Born in Athens, Alabama, and educated in the United States and in Europe, GUY MARTIN lives in Berlin, Prague, and a town in the Deep South. The author of *Garden & Gun*'s Ask G&G column, Martin has no active Facebook, Twitter, or other social media accounts, except for satiric ones under assumed noms de guerre.

Frances Mayes

FRANCES MAYES's *Under Magnolia* is a memoir of growing up in Georgia. She wrote three Italian memoirs, beginning with *Under the Tuscan Sun*. A novel, *Women in Sunlight*, will be published in early 2018.

Jon Meacham

JON MEACHAM is the author of *Franklin and Winston*, *American Lion*, and *Thomas Jefferson: The Art of Power*, among other books. Born in Chattanooga, he is a distinguished visiting professor at Vanderbilt University and lives with his family in Nashville and Sewanee, Tennessee.

Dave Mezz

DAVE MEZZ is a deputy editor at *Garden & Gun* and has been with the magazine since 2008. Born in Chapel Hill, North Carolina, he's a graduate of Carleton College and attended the Missouri School of Journalism. An avid fisherman, he's known for surgical precision with a fillet knife. He lives in Charleston, South Carolina.

Jonathan Miles

JONATHAN MILES is the books columnist for *Garden & Gun* and the author of the novels *Dear American Airlines*; *Want Not*; and *Anatomy of a Miracle: The True Story of a Paralyzed Veteran, a Mississippi Convenience Store, a Vatican Investigation, and the Spectacular Perils of Grace*.

Adrian Miller

ADRIAN MILLER is a food writer, former attorney, former politico, and certified barbecue judge who lives in Denver. His first book, *Soul Food: The Surprising Story of an American Cuisine, One Plate at a Time*, won the 2014 James Beard Foundation Book Award for Reference and Scholarship. His second book, *The President's Kitchen Cabinet: The Story of the African Americans Who Have Fed Our First Families, from the Washingtons to the Obamas*, was published on Presidents' Day 2017.

Jessica Mischner

JESSICA MISCHNER is a writer, editor, and content strategist. From 2009 through 2015, she was a contributing editor and then senior editor for *Garden & Gun*. In addition to *G&G*, her work has appeared in the *Wall Street Journal*, *Domino*, *Food & Wine*, *Gourmet*, *Elle Decor*, and *Travel + Leisure*, among other publications.

T. Edward Nickens

A freelance journalist for nearly thirty years, T. EDWARD NICKENS is a judge for *Garden & Gun*'s Made in the South Awards and a frequent contributor to the magazine, an editor at large for *Field & Stream*, and a contributing editor for *Audubon*. He splits time between Raleigh and Morehead City, North Carolina, with one wife, two dogs, a part-time cat, eleven fly rods, three canoes, two powerboats, and an indeterminate number of duck and goose decoys.

Dacey Orr

DACEY ORR is the assistant online editor and producer at *Garden & Gun*. An Atlanta native and a graduate of the University of Tennessee, she worked as an editor and producer at *Paste* magazine and has contributed music and culture stories to the *Village Voice*, *Nashville Scene*, and the Bluegrass Situation, among other outlets.

Joe Nick Patoski

JOE NICK PATOSKI authored the book *Willie Nelson: An Epic Life* and has written about Willie Nelson for more than forty years. A former staff writer for *Texas Monthly*, he lives in the Texas Hill Country near Wimberley.

Roger Pinckney

ROGER PINCKNEY is a Lowcountry legend, a juke-joint poet, a partisan of pines, a patriot of palmettos, a prince of porpoises. He is the author of thirteen books of fiction and nonfiction and hundreds of newspaper and magazine articles.

Jed Portman

JED PORTMAN is a Charlottesville, Virginia–based writer and former *Garden & Gun* editor who discovered passions for food and drink at a young age—thanks to the famous fried chicken at the Golden Lamb, his father's family restaurant in Lebanon, Ohio, and his mother's strategic reserves of Cheerwine and Stan's pimento cheese.

Will Price

WILL PRICE is a freelance writer and novice cook born and based in Atlanta. He's a proud alumnus of Georgia Southern University and takes cast-iron cookware far more seriously than he should.

Kathleen Purvis

KATHLEEN PURVIS has covered food and restaurants for the *Charlotte Observer* for more than twenty-five years. She's the author of books on bourbon and pecans in the Savor the South cookbook series, and her third book, on Southern craft distilleries, comes out in spring 2018 from UNC Press.

Hanna Raskin

HANNA RASKIN is the James Beard Award–winning food editor and chief critic at the *Post and Courier* in Charleston, South Carolina. She started her food writing career in Asheville, North Carolina, a city she profiled for the first issue of *Garden & Gun*.

Erik Reece

ERIK REECE is the author of six books of nonfiction, including *Utopia Drive: A Road Trip Through America's Most Radical Idea*. His book *Lost Mountain* won Columbia University's John B. Oakes Award for Distinguished Environmental Journalism. He lives in Nonesuch, Kentucky.

Julia Reed

JULIA REED is a contributing editor for *Garden & Gun* and writes the magazine's column the High & the Low. She is the author of six books, including *Julia Reed's South: Spirited Entertaining and High-Style Fun All Year Long*; *Queen of the Turtle Derby and Other Southern Phenomena*; and *The House on First Street: My New Orleans Story*.

Phillip Rhodes

PHILLIP RHODES is the executive managing editor of *Garden & Gun*, where he produced and coauthored *The Southerner's Cookbook*, a *New York Times* best seller. Prior to that, he worked at *Cooking Light* and *Men's Health*, where he contributed to the best-selling Abs Diet series of books—despite having no abs to speak of. He was born in Rutherfordton, North Carolina; was raised in Gatlinburg, Tennessee; and now lives with his partner in Charleston, South Carolina.

Steve Russell

STEVE RUSSELL was raised on a family farm in West Tennessee. After working at *Maxim* and *Playboy* in New York City, he fled southward again in desperate search of good biscuits. He now resides with his wife, Natalie, and their two children in Charlottesville, Virginia, where he publishes *Edible Blue Ridge*, a locavore food magazine.

Hampton Sides

HAMPTON SIDES is the author of the best-selling histories *Ghost Soldiers*, *Blood and Thunder*, *Hellhound on His Trail*, and, most recently, *In the Kingdom of Ice*, which recounts the heroic polar voyage of the U.S.S. *Jeannette* during the Gilded Age.

John Sledge

JOHN SLEDGE is senior architectural historian with the Mobile Historic Development Commission and a member of the National Book Critics Circle. He is the author of six books on history, architecture, and literary criticism. He and his wife, Lynn, live in Fairhope, Alabama.

Bill Smith

BILL SMITH, the chef at Crook's Corner in Chapel Hill, North Carolina, is the only James Beard Foundation America's Classic chef to also have been named a finalist for Best Chef Southeast (twice). The author of the cookbooks *Seasoned in the South* and *Crabs & Oysters*, he is currently at work on *Seasoned in the South, Volume II*.

David Thier

DAVE THIER is a freelance writer covering food, music, video games, and everything in between. Originally from Massachusetts, he has lived in New Orleans, Savannah, and Nashville, and currently resides in Philadelphia.

Jeff Vrabel

JEFF VRABEL's work has appeared in *GQ*, *Men's Health*, the *Washington Post*, and *Success*, among other publications. A former and hopefully future resident of Hilton Head Island, he now lives in Indianapolis with his wife and two sons.

Daniel Wallace

DANIEL WALLACE is the author of *Big Fish* as well as five other novels, including his most recent, *Extraordinary Adventures*. He directs the Creative Writing Program at the University of North Carolina at Chapel Hill.

Robb Walsh

Three-time James Beard Award winner ROBB WALSH is the author of *The Chili Cookbook*, *Texas Eats*, and *The Tex-Mex Cookbook*. He is a partner in El Real Tex-Mex Cafe in Houston's Montrose neighborhood and a cofounder of Foodways Texas, a nonprofit dedicated to preserving Texas food history headquartered at the University of Texas at Austin.

Logan Ward

LOGAN WARD is the author of *See You in a Hundred Years*, the true story of his family's immersion into 1900-era farm life in the Shenandoah Valley. He lives in Virginia with his wife and two children.

Holly Williams

HOLLY WILLIAMS is a critically acclaimed singer-songwriter and a successful Nashville entrepreneur. She owns the popular retail spots White's Mercantile, a general store for the modern-day tastemaker, and H. Audrey, a finely curated women's clothing boutique. She is also a mama to three little ones.

INDEX

pimento cheese, 237
Pinckney, Eliza Lucas, 136
Pinckney, Roger, on quail, 248
pirates
    Blackbeard, 25–26
    overview, 237–238
pirogue, 238
pit masters, 238–239
places. *See* bars; bridges and roads; geographic formations; museums and tours; regions; restaurants and eateries; *individual names of states*
plants. *See also* trees; *individual foods*
    bluegrass, 27–28
    boxwood, 33–34
    Camellia, 41
    Confederate jasmine, 57–58
    cotton, 60
    creeping fig, 63
    indigo, 136
    kudzu, 159
    mangrove, 181
    Noisette rose, 212
    okra, 217–218
    palmetto, 227
    poke, 241
    ramps, 250
    Spanish moss, 289
    spartina, 290
    Venus flytrap, 317–318
    vidalia onions, 319
    wisteria, 336
plate lunch, 188
Plessy v. Ferguson, 143
pluff mud, 239–240
po'boys, 240
poke, 241
political figures. *See* celebrities
Polk, Noel, 182

"Polk Salad Annie" (White), 241
Po' Monkey's, 241–242
Porch House concept (Lake Flato), 163
pork
    bacon, 18
    barbecue, 19
    Benton and, 21
    boudin, 31
    chitlins, 52
    country ham, 61
    cracklings, 62
    Cuban sandwich, 64–65
    cure masters and, 65
    fatback, 94
    Frogmore stew, 106
    gumbo, 119
    jowl, 146
    kil't greens, 155
    lard, 165
    offal, 216
    Ossabaw hogs for, 220
    overview, 242
    pigs' feet, 236
    redeye gravy, 252
    sawmill gravy, 267
    trotters, 310
    whole-hog barbecue, 333
    wild hogs and, 334
potlikker, 242
Presley, Elvis
    Graceland, 114
    overview, 243
    Parton and, 229
    Perkins and, 235
    Sun Studio and, 295
Price, Reynolds, 318
Pride, Charley, 243–244
Priestley, Joseph, 138
Prince, Thornton, 206
Prince's Hot Chicken Shack, 206

Prine, John, 291
Prudhomme, Paul, 245, 253
    redfish popularity and, 253
punch, 245–246
Punch (Wondrich), 245
Pursley, Ken, 187
Purvis, Kathleen
    on biscuits, 24–25
    on bourbon, 32
Pusser's Rum, 226

Q
quail, 248–249

R
Rabun Gap-Nacoochee School, 100
race issues. *See* civil rights movement; slavery
radio program, *King Biscuit Time,* 157
Rainey, Ma, 249
ramps, 250
Randolph, Mary, 96, 178, 218
Raskin, Hanna, on Asheville, North Carolina, 9–10
Rausse, Gabriele, 321
Rawlings, Marjorie Kinnan
    overview, 250
    writing by, 64
Rawls, Wilson, 332
red beans and rice, 251–252
Redding, Otis, 252
redeye gravy, 252
redfish, 253
"Rednecks" (Newman), 112
Redouté, Pierre-Joseph, 212
Red Rock Cola, 289
Red's, 253
red wolves, 253–254
Reece, Erik, on Berry, 22–23
Reed, Ishmael, 49

seafood (*cont.*)

  étouffée, 90

  Frogmore stew, 106

  grouper, 117–118

  gumbo, 119

  lionfish, 169

  mudbugs (crawfish), 198

  mullet, 198–199

  oysters, 222

  pea crabs, 232

  redfish, 253

  she-crab soup, 273

  shrimp and grits, 274–275

  soft-shell crabs, 280–281

  stone crabs, 294–295

Sea Islands, 269

sea turtles, 269–270

Seeburg, Justus P., 147

Seelbach cocktail, 270

seersucker, 270–271

Seger, Adam, 270

segregation, 271

Sewanee, 271–272

Seward, William H., 53

shag, 272–273

Shearer, Harry, 150

she-crab soup, 273

Shepard, Sam, 293

Shindig in Florence, 254

Shines, Johnny, 145

shrimp and grits, 274–275

sideboard, 275

side dishes and miscellaneous foods

  aspic, 10

  benne seeds, 21

  biscuits, 24–25

  butter beans, 38

  Carolina gold rice, 42

  collards, 56

  field peas, 95–96

  fried green tomatoes, 105

  greens, 116

  hash, 123

  kil't greens, 155

  okra, 217–218

  pilau, 236–237

  poke, 241

  potlikker, 242

  ramps, 250

  rice, 251–252

  slaw, 276

  sweet potatoes, 297

  tomato pie, 307

  wilted greens, 336

  Wonder Bread, 336

  Zatarain's, 342

Sides, Hampton

  on Lorraine Motel, 172–173

  on Memphis, Tennessee, 189–191

Signa, Charles, Jr., 78

Signa, Charles, Sr., 78

Signa, Dominick "Doe," III, 78

Signa, Dominick "Doe," Jr., 78

Signa, Dominick "Doe," Sr., 77–78

Signa, Florence, 78

Signa, Jughead, 77, 78

Simmons, Philip

  overview, 275

  wrought iron and, 337

Simone, Nina, 276

Sinatra, Frank, 146

Sippin' Safari (Berry), 343

Skinner, Leonard, 286

slavery. *See also* Civil War; *Civil War, The* (Foote)

African Methodist Episcopal (AME) Church and, 4

  benne seeds and, 20

  in Black Belt of Alabama, 26

  blues and, 29

  Carolina Gold rice and, 42

  in Charleston, South Carolina, 45

  cotton and, 60

  Creole origins compared to, 63

  Gullah/Geechee and, 119

  indigo and, 136

  jazz and, 139

  Jefferson and, 142

  Juneteenth, 148

  Lewis and Freetown (Virginia), 166

  Mason-Dixon Line and, 184

  Newman on, 113

  in New Orleans, 103, 210

  peanuts and, 30

  Tubman and, 310

slaw, 276

Sledge, John, on Mobile, Alabama, 194

Sledge, Percy, 200

sleeping porches, 276–277

Smart-Grosvenor, Vertamae, 277–278

Smith, Bessie

  overview, 279

  "St. Louis Blues" (Handy) and, 122

Smith, Bill, on Neal, 206–207

Smoltz, John, 14

snack foods. *See also* desserts

  cheese straws, 50

  Frito Pie, 105

  kolaches, 158

  Kool-Aid pickles, 158

  nabs, 204

  Zapp's Potato Chips, 342

snakes, 279

sno-balls, 280

snowbirds, 280

soft-shell crabs, 280–281

Soldier's Pay (Faulkner), 104

Ward, Logan
  on Blue Ridge Parkway,
    28–29
  on Jefferson, 141–143
  on McAlpine, 186–187
  on verandas, 318
Warner Bros. Records, 112
Washington, D. C., 325–326
Washington, George, 34, 95,
    126, 231, 232, 260, 305
Waters, Muddy, 326
Watson, Doc, 326–328
Watson, Nancy, 327
Watson, Rosa Lee, 327
weapons
  Bo Whoop, 33
  double guns, 79
  dueling and, 82–83
weather and natural disasters
  earthquakes, 86
  humidity, 130–132
  Hurricane Katrina, 132,
    150–151
  hurricanes, 132
Weeki Wachee mermaids,
    329–330
Wein, George, 139–140
Wells, Dean Faulkner,
    221–222
Wells, Ida B.
  Jim Crow and, 143
  overview, 330
Wells, Larry, 221–222
Welty, Eudora
  on humidity, 130–131
  overview, 331
  on sleeping porches, 277
  on verandas, 318

Western swing
  overview, 332
  Wills and, 335
Where the Red Fern Grows
    (Rawls), 332
White, Jack, 175
White, John Paul, 201
White, Tony Joe, 241
White Elephant Saloon, 279
White Lily flour
  Dupree and, 83
  overview, 332–333
white sauce, 333
whole-hog barbecue, 333
Widespread Panic, 12
wild hogs, 334
Williams, Addie, 189
Williams, Hank, Jr., 334
Williams, Hank and family
  Grand Ole Opry and,
    115
  honky-tonk and, 127
  overview, 334–335
  pirogue in "Jambalaya,"
    238
Williams, Holly
  on Grand Ole Opry,
    114–115
  recording by, 334
Williams, Hosea, 87
Williams, Shelton Hank, III,
    334–335
Williams, Tennessee, 82, 104,
    131, 335
Willis, Virginia, 217
Wills, Bob
  overview, 335
  Western swing and, 332

Wilson, Angelish, 189
Wilson, John Lyde, 82
Wilson, Wesley, 236
Wilson, Woodrow, 194
wilted greens, 336
Wind, Herbert Warren, 5
wine. *See* alcoholic drinks
wisteria, 336
Wolfe, Thomas, 10, 277
womanism, 325
Wonder Bread, 336
Wondrich, David, 245
Woodson, Mary, 116
Woolworth's, 173
World of Coca-Cola, 56
writers. *See* authors
wrought iron, 337
Wuxtry Records, 11–12
Wynette, Tammy, 146

X
XXX, 340

Y
ya-ka-mein, 340
y'all, 340–341
yardbird, 341
yarn, 341
Yearling, The (Rawlings), 250
Young, Neil, 175

Z
Zappe, Ron, 342
Zapp's Potato Chips, 342
Zatarain, Emile, 342
Zatarain's, 342
zombie cocktail, 343
zydeco, 343